SECRETS OF A
FAMILY ALBUM

Also by Isla Dewar

Keeping Up With Magda
Women Talking Dirty
Giving Up on Ordinary
It Could Happen To You
Two Kinds Of Wonderful
The Woman Who Painted Her Dreams
Dancing In A Distant Place

SECRETS OF A FAMILY ALBUM

Isla Dewar

review

Copyright © 2004 Isla Dewar

The right of Isla Dewar to be identified as the Author of
the Work has been asserted by her in accordance with
the Copyright, Designs and Patents Act 1988.

First published in 2004
by REVIEW

An imprint of Headline Book Publishing

10 9 8 7 6 5 4 3 2 1

Apart from any use permitted under UK copyright law,
this publication may only be reproduced, stored, or transmitted,
in any form, or by any means, with prior permission in writing
of the publishers or, in the case of reprographic production,
in accordance with the terms of licences issued by the
Copyright Licensing Agency.

All characters in this publication are fictitious
and any resemblance to real persons, living or dead,
is purely coincidental.

Cataloguing in Publication Data is available from the British Library

ISBN 0 7553 0081 5 (hardback)
ISBN 0 7553 2014 X (trade paperback)

Typeset in Cochin by Avon DataSet Ltd,
Bidford-on-Avon, Warwickshire

Printed and bound in Great Britain by
Clays Ltd, St Ives plc

Headline's policy is to use papers that are natural, renewable and
recyclable products and made from wood grown in sustainable forests.
The logging and manufacturing processes are expected to conform to
the environmental regulations of the country of origin.

HEADLINE BOOK PUBLISHING
A division of Hodder Headline Limited
338 Euston Road
London NW1 3BH

www.reviewbooks.co.uk
www.hodderheadline.com

For my family

Beauty and Acceptance

'Some people are universally beautiful,' Mattie said. 'And some people are beautiful only to those that love them.'

A conversation four Christmases ago: sitting on the bus, going home after work, Lily remembered it well. The streets the bus rumbled through were lit, shops aglow with festive decorations. Faces looking in at her, people waiting for other buses, or moving through the pavement bustle, chilled, bored, impatient. It was a bitter London night, traffic crawled, horns blared, voices cut through the dark, 'Taxi!' Everyone was wanting to get home.

They'd been at Lily's other home, in Edinburgh, when Mattie had said that about beauty. She and Art, her husband, had come north, as they did every year, to spend the day with her family in the old house where she'd been brought up.

It was always a comfort, this house, the feel of it, its sounds – the shudder of the central heating pipes, the creaking board on the stair, five steps up, the hum of the fridge in the kitchen, the rattling window in the dining room. The radio was always on, usually tuned to a classical station. Lily could never hear Mozart without thinking about her childhood home, and its smells. Mattie's cooking, lavender room spray, and another smell, an indefinable mix that was always in the air: old wood, coal fires, the scents of lilies or roses in the vase on the dresser, the lingering wafts that trailed in the air after Mattie or John or Grandpa, Dior perfume, the chill from outdoors that hung on John's woollen jersey when he came in from the garden. All that and more combined to make the smell that was the smell of Lily's childhood, soft, enfolding, familiar. She loved it.

It was an old house, rambling, draughty, spacious. It backed on to Edinburgh Zoo. Its garden was a haunt for magpies and occasional badgers and foxes. Something Mattie and John, Lily's

1

mother and father, considered an asset, along the lines of a conservatory or a double garage, despite the damage they did to their compost heap. Inside was a huge hallway with a staircase leading to a large landing. Here there were five bedrooms and a bathroom with an old Victorian clawfooted bath with a shower attached. Downstairs was the kitchen, a big room, dominated by a pine table that was constantly cluttered with newspapers, bills, books, cups. On the other side of the hallway, a dining room, and off that the living room, bay windows looking out over the garden, a coal fire, and a long-lived denim-covered sofa, bought from Habitat in the seventies, where Lily had curled reading *Little Women* and *The Lion, the Witch and the Wardrobe*, and other books. On this sofa she had fallen in love with Jane Austen, and had, with her brother Rory and sister Marie, thrilled at the adventures of *The Bionic Man*, *Knight Rider* and *The A-Team*, and done some seriously heavy petting with Richard Hardcastle, her teenage sweetheart.

This house was filled with memories. There were secret haunts and hiding places here. The cupboard under the stairs where Lily had always gone when she needed solitude, an hour or so of peace away from her boisterous younger siblings. The sill at the window on the landing, wide enough to sit on, draw up your knees, gaze out at the world, and dream.

Everything was just as it had been when Lily left, over fifteen years ago. The door on the kitchen unit still needed fixing, the tiling in the bathroom still stopped three inches short of the door. John had been promising to finish it for years. Years and years, and hadn't got round to it. The front gate still squeaked. The back door still needed a bang from the hip to make it open. Oh, the comfort of all this. The joy of returning to find the old quirks she'd been intimate with all her life, still in place. Lily felt safe here. It was home.

Lily, drifting and dreaming, her head on the window of the bus she was travelling on, looked round. An old man had, at some point, sat down next to her and was reading a paperback book. She wondered what it was and craned over to see if she could read the title. She couldn't, not without him noticing her curiosity, anyway. She always meant to read on buses, but somehow the movement around her, people getting on and off the bus, the unsteady stop, start, trundle of the vehicle, always disturbed the rhythm of her concentration. On buses and trains, Lily always moved into her own thoughts.

That year, the year of the conversation about beauty and acceptance, Lily and Mattie had lingered at the table after everyone else had gone out to walk off their meal. Mozart's third violin concerto was on the CD player. The cloth that spread before them was littered with festive debris, nut shells, empty bottles, pudding plates, some only half emptied because eaters had declared themselves too full, too bloated to manage another bite, remnants of pulled crackers, discarded paper hats, glasses, coffee cups, a bottle of vintage port. Mattie had poured herself a second glass, offered the bottle to Lily, who'd refused and filled her glass with the last of the champagne.

Yes, it would have been five Christmases ago, because Andy had been there, he hadn't left Marie yet. And Rory's hair was still long, he hadn't met Isabel, who would insist he had it cut. And it had also been the first time they took a bet on how long it would take Mattie to mention the sledge.

The following year had been full of news, the phone ringing, Mattie pouring her worries out to Lily. 'Andy's left Marie. He's just gone. What is she going to do? *And* she's pregnant.'

Only a few weeks later, another call, 'Rory's met some French woman. He brought her here last night. She's very chic. He's going to live with her in Paris. She's ages older than him, thirty-six, three years older than you. He's had his hair cut. It's a sign,' Mattie said. 'Actually . . .' Then she'd stopped. She had been going to say that actually Rory's Isabel had reminded her of Lily.

It had struck her as she spoke that Isabel looked a bit like Lily, wore similar clothes, had the same haircut. And there was something about the way she fussed over Rory, told him to put on his jersey when he was going out to buy milk when they'd run out.

'Is cold,' Isabel had said. 'You'll get a chill. Put on the sweater I bought you last week.' Remembering that, Mattie thought, My God, Lily used to fuss over him in exactly the same way.

'Actually what?' Lily had said.

Mattie, recovering from this revelation, said, 'Actually, I think she may rule his life.'

Lily had, at the time, thought her brother could do with someone who'd rule his life. Oh, the relief that he'd at last cut his hair.

Then, later that year, Lauren had been born. 'She's gorgeous,' Mattie crowed, weeping, 'just gorgeous.' John, Lily's father, had looked after Marie's two older children, Tod and Agnes, while Mattie attended the birth. The experience had rendered her sobbing and emotionally wrecked. 'I've never seen anything like it. I never knew it was like that. Well, I did know, I've had three myself. But when you are giving birth you are sort of out of it. I saw the little head appear, and I cried. I cried and cried. And there she was, a little person, a whole new human being. It's a miracle. I can tell you, I really bonded with that baby.'

And that was the first jarring pang of jealousy Lily had ever felt. It sliced through her. Of course, she chastised herself for it. This new baby was her niece, she should love her. And anyone coming into the world in these times we are living through, she told herself, needs all the bonding it can get. But there it was, the envy. If her mother was going to really bond with somebody, really think someone to be gorgeous, Lily wanted it to be her.

So there they'd been, Lily and her mother, that Christmas five years ago, before Andy's mysterious departure, Rory's passion for an older French woman and Lauren's appearance in the world, discussing beauty and acceptance. Lily couldn't recall how the subject had come up.

'Love changes beauty,' Mattie'd said. 'When you love a truly beautiful person, they cease to be perfect and you love them more because you, and only you, know their flaws. That's what makes them yours, the secret of the flaws. And when you love, for want of a better word, an ugly person, they become beautiful to you. That's part of the love, the fact that you know they are beautiful.'

'People's features change when you love them. They become precious. And once you really know them, have held that face close and kissed every bit of it, you'll never recapture how it looked to you the first time you saw it,' Lily had said.

'Oh, absolutely.' Mattie had nodded furiously. 'But sometimes you see a face for the first time and know that is the face for you.

And sometimes a face just grows on you, and there it is in your life, and your days would be empty without it.'

'I know,' said Lily. 'I didn't think Art was beautiful at all when I first met him. Now I wonder how I could have missed it.'

Lily smiled now, thinking of Art. And noticing a woman across the aisle of the bus noticing her, she stopped and looked out of the window. The streets were familiar; soon she'd get off and walk the rest of the way home.

'Art is beautiful,' Mattie had said. 'I thought that right away when you first brought him here. But I knew it was a slow beauty. One that sort of caught up with you the more you looked at him and spoke to him. That Mark Tilley you were with before him was a seriously handsome chap, but the more you let him into your life, chatted with him, heard what he had to say, the less handsome he became.' She'd been, on account of the vintage port, more than a little tipsy.

Lily had looked into her glass. She did not like to think about Mark Tilley. For three years their lives had been entwined, they'd been Mark and Lily. An item. At social gatherings one was rarely seen without the other. Then he'd asked her to marry him, and she, almost as much to her own surprise as his, said no.

'No?' he'd said. 'No?'

'I don't want to marry you, Mark. Ever,' Lily told him. She'd meant to say it gently, but it didn't come out that way. She'd sounded brusque.

'Well,' Mark had said. 'That's me told. That's that then.' They'd been at the door of her flat, and he'd turned and walked away.

'Wait,' she called. 'What do you mean, that's that? It's over? You're not going to see me again?'

He stopped, turned, looked back at her. 'Yes. It's over. What's it all about, Lily? I thought we'd marry. Have children. The full catastrophe, as they say. And it would be wonderful.'

Lily had said, 'Couldn't we just cut to the catastrophe without the ceremony first?'

Mark had smiled. 'No, Lily. I don't think so.'

Lily had thought, he knows. He knows. He'd been testing her, and she'd failed. Will you marry me, Lily? Do you love me enough to take my name? Though hardly anybody she knew took their husband's name; he'd just wanted to see if she would. She'd have been Lily Tilley, and she couldn't bear the thought of it.

Thing was, she had, all her life, wanted to change her last name. At university her friends had said she could easily change it by deed poll. Indeed, they had all spent gigglish evenings thinking of names Lily could choose. Pasternak, they'd thought. Steinbeck. 'Austen,' Lily had said, dreamily. 'That's lovely. Or Woolf. Lillian Woolf. I sound important, intellectual.' But somehow she couldn't do it. She was sure John and Mattie would be hurt, and she didn't want to offend them.

She'd been Lily White, daughter of John and Mattie White. Lily White, how she'd been taunted at school. *Lily White is a shite. Oh, Lily White got a fright, in the middle of the night.* If she'd been naughty, teachers would peer at her imperiously. 'Not as pure as your name suggests, Lily.' She'd longed for years to dispense with that last name, and had thought she'd do what none of her friends were prepared to do, take her husband's name when she married. But Lily Tilley? She didn't think so.

She'd said no to him. That had indeed been that. She hadn't seen or heard from Mark again.

For some time she'd felt dreadful about it. The way the no had come out. Strong and loud, no denying it was a refusal. She thought she was shallow. She could have said yes, and kept on being Lily White. What was wrong with that?

In the end she'd confided in Marie, her sister. She couldn't tell her mother about the name shame.

'You said no because it was what you really felt. Nothing to do with your name. For the first time in your life you truly expressed your emotions. No, you said. Because you knew marriage to Mark wouldn't work. He was a pompous arse. Never liked him.'

Some months later Lily met Art. Arthur Raphael. She'd married him, taken his name. Now they'd been together for almost nine years. No children, which was an issue. But more of an issue with him than it was with her.

Lily still squirmed whenever Mark Tilley was mentioned. As Mattie had mentioned him then.

'People want to be beautiful,' Mattie was saying. 'And they want to be rich. But I'm past all that. I want acceptance.'

'Acceptance?' asked Lily. 'What do you mean?'

'I want to be accepted for who I am, what I am wherever I go. Just that. In the supermarket, in the park, in the street, in my music class, my book group, I want people to think there goes Mattie White and she's just fine.'

'I'm sure people do that already,' Lily had said.

But Mattie had shaken her head. 'No. There's always criticism, nasty thoughts, rumours, speculations and hints. I know, I know, it's the same for everyone. But I've had enough of it. I want to live in a world where we all just accept one another. I've come to think beauty is over-rated.'

'Over-rated,' Lily said, now. 'I don't think so.' The man she was sitting next to stopped reading, raised his head, turned and looked at her. Lily looked down into her lap, embarrassed. It would soon be time to get off, thank goodness. Art would already be home, in their flat. He'd have showered, and changed into fresh clothes, which would be the same as the clothes he'd have shoved into the laundry basket in the bathroom – jeans and a T-shirt. He'd be in the kitchen now, preparing supper. His hair would still be wet. The radio would be playing. He'd be chopping onions. He was a better cook than she was, more flamboyant, adventurous. Lily needed proper measuring spoons, a recipe to consult at regular intervals. Sometimes songs on the radio interfered with her thoughts and she had to switch it off lest she made a mistake and her dish turned out wrong. Art's food never turned out badly, he always seemed to know exactly what he was doing.

On the subject of beauty and acceptance Lily had said to Mattie, 'Hmm.' She knew this to be true. But still, to be utterly beautiful would be wonderful. It would make up for being shallow and foolish, which was what she secretly thought she was. Mattie had been about to ask what hmm meant, but hadn't because the room filled up with sound and bustle and people with the stark scent of winter still clinging to their coats.

The walk hadn't lasted long, it was cold outside. Lily's brother Rory, her sister Marie and her two children, and Art were back, stamping their feet, rubbing their hands and casting glances at the table. They could eat something; after the walk there was room for a little tasty mouthful or three.

Art took a slice of pudding and poured himself some wine. He was off to watch the film on television. 'That's what you need on Christmas Day, a good rubbishy film with a good rubbishy happy ending.' And Lily agreed, and went to curl on the sofa next to him.

In fact, Lily was clever, an academic, Doctor Raphael (Doc Lil, Art called her). But it was the cleverness of someone who knew how to read, how to distil facts, form opinions and critiques and write them exquisitely and accessibly. She lectured part time in English at London University, something she didn't think she did very well. She often stopped mid-sentence and stared at her students, who lolled this way and that, took occasional notes, gazed out of the window. She'd say, 'Is anyone listening? Has anyone grasped what I'm talking about?' And she contributed to a series of educational books, *Writers Unravelled: Understanding Authors.*

'Opening up the classics to new generations of readers,' Lily said.

'Kafka for beginners,' Art said.

The books sold to schools and colleges across the world, and made Lily a fair amount from royalties.

'A good source of income, that I'm quite proud of,' Lily said.

'Nice little earner,' Art said.

It was what Lily wished she could say. It had a certain indiscreet charm. And people who spoke that way were all the things Lily wanted to be. Street-wise, they had natural savvy, nous. Writing books about dead writers for schoolchildren who, Lily suspected, wanted to read neither the dead writers nor books about them, was a dreamy thing to do, made her feel unworldly. Words were no challenge, she swam through them effortlessly. But life bothered her. She could not cope with car dealers, plumbers, window cleaners, she got short-changed in bars. She was easily taken in.

Until Art had come along she'd driven dud cars, had dripping taps and dirty windows, and had stood rapping her knuckles on bar counters saying, 'Excuse me, I think there has been a mistake.' Her unworldliness infuriated her. And it showed. She yelled, she demanded. 'I absolutely *demand* you look at this heap of a car you sold me,' she'd said to the man at the garage where she'd bought a Fiat that had turned out to have a dodgy gear box. The salesman had shrugged and told her the three months' guarantee period was up, and really she should depress the clutch every time she changed gear. She'd huffed, puffed, ranted and raged. And threatened to report the garage to whoever it was you reported garages that sold dud cars to. But in the end she had left feeling outraged and more than a little foolish.

She knew, she just *knew*, that if she was beautiful none of these things would happen to her. Beautiful people were exempt from being duped, they did not have to be street-wise, or smart. Despite being old enough to know better, Lily believed this. She wanted to be beautiful. Though, because it was Christmas, and she was feeling champagne-mellow, she'd agreed with Mattie on the matter of acceptance over beauty. 'Being accepted wherever you went would be lovely,' she'd said. But reluctantly. She wanted more than acceptance; adoration would suit her nicely.

Her husband, Art, was adored. Everybody loved Art. He ran a post-production company in Soho. A small outfit, ten people working mostly on pop videos and occasional adverts. He was handsome, but in a roguish way. Not stunning, just, as Lily put it, his face had been assembled almost perfectly.

In fact, his nose was slightly squint, though you had to stare to notice it. But as faces go, Art had been blessed. His was open, swift to smile, dark eyes, and eyelashes that were the envy all the females who saw them. 'Not fair,' they'd say. 'What does a man need with lashes like that?' He was tall, long legs usually encased in jeans. Above them, a T-shirt. Always plain, black or white. He only wore suits for business meetings. He had three, and in one of the pockets of every jacket was a rolled-up tie. For as soon as he hit the street after spending time with potential clients, he'd whip off his tie, roll it up and shove it in his pocket, before opening the top button of his shirt. 'Bloody ties,' he'd say. 'Hate them.'

He was easy to like. He liked people, so people tended to like him back. They called him a lovely bloke. Which pleased Lily – for Art was hers – and filled her with envy. It was what she wanted to be – a lovely bloke. Except the bloke bit annoyed her.

'There is no female equivalent to bloke,' she complained to Art. 'Men get to be, well, men, chaps, gentlemen, lads, boys and blokes. We don't have a blokey word for us. A bloke's not a boy, a man, but affable and, well, male, terribly male. Women are women, ladies or girls . . .'

'But they ain't blokes,' said Art. 'Thank goodness.' And he smiled.

Which made Lily smile, and forget the rest of her tirade, which had been going to be lengthy. Art could always do that.

At last the bus reached her stop. Lily got off and walked the rest of the way home. She made her way through the thick bustle of Islington, to the quiet, expensive, tree-lined street where she lived. She wondered what Art had prepared for supper. She thought that he would never have to choose between beauty and acceptance, for he had both already. She wondered what that might be like, as she considered how she had neither. Then she wondered what Rita Boothe would choose.

Her heels clicked along the empty pavement. She walked past houses, wide bay windows, curtains open. Inside living rooms were lit, televisions on; she could see plants, bookcases, large sofas. Lifestyles being lived.

Rita Boothe, she thought. Terrifying. The woman was known to be brusque, abrupt, a curmudgeon. And tomorrow Lily was going north to St Andrews, about an hour's drive from Edinburgh, to interview her for a chapter she had been invited to write in a book about lost icons. People who had in the past failed to make their mark and had, instead, become victims of their times. Rita Boothe, writer, photographer, journalist and cook, fitted the bill perfectly. Lily was nervous about meeting her. She didn't think Rita Boothe would give a fig about either being beautiful, or being accepted. There was a freedom in that. Lily knew she would never achieve it.

Arthur and Lillian

In bed, after sex, Lily and Art often played games. If people were cars, fish, weather, dogs, puddings – what would they be? Lily would be a Mini, a Koi, a windy but sunny day in early spring, a saluki, a sorbet, which disappointed her (though she had to admit it was true); she wanted to be a vanilla ice with a splash of amaretto drizzled over it. Art would be a vintage Jaguar, a salmon, a balmy autumn afternoon, a labrador, an apple pie flooded with sweet, thick homemade custard.

There were other ifs. If you only had ten minutes left to live, what would you do? 'Find you, wherever you were,' Lily told Art.

'If,' Art asked Lily that night, 'you could have anything. Anything at all in the world. A Porsche, a villa in Tuscany and a private Lear jet to get to it, an endless wardrobe. Or the power to cure all sickness – cancer, AIDS. Or to end world poverty. But to have that you had to *vow* never again to buy or use, in any shape or form, moisturiser. What would you choose?'

How Lily had squirmed. 'Oh, I'd end all sickness,' she'd said. But in her head a horned demon had squealed, protesting, 'Liar. Liar. You'd have the moisturiser. You'd never forsake that.'

She and Art were in bed in their perfect bedroom, in their Islington flat. Pale, pale walls, Persian rugs on polished floors, charcoal-grey velvet curtains. They had, for the past half-hour, been Arthur and Lillian, not Lily and Art, which was how their friends and relatives knew them. Arthur and Lillian were an earthier couple altogether. Arthur was willing, always willing. And sometimes a little incredulous at Lillian's sauce, her cheeky suggestions. She was the upstairs maid. He the *chauffeur*. He was a stud. She was brazen, a goer. It was their private joke. A secret they shared. Things they did in the dark. Sometimes, at dinner parties, they would slip from their sophisticated Lily and Art shells, and let Lillian and Arthur have an airing.

'Great asparagus, Lillian,' Arthur might say.

And Lillian would slide a glossy spike between her lips, and say, 'Absolutely yummy, Arthur.'

Their friends would ask what they were on about, knowing it was something sexy. But Lily and Art never let on. They had mischievous, deliciously dirty, wicked alter egos, their bedroom beings. To let anyone into this exclusive intimacy would have spoilt it.

'So,' Art asked, 'what would Mattie do in the moisturiser debate?'

'Oh,' said Lily. 'She'd tie herself in knots trying to find a way to have all the things she wanted *and* have the moisturiser. She has delusions of being a great manipulator and negotiator.'

'Yes,' said Art. 'But in the end, what would she choose?'

'Things,' said Lily. 'Lots of stuff, sofas, cars. I think she secretly longs for classy consumer goods to hide behind. Though right now she hasn't got any.'

'And what would Rita Boothe decide?' Art asked.

'I don't know,' said Lily. 'I haven't met her yet. But from the sound of her cracked old voice, I suspect she'd try to save the world. I don't think she'd give a fig for moisturiser. Her face probably hasn't seen a lick of Oil of Olay for the past thirty years. I'll let you know when I get home the day after tomorrow.'

A few days ago Lily had phoned her mother to tell her she was coming to Scotland to interview Rita Boothe in St Andrews, and she would be looking in to say hello on her way back. She'd been surprised by Mattie's reaction. Rita Boothe had been one of her heroes. Lily had thought her mother would swoon with delight and envy, and had delayed the call, relishing this. But Mattie had gasped, then was silent. A long telephone silence, such an awkward thing when one person is saying nothing and the other is swimming through the hush, and each can only guess at the other's expression. Mattie imagined smugness. Lily, horror.

Lily was right. 'What?' she said.

'What do you mean, what?' said Mattie.

'You've gone all silent. I thought you'd be pleased. I thought Rita Boothe was your heroine.'

'She is. Well, was. Years ago. I mean Rita Boothe, nobody's heard of her these days. Why are you writing about her?'

Lily sighed. 'It's for a book. The *Lost Icons* series. I told you, I'm sure I did. Anyway, the book's not so much about her as the times she lived through. The whole series is about people who missed their mark, who should have had an *effect* on their times but instead became a victim of them.'

'Well, don't accuse Rita Boothe of being a victim. She'll whack you one on the jaw.'

'I wasn't going to. I want to write about her sympathetically. I think she was misunderstood.'

Mattie laughed. 'Misunderstood. Oh, I love that. If you are writing about the times she lived through, when she was actually famous, is it absolutely necessary to go and see her?'

'Of course it is. I get the impression you don't want me to meet her.'

'Do you? Why is that?'

'You went awfully quiet when I said I was.'

'I was doing something, is all,' said Mattie.

'What?' asked Lily.

'Um,' said Mattie, racking her brain for something to tell Lily. She hadn't been doing anything. Her silence was a result of the shock she'd felt when her daughter had told her she was going to meet Rita Boothe. 'I can't remember,' she said.

'Mattie,' said Lily, filled with a rush of affection, 'what are you like?' And she rang off.

'I don't know what's got into Mattie,' she said to Art that night. 'When I told her I was going to meet Rita Boothe, she went all funny and silent. And when I asked her why, she said she was doing something, and when I asked her what she was doing, she said she couldn't remember.'

Art had smiled. 'That's Mattie.'

Lily smiled too, then. 'So it is,' she said.

Lovely Mattie, spacious old Citroën of a person. A trout leaping from a still lake on a dewy morning to catch a fly, and missing. A crisp day in October when the leaves are golden. An old English sheepdog. A bread-and-butter pudding. Comfortable, dreamy, beloved, room for everybody in her life. And lovable. Who could not love Mattie?

That night, they might have continued thus, deciding what their friends and relatives might do should they ever have to sacrifice their vanity and forsake moisturiser to save mankind. Art wanted to, anyway. It amused him, and he loved to talk. Loved the sound of their soft, end-of-the-day voices rubbing against the dark. But sleep was taking Lily, her head was swimmy with it. She was settling in for the night, tugging the duvet round her, blocking up small places where draughts might seep in. She was an organised sleeper. An organised everything. So she tucked and tugged, and smoothed her pillow, preparing the bed, making herself comfortable.

Art kept on talking, though the tucking and tugging irritated him, but only a little. 'Do you have to do that?'

'Yes, I'm getting comfy.'

'You're in bed, you should be comfy already.'

Lily always claimed Art knew nothing about sleeping. In fact she told him that before he'd met her he'd been a miserable sleeper. 'I taught you everything about sleeping.'

Art agreed. Before Lily, he'd climbed into bed, pulled the duvet over him, and slept a sound and satisfying eight hours. Then he'd woken up, thrown off the covers, got out of bed, and started his day. But life was no longer that easy. Now Lily was with him everything had to be perfect, even the simple business of falling asleep.

'I need to be the right temperature to sleep properly,' Lily said. 'It has to be properly cosy. There are degrees of cosiness. First you get into bed and it's cool and soothing and you think, why didn't I come here earlier? This is lovely. Then it begins to get warm and you get into sleeping position. Sort of on your tummy, sort of on your side, one leg straight, the other bent. Then it starts getting cosy, and that's lovely. Snoozy. Then it gets toasty, and that's the perfect condition for sleeping.' She sighed.

Sometimes, despite loving Lily, Art longed to be again the Art he used to be. The man who slid into bed and removed his boxers under the duvet. Who had piles of books and coffee cups on the floor beside him. Who simply shut his eyes and drifted off to the happy place he went when he slept. But somehow Lily's pursuit of perfection in everything had infected him; now he too needed to get into the right position, to stop up all draughty spots and become toasty cosy.

He didn't really like this in himself, thought it soft, persnickety. Furthermore, he had come to think of the bed as Lily's rather than something that belonged to them jointly. She was too fussy, demanding her proper share of both duvet and sleeping space. 'Your leg is trespassing on my side, I can't get to sleep for it being there.' He'd remove his leg. Then again, the kitchen he also thought of as belonging to Lily. The dining room and the living room were also hers. Now he thought the only bits of the flat that were truly his were his study, and the seat at the far end of the sofa where he sat nightly, reading the paper, watching television, snoozing.

'Lily might end all sickness,' he said. 'But Lillian would definitely have the moisturiser.'

There was breathing beside him. He looked at his wife. She was sound asleep, her face smooth, fallen into a gentleness only he knew, the creases and tightness of the day gone. He sighed. Nobody to talk to, and there was the regret that he was once more in bed with Lily. Lillian was gone and would not return to him for at least three or four nights. Lily was organised about Lillian's appearances. He sighed, smoothed his pillow and settled into the perfect sleeping position.

In the morning, Lily rose early and packed her overnight case. She had a long journey ahead, an hour's flight, then a car drive up the coast. She wasn't looking forward to it.

Art was up too. Wearing his boxers and today's T-shirt, making coffee and insisting Lily, who was not a breakfast person, eat some muesli before she left.

'You'll get hungry and eat some of the dreadful aeroplane food. Then you'll complain about it for weeks.'

Lily nodded, and complied. Then she went to the bathroom to fix her lipstick, and left her coat and bag by the front door while she waited for the minicab she'd ordered to take her to Paddington to catch the Heathrow Express.

'I'll be home tomorrow,' she said to Art. 'I wish you were coming too.'

'So do I,' he said. 'I hate it when you're not here.'

Isn't it funny? Lily thought. Someone becomes so much a part of you, you don't feel whole when they're not there.

Once she'd loved going places alone. A stranger in a strange place, she'd wandered new streets, looked at new buildings, soaked in new atmospheres. When studying for the PhD, she'd travelled a lot, and always on her own. She'd loved it, the freedom of it. Nobody to answer to, nobody to please but herself. Now, when visiting new places, she longed for Art to be with her. So she could talk to him, listen to what he thought of where they were. She would walk strange and different streets, staring about her, and thinking, Art would like that. She'd notice other visitors, walking arms linked, smiling to one another, staring at this, pointing at that. That was the thing, when you were with someone, when you shared a new experience, you stared and pointed. When you were alone, with nobody to point things out to, you only stared.

Self-Awareness Sucks

A cold day. Lily eased herself from her car, and stood looking around. The rain had not long stopped. There was restlessness after the deluge. Bitter squalls rattling winter trees. Bird song turning vibrant, frenzied in damp air. Sparrows in beech hedges comparing hysterical notes, asking if that was it, or was there more to come? Shivering droplets lining bare branches. A sniff of wintrier weather than rain in the air, mingled with the salt tang that came off the sea.

The last time Lily visited St Andrews had been on a family outing when she was about ten. It occurred to her now that Rita Boothe must have been living here then. Before going to her interview, Lily drove around, sightseeing. She wanted a look at the town where Rita lived, the streets she tramped, where she might shop.

It was much as Lily remembered, an eclectic mix of shops, beautiful old buildings. That was why they'd come here all those years ago on that family outing, to look at the buildings. Mattie had taken Rory and Marie to the West Sands to play, paddle in the sea, build sand castles. John and Lily had gone to seek out some fabulous architecture. He'd taken her hand, they'd explored tiny lanes, peered up at the skyline; they'd stared and pointed. He'd bought her a pistachio ice cream at Luvian's.

Today, it being December, Christmas in the offing, the trees in South Street were draped with lights. More lights hung overhead, slung across the width of the road. The place twinkled. Christmas trees were propped on the wall outside the fruit shop and the market garden. Chairs and tables spilled from restaurants on the pavement, though none were occupied. Too damp after the downpour. She turned out of South Street, heading for Market Street, bumped over cobbles in the square. More restaurants, a video shop, exquisite old buildings and students strolling through the afternoon, mobile phones clamped to their ears. Lily wondered what Rita Boothe made of it all. She turned out of Market Street and headed for Rita's house.

Stiff after two hours sitting, driving, she groaned relief at being upright and gently massaged the muscles above her knees. Then reached into the passenger seat for her bag, a cavernous thing but organised within – two notebooks, a selection of felt-tip pens, her tape recorder, lipstick (Dior, a pale brownish), foundation cream (Estée Lauder), mobile phone (dark red, and very tiny), paracetamol, comb, Issey Miyake perfume, personal organiser, keys and wallet. Before heading up the path to ring Rita Boothe's doorbell, Lily looked round.

It was a good street. In fact, a beautiful street. Not at all what she'd imagined. Though, if asked, she'd have found it hard to put her imaginings into words. 'A street,' she might have said. 'Uniform buildings, lampposts, hedges, railings. Nothing much, probably bland. A lot of streets are.'

But this place, tucked away in St Andrews, was lovely. Terraced, but none of the houses were the same, as if two or three hundred years ago someone had built a home, then a while later someone else had built another home attached to it. Only the second home bore no resemblance to the first. It would have one more storey, a flight of steps leading to the front door. After that, over a hundred or so years, more houses had been added, not one resembling any of the others. Every single building was listed.

Trees lined the edge of the pavement. In front of every home a tumbling of growth, lavender, roses. Though it was December, some blooms still shone in the greying afternoon. Lily looked up. Hulking clouds were gathering. The sparrows were right to worry, there was weather coming. Wind sped round her legs, lifted her skirt, flung her hair round her face. She shoved it back into place. Smiled, a small twitch at the corner of her mouth. This was a wonderful street. It was the street where Rita Boothe lived.

For over twenty-five years, ever since she'd been ten, Lily had been fascinated by Rita Boothe. The woman was a legend. Among her many, many quotable remarks had been her famous outcry – Self-Awareness Sucks.

In the early seventies, and well past forty, at a time when all her contemporaries had left such things behind, Rita had taken acid and gone into therapy. On being interviewed about what enlightenment these experiences had brought her, Rita said, 'Well I always knew there was more to me than meets the eye. I wanted to get in touch with the woman within the woman. And now that I have, all I can say is that what meets the eye may not be breathtaking or even comforting, but it's a hell of a lot better than what doesn't meet the eye. And having been to the depth of me and met the woman within the woman, I can tell you, self-awareness sucks.'

The phrase had caught on, briefly. The notion of self-awareness sucking was discussed in newspaper feature pages, on a radio programme, in bars, in railway carriages. The words had been printed on T-shirts that hadn't sold, because the sort of people who wore their philosophies emblazoned across their chests did not agree with Rita. They were young, Rita wasn't. They thought self-awareness next to inner godliness, enlightenment. The idea of it sucking was the opinion of a middle-aged curmudgeon who did not understand, or worse, was afraid to address her own inadequacies. Still, Rita's thoughts on her inner self found their way into several minor books of quotes. She had her fans, Rita Boothe. Lily's mother, Mattie, was one of them.

Now Lily stood at Rita's door and rang the bell. It was a blue door, deep lavender blue, and the bell was polished brass. The little tumbling garden between the front of the house and the pavement was neatly planted.

This didn't seem like the residence of the woman who had written the famous, and now long-out-of-print, book, *The Joy of Filth*. It had been a history of housework and a call to all women to stop doing it. *There are memories in all our stains*, Rita had written. *Why are we so eager to get rid of them? Why are we so obsessed with cleanliness? What comfort is there in the sterile, unlived-in home?*

Mattie had read, and believed. And stopped cleaning.

The woman who appeared in the doorway was small, wiry. Piercing blue eyes. Her hair was pale blonde, woven loosely into a plait that was pinned up at the back. She wore linen slacks and a grey roll-neck jumper. She was stylish and severe. Here was someone, Lily thought, who did not suffer fools gladly. Indeed, here was someone who did not suffer anyone gladly.

'You'll be Mrs Raphael,' said Rita.

And Lily nodded. 'Yes. Thank you for agreeing to see me.'

'It's distracting,' said Rita, standing aside to let Lily enter. 'Knowing someone is coming to see me distracts me from my day. I don't like to start something when I am aware I'm going to get interrupted.'

Lily apologised and said she wouldn't be long, but there were one or two things she wanted to talk about.

'My dear,' said Rita. 'You fool yourself. The one or two things you want to talk about will lead to three or four things, which will lead to even more things. You are going to be here for a very long time indeed. And I am going to be distracted beyond belief. Go make yourself comfortable in the living room. I shall fetch us a pot of tea.'

She waved Lily into the room at the end of the hallway, and strode in the opposite direction towards the kitchen. The living room surprised Lily. It was light, spacious. A fire crackled in the hearth. Logs were stacked neatly beside it. There was a pale blue linen-covered sofa near the bay window, behind it a table lined with plants, all flourishing. Either side of the hearth was an armchair. There were books. A CD player with two rather splendid speakers each side of it. The room was modern, surfaces shone. It was welcoming, inviting. Considering the sofa too perfectly plumped to actually sit on, Lily chose one of the armchairs, sat down and fished her tape recorder, a notebook and pen from her bag.

Rita appeared, bearing a tray laden with cake, a pot of tea and two cups, which she placed on the table. She poured tea. 'Sugar?' she asked.

Lily shook her head.

'Milk?'

Lily shook her head.

'Cake? No, I'm not going to give you the opportunity to refuse. I made this cake specially for you coming. It would be rude of you not to have a slice.'

Lily nodded. 'Cake would be lovely.' She was handed a cup, dark blue porcelain, and a matching plate on which lay a slab of cake and a silver dessert fork. 'Thank you.'

'It's a pleasure,' said Rita, sitting in the chair opposite. She crossed her legs, held her saucer in one hand, and raised her cup to her lips, sipped.

Lily noticed she had not helped herself to a slice of cake. 'Do you mind my tape recorder?' she asked.

'I most certainly do,' said Rita. 'Terrible things. Too accurate by far in the gathering of information. You need to write things down. Note my expression, the rhythm of my speech. Put that thing away.'

Lily obeyed. Sipped some tea, and put a sliver of cake on to her fork, then into her mouth. It was the best cake she'd ever eaten. Moist, light, sweet and slightly lemony. 'Oh,' she said, not really meaning to let the surprise show. 'This is delicious. And this is such a lovely room.'

'Not at all what you'd expect from the author of *The Joy of Filth*,' said Rita. 'I suppose you were steeling yourself to meet years of dirt, thickly stained carpet, grubbiness.'

Lily swallowed, and put more cake on her fork. 'Not at all,' she said. Lying.

'My fault, really,' said Rita. 'Silly title. I meant why clean what will only get dirty again? Do it when you must. I should have called it *There Is No Rapture in Dusting*. Or perhaps, *If You Find Rapture in Dusting, You May Need Help*. There were those out there who thought it to be a paean to pornography.'

Lily jotted this down. 'My mother loved that book.'

'Excellent. Your mother has a name? She is not just called Mother or Mum, I presume.'

'Mattie,' said Lily. 'Matilda. Matilda White. Though she was Mattie Cameron before she married.'

'Matilda Cameron,' Rita mused. 'Sounds familiar. I do vaguely recall a Mattie. But there have been so many people. So many passing through the years, can't remember them all.'

Rita took Lily's empty plate from the arm of her chair and placed a second slice on it. Normally Lily would have refused; she was very careful what she ate. But this was meltingly special. 'It's so good,' she said through a mouthful. 'What is it?'

21

'Apple and carrot,' said Rita. 'But it's the smeck of cinnamon and lemon peel that makes it.'

'Smeck?' asked Lily. Smeck? She'd never heard of a smeck. Was it perhaps some Polish spicy thing, a rare mix of cinnamon and lemon. Or a liqueur?'

'You're not alone there,' said Rita. 'It would appear nobody has heard of a smeck. There were complaints when my cookbook came out. A smeck.' She waved her fingers in the air, as if adding a pinch of something to something else. 'A smeck.'

'Cookbook?' said Lily. 'You've written a cookbook?'

'*Recipes for More Than Food*. Sold. Then didn't sell. People said the quantities and timings were erratic. Things burnt, things were underdone.' She shook her head. 'I don't know.' She got up, crossed the room to the cupboard behind Lily, and brought out a large glossy book. 'There,' handing it to Lily. 'Unusable, they said.'

Lily considered the book. It was a wonderful thing. On every page was an illustration of a fat, leaping nude, waving, smiling. Some were gathered round a table eating with gusto. There was joy. Lily read.

Welsh Rarebit
A fabulous hearty snack. Perfect for after a winter walk, or when you come home from the cinema or the theatre. Softly creamy melted cheese, tangy on a thick slice of good bread.

Wodge of thickly stodgy bread
A wallop of grated cheese
A good dod of mustard and maybe a smeck of paprika
A whack of Tabasco and Worcestershire sauce
A hefty glug of good hearty ale

Cooks were advised to mix the ingredients together, whack them on to the bread and stick under the grill for as long as a lingering kiss. *That ought to do it*, Rita had written.

'As long as a lingering kiss,' said Lily. 'How long is that? I mean, some people's lingering kisses last longer than others.'

'Surely one would know when the cheese had brownly melted.

The smell. I didn't advise anyone to leave the kitchen while kissing. And a lingering kiss is more than a peck, and not as long as a snog. A snog would probably lead to bed, and the cheese would undoubtedly burn. Going to bed whilst some dish is cooking would probably involve a casserole. But a quickie, on the kitchen table, perhaps, might be perfect timing for, say, watercress soup.'

Lily felt her jaw drop. As someone who needed precision, exact quantities, exact timings in her cookbooks, she didn't know what to say. So she asked why Rita had claimed that self-awareness sucked.

'Isn't it obvious?' said Rita. 'You go poking about in your psyche, rummaging in the depths of yourself. And what do you find? Dubious motives, greed, envy. Other ghastlier things. Oh, some say your failings are the result of childhood traumas, or infant defeats, or your parent's absurdities. But my mother and father were lovely. I adored them. Well, I came to adore them. Certainly by the time I went into therapy I adored them. No, I'm afraid the lust and longings, the avarice and jealousy I discovered were all of my own making. I looked deep into the inner woman and saw somebody I didn't much like.'

Lily smiled, and scribbled. '*The Joy of Filth* was your first book?'

'Of course not. My first book was *Limousine Nights.*'

'I've never heard of it,' said Lily.

'It was briefly notorious, but mostly for missing its time. I took so long deciding which photographs to use, and how I wanted the pages laid out, the sixties were long gone. We were into the seventies, and punk. The whole groupie thing had changed completely. The new groupies were far more outrageous, rawer, and at the time, a lot more interesting.'

'Right,' said Lily. 'How did you feel about this?'

'Bloody stupid,' said Rita. 'I missed the effing boat.'

Missed the boat, Lily scribbled in her notebook.

Rita revisited the cupboard the cookbook had come from and brought out a copy. 'Here it is. Not a bad book, if I say so myself.'

Lily flicked through the pages. Stared at the photographs. The late sixties. Long-haired people crowded on to beds, lay on sofas, sat on chairs covered in ornate throws, behind them huge

Aubrey Beardsley posters. There were spliffs, there was booze. She flicked some more. Something familiar caught her eye. A photo of a young woman wearing black fishnet stockings that stopped just short of the top of her thighs, a feather boa wrapped round her neck. She wore long black opera gloves, rings glinting on her darkly clothed fingers, a bottle of Jack Daniels in her right hand. She had tattoos on her thighs, *Kama Sutra – Harley Davidson Position*, said one. Another was a beautiful dragonfly. Lily stared. The woman in the photograph was exquisitely lovely. Her smile mischievous and haunting. The woman in the photograph was her mother.

Lily spread her fingers over the page and gazed at the picture. Outside, wood pigeons in the trees at the end of the garden softly warbled. Logs shifted in the grate. She stroked her mother's glossy gravure cheek.

Rita was regretting having let Lily into her house, regretting having let Lily glimpse her past life, which was, she thought, a headlong rush towards failure. She always got things wrong. She said the wrong things. Mixed with the wrong people. Went to the wrong parties, or turned up drunk at the right ones. The whole networking business had baffled her back then when she was making her way, and baffled her now. Even though she considered she had no longer any way to make. Her mistakes haunted her, and she didn't want to talk about them to anybody.

All that, and Lily had hardly started, and it was by now halfpast three. Her favourite time of day, when in December dusk was gathering, and she liked to sit here, in this room, and watch the starlings. They congregated in their hundreds, maybe thousands, on the bare branches of the sycamore at the bottom of her garden. They'd sit, chorusing. The noise when she opened her window was always astounding – a thick throaty warble, a thousand clustering voices. Not a song, definitely not a song. And they were so still, but when she looked through her binoculars there were always a few battling for a perch, knocking others off. But in time that would stop and they would all be still, and all facing the same way so the tree looked as if it was covered in strange black fruit. Then as one they'd take off to whoosh, whirl and dip over the rooftops, round and round till they finally sailed off to their roosting place, wherever that was. Rita didn't know.

What fascinated her was the number of them. All arriving at the same time, and pressing together. She wondered if they all got along. Or if somewhere there was a starling that had been ostracised because nobody liked it. Or if there was a starling that made lewd jokes, and belched and farted and annoyed the others, but they just said, 'Oh, don't mind him, he's like that.'

It was about acceptance. Rita wanted to know what that was like. She'd never moved with a crowd. She'd been an only child, and sickly, kept in, safe from the rough and tumble of other children. Then a loner. One marriage that didn't last. Then an affair that produced a son who rarely kept in touch. She thought that nobody liked her. So she was drawn to the camaraderie of starlings. To fly through the evening with a multitude who knew you for what you were, and didn't think about it. An acceptance of starlings. It would be a comfort to be part of such a thing.

'What's wrong?' she asked, noticing Lily staring at the book.

Lily held it up, pointed to the photograph. 'My mother.'

Rita leaned forward in her seat, peering. 'She's beautiful.'

Lily agreed. And did not remove her gaze, trying to take it all in. All the secrets that the moment's freeze frame did not give up. Who else was there? Where was she going? What was she thinking? What did those white leather seats feel like against her naked back, her naked bum?

'You're shocked,' said Rita. 'You didn't know your mother had a past.'

Lily shook her head. She knew all about Mattie's life, the nine or so months she'd spent chasing rock stars. Mattie was open about it; she told all sorts of people. 'I used to be a groupie,' she'd say.

And whoever she was talking to would look at her with disbelief. 'You did?' they'd say, taking in this woman with thickening hips, sagging breasts, who moved though her days wearing pull-on pants and baggy shirts. Then they'd look harder and see the full lips, the blonde hair still long, but rolled up untidily at the back, and they'd think, Well, maybe.

It was Mattie's smile that captured Lily's attention. It was complete, abandoned, total enjoyment. Lily realised she had never smiled like that, she always kept a little bit of herself back. She needed to be in control of herself. She stared at the photo, got momentarily lost in it, forgetting that Rita was watching.

Rita vividly remembered taking that photograph: 1967, it had been, a hot day. The window and sun-roof of the limousine had been open. She'd spent some time getting shots of the four or five girls that were with some band she couldn't remember the name of. What she did recall was that the band's manager, a young man, painfully thin with hair down to his shoulders, was angry that she wanted to photograph the groupies and had insisted, somewhat aggressively, that she shoot a couple of rolls of the boys, as he called the bunch of musicians he represented.

'I have no interest in them,' Rita remembered saying. 'A stereotypical group of boys who sing stereotypical songs about love and freedom. Things they are far too young to know anything about.'

The manager had said that if that was what she thought, she could get out of the fucking car.

So she agreed to photograph the band. She had adjusted her lens so that they were blurred in the front of her shot, the groupies crystal clear in the long back seat behind them. They had all been giggling. Rita had loved that. She loved the sound of women laughing.

Sitting slightly apart was a girl who seemed more aloof, or was she just shy? Rita had noticed how beautiful she was, and had wanted to take her on her own. But the girl had refused. 'Oh come on,' Rita had wheedled. 'It'll only take a second. Please.'

The other girls had joined in. 'C'mon, Mattie, let her do you. She's done us.'

The girl had smiled. Then the other girls had told Rita that Mattie was the one. She had slept with everybody. Rita had said, 'Goodness.' Then pleaded with Mattie again. 'Please,' she smiled.

Mattie had shaken her head. But Rita had insisted. 'Go on.' Then she'd opened the cocktail cabinet of the limousine and handed Mattie a bottle of Jack Daniels. 'Have a slug, loosen you up.'

'Don't do alcohol,' Mattie had said. 'It ruins you. Rots your liver and that.'

Then Rita had said, 'Oh please, Mattie. You have such a wonderful face. It's more than beautiful, it is full of life and wonder. I don't think I've ever seen such an expressive set of features anywhere before.'

Mattie had looked at her, amazed. And seemed almost overwhelmed. 'Really?'

'Really,' said Rita. 'I'd love to photograph you. It would be an honour.'

So Mattie had agreed. And sat stiffly waiting the click, and the release from torture.

'Relax,' Rita had said. 'Suddenly you look like you're stuffed.'

Mattie had laughed. Taken a small swig of the Jack Daniels. Excellent, Rita had thought. Then she asked, 'Have you slept with John Lennon?'

Mattie had laughed harder. Swigged again. Then said, 'John Lennon. Oh yeah.' And she'd stood up, removed the long calico dress she'd been wearing, picked up a feather boa that some other girl had left on the seat beside her, wrapped it round her and said, 'Take me like this.'

Oh joy, Rita thought. This is what I want. 'Think of John,' she'd said. 'Your night of passion together.'

Mattie had laughed and laughed, and looked at the camera with complete abandon. Rita got the shot she was after.

My goodness, she thought now. That was years ago. I was thirty-five. I thought the world was mine. I smoked, rolled my own. I lived in Notting Hill. Though it wasn't fashionable then. I should have hung on to that flat. I mixed with people, though I was always on the edges of the in-crowd. I drank. I had friends. Three lovers, Tunji, the African who lived downstairs, Frank, a film producer, and Ray, who did something in advertising. She'd had a best friend, Richard, and hadn't yet made the mistake of sleeping with him. She took photographs for Sunday supplements and was planning to do her own cookbook, illustrated with fat and happy nudes. Thirty-seven years ago, she thought, I had it all. She came to herself, realised she'd been dreaming. That was her curse, dreaming. She often drifted off when people were talking to her, and missed what they were saying. And instead of apologising, she always snapped some swift response. 'I totally disagree. I think you are being judgemental.' 'Your opinions are ill-conceived and subjective.' And had earned herself a reputation of being opinionated and difficult.

Lily, to her relief, hadn't realised that Rita had slipped off into her own thoughts, and was still staring at the photograph. Rita watched for a moment.

'You're jealous,' she said.

The accusation was too quick, too accurate. Lily had no time to gather her thoughts and deny it. She nodded.

'You're jealous, and you're ashamed of yourself for being jealous. You know you should only be glad at your mother's beauty, at her utter enjoyment of what she's doing.'

Lily nodded again.

The old lady placed her cup carefully on its saucer, looked primly across at Lily. 'Like I said, self-awareness sucks.'

'It's just,' said Lily, 'that yesterday I was remembering a conversation I had with my mother some years ago. It was about beauty and acceptance. She wanted to be accepted by everybody wherever she went. No speculations, hints, rumours. Now I know why she wants that. She can reject beauty easily, she has been beautiful. She knows what it's like.'

Rita said, 'Ah. I think I would choose acceptance too.'

Lily smiled. She asked a few more questions, then decided the interview was over. She had all the information she wanted. Rita walked with her to the front door.

They said their goodbyes. Then, just before she made her way to the car, Lily turned, and said, 'Oh. By the way, I forgot to ask. How old are you? If you don't mind.'

Rita smiled. She'd been waiting for this. She was seventy-two, and surprised by that. Looking in the mirror she saw a woman she recognised. But it wasn't the person she imagined she looked like when she wasn't staring at her reflection. This person looked like some distant relative she knew, but only slightly. 'I am not as old as my knees,' she said. 'They are at least twice as old as I am. And considering the world I am now moving through, its twists and turns, its standards, its technology and how little I understand,

and how confident I was years ago, I'd say that I was a lot older when I took that photograph of your mother. I am, as the song goes, younger than that now.' And she shut the door.

Nice Isn't Nice

It was a typical morning for Mattie. She rose at seven thirty, made coffee and stood by the window in the kitchen, drinking it, staring out. The day was murky, December grey. She reminded herself that it would soon be Christmas. And it didn't look like Christmas, didn't feel like Christmas.

She was one of four children. Three sisters and a brother. Two of the sisters had produced two children, her brother four, and she a further three. Eleven in all, then. Six of that eleven had now added a further seven children. And when you included all the assorted wives and husbands – both present and ex – it made for . . . Mattie stared blankly ahead, counting. An awful lot of people, she concluded, nodding. Definitely far too many to count. But however many there were, they made Christmas horribly expensive. 'So many presents,' she said. This needed a list.

She fished the gas bill from the pile of papers on the table, a pen from the pocket of her dressing gown, and started on the back of the envelope. *Pay gas bill*, she wrote. Then, *Turkey. Sprouts*. She paused, thinking, What else? Noticed that the lilies in their vase at the centre of the table were wilting, and should be thrown out. Wrote, *Lilies*. The morning paper rattled in the letter box. Mattie stopped making her list and went to fetch it.

On her way to the front door, she saw the remote control for the television lying on the kitchen dresser. She'd had it in her hand, she remembered, when, last night on her way to bed, she'd come in here to check the cooker was off. She picked it up, meaning to return it to its place beside the television, but went to collect the newspapers instead. Here, she put the remote on the hallstand as she stooped to gather her *Guardian* and *Scotsman*, and, pausing to look at the headlines, forgot about it. Clutching her papers, she headed into the living room, knowing she had business there, but on arrival stood looking dumbly around. *Why am I here, exactly?*

She saw the roses John had bought her for their anniversary last week drooping slightly, and knew she ought to refresh their water. She crossed the room to pick them up from the top of the piano, and as she did so noticed the thick layer of dust on the Venetian blinds. She pulled the sleeve of her dressing gown over her hand and dragged it across a couple of the slats, examined the wipings. She would have to dust. She picked up the vase of roses and returned to the kitchen. Put the roses beside the sink, and returned to her list. *Dust blinds*, she wrote. Then, *Wrapping paper and mince pies (ready-made)*.

One of the front-page stories was about the scandalous cost of mobile phone calls, which reminded Mattie that she'd meant to get in touch with Lily to find out how she'd got on with Rita Boothe. *Lily*, she added to the list. Then, *Chestnuts*.

She heard John coming down the stairs, turned to smile at him as he came into the room. 'Hello.'

'Hello, you been up for long?'

She shook her head. 'I'll make coffee. Grandpa awake?'

He shook his head. 'He snores on. He had dreams last night.'

'*Moby Dick*?' said Mattie.

John nodded. Grandpa White had come to live with John and Mattie fifteen years ago, two years after his wife died. He'd been seventy at the time, and when the offer of a home had been made nobody had thought he'd live longer than another five years or so. But living, or surviving as he put it, was something he was good at. He was a fixture in the house, had his own cup, his own chair, his own workshop in the garage where he made things, or planned things he might make were his hands steady enough. Over the last two days he had been rereading *Moby Dick*. It had captured his imagination, both waking and sleeping. He had dreams of waves, thunderous seas. And caught in foaming turbulence, his long-dead wife, Sylvia, drowning, calling to him. In the depth of the dark from his boiling, frothing slumbers, he'd shout her name, a long, curdling cry, waking Mattie and John.

She got up to make coffee, and John sat down in her chair, considered her list.

'Ready-made mince pies?'

'I think so,' said Mattie. 'Last year I made three trays, and they just lay there. Nobody wanted one. They said they were too full. So if nobody eats them, what's the point of standing making them?'

'Why bother having them at all? Just cross them off the list.'

'You can't do that. It's Christmas. You've got to have mince pies. Christmas isn't Christmas if you don't have mince pies, even if nobody eats them.'

He knew from experience, thirty-seven years of marriage, there was no point arguing about this. Mattie had decreed there would be mince pies. There would be mince pies. Even if nobody ate them. He took up the pen and continued the list. *Crate champagne. Cheese. Brandy butter. Check tree lights*. Then he started to doodle a row of pound signs down the side of the envelope. 'This is going to cost.'

'Christmas always costs.' Mattie put two slices of bread under the grill.

In unison, they sighed. Money was an unpopular subject. They had recently discovered that the pension fund they had been paying into for years had suffered substantial losses on the stock exchange. They had been expecting a large lump sum, followed by a handsome monthly payment they'd hoped would see them into a full and exciting retirement. A firm but apologetic letter from their insurance company told them there was to be no lump sum, and their monthly payments had been more than halved.

'Not quite penury,' John had said. 'But nearly.'

'We won't be getting a conservatory, then,' Mattie had said. 'Or going on our trip across America.' She had, anticipating a juicily large cheque, ordered a new red velvet sofa, and had spent happy evenings studying holiday brochures and kitchen catalogues. They'd debated which new car they would buy. John thought a Volvo would see them into old age. 'Reliable,' he'd said.

Mattie had shaken her head. 'I have not scrimped and saved and put money away to do safe and reliable things. I want fun. I want a yellow Alfa Romeo convertible. I want to go to the South of France in it.'

John had smiled, and nodded. 'Why not. You only live once.' An Alfa Romeo it was to be, then.

Three days after the car conversation, the letter had come. And the order for the red velvet sofa was cancelled. 'I loved that sofa,' said Mattie.

Still, they did not take the matter lying down. They had made an appointment with a fund manager and gone in to demand what money was still due to them in a lump sum. They were shown into a small office, a desk with a computer, behind it a chair, in front of it two more chairs. The walls were an approved tranquil green. 'This does not bode well,' Mattie had said. 'This is definitely a C-list office.'

They had been joined after a fifteen-minute wait by a woman of about twenty-six. She told them she was Brenda, though they could see that on the badge on her lapel. She called them John and Mattie, sat behind the desk, got their files up on the computer and asked how she could help. To Mattie, this woman seemed crisp and cheerlessly friendly. Our Brenda's been on a course, she thought. How to deal with irate and mildly batty customers. Eye contact, body language assertive, but never aggressive. Stand your ground. Repeat salient points. Use first names. Don't give them any money.

John explained the situation. She sympathised and said that many, many other people were in the same boat. Times were hard for savers.

'Oh well, that's all right, then,' said Mattie. 'If there are other people similarly let down, perhaps we could all get together and have tea parties. We certainly couldn't afford booze.'

John put a silencing hand on her knee and asked if they could forgo the monthly payments, and have what was due to them in one lump sum. He was refused. The contract they had signed was for a pension to be paid monthly.

'The monthly sum you are offering us is less than half the amount we have been paying in,' said Mattie. 'We might as well not have bothered. We might as well have spent the money when we had it. Where is the money, anyway?'

She was told it had been lost in certain unfortunate investments.

'Lost to whom?' Mattie wanted to know. 'Who has it?'

'It isn't like that. Money is invested. It's figures on paper. In a way you could say it isn't real money.'

'It was real when we paid it over to you. It was our earnings.'

The woman shrugged and looked to John.

'Somebody must have our money. I'd like to know who. That person is probably right now sitting on my sofa in my conservatory with my Alfa Romeo at the door,' Mattie insisted.

The woman looked down at the shiny surface of the empty desk. 'I'm sorry,' she said. 'But the monthly sum paid out to you will be paid until you die.'

'What if we go outside right now and get killed by a passing bus, or a falling piece of masonry, or a deranged madman with a machine gun?'

'Then it will pass on to your children. It is guaranteed for five years.'

'Five years. What happens to the rest of it?'

The woman shrugged.

'Theft,' shouted Mattie. 'Theft. You have purloined our money, and if we die you are going to keep it. Theft.' She fished in her huge handbag and brought out a calculator. Punched furiously. 'I will have to live for another thirty years to get our money back. I wasn't planning on that.'

John looked surprised. 'Weren't you? I was.'

'Nobody likes to think about dying. But at least if Mr White goes before you, you do have some provision.'

'I will die when I choose,' said Mattie. 'But when I do, I will die knowing I haven't cheated someone of their life savings. I will leave this earth with a clear conscience. Which I suspect is more than you will do. Do you have a pension fund?'

'As a matter of fact I do,' said Brenda.

'With this company?'

'It comes with the job.'

'Do you have one that doesn't come with the job?' Mattie needed to know.

'Yes.'

'With this company?'

Brenda looked out of the window. This wasn't going well. There had been nothing to cover this question on the course she'd been on. 'Um,' she said.

'Hah.' Mattie was triumphant. 'Thought not.'

'I pick my investments carefully,' said Brenda. And regretted this.

John and Mattie gasped.

'You're implying we didn't,' said John. 'And what, I wonder, will your employer make of that?'

Brenda shrugged. She had the feeling she was shrugging a lot during this meeting.

'Shrug, is that all you can do?' said Mattie. 'I find that very juvenile. Is there, perhaps, an adult we can talk to?'

'I am an adult,' said Brenda. 'And I find your attitude very hostile. Rudeness isn't going to get you anywhere.'

'I have been told that your company has lost our money. And now our pension is hardly enough for groceries, never mind council tax, electricity, phone bills, never mind holidays and Christmas. But at least when I die, in penury I might add, I will know I have lived. I did not sit in an office day after day wearing a cheap chainstore suit, with a name badge pinned to the lapel. I have seen things, I have done things.'

If she'd been pushed on this point, Mattie would have had difficulty bringing to mind what exactly she'd seen or done. But one thing, at least she hadn't squandered other people's savings on the stock market.

'You will probably die while wearing that suit. Maybe of guilt while sitting behind that desk. Or maybe while slipping up to your drab office in the lift hearing in the distance the stifled giggles of office girls gathered at the photocopy machine, and with the taste of out-of-date onions from the burger you had for lunch stale in your mouth.' She stood up, glared. 'I have been robbed and cheated and let down and lied to, but at least I have lived honestly.'

Brenda was about to say she was glad to hear it. But didn't. Mattie stormed from the C-list office. John looked sheepish. 'She gets a bit heated from time to time,' he explained.

Then he, too, left. At the front of the building he found Mattie sitting on the steps. 'I loved that red sofa,' she said.

Now John sighed, remembering Mattie on the steps, coat spread behind her, head in hands, sobbing. And how he'd felt, hopeless, unable to do anything to fix things for her. All his life he'd tried to get for Mattie the things she wanted. Though she never asked for anything, he knew she had longings. He'd catch sight of her leafing through a magazine, stopping to look at a glossy photo of a room, a car, a holiday destination, a fridge, perfume, make-up, oh, all sorts of things, and he'd feel a pang. If he couldn't somehow acquire this thing for Mattie, he'd feel he'd let her down. In all his years of marriage there had been a lot of pangs.

A song came on the radio, Sting singing 'I'll be watching you . . .' Idly John wrote, *I'll be watching . . . I'll be watching . . . I'll be watching.* Then, realising he'd been writing on the back of the gas bill envelope, he wrote, *Pay gas bill,* not noticing Mattie had written it higher up the list.

Mattie placed a plate of toast, marmalade, honey and butter on the table, then sat on the chair across from John's. 'It's not the same,' she said.

'What?' asked John.

'Christmas. Without the kids it's not the same. About now they'd be getting all excited. Doing carols at school. Putting up decorations here in the kitchen, in their rooms.'

John wrote *Decorations* down on the envelope.

'Writing letters to Santa,' continued Mattie. 'Then writing revised letters to Santa when they changed their minds. I miss it. I miss them. The row of little coats by the front door. Their noise and chatter. Their programmes booming on the television. All gone. It's as if my children are dead.'

'Don't be silly,' said John. 'They've grown up. Moved on. They've got their own lives, you should be proud. You did a good job with them.'

'But they're not children any more. The people they were, the children, are gone. It's like they're dead.'

'Not dead,' said John. 'Just faded away.' And he wrote *Faded away . . . faded away . . . faded away.* Mattie briskly buttered her toast, spread it to dripping point with honey. Took a bite, then officiously took the list from John. 'Let's see how you are getting on.' She persued it, saw he'd mentioned checking the tree lights, said, 'Excellent.' Wrote, *Excellent. Potatoes. Onions. Garlic. Bacon,* she added. Now she was getting somewhere. She paused, thought about her lost sofa. *Comfort,* she wrote. *Luxury. Peace.* She thought about her Alfa Romeo, wrote, *Freedom*. Goodbye to all of that. Remembered the woman at the insurance company and said, 'That was terrible, what I said to that Brenda.'

'I thought it was quite good. All that stuff about not having squandered other people's money.'

'But the things about dying while wearing her suit. In the lift. That was terrible.'

John nodded. 'You did go a bit far there.'

'I feel awful about it. Perhaps I should write and apologise.'

John shook his head. 'Never explain. Never say sorry.' He'd read that somewhere and was meaning to follow it as a sort of philosophy, but always forgot. He always found himself explaining or saying sorry.

'Then there's Marie. I feel awful about that. Just awful,' said Mattie.

John and Mattie's youngest child, Marie, lived on a council estate with her three children. She'd married Andy, a gym teacher with a passion for mountaineering, when she was nineteen and four months pregnant.

It hadn't been one of the finest moments of her young life, telling her mother she was expecting a baby. Eighteen months out of school, a year into a course that included word-processing and accounting, sitting at the kitchen table, weeping. 'I'm going to have a baby.'

'You're what?' Mattie had said. 'For heaven's sake, how stupid can you get?' There had followed a long diatribe about being careful, using condoms, taking the pill. 'Or simply,' Mattie said, 'learning a bit of self-control.' Then she'd said, 'Well, we'll just have to make the best of it. It'll be wonderful having a little one about the place again.' And she'd sighed. This hadn't been what she'd wanted for her daughter.

For two years after they'd married, Marie and Andy lived with Mattie and John. Marie finished her course, while Mattie cared for Tod, the baby. At last, with a second child on the way, the couple had been allocated a council house about ten minutes from this old Victorian house that Marie had lived in all her life.

'So we'll be nearby,' Marie had said. 'We'll see you all the time.'

'So you will,' Mattie smiled. But she was miserable. She'd loved having her house full. Loved the clatter of people coming and going, voices in the hall, in the living room, the warmth of evening meals when everyone gathered round the table, helping themselves from the serving dishes she laid out, stews, vegetables, fat golden puddings.

In the dark, in bed, the night before Marie and Andy and little Tod left to live in their own home, Mattie cried. 'Why can't everyone be happy and live in one big house together?'

John put his arm round her. He couldn't really answer that. 'Dunno. The pursuit of happiness is a mysterious thing. You have to let your children go do it on their own.'

He'd kissed his wife's sodden cheeks, dabbed her eyes with the duvet cover and told her that now was their time. 'Time to get back to being us again.' And in a few years their pension would come through, and, then how they would fly. The fun they'd have.

So Marie and Andy began pursuing happiness in their own four-roomed, two-up, two-down home. Mattie looked after Tod every day when Marie got a job with Bartlett, Bartlett and Hogg, architects. 'I'm an underling,' she'd say. 'I take bits of paper from one person to another. I do letters, I make tea. I take the post down to the mail room.' But she wasn't an underling for long. Over the years she rose to become PA to Ronald Hogg, and along the way produced Agnes, her second child. With two salaries coming in, she and Andy were able to save. 'Soon we'll have enough for a deposit on our own house,' she'd told Mattie. 'Next year, hopefully.'

Then, four years ago, a couple of weeks after that conversation, Andy had gone, leaving Marie alone with two children and pregnant with their third child. For a fortnight Marie hadn't said anything to her family. She'd come and gone from her parents' house without saying a word about her husband. Till one day Mattie said, 'We haven't seen Andy in a while,' and Marie had said, 'He's gone. He left us.'

Oh, the surprise, and endless questions. 'What do you mean, left you? Why?' And Marie would say, 'He just went.' But it was said firmly, and she'd turn away and start doing something, tucking

Agnes's shirt into her trousers in such a way that anyone asking knew that no information about Andy's dramatically sudden departure would be forthcoming.

John and Mattie, Art and Lily, and even Rory, Marie's brother, had all spoken about it at length. Had Andy been having an affair? Had the marriage not been as loving as it had seemed? Why would Andy just go? He had seemed such a down-to-earth, caring man who adored his children and his wife. It was a mystery. Obviously Marie was distressed, but whatever the reason he'd left her, she was keeping it to herself. So now the family never mentioned it, at least when Marie was around. When she wasn't, they puzzled and wondered.

John and Mattie had promised her some money, enough, they'd said, to add to her savings so she could put down a deposit on her own home, when their fortune came. They figured they could afford to dip into their own savings, which were fairly minimal. But after the dreadful meeting in the C-list office, they knew they'd need all the money they had – the reduced pension, Mattie's state pension, the few thousand in their bank account – to get by themselves. They'd had to phone Marie and tell her they could not give her the money they'd offered.

Now, remembering that call, Mattie wrote, *I feel just awful.* Then she added, *Cream. Bottle of brandy for Grandpa. Stuff for trifle.* She heard the front door open, voices. Children running down the hall, and bursting, pink-faced, into the kitchen. Lauren, Agnes and Tod.

They came every weekday morning. Marie would drop them off before going to work. Mattie would make them all breakfast. Then she'd take Agnes and Tod to school, and pick them up again at half past three. Meantime, Lauren was hers to play with, dote on. Next year Lauren would start nursery school. And that, Mattie thought now, would be another one starting to fade away.

They gathered round the table as Mattie fetched packets of cereal. Muesli for Marie, Rice Krispies for everyone else. Bowls, milk (organic) and sugar, which Marie disapproved of. The children ate.

Marie took up the list, scrutinised it. 'Getting organised for Christmas?'

'It's only weeks away,' said Mattie. 'I don't know, it hardly seems any time at all since last Christmas. You just seem to blink and here it is upon you all over again. Have a look, see if we've forgotten anything.'

Marie ignored the asides, the remarks, and concentrated on the trifle. She divided this into sub-sections. *Trifle, sub-section one: sponge fingers, fruit (bananas and oranges), cream (whipping). Sub-section two: sherry, good enough to drink on its own. Or Madeira. Sub-section three: remind Lily to bring bowl.*

By then it was time for her to go to work. She kissed her three children and John. Mattie came with her to the door, saying that it was icy out, and Marie should take care when driving.

She stood at the door, waving goodbye, thinking what a wonderful mother her daughter was. She didn't know how she managed. Three children, she thought, such a lot to cope with. But Marie was wonderful, and how she'd changed since Andy had left her. She had found herself. When she'd been a teenager, Marie had been a handful. But Mattie knew she'd only been doing what her friends did, wearing what her friends wore. She'd needed to fit in. Peer group stuff, Mattie thought. But there was a fire about Marie now. She took control of situations, she had opinions. And how good she was at her job! PA to an architect. She took phone calls, she wrote letters, she organised meetings, she could read plans. Why, Mattie thought, that office would fall apart without my Marie. She almost runs the place.

Marie got into her car, and waved back. She wondered why Mattie felt just awful and hoped she wasn't ill. Now she thought about them, the other asides on the list were a little upsetting – faded away, freedom, peace, comfort? What did it all mean? Were Mattie and John going through some sort of middle-age crisis? Perhaps they felt they were getting old, too old to care for young children, and wanted freedom, comfort before they faded away. Oh dear, she thought. What was she going to do? She needed Mattie and John, without their help she couldn't go out to work. She certainly couldn't afford child care. She crunched the gears of her car, moved out into the traffic without checking her mirror, without signalling, and into the path of an oncoming Saab, which hooted violently as it shot past. She didn't see the driver's face, but his gestures indicated how stupid he thought her to be.

Seeing this, Mattie's hand flew to the mouth. 'Careful,' she shouted. She watched till Marie's car disappeared round the corner, then returned to the kitchen, deciding she wouldn't mention Marie's near-accident. She didn't want to worry the children.

Ten minutes later she left to take Tod and Agnes to school. John took Lauren out into the garden to fill the bird feeder.

Grandpa came down, found the kitchen empty. He boiled himself an egg, made some toast, sat slowly eating, mouth open to let his spoonfuls cool. He looked at the list. Took the pen, scored out *brandy*, replaced it with *whisky. Which I prefer*, he wrote. And added a couple of things he wanted, *A plump naked woman and a gleaming black stallion.* He might be old, but he could dream. Then, noting the double entry, *pay gas bill*, he shuffled to the kitchen drawer where he kept his cheque book. He found the bill in the pile of papers on the table, and wrote a cheque for the amount owed.

He heaved on his outdoor shoes and pulled a thick jumper over his shirt. He moved at snail's pace into the hall, where he put on his heavy coat, his scarf, his furry cap with the ear flaps, and gloves. He noticed the television remote Mattie had left on the hallstand when she collected the mail, and picked it up. Stood holding it. What to do? Cocooned in his thick coat and everything else, he felt hot. Sweaty, in fact, which made him grumpy. He was certainly too hot to walk all the way down the hall to the living room. It seemed miles away. So, still holding the remote, he opened the front door and left the house.

Outside the air was morning fresh. Chilled. He walked to the postbox on the corner, carefully watching the pavement for ice. A slip could be disastrous. At the postbox he used his teeth to grip his glove as he slid his hand free, then fished in his pocket for the gas bill, and brought it out and put it into the hand that was already holding the remote control, as he took his glove out of his mouth.

It was all over in a second. He didn't mean to, but it was as if the movement of hand to postbox mouth was somehow irreversible. He posted the letter and the remote at the same time. Down it went into the red depths, irretrievable. Lost for ever. He looked at the letter box glumly. What had he done? He knew he would not confess to this. Tonight, when the bickering about the whereabouts of the remote started, he would say nothing. He would read his paper, and when asked, would look slightly bewildered and innocent. It would have nothing to do with him.

Mattie dropped Agnes and Tod at the school gates. Sat in the car watching them blend into the moving morning mass of brightly coloured children. How time passes. It did not seem long ago when she was running through the playground herself. Six years old and living a little life filled with hugely important things – a new pencil, a bright red plastic bangle.

Now here she was watching her grandchildren do the same thing, only their important things were more sophisticated and expensive. She was filled with melancholy. It had arrived, this feeling, not long after the meeting in the C-list office. At first anger, then depression, now this slow, lingering sadness.

It was an isolating thing, this melancholy. Both she and John suffered it separately. One would sigh, and the other would hear it and know why that sigh had happened. But they didn't talk about it.

John was miffed. He didn't want a convertible, or a conservatory. He was relieved he wasn't going on a trip across America. The thought of it had filled him with dread. All that moving about, sitting on trains, waiting for trains, worrying that they'd miss trains. Thank God he had been excused that. And secretly he'd hated the red velvet sofa. He was simply irritated at himself for trusting his money to a bunch of inept stuffed shirts in suits, and for somehow failing to get Mattie the things she longed for.

Mattie was the one who wanted things, John thought. And a sudden flash of anger streaked through his guilt. Damn you, if you want all that stuff, go out and get it yourself. Get a job, I did. And it wasn't always pleasant.

Mattie just thought the whole thing typical. She never got what she wanted. It was always the same, the thing, an object of desire, dangled just out of her reach. And then, when she thought she could have it, when it was in grasping range, it was whipped away.

She thought of her youth. Her golden days, when the world was buttery, full of lipstick and opportunity. She'd thrown it away. Frittered her young life away trying to be nice, wanting everyone to like her. Pah! she thought. What a vile thing to want to be. What was nice? A slippy thing, not good not bad. Just safe, slightly sweet. Nice, who was nice? People who didn't speak out, didn't grab their chances. But kept their opinions quiet lest they offend, lest they lose a friend who wasn't a real friend anyway. A view was nice, a pudding might be nice, a puppy, a kitten – nice. But people weren't nice. People were jealous, greedy. People told lies. In fact, nice was a lie. Nice was hypocritical. Nice wasn't very nice.

She knew when all this being nice had happened. Knew the moment she'd let her youth slip away. She'd done it with two words. I will.

Looking for the Remote Control

Lily stayed overnight at Russack's Hotel. A genteel place which she found quietly comforting. It made no demands on her other than that she be polite, which she was at all times, anyway.

She wore jeans and a sweater to the dining room. Sat in a corner, a book propped against the salt and pepper grinders, a defence against other diners. She felt it helped give the impression that she wasn't eating alone because she was alone, but because she chose to be alone. She felt that in the opting for solitude lay the difference between being unwanted and being self-contained and interesting.

The menu tonight suited her need for comfort. Lily ate fish pie and followed it with plum crumble. Ideal fare for someone out alone on a bitter night. She felt she needed some stodge, she was eating for solace. The book wasn't working. She did not think she looked self-contained and interesting; she looked lonely. She chewed slowly, staring out of the window, at the golf links and the sea beyond, thinking. But not in the organised, well-ordered way she liked to think, or at least, flattered herself she liked to think. She forked the creamy mix of fish and potato into her mouth, felt the pleasing solace of it, and her mind filled with pictures of Mattie.

Mattie had taken responsibility for the loss of the television remote. It was all her fault. She remembered finding it in the kitchen, carrying it with her as she went to pick up the morning paper, putting it down on the shelf of the hallstand. Then nothing. There was a void, a blackness where her movements with the remote ought to be. She'd retraced her steps to the hallstand, seen the empty shelf and stood looking blankly into the middle distance, wondering, What the hell did I do with it?

The search had been relentless. Frantic, when they checked in the newspaper and discovered that because the television was stuck on Channel Five, they were doomed to an evening of dire films – one about an invasion of earth by aliens from outer space who took over people's bodies, the other an erotic thriller which was neither erotic or thrilling. 'Just people humping one another in various places and various positions,' said Mattie.

'There must be some other way of changing the station without using the remote,' said John.

'Surely,' agreed Mattie.

They'd studied their sleek set, looking carefully for some button they could push that would open a tiny door and reveal a set of manual controls. But they couldn't see anything. They ran searching fingers over it, poked it here and there. Nothing happened.

'It has to be somewhere,' said John. 'You *must* be able to get into it. What about when it needs fixing?'

'They don't fix televisions any more,' said Mattie. 'They just tell you that it'd be cheaper to buy a new one.'

'Buggered if I'm buying a new one,' said John.

So the hunt resumed. They looked under the cushions on the armchairs and sofa. Then under the armchairs and sofa. Mattie slipped her hands down the sides of the armchairs and sofa. She found four fifty pences, a button, several Mars Bar wrappers, a packet of Polo mints (unopened), many pennies, a watch (long lost), a comb, six five pences and a small black plastic thing. She didn't know what it was, but in case it was some important part of something, she put it in the drawer in the pine dresser along with the other things she had over the years come across and didn't know what they were, but which might be vital to the working of something, she couldn't imagine what. She did not find the remote control.

She broadened the search. She rummaged through pockets, upended boots, took books from the shelves to peer behind them, rifled through the drawers in the kitchen, looked into the fridge. 'Surely it couldn't be here.' She went outside with a torch to see if it had somehow found its way into the front garden. Maybe she'd had it in her hand when she left to take the children to school, and dropped it. She hunted inside the car, under the beds, in the beds, in the wardrobe, in the bathroom. She looked in the shed, thinking John might have carried it out there. 'Unthinkingly,' she said. 'You might have forgotten you were carrying it.'

'I do not forget I am carrying something and drop it. Do you think I've gone ga-ga?' said John. 'I haven't laid eyes on the damn remote since last night.'

Grandpa had decided over an hour ago to go to bed. 'In my day televisions had proper knobs on them and you turned them. Those were proper times. You measured things in feet and inches. You got a pound of tomatoes. And you paid for them with proper money. We were happy then. You had milkmen who whistled, and children were polite.'

Mattie and John glared at him.

Guiltily, grumpily, he'd climbed the stairs and disappeared into his room. He sat at his desk, switched on his computer and emailed Nina in Prague. They'd met in a chat room two years ago, and now corresponded daily. It worried him that she was under the impression that he was a forty-two-year-old architect with a full head of hair. But it did not cross his mind that if he lied, so might she.

Nina had told him she was thirty-five and a ceramics designer. She was sixty-eight and a retired butcher's assistant. She told him she liked older men.

Not this old, thought Grandpa.

All in all, the deception cheered them both. And ensured neither had any intention of meeting the other.

Grandpa told Nina about the television remote. How he'd inadvertently posted it.

It just sort of happened, he wrote. *It was in my hand with the letter, and whoosh, down into the postbox it went. Landed with a thump. I stood looking at the hole thing you put letters into and knew there was nothing I could do about it. Now Mattie and John are downstairs having a real ding-dong about it and who lost it. I can hear them all the way up here in my room. Do you think I should go down and tell them? Only things are a bit fraught in the family right now, what with one thing and another. And Christmas coming up and all.*

Hope all's well with you.

Cheers, Martin.

Nina responded quickly. She usually did, spending many hours every day corresponding with people across the globe, most of whom thought she was a ceramics designer, though one or two had been told she was an actress concentrating on character roles. *My days as a leading lady are long past,* Nina had written.

Hello, Martin.

I think it best you keep the secret of the television remote to yourself. This way it will become a family mystery, a sort of legend your children can talk about all their lives. (She had assumed, when Grandpa first told her about Mattie and John, that they were his nine- or ten-year-old children; he had not enlightened her about this.) *Also, if they are fighting, they might unite and turn against you. Best keep quiet, though this might mean you will have the stress which can give you the ulcer in the stomach. I have no children myself* (She had five), *but my sister has many. I have watched her and I know they can be of trouble to you. I used to think the way to bring up the children was to be kind and good and tell them always the truth. But now I think the best way is to sometimes give them the bribes and tell them the lies. This way you will not have the stress and you will not get the ulcers.*

Love, Nina.

Grandpa was relieved. He did not want to admit to having posted the television remote. It would just serve as some sort of confirmation of his senility.

Emotionally Chic

The bedroom at the hotel had a crumbling opulence. It had what Lily called an old-world charm. She loved it, but not enough to want anything like it in her own home. The wardrobe was cavernous and ornate; she thought her coat looked lonely hanging in it. The bed was huge and high, and Lily had to clamber into it. No duvet, but a thick, and very comforting, layer of blankets. Perched in it, over three feet above the pinkish carpet, Lily could see out to the other side of the bay. Clusters of lights, a winter moon luminescent in the icy sky. She didn't draw the curtains, she loved the view too much. She checked her watch, ten o'clock. She sighed. It was going to be a long night. She never slept in hotels.

She phoned Art. 'Hi, how are you?'

'Hi, Lil. I'm fine. Had a good day? How was Rita?'

'She'd be charming if she wasn't a bit scary. And I was wrong about the Oil of Olay. She has beautiful skin.'

Lily could hear a roar in the room. In her absence, Art would be indulging in sports programmes, which she hated. It sounded like someone had just scored a goal. She knew Art would be watching it and not really paying attention to her.

'I'm lonely,' she said. And as the words came out, she realised how lonely she was. Not just here, in this hotel room. But everywhere she went. She was lonely even when she was with Art. All this pursuing of perfection in everything she did was isolating.

'Never mind,' said Art. 'Home tomorrow, and I'll make up for it. What's the hotel like?'

'Old, but comforting. Huge bed, and high off the ground, makes me feel like a little girl.'

'Cool,' said Art. 'Wish I was in it with you.'

'Do you know,' said Lily, 'in a way it reminds me of Marie's

48

house. Sort of ramshackle and homey. The way Marie's rooms are thrown together out of things she's been given or has come across in second-hand shops.'

'The girl has her own style,' said Art. 'And her own way of thinking.'

'She's cool in her way,' said Lily. 'Especially in how she thinks. The things she says.'

'She's emotionally chic,' said Art.

He'd done it again. Said something Lily wished she'd said. So she grunted. 'Yeah. That's it.'

'When will you be back tomorrow?' asked Art.

'Late afternoon. I'll drop in on my folks before heading for the airport.'

The roar behind Art deepened; she could feel his frustration at not being able to give the football his full attention, and bade him goodbye. 'Love you.'

'Yes, love you too,' he said absently, a distracted, automatic response. His attention was with the football, which was hotting up. He rang off.

Lily lay back on the bed, looked at the moon, and thought about Art. She could picture him. He'd be lying on the sofa, wearing his Dockers and that blue sweatshirt with the fraying sleeves, no socks or shoes. He'd have his feet up on the red and black silk cushion. He had beautiful feet, long toes, which he'd wiggle with pleasure.

Art was good at pleasure. Lily wasn't. She never could, except when sleeping, relax. After twenty minutes or so of sitting, she'd think of something she ought to be doing, or she'd notice the curtains needed straightening, or there was a mark on the carpet that needed cleaning. It would bother her, nag her, taunt her, and eventually win. She'd get up, go to the kitchen for a spray can of Vanish and a cloth, and erase the stain. 'Do you have to?' Art would say.

Art could relax effortlessly. More than that, he planned his leisure, engulfed himself in it. Tonight, for example, knowing there was a replay of the match on television, he'd have avoided the news so he wouldn't hear the result. He'd have made a sandwich in advance, so that he'd be settling down as the title music came on. Lily could never manage this. She was always still making her snack when any favourite programme started, so she'd miss the sometimes vital opening section. Or she'd make it too soon, and have it eaten before the credits stopped running. 'Too jumpy, Lil,' Art would say. 'You got to work at your relaxation techniques.'

It seemed to Lily that she was the flaw in her perfect world. The flat was immaculate, facing sofas, beautiful plants, every single thing in it, down to the sheets and teaspoons, chosen and bought with care. Actually, more than care – precision. Everything had to be right. And having achieved this, Lily in some way felt her home to be more than her, better than her. She didn't fit in. She felt, and she never told anyone this, that she wasn't good enough for it. Evenings she would wear a satin robe and sit curled on the sofa reading a book, hoping to appear at ease, sophisticated.

It was a façade. She'd read a few lines, resettle herself, moving her legs from under her. Read a little more, then rearrange herself again. Unlike Art, who draped himself naturally on the sofa opposite, she just couldn't get comfortable. She'd squirm and sigh and think that really she oughtn't to be sitting down at all. Not when there were things to be wiped, dusted, floors to be kept immaculate.

'Pack it in, Lil,' Art would say when he saw her get up to put her row of black vases into a disciplined line. 'What do you think? A crack squad from *Homes and Gardens* is going to burst through the door and smack you about for not having the flat up to absolute photogenic snuff?'

She sighed. She wanted to be cool, like Art. Emotionally chic, like Marie. And what was she? A worrier, a wiper of things that didn't need to be wiped, a fusser. A woman with face drawn in constant battle with dirt. Moving in a finicky bustle, keeping perfect order. And, in her case, using her beautiful home as a front, somewhere she didn't so much as mellow out in, more hide in. For if the flat she inhabited was perfect, who would guess how inadequate she secretly was?

To the outside world Lily and Art were a wonderfully compatible couple, stylish, fashionable. But there were undertows.

The first undertow was Art's objection to Lily's obsessive tidiness. He deemed her anally retentive, and would leave things for her to tidy – newspapers on the kitchen table, coffee cups on the floor beside the sofa in the living room, shoes wherever he kicked them off. An act of defiance. The perfectness of Lily's vision of home life annoyed him. 'This is where we hang out. Actually live. Can't we do that? Live? Instead of perfecting our lifestyle?'

There was the hours he worked. He often stayed in the office till two or three in the morning. Lily liked him to be home in the evenings, so they could share quality time discussing their separate days over a cholesterol-free meal and a glass of wine. There was his moodiness. He could sink into blackness, despair. 'God dammit,' he'd say, 'what's the point of it all? Why do we do it? Work our arses off snipping, cutting, perfecting to produce a ninety-second piece about the virtues of some cat food or frozen peas. I mean, in the end, who really cares?'

Lily would say, 'You do.'

He'd say, 'Only for the time it takes to work on the film. After that I think, What's that all about? Wouldn't it be great, Lil, to give it all up? All this meaningless stuff. We could go live somewhere in the country, grow our own food. You could still write. I could work the garden. I could provide for us in a real, worthy way. There'd be a purpose.'

In theory Lily agreed. It was the countryside she didn't see the point of. Fields, acres of nothingness, wind, rain, no shops. All this was terrifying.

But the main undertow was the children thing. Art wanted them, and so did Lily. If only she didn't have to give birth to them. Children she liked. Especially when they got old enough to talk to, converse with. Babies scared her. They were little, incredibly little. They were unpredictable. They were incontinent. Their digestive systems were unreliable. They lacked self-control, and were prone to letting rip and howling if they did not get their own way.

There was the business of the actual pregnancy. Lily had friends who'd told her about it. Secretions, bloatedness, swollen ankles, heartburn. It didn't seem pleasant at all. Then there was the actual birth. She'd heard tales – hours of pain, shouting, swearing. Could that be true? It didn't seem at all polite. And a baby – broken nights, teething problems, feeding rituals. And all the stuff. She'd had friends visit with new infants and all the things they needed – a pile of incomprehensible things larger by far than the small being they were supposed to accommodate. Where, in this wonderful flat, was she to put it all?

But what scared her most of all was the baby itself. Toothless, bald and demanding. And the way they looked at you, that long, guileless, knowing stare. Lauren did that. She sucked her thumb and looked at Lily, wide-eyed, unblinking. It made Lily squirm. The girl can see right through me, she'd think. She knows, she just *knows*, what an anally retentive, uptight fool I am.

'I hate the way Lauren stares at me,' Lily had said to Art. 'It's as if she understands everything about me. It's uncritical, yet it makes me doubt myself. There's something almost religious about it.'

'Don't be silly. She's a kid, she's just looking. She probably isn't thinking anything. Smile at her. Make her laugh. Reach out to her. Reassure her. She's a little girl in the same space you are in. Let her know you love her. Join in the moment, Lily. Can't you just join in?'

Join in, thought Lily, how the hell do you do that? She reached for the breakfast menu that had been left on the bedside table. She thought she would have porridge, and smoked haddock with bacon, maybe a poached egg too. Hoped there was decent bitter marmalade to layer on her toast, and wondered if the coffee would be stewed. Perhaps tea would be safer. She didn't know what was getting into her. She was becoming obsessed by food. Normally she ate like a bird. She looked at the clock again. Half past ten. Hours to go before she went down to the dining room. It was going to be a long, long night.

Halfpast ten in the evening, Marie was asleep on her sofa, the television on – an erotic thriller that, had she been awake, she would have turned off. She lay curled, holding a cushion to her stomach. The room was hot, and sweat beaded her forehead and upper lip. This happened every night. She'd pick up her children from Mattie and John's, bring them home. They'd fall into the quiet rhythm of their evening routine. Tod peeled the potatoes or put the pot on for spaghetti. Agnes set the table, filled glasses with milk or orange juice. Marie grilled chops, or, if they were having pasta, prepared the sauce. Afterwards Agnes would help bathe Lauren, and Marie would put her to bed, read her a story. Then, when she was sleeping, Marie would come downstairs to help Tod and Agnes with their homework, do the supper dishes and tidy up. She'd shove dirty clothes in the washing machine, iron clothes for tomorrow, all the while reminding the remaining two offspring it was past bedtime. When all this was done, it was usually after nine, which Marie considered too early to go to bed herself. So she'd sit in front of the television, and always, always fall asleep. Roundabout midnight she'd wake, stretch stiffly, switch off the television and the lights, and stumble groggily to her bedroom.

Tonight, though, her sofa dreamings were interrupted by the phone. For a few moments before its insistent shrill bit into her slumbers, it joined them: she dreamed the phone was ringing. So when she woke she had a few moments when reality was suspended, and soft fragments of her dream still hung about her, her head still numb from thick, gluey sleep. Was the phone ringing, or not? It was, and who could be calling at this time of night?

'Have any of the kids got our remote control?' Mattie said. She never did announce herself, thinking that anyone she phoned should know it was her.

Marie, still surfacing, said, 'Huh?'

'The children.' Mattie sounded crisp. Irritated even. 'Have they by any chance picked up our television remote and taken it home?'

'What?' said Marie. 'Television remote? No, I don't think so.'

'Could you check?' asked Mattie.

'You mean go through their schoolbags and pockets? That's a bit intrusive, don't you think?'

'No, I don't think. I did it all the time to my children.' Forgetting that she was speaking to one of them. 'It was a very effective way of keeping an eye on them.'

'It's spying,' said Marie.

'It's maternal concern,' Mattie insisted. 'Now go and look for our remote.'

Marie put down the phone, walked through to the living room, stood with her arms folded for a few minutes, thinking, This is the nuttiest thing my mother has ever done. She had no intention of raking through her children's pockets. After a while, she went back into the hall, picked up the receiver and said, 'No, Mum. There is no remote control here. What's this all about, anyway?'

'Tell you in the morning,' said Mattie. And rang off.

Marie stood a moment staring at the phone, puzzling. What *was* that all about? She shrugged, but didn't really care. She'd find out in the morning. She went to bed. Lay wondering, as she always wondered, why she hadn't come here sooner. She spread her limbs, luxuriating. Then drifted off.

An hour later she was woken by Lauren climbing into bed beside her. She did this every night. The child huddled against her, complaining she didn't like the dark.

Marie told her what she always told her, 'Shut your eyes and the darkness will go away.' Which she knew was really silly. But it worked.

The child's body soft against her, Marie was swept back to sleep.

But sometimes she would put her head against Lauren, drawing comfort. The chubby three-year-old's arms would enfold her, and a little hand would gently pat her head. Lauren doing what Marie did to her when she fell down, or some kind of pain broke through her normally joyful life. A pat and a silvery child's voice saying, 'There, there,' was so soothing. In the morning for a few precious minutes before she had to force herself from the warmth of bed, Marie would watch her child. She loved the way children slept, arms up on the pillow, fists clenched, lips moving – a slight sucking. Theirs was a fat sleep, ample, deep, satisfying. A restorative thing that set them bouncing into each new day. How Marie envied that.

But for the moment, and before sleep took her, Marie prayed. It was something she did all the time. It had started some months after her husband left, and hadn't stopped. It wasn't a carefully constructed plea for mankind, for the stopping of wars, the feeding of the hungry, the healing of the sick. It was a quiet mantra. Lord God, have pity on me. It wasn't something she'd even planned to do. She wasn't religious, didn't think she really believed in a supreme divine being. The prayer just happened. One day, washing the dishes after supper, she'd said it for the first time. And from then on had kept saying it. It got shorter, though. Now she just said, 'Help me.' Had said it so often her lips didn't move, she no longer thought it.

Of course she knew why she said it. There was a moment coming that she was dreading. It was inevitable, this moment, there would be no avoiding it. One day Andy would come back to her. She might get a letter, he might phone. But one way or another he would get in touch, and he would want something. A divorce, the house, to return to his place in the home as her husband and father of his children, she didn't know. What she did know was that she had changed in the time she'd been without him.

They'd married too young. They'd started being man and wife without really thinking about it. They had carried on the lives they had seen their own mothers and fathers living. They had brought nothing of themselves into the relationship, doing what they thought married people did.

And now, she had grown up. She'd had to. She had sought promotion at work, she needed the money. She had organised her children into a routine of helping in the house. Evenings they moved about, doing their chores, talking, telling one another their days. Complaining, bantering, bickering, planning, exchanging news and jokes. She now knew them better than she had before Andy left. No, it was more than that. She needed them.

How would Andy fit into all this? Marie felt there was no room for him any more. She'd closed the gap he left. And she had changed. She now thought that if she was looking for a man, the man she'd seek would not be Andy. She wasn't looking for a man, though. But some sex now and then would be good.

So she said her prayer. It had become constant, and moved within her in time with – in place of? – the beating of her heart.

❊　❊　❊

Mattie returned to her living room. 'Well,' she said. 'That's that. Marie does not have the remote. It has gone. Disappeared off the face of the earth. We're left with that appalling film. Other than that, there's nothing left to do but switch off the television and have a chat.' It was said with the panicky desperation of a woman who thought she was going mad, or facing the first signs of dementia. It was the void that distressed her. The remembering putting the television remote down on the hallstand, and the blackness of not recalling picking it up again and putting it down someplace else. There was a hole in her brain where her memory ought to be.

Having completely forgotten what she did with the remote control (it did not once cross her mind that perhaps someone else had removed it from the hallstand), Mattie now tested her memory with other things. The name, for example, of her first boss. The sixties-slender, blonde, panda-eyed manager of the King's Road boutique where she'd been more than a mere underling. The underling of underlings, who'd made tea, run to the chemist for Panadol and scrubbed the staff loo. A crisp and perfectly detailed picture of the woman came into Mattie's mind, but her name was gone. It, too, seemed to have disappeared into the same black hole as the whereabouts of the remote. Other things had gone too, the name of her primary school teacher, the name of her Auntie Effie's house, the author of that book she so liked, who was it? What was the book called? She'd forgotten. It was a clear sign she was going, not mad exactly, but a bit dotty. Madness would follow. It was in her family. Her Uncle Tom had gone barking. Had ended up riding the buses holding a notice – *God doesn't like you, and neither do I* – pressed to the window for passers-by to read.

It was with this dread seeping through her that she'd said, 'There's nothing left to do but switch off the television and have a chat.'

John misunderstood. He took the clipped tone to mean that the last thing in the world she wanted to do was have a chat. Especially with him. He wasn't in a pleasant mood anyway. He'd been looking forward to watching the football, followed by a rerun of *Frasier*.

The clumsiness of the erotic thriller appalled him. A thriller it wasn't. Erotic it wasn't. But maybe there was something about those carefully choreographed tongueful kisses, the gorgeously lean and toned bodies, moaning, sighing, stretched with longing, that reminded them both that once that was what they used to do. That was what they ought to be doing now upstairs in their bedroom, expressing their long mutual adoration, not verbally but physically, sweatily. Pouring into one another a passion, hot and breathless.

But John was tired, and angry at himself for not understanding the ways of modern technology – how to get into that smooth-fronted silvery shiny thing on the stand across the room and change the station without using the remote. There must be a button he could press somewhere within its sleek and mocking case.

Mattie was just furious. Panting and verging on crazed. Her search had moved from thorough to silly, from frantic to savage. She had retraced her steps to and from the hallstand over half a dozen times and always drawn a blank. She was going senile, and would never again savour the sweet delights the tanned and sculpted people on the telly were savouring.

The argument, John was to say later, was an argument waiting to happen. It had been hovering round them for weeks. The raging undertow beneath the sighs. It took them by storm, set them reeling. Grievances from years ago were hauled up, and aired. Insults were hurled, they sliced and gashed. And it had started in such a small way.

'You're just mad because you can't watch the football,' said Mattie. 'Who'd want to watch it anyway? Bunch of men kicking a ball about a field. It's boring.'

'Only to someone who doesn't understand it. Someone who is too stupid to grasp the speed and skill and absolute beauty of what they are seeing.'

'Are you calling me stupid?'

'Are you so stupid you have to ask?'

'No. I just thought that if that is what you think, you might have the courage to say it out loud.'

'I thought I just had. OK, you're stupid. You're so stupid you can't remember what you did with the television remote control.'

It stung, this insult. Yet Mattie had invited it. Go on, go on, tell me I'm stupid, I deserve it. Burdened with guilt, she instinctively moved towards pain. But when it came, she didn't take it well. 'That's a horrible thing to say. How could you?'

'You asked for it.'

'I may have done. But you might have had the courtesy to deny it. You might have said, "Of course you're not stupid, Mattie."'

'Didn't, though, did I? You're so manipulative, Matilda.' He always called her Matilda when they argued, he knew she hated that. 'You try to turn conversations, arguments in your favour. So people will pity you, put their arms round you and say, "There, there." Well, that's not going to happen. Not this time.'

Mattie said nothing.

'You think you can get away with anything by being slightly charming, slightly forgetful, a happy-go-lucky cheery mum person. But that's not you at all. You're using this it's-only-me act to run away from things,' John continued.

'I am not,' said Mattie. It came out a lot louder than she meant it to. 'What things?'

'Responsibility. Yourself. Life. This happy-mum-I-don't-matter rubbish is an excuse.'

'For what?' said Mattie.

'For all the things you don't do. Are scared to do, or too lazy to do. I don't know, you tell me.'

'Scared?' shouted Mattie. 'I'm not scared. Lazy? What do you mean?'

'You're lazy. How else do I say it? You don't *do* anything, Matilda.'

'What do you want me to do? Go down the mines? Tote dat bale? What?'

'Clean. You could clean the place. It's filthy.'

'It never is,' Mattie said. 'Where is it filthy? Show me.'

John took her arm and led her to the long pine sideboard (five pounds from a second-hand shop in 1978). Mattie had lovingly stripped and polished it. On the surface was a thick blackened mark.

'That's not filth,' Mattie said. 'That's not a stain. That's candle grease.'

Mattie and stains. A complex subject. Some of the marks in Mattie's house were stains, some were memories, life marks she called them. Only she knew which were which. But the rule was stains were wiped away, life marks stayed. The candle grease was a memory. Why John didn't understand that was a mystery to her.

'It's from when Linda and Marc came to dinner, remember?' She looked at John eagerly, trying for the umpteenth time to instruct him in the basically very simple art of differing between stains and life marks. 'We lit the room with candles and played all our favourite old records, Dylan, James Taylor. Oh, we had a lovely time.'

'That was over ten years ago. I think Linda and Marc would understand if we removed the candle grease from the sideboard. I don't think they'd be insulted.'

'There's no need to get rid of it. It's not really a stain, it's candle grease.' Mattie said this loudly, as if explaining something to someone rather deaf and rather old. Which did nothing to ease John's temper. He cast his eyes up, saw the large brown potato-shaped mark on the ceiling.

'And that,' said Mattie, following his glance, 'is where Rory squirted Coca-Cola. He'd filled his water pistol with it.' She smiled fondly up. Ah, memories.

There were rules in this household. They were not written down, these rules. Never discussed. But they were there. One of them was that all chores requiring a trip up a ladder fell to John. Mattie said quite firmly that she did not *do* ladders.

Recently John had started to regard his possessions with a certain despair. They were old, and had started to look it. He now could no longer see chairs, curtains, carpets without noticing the marks time and use had left on them. They had come to represent the uselessness of his life. Years spent working, earning, and this was what he had to show for it. An old house in need of repair, filled with things in need of repair. Standing at the door, a six-year-old second-hand car, in need of repair.

He looked round the room. The evening newspaper was spread over the sofa, and he hated that. But tonight the mess was worse than ever. Mattie's findings after her obsessive search for the television remote were scattered across the floor – sweet wrappers, old television guides, magazines. He stood viewing the mess and the red mist descended, fury. Is this it? he thought. All that coming and going to and from the office, drawing plans I hated, in an overheated place, with people flirting and telling stupid jokes, and girls in skimpy skirts talking about their boyfriends and their holidays, for this?

'Is this it?' he said now. And there was nothing kind in the way he said it.

'What?' said Mattie. 'Is what it?'

'This.' He spread his arms. 'This room. That sofa. These curtains. The kitchen with that unit door you can't open because it's off its hinges. The cooker with that grill pan you haven't washed in fifteen years.'

'Fifteen years. That's a lie. I washed it last week. I remember because it was when Grandpa wanted sausages, and I had to go to the supermarket at half past six to get them, and it was raining and—'

'The huge pile of laundry on top of the tumble-dryer. The scattering of newspapers spread over the kitchen table—'

'If the laundry annoys you, why don't you do the ironing?'

'Well, it would leave you free to move slowly from room to room with a glazed expression contemplating some minor dilemma in *ER*. I wouldn't want anything like ironing to take you out of your cosy world, Matilda.'

'If you did the ironing it would give you a break from mooning around all day, complaining and making too much tea and getting in my way.'

'Ironing's your job. I have retired. I am taking it easy after years and years of plodding on and plodding on. And nobody noticing or caring as long as I kept the money coming in. A workhorse and you'll get your oats.' He paused, glared. 'Maybe.'

'You can be really nasty when you want to be, John,' said Mattie. 'Nobody thought you were a workhorse.'

'What *did* you think I was? I'd come home from work and you'd all be sitting round the kitchen table, eating, laughing, chatting. Never thought to wait for me. And you'd look up at me as if some intruder had entered. "Hello, it's me, John." And you'd stare as if the beast was here. The thing. Part of the furniture, a chair. And what had you been doing all day?'

'Cooking, cleaning.' Mattie was defensive.

'What did you clean?'

'I don't keep a cleaning diary, John.'

'Just as well. The pages would be blank.'

'Are you suggesting I'm filthy?'

'Yes,' said John. He spat the word.

'I work my fingers to the bone making meals out of nothing to feed this family. That includes your father. If you had brought home a decent living, such as a—'

John cut her short. 'So you see me as a meal ticket.'

'Well,' Mattie was shaking, 'you certainly haven't given much in any other department over the years.'

'If you opened your legs as much as your mouth, perhaps I'd have been motivated.'

Even as the words came out, John regretted them. He knew they weren't true. It was a smutty, schoolboyish remark. The sort of cheap humour he'd heard at the stag night he'd gone to a couple of months before he retired.

One of the men in his office was getting married, and had hired a room in a West End club, a shiny, throbbing place where conversations were throat-achingly yelled over deep bass thumping music. A stripper dressed as a policewoman came along. She put a ghetto-blaster on the floor and slowly, slowly, to the tune of 'Big Spender', removed her uniform till she wore nothing except a pair of black stockings and a suspender belt, then she had straddled the bridegroom-to-be, and gyrated singing along with the song. There had been jokes, wild bawdy jokes. Their blatant crudeness had shocked John. All round him younger men had laughed and laughed, till one by one they'd noticed his simmering scowl, and one by one they'd stilled into uncomfortable silence. Not long after that John had left, but trudging home through the soft summer dark he'd thought himself a fool. It was a night out, a laugh, what did a few silly dirty jokes matter? He was no prude, but the jokes tonight were dirtier than the jokes he'd told when he was young. The clothes these colleagues wore were smarter than the clothes he'd worn when he was their age.

Smarter, too, than what he was wearing now, the suit he'd bought for Lily's wedding. Their cars were newer, shinier, their chat was fast, their jokes no-holds-barred raw. They spoke freely about their sex lives, the things they did, preferred positions, partners' proficiencies and inadequacies in brazen detail. Something John never did. Not that he hadn't done the things his young colleagues bragged about, he just never mentioned them. Not even to Mattie. And she didn't mention anything either. They had naughty adventures in the dark, eight hours' sleep, some toast and coffee when they woke, and went off into their separate days.

Confidence, he thought. It was all about confidence, something he never really had. Not that he wasn't good at his job. He was, he knew that. But he was a draughtsman, never an architect. He'd failed his exams twice, and that was when the confidence slipped away. When he'd worked with a small firm, he'd been an important part of an enthusiastic group of people. In this job, with a huge company, he melted into the background. Now he was part of a team, with a team leader. It sounded like he was playing hockey, for God's sake.

He was ill at ease with the times he was living through. The clothes, the music, the gadgets. He had a mobile phone but rarely used it, and kept it switched off so as not to run down the battery, and he had never once sent anybody a text message and had vowed he never ever would. Such strange stilted exchanges, shortened words interspaced with numbers – thnk U, fck U 2. Emails he hated and never could understand why people didn't just phone him and chat. People had such powerful communication tools, and nothing to say.

And the language – I have a window on Tuesday, that sort of thing. Why didn't people just say they were free on Tuesday. Another thing he hated – when someone said, 'At the end of the day . . .' At the end of the day, we have to conclude. When all's said and done, at the end of the day.

'And another thing,' he'd said to himself as he headed home. 'I hate how nobody gets to be depressed or negative any more. It's all up, it's all positive. Which, at the end of the day, is very depressing, now I think about it.'

He'd felt old and censorious and more than a little shabby. He'd been left behind. It was time to go. A week later he'd taken early retirement. Why not? he'd thought. He'd been wise enough to let Mattie nag him into investing in a private pension plan, that soon would make him more financially comfortable than he'd ever been.

But, right now, he was furious. The erotic thriller played absurdly behind them. The football was long over. He didn't even know the score. And so he'd said a stupid smutty thing to hurt the person he loved most. He knew that was what people sometimes did; in moments of blood-pumping wrath you lashed out and hurt the one person you wouldn't want to hurt, but who was probably the only person it was safe to hurt. The person you knew loved you back.

'Motivated? You?' shouted Mattie, now. 'When have you ever been motivated to do anything? You came home, you sat in the chair—'

'Warmed by your arse after watching soap operas—'

'And,' Mattie blustered on, 'you never did anything. You never fixed the wobbly banister, you never ever finished tiling in the bathroom, you've been saying for years you'd paint the dining room. Too tired from business lunches, I suppose, Mr Not-Quite-An-Architect. Mr Not-Quite-An-Anything.'

Very, very quietly John said, 'Better an almost-been than a never-was, Matilda.' And walked out of the room.

Mattie heard him climb the stairs and go into the bathroom. She stood perfectly still as if the verbal chaos they'd created was still hurtling round her. She heard taps turned on, the rush of water through pipes, the toilet flush. Then John going into the bedroom. It was only her and the romping naked adults in the room. She switched them off. And looked round. She had to agree, she'd made some messes in her time, but the debris left after her frenetic hunt for the television remote was one of her best. The room looked as if it had been ransacked by drunken underage burglars. Even though she was by nature tolerant of upheaval, this shocked her.

She started to slowly pick things up. When the floor was cleared she vacuumed it. Then she dusted and polished the coffee table and the pine sideboard and spent some time getting rid of the beloved candle grease stain. She wiped the Venetian blinds. After that, she went to the kitchen, packed the dishwasher with the supper dishes, and wiped the tops of the units, then the fronts of the units. She cleaned out the fridge and gave it a wipe, too. Then she got her bucket and mop and washed the kitchen floor. After that, she did the windows. This would show John. She decided she would stay up all night cleaning, then he would come down in the morning and feel just awful for telling her she was filthy.

It was a foolish decision. For if she'd followed John to bed, they would have turned to one another in the warmth and the dark. They would have held each other, and she might have cried a little, and if she had, he would have comforted her and told her he was sorry. Then she would have told him she was sorry, too. They would have made love. They would have forgiven one another. Arguing might be hell, but worth it, for making up could be glorious.

But tonight Mattie was a martyr. Giving up the comfort of her bed to scrub and clean, and to show John what a fine woman and splendid housewife she was. Though mostly she worked through the night to make him feel guilty. As she wiped and scrubbed she imagined John coming down in the morning to be amazed at the shine and sparkle she'd created.

'Oh you shouldn't have,' he'd cry.

And she would say, 'I wanted to. I wanted you to have the pristine house you long for, so I stayed up all night cleaning.'

He would then be filled with remorse at the cruel things he'd said, and insist she sat in the living room with her feet up while he ministered to her, bringing her tea and toast, and telling her tenderly that she was a fool, but a lovely, lovely fool.

Spurred by this vision, Mattie worked into the small hours. So they didn't hold each other, they didn't apologise, and didn't seal that apology in the soft snug of their bed with a kiss, with love.

When Mattie did at last fall asleep it was in the chair in the living room, wearing a blue and white striped apron and clutching a spray can of upholstery cleaner in one hand and a small yellow

64

sponge in the other. She woke at six, the sky reddening and the first birds singing. Stiff, aching and shivering, she shuffled upstairs to bed, peeled off her clothes, snuck under the duvet. And slept.

At quarter to eight, the insistent ringing of the doorbell woke John. It was Marie and the children, wondering what had happened. Why was the house still dark, curtains drawn? Was someone ill?

John, still rumpled from sleep, scratched his head and told her nobody was ill. Mattie seemed to have over-slept. As Marie prepared breakfast, John went upstairs to dress. Then he took Tod and Agnes to school. Grandpa played with Lauren. Nobody really noticed how clean the house was, though Agnes remarked that the kitchen smelled funny, sort of bleachy. Marie said it did, didn't it? Grandpa and Lauren spread newspaper on the kitchen table and did some finger-painting. When John returned from dropping off Agnes and Tod at school, he made himself bacon and eggs and dumped the frying pan, then his plate and coffee cup in the sink.

Upstairs Mattie slept. Head drowning in her pillow, mouth open, a small spill of drool easing its way down her chin. She smelled of bleach. By the time she woke, and came downstairs, the house was inching towards being messy again. She ached all over, long-dormant muscles protesting at their sudden awakening. It hurt to move, to fill the kettle, to reach to the top shelf for a cup. To work through the night, scrubbing and wiping just to make your husband reel with remorse, was, Mattie knew, now that daylight and sanity were here, stupid. More than stupid, seriously stupid.

She made herself some coffee and walked slowly to the living room, where John was reading the paper. He had by now noticed how shiny and tidy his home was, he'd spotted that the famed candle grease stain had been removed from the sideboard. And had felt a certain pleasure at the new gleaming surface, and at the same time a small pang at the passing of a long-term household landmark. He'd miss that stain.

Of course, he realised that Mattie must have worked long into the night to achieve this degree of cleanness. He realised, also, that she'd done it to make him feel guilty. To make him feel just awful about the things he'd said. Well, he did feel awful. But he wasn't going to be manipulated into admitting it. So when Mattie came, shuffling on weary legs, into the room and sat with a deepening sigh on the sofa, he did not look up. He did not say, 'Mattie you fool. You didn't have to do all this.' He did not remark on how pleasant it was to sit in a pristine room smelling of lavender wax and not to have to remove a whole clutter of newspapers from the chair before he could sit down. He didn't give her a hug and a kiss, and promise himself he'd buy her some sort of a peace offering. He carried on reading his paper.

Mattie said nothing. She did not complain of aching bones. She did not ask him to congratulate her on her splendid skivvying skills. She drank her coffee. She sighed several times to let John know she was there. When he did not respond, she stopped. They sat ignoring each other. This silence was not a quiet, companionable thing. It was thick, spiked with resentment, nasty, full of the words they'd said last night. Long-time lovers and friends do not have to use words to communicate. Mattie and John, in this stiff and quivering quiet, were telling one another that the arguing was not over. Neither was ready to forgive. There was more hurt to come.

Mattie rose and left the room, taking her cup with her (normally she'd have left it lying on the floor and would have retrieved it sometime later, maybe even the next day, when she was looking for a cup). After a few moments John followed. He stood in the doorway of the kitchen, watching Mattie washing up. Even from behind she said, 'I am not speaking to you, John White.' He could tell from the stiff way she held herself, and from the busy elbows moving in and out, up and down as she washed the dishes. That, and the fact she'd opted to wash the dishes in a manner that suggested grandiose suffering, rather than just stack the dishwasher.

He thought she was behaving foolishly. Mr Not-Quite-An-Architect, Mr Not-Quite-An-Anything, he thought. Below the belt, Mattie. It'll take more than a smile and a peck on the cheek to fix that one. More than a plate of roast pork and crackling, his favourite meal. In fact he couldn't imagine what it would take to make him feel that Mattie didn't consider him a failure. But it

would be a lot. Meantime, he would not forgive. After all, she'd
started it.

Mattie pulled a fork from the foamy depth of her washing-up
bowl, and viciously wiped yolk from its prongs. Better an almost-
been than a never-was, Matilda. How cruel, how nasty. And he
thought her stupid, and a slut. She clenched her jaw, narrowed
her lips, felt her heart harden. He'd have to crawl across the floor
before she forgave him. After all, he'd started it.

Catch-up Conversations

Lily felt queasy. She drove down the motorway approaching the Forth Bridge, which would take her into Edinburgh, at a sedate fifty miles an hour, hugging the inside lane. She yawned. She'd had a restless night, and had been woken at six by a strange thwacking sound she could not place. She'd slid from bed and crossed to the window. Through the morning gloom she could see, on the golf course, only yards away, a group of men teeing off. She watched them settle their stance, eye the ball, swing, and wallop it. There was the hollow whack of driver on ball and the thin whoosh of something small and hard ascending at speed. Golfers, she thought, at dawn. Well, it was St Andrews. That was what people did when they came here.

Every now and then, as she drove, she'd touch her stomach and draw in her breath. Too much food in there. She didn't know why she had eaten so much. It had been a compulsive and comforting placing of soft, tasty and nurturing things into her mouth, that led to her eating a plate of porridge (neatly sprinkled with brown sugar), smoked haddock, bacon and egg, two slices of toast liberally spread with Oxford marmalade, and two cups of tea. For someone who normally breakfasted on a glass of fresh orange juice and an abstemious low-fat yoghurt, this was a blow-out. She belched.

It had stopped raining, but the effects of the deluge Lily had driven through on her way south were there on the road. A glistening couple of inches of rain water covered the tarmac. The car tyres swished through it.

She drove on to the bridge. High above shining water, elated and fearful. For if this suspended construction was ever going to snap in two, it would surely do it when she was driving across it. If she looked to the right, she could see the river Forth stretching out, widening towards the sea, and glancing left she saw the old railway bridge. The complex red structure that from a distance up the motorway rose high to complement the hills behind Edinburgh. A train rattled across it. Lily remembered briefly dating a man who painted this bridge. He was tall, wore checked shirts and read a lot of Hemingway. They'd had three heated, passionate months together, then drifted apart. She wondered what had happened to him. Was he, perhaps, standing on a platform dangling far above the river, busy with large brush and pot of red paint? And wasn't it funny how you could be so deeply intimate with someone, then never see them again?

The sky was darkening, more rain on the way. The air was translucent, heavily damp. The person who'd had the hired car before Lily had switched the radio to a classical music station which she hadn't bothered to change. So something deep, sombrely unmelodic droned out, filling the car, and Lily, with a sense of impending doom. This was magnified by the emptiness of the road. Coming off the Forth Bridge and on to the dual carriageway that led into town, there was not another driver about. Lily wondered if something catastrophic had happened and only she in the whole world didn't know about it.

She looked in her rear-view mirror, saw a car speeding towards her. As it whooshed nearer, the driver flashed the headlights and banged the horn. Great walls of hissing spray flew out from under the tyres, and as the car shot past Lily's, the deluge drenched her windscreen, obliterating her view of the road ahead. She switched on her wipers, and saw the hooligan car hammer into the distance, and a small figure at the wheel, waving wildly. It was, Lily realised, Rita Boothe.

Where was she going? Lily wondered. And at such a pace. It seemed so glamorously hectic. She wished she was going where Rita was going, and not on her way to pay a fleeting visit to her mother and father. Still, small comfort. If something catastrophic had happened, then judging from her vivacious driving habits and overly friendly motorway greeting, Rita didn't know about it either.

Lily continued her careful way into Edinburgh. She felt some relief as she crossed the intersection that took her off the dual carriageway and on to the Queensferry Road. There was traffic here. It was always a busy spot, cars going into town, cars coming away from the centre heading north to the Bridge, cars going to the city bypass. So nothing drastic had happened, the world was carrying on – business as usual.

She moved through the traffic lights, and turned right past rows of thirties bungalows, then on to the Corstorphine Road. Suburban shops, wine shops, hairdressers, newsagents and people moving along the pavements. It was all comfortably familiar, her old stamping ground.

She turned at last into the small cul-de-sac where Mattie and John lived. The houses here were large, expensive, though they hadn't been when Mattie and John bought theirs. Most of them had been renovated, new front doors, landscaped gardens. Only the house that Lily stopped outside remained as it had been in the sixties. The paint on the window frames was peeling a little, the roof sagged slightly. The huge rowan tree in the garden needed lopping. The hedge bulged on to the pavement. But there was something about it that attracted the eye. It had a solidity, a gentle oldness. The astragal windows over the front door, the carved wooden swan at the upstairs window, the huge aspidistra at the one downstairs. The battered, weathered nameplate on the gate that read THE WHITE RESIDENCE. This, Lily had no doubt, was the loveliest house in the street.

She got out of the car, gathered up the selection of cheeses and bottle of malt whisky she'd bought them in St Andrews, shut the car door, locked it, walked to the front gate. A rush of nostalgia when she heard that old familiar squeak as she pushed it open. Up the path, past Mattie's flower beds. Now dormant, but in summer a thick fusion of colour – delphiniums, roses, salmon-pink verbascum, red poppies – to the front door. A smile to the huge tub of dark blue and white winter pansies and scarlet cyclamen. She rang the bell, and, not bothering to wait for anyone to answer, went in.

'It's me,' she shouted. She had shouted this every time she'd entered the house for the past twenty-eight years. When she'd come home from school, or from visiting one of her childhood pals, she'd throw open the door, and announce herself.

She stood in the hallway. Home. She breathed it in. There was that smell – the indefinable aroma that always stirred something deep within her. Lily had travelled far to distant countries – India, Japan, America, France – but nowhere had she found a scent that made her feel safe, wanted, like the scent in this house did. Only, she sniffed again, it was different. There were undersmells of bleach and cleaning agents. She looked down, saw that the lovely old red and ochre tiles were gleaming. There were no coats hanging over the end of the stair banister. There was a stillness. There was an atmosphere, something was wrong. 'Hello,' she shouted again.

'In the kitchen,' Mattie answered.

Lily found her mother not sitting at the table doing the crossword or reading, her normal morning activities, but kneeling on the floor polishing the lower panels of the stripped pine door. 'What are you doing?'

'I'm cleaning,' said Mattie. 'I've taken a notion to scrub and polish. There's something comforting about it. It's soothing to see the surfaces I'm doing coming up all shiny.'

Lily looked round. The table where Grandpa and Lauren had been finger-painting was now cleared, wiped and had a bowl of oranges sitting dead centre. Nothing else. No newspapers, mail, books. This was disconcerting. There were no dishes in the sink, no crumbs on the units, the floor sparkled. Lily's uneasiness deepened, shifted inside her. Yes, definitely, something was wrong.

'Put the kettle on, there's a love,' said Mattie. She remained kneeling and polishing.

Lily filled the gleaming kettle and switched it on. 'Where's Dad?'

'Outside in the shed,' said Mattie, still polishing.

'It's December. And freezing. What's he doing out there?'

'Don't ask me. I have no idea what he does in that shed. He goes out there, stays away for hours, then comes back in again. Who knows what he's doing?'

Lily said she'd snip out to say hello while the kettle boiled.

Mattie said, 'Good idea.' And seemed to Lily to start polishing harder.

In the shed, John was sharpening his spade. Lily, until this moment, didn't know spades needed sharpening. Still, at least he stopped to give his daughter a hug and kiss, which was more than her mother had done. They swapped news.

Rory, Lily's brother, called these exchanges of recent personal events catch-up conversations. He hated them. 'Every time I go home,' he said, 'it's all platform kisses and catch-up conversations. Why? It takes days sometimes to get down to some decent talk. Sometimes you don't get any real chat in till it's time to go home.'

He lived in Paris. He had planned to move further from his family, Australia or America, but had met and fallen for Isabel, a Parisienne of astounding beauty – long gleaming black hair, and lips to die for (according to Rory) – who thought her native city the only place in the world worth living in. She was so fixed in this notion, she regarded anyone who did not live in Paris with a certain scorn. They were definitely inferior beings with very little taste and no sophistication at all. Rory's suggestion that they move to San Francisco or Melbourne was met with a tantrum, and Isabel was good at tantrums. 'Montreal, then,' Rory had proposed, an excellent compromise. It was French, though in a Canadian sort of fashion, and at the same time a suitably extreme distance from his family. Isabel abandoned the tantrum and gave him the icy stare. They remained in Paris.

'I've put the kettle on,' said Lily. 'Are you coming in for a cup of tea?'

John said he'd be along in a minute. But Lily had the feeling he wouldn't, and asked if anything was wrong.

'No,' said John. 'Nothing's wrong. Nothing at all. What makes you think something's wrong, just sharpening my spade. Got to keep the tools in order. Good heavens, Lily, just doing a few chores. Nothing's wrong.'

Lily thought he protested too much. Something *is* wrong, she thought.

Back in the kitchen, Mattie had made tea and set a plate of home-made biscuits on the unnervingly pristine table. They were the usual Mattie fare, short on looks, but tasty. Mattie's cooking was superb; her baking left a lot to be desired. Her cakes, John said, resembled children's sandpies. They were shapeless and usually sagged in the middle, but her family ate them anyway. Mostly so as not to offend Mattie, who took all refusals of cake as a personal insult. Lily knew she would have to eat a biscuit, probably two. If she didn't Mattie would sulk, not openly, but in a stiff-body-language way. And would mention the declined biscuit at some later date. Eating Mattie's offerings was one of the house rules, along with the obligatory catch-up conversations.

Lily sipped her tea, and nibbled the misshapen offering. 'I'm not terribly hungry,' she said. 'I had a big breakfast at the hotel.'

'When did you have breakfast?' asked Mattie.

'Nine o'clock.'

'And it's now after twelve. You'll be hungry again. You'll be staying for lunch.' It was said like that, not so much an invitation as an order.

'I have to get to the airport.'

'When?'

'Three at the latest.'

'You've time for a plate of soup. I made some this morning. Carrot.' She waved in the direction of the giant soup pot on the cooker. Lily knew she was doomed to soup. There would be no getting out of it.

Mattie rose, went to the cooker to heat up her pot, and as her back was turned Lily slipped the biscuit into her handbag.

Mattie leaned against the kitchen unit and looked at her daughter. 'Have you finished that biscuit already? You better take another. You're too thin. You could do with some feeding.'

Lily dutifully took a second lumpen, but golden, oaty round from the plate. And when her mother's back was turned, slipped it into her handbag beside the first one.

'I saw a photograph yesterday,' she said.

'Oh,' said Mattie. 'Where?'

'In a book Rita Boothe showed me. It was a photo of you. You were in the back of a limousine and you weren't wearing very much. You had a bottle of Jack Daniels.' Her tone was accusatory. She didn't have to voice her disapproval, it was there in the way she spoke.

Mattie smiled. 'Oh goodness,' she said. 'Happy days.'

'Whose limousine was it?' Lily asked.

'I have no idea,' Mattie told her. 'I can't remember. Like the saying goes, if you remember the sixties, you weren't there.'

'You looked like you were having a wonderful time,' said Lily.

'It was the sixties,' said Mattie. 'Everyone was having a wonderful time. It *was* a wonderful time.'

Mattie drifted off, remembering. It had been a hot day, and she'd been wearing a calico dress and very little else. Rita had come to photograph not the band she'd been following at the time, but the groupies. The manager, she remembered, had been furious.

Of course, she'd wanted to be photographed, but had sat apart from the rest of the girls, looking, she hoped, mysterious. Praying Rita would find her more intriguing than the others. Then, when Rita did notice her, and did want to capture her on film, she'd refused, thinking this would add to her allure, and anyway, refusing to be photographed was what interesting people did.

Then Rita had said her face was full of wonder and life. How she'd thrilled at that. It had stayed with her all her life, a little precious memory kept in a secret place. She would take it out when she was feeling low, and finger it, turn it over and over, cherishing it. She had adored Rita Boothe ever after.

Rita had asked her if she'd ever slept with John Lennon. How she'd laughed at that. Laughed and laughed. What the hell, she'd thought. If she thinks that, I might as well go for it. So she'd stripped off her dress, flung someone's feather boa round her neck, swigged the Jack Daniels she'd been given, felt it go straight to her head – she rarely drank in those days – and gave in to the moment. Her face was full of wonder and life. She was beautiful. Click went the camera, and there was that moment preserved for ever. Wasn't it strange how things happened? She hadn't thought about that photograph for years. Only the compliment that went before it. Now Lily had seen it, and was clearly shocked.

John Lennon, she thought. Huh.

'You were a groupie,' said Lily. She sounded horrified. In fact, she was jealous.

'I know that. You know that. I have never hidden my past from you or Rory or Marie. I have always been absolutely honest with all of you.'

'If you saw a photo of me looking like you looked in that photo of you, you'd have grounded me for life.'

'I most certainly would have done. I have been there, seen the dangers. A mother tries to protect her children from the pitfalls of her own experience.'

'Huh,' said Lily. 'It was sex and drugs and rock'n'roll for you. And homework, cocoa and being in by eleven o'clock for us.'

'Exactly,' said Mattie, laying out the soup plates. She went to the door, opened it, shouted, 'SOUP,' and returned to laying the table.

Sex and drugs and rock'n'roll, she thought. I should have been so lucky. Sex – she had been young and very inexperienced. Not wanting anyone to know her inadequacies, she had demurred at many offers of a roll in the hay. In fact she had been so quiet when sex had been discussed by her fellow groupies, they'd decided she thought they were novices. She'd gained a reputation as a woman of vast experience, someone who knew a trick or three, but was too sophisticated to talk about it. As a groupie, she'd grouped, definitely that, and grouped around famous men. But nothing of an intimate nature had ever taken place. Except for once with a drummer with a band that had fleetingly made the charts, then disappeared for ever. He'd been even more inexperienced than her, and not wanting to appear less than wildly laddish had hinted at her prowess. She'd come across him years later in a newspaper at the garage where her car was being serviced, in one of those whatever-happened-to articles. He'd quit the music business and opened a hairdressing salon. He seemed quite wealthy. And he did not, to her relief, mention her. Sex, drugs and rock'n'roll? Well, not really. No sex anyway.

Drugs? They scared her. She'd smoked a little dope. But anything else was out of her league. Dropping acid? Seeing rooms melt? No thanks, she'd thought. I'd rather have a cup of tea.

Rock'n'roll? That she still liked. Of the three, that had been her favourite, and the only one she'd indulged in. Even now she'd thrill at the opening bars of Jimi Hendrix's 'All Along the Watchtower'. Hearing them made her stop in her tracks, and for a moment she'd feel something exciting was going to happen. Though it never did.

'I didn't want you to . . .' Mattie stopped. Thought about this. She hadn't wanted Lily to be like her. True, but she wasn't going to admit that. She hadn't wanted Lily to fritter away her young life being silly. She hadn't wanted Lily to spend her days wishing something would happen, which was what she herself had done. Which was what she still did. Only now she knew that events of the magnitude she wished for didn't just happen, you made them happen. Except she didn't know how to do that.

'I wanted you to have direction in your life. To know who you are and what you want, and how to get it.' Mattie was pleased with this. 'Yes, that's it.'

She ladled out the soup, thinking that she still didn't know what she wanted. Knowing that as a young girl she'd been scared, and she was still scared. And if she could only grasp what it was she wanted, and what exactly she was scared of (for she never really could define that to herself), then everything would be fine.

Grandpa and Lauren came through from the living room, where they'd been playing computer games. Grandpa kissed Lily, and settled at the table beside her. Lauren sat next to Mattie, who tied a bib round her neck. The child gazed with wide and innocent eyes at Lily, who squirmed, then, remembering Art's lecture, smiled and said, 'Hello, Lauren.'

The child continued to stare, her mouth twitched. For an awful moment Lily thought the little face across the table was going to crumple, and tears would flow. But no, Lauren returned the smile. It was a wholehearted thing, this smile. It moved up from her lips, dimpling her cheeks, to her eyes, that shone, and down through her whole body. She glowed glee. Then, hit by a sudden bout of shyness, Lauren turned and hid her face in Mattie's shoulder.

'That's your Auntie Lily come to see you,' said Mattie.

Lily was triumphant. She'd made a three year old smile. She couldn't have felt more proud if she'd scaled Everest, won Wimbledon or sailed the Atlantic single-handed. She gave Lauren a little wave, a small flutter of her fingers. 'Hello,' she said again. Noticing that her voice had gone an octave higher than usual. The child grinned and hid her face again.

Mattie, knowing a game was in the offing when everyone should be settling down to the serious business of soup-eating, said, 'Now, now. Let's not get silly.' She scooped a spoonful of the carroty brew from Lauren's plate, and guided it into her grandchild's open mouth.

To let Lily know they were adult, and should concern themselves with adult matters, she asked if they should bother with
proper napkins, or settle for paper this Christmas. 'There's such
nice designs these days,' said Mattie. 'And you can just throw
them out afterwards. No laundry.'

Lily agreed, adding that they could use a paper tablecloth, too.
But Mattie insisted a good Christmas table needed proper linen,
and candles. 'It has to be special,' she said. Lily agreed, and gave
Lauren another little smile. Checking if this smiling thing was the
start of something special, or just a one-smile stand.

Then Mattie asked after Art, and Lily told her he was fine, and
had just bought a new suit. Mattie said that was nice and what
colour was it. Lily told her charcoal grey. 'Nice,' Mattie said again.
Then, 'Good girl,' to Lauren. 'You'll soon be big and strong eating
up all your food.'

Grandpa crumbled bread into his soup. Lily commented that
John hadn't come in for lunch. And noted that Mattie wasn't
eating.

'Oh, he'll be along,' said Mattie. The spoon in her hand moved
fluidly from plate to Lauren. The child sat gripping the sides of
her high chair, mouth agape, eyes wide and fixed on Lily. 'And I'm
not that hungry.'

Grandpa stopped crumbling and looked at her. Mattie did not
meet his gaze, and said that she might buy a goose for Christmas
dinner, though they could be a bit greasy, then told Lily not to
forget the bowl for the trifle.

Lily noticed the look, but was too busy being pleased with
herself for extracting a smile from Lauren to think about it.

She imagined herself in a new role of interesting aunt. She
would come to see her nephew and two nieces bearing exciting
gifts, she would take them on wonderful days out, encourage
them to express themselves, side with them in arguments with
their mother and grandmother. She wondered what sort of outfit
this would require. Something glamorous and flamboyant, but
not too over-the-top. She didn't want them to be embarrassed to
be seen out with her, when, for example, she took them to new
and controversial productions of Pinter or Chekhov at the
Traverse Theatre. Though it might be a few years before she

could do that. Tod, Marie's oldest, was nine and still absorbed by football and his PlayStation. Agnes was a drama queen, though Lily loved her dearly, and very ambitious. She was going to form a girl band with her two best friends, Laura and Kim, when she grew up. 'I'll stay with them for two years before going solo,' she'd told Lily. Good heavens, Lily had thought. The girl's got it all worked out. She's seven. What did I want to be when I was seven? She'd thought about this. Eight, she concluded. Kids these days, so sophisticated.

Lauren was three. Who knew what she'd be like in a few years, but Lily had hopes. She might buy the child a copy of *Little Women* for future reading. She started compiling a mental list of books for Lauren to grow up with. It started with *Winnie the Pooh* and ended with *Trainspotting*, taking in *To Kill a Mockingbird*, *Catcher in the Rye* and *The Railway Children* along the way.

Mattie disrupted her musings, saying that usually she tried to get Lauren to feed herself, but that tended to be messy, and today they were in a bit of a rush what with Lily needing to get away to the airport, and her being caught up with her cleaning.

As a conversation this was a low hum, an exchange of not very interesting thoughts and information, the sort of chat that drove Rory into a fury. Lily imagined him here today. He'd slap his hand on the table and look round wildly. 'Is this it? Is this all we can say? There are wars going on out there in the world. There are books, films. There are people dying of hunger, and we are sitting talking about paper napkins and trifle bowls! My God!' And everyone would stop eating and look at him feeling embarrassed, guilty and conversationally inadequate.

Grandpa finished his soup, said thank you to Mattie and he was going upstairs for a nap. He kissed Lily goodbye, and slowly left the room. Lauren wriggled from her seat and ran back to the television. Lily said she really ought to be on her way. She fetched her coat and handbag as Mattie went to tell John.

Mattie opened the back door, shouted, 'Lily's going.' And shut it again.

By the time John appeared, Lily and her mother, who had scooped up Lauren from her spot in front of the screen and carried her to say goodbye to her Auntie Lily, were outside the house on the pavement, having an argument about the biscuits Mattie had wrapped in greaseproof paper and was insisting Lily take home to Art.

'No,' said Lily. 'I've no room for them in my bag.'

'Of course you do,' said Mattie. 'I wrapped them for you. Something to eat on the plane, and Art likes a biscuit.'

'I don't want anything to eat on the plane,' said Lily. 'And the kids might like them.'

'I can make more,' said Mattie. 'I made them for you. And Art would like them. It's nice to think someone's thinking about you.'

'I know it is. But, really, Art doesn't eat biscuits.'

'Of course he does,' said Mattie. 'Everybody eats biscuits.' And she shoved her parcel into Lily's hands.

'I don't want them. Dad might want them.'

'No he doesn't,' said Mattie. 'You take them. Homemade. You don't get that in London.'

'You do, actually,' said Lily. 'You get all sorts of things there.'

'But you only get my biscuits here. Take them.'

John stood watching, and was for a minute tempted to join in, taking Lily's side. But he thought the better of it. Relations with Mattie were strained enough.

Lily took the greaseproof package. She kissed John, then Mattie, then Lauren. Within her something stirred when the child put two puckered lips on her cheek, then ducked back, hiding her face in Mattie's neck.

Lily put the biscuit package on the passenger's seat and drove off. In the rear-view mirror she saw Mattie and John watching her go, waving. They were standing some distance apart, then Mattie disappeared into the house. John stood alone, waiting for the car to turn the corner, his hand raised. Lily thought he looked lonely. But she couldn't really figure out why.

Free-Range Rita

The window of Sebastian Boothe's Newcastle flat stretched from floor to ceiling. He loved to stand at it, hands in pockets, looking out at the river, surveying the day. Today the water was pewtery grey, reflecting the sky, and choppy. It wasn't looking its finest. He lived on the Quayside. The building was stylish, modern. Across the water he could see the new developments going up. Getting bigger, bolder by the day, he thought. To his left along the embankment were the Tyne Bridge and the new Millennium Bridge, though he had to press his cheek to the pane to see them. Below him the walkway which thronged on Friday and Saturday nights with shifting waves of young people moving from bar to bar, club to club. The sound-proofing kept out the hollers and squeals of partying, but Sebastian knew a good time when alone and watching one from above. When it came to that kind of enjoyment, looking on was what he did best. He never was one for joining in. He liked his life here. The flat, sparsely furnished, piles of books against the far wall. He hadn't yet found time to put up shelves. And a few minutes' walk away were bars and restaurants. Every morning he'd take his newspaper, and stop for coffee at Est Est Est. On good days he'd sit at a table outside, reading the latest reviews, sipping a cappuccino, before walking up through town to the university, where he lectured in geology.

Yes, right now, things were good. No complications. No women. And enough money to eat out most nights, and indulge himself in wine and the occasional cashmere sweater.

He saw a silver Golf draw up in the parking area below. A small, determined woman got out. She looked familiar. Oh my God, he thought. That's my mother. His first instinct was to hide, to throw himself to the floor so she wouldn't see him, then when she rang the bell, he wouldn't answer. She might think he was out and go away. But by the time he'd decided upon this evasive action, Rita was looking up at the window, and smiling. She'd seen him. No hiding then, he thought.

Not that Sebastian didn't love his mother. He did. He just loved her more at a distance. Anything over a hundred miles suited him just fine. Every mile over that was a bonus, and for each one his love got deeper.

Rita rang the doorbell, Sebastian took his time about answering it.

'What took you?' said Rita. 'You saw me arriving. You could have been at the door waiting for me.'

Sebastian shrugged. 'I was preparing myself mentally. I wasn't expecting any visitors today.'

'What do you mean, preparing yourself mentally? I'm your mother, you shouldn't have to go through any emotional acrobatics to get yourself ready for me.'

'I know. I know,' said Sebastian. 'But sometimes, you know . . .'

'No.' Rita shook her head. 'I don't know. Tell me.'

'I mean, sometimes, if I don't pick up the phone, or answer the door, it doesn't mean I don't want to talk to you or see you, it means I don't want to talk to you or see you, or anybody, at the moment. I might be thinking, or reading, or listening to something interesting on the radio, or revisiting shameful moments in my life. I'm just temporarily hiding away.'

'It sounds like you are suffering from some sort of melancholy. Have you been drinking?'

'No. I've been relaxing.'

'Sounds self-indulgent,' said Rita.

They were still in the hall. Only minutes in one another's company and already uncomfortable. He was standing six feet away from her, she noticed, but then, she thought, he always stood or sat six feet away from her. She knew why, and it shamed her. She considered herself to have been a dreadful mother. In fact, she was so scathing about her abilities as a mother, she often thought, I would have hated it if I had been my mother.

Every now and then moments from her mothering past would flash into her mind, and she would writhe in embarrassment. What had seemed reasonable at the time, when Sebastian was a child, seemed dreadful now. She hadn't cut his hair till he was nearly four, and by that time it was down to his shoulders. People thought he was a girl. 'I'm a boy. I'm a boy,' he would shout. When he was five, she'd lined him up with his friends on the sofa and insisted they listed to Maria Callas, hoping they'd benefit in some way by hearing the wondrous voice, as she called it. They hadn't. They'd squirmed, wriggled, fiddled with toys, then asked politely if they could go now. She had been a broccoli tyrant, insisting he eat the stuff. And when it came to frozen burgers, potato waffles and fish fingers she had been a despot, standing at the ice compartment in the supermarket ranting about E numbers and toxic ingredients. Other shoppers had backed away. Sebastian had in time refused to go into the supermarket with her, and would sit in the car reading his Roald Dahl books while she shopped. His friends had all been scared of her.

It hadn't crossed Rita's mind that having produced one child might lead to her having to mix with more children, other people's children. 'What I dislike about them,' she explained to Sebastian, 'is that they are all so childish.'

Sebastian, seven at the time, old for his years, had told her that his friends were childish because they were children. 'It's the way of things.'

So Sebastian had a wide circle of friends who never came to his house, but welcomed him in their own. This suited Sebastian very well. Out of Rita's critical gaze he could watch cartoons on television, eat beefburgers and chips and play the sort of silly kids' games children played without her intervening or, oh, the embarrassment and shame, joining in.

So here he was. Tall, gentle, still blond, thirty-four, cropped hair, small rimless spectacles, loathed opera and not particularly fond of vegetables. And with a wide circle of friends he had no intention of ever introducing to his mother.

There was, of course, the matter of Sebastian's father, Richard. He'd been an old friend of Rita's. After years of matiness, drinks together, exchanging gripes and sorrows, tales of lost love, tangled relationships, hopes and dreams, they had on one drunken evening fallen into bed together. The affair was passionate, lasted a week and fizzled into silence.

'It was,' Rita explained to Sebastian, 'foolish. A person should never sleep with their best friend. Suddenly there you are in the kitchen together and you both realise you know too much about each other to ever just be mates again. Like he knew I like to go on top, and the sorts of noises I make when I—'

'Mother,' said Sebastian, who was now ten and very, very old for his age, 'there are some things a child just does not want to know about his mother.'

Rita had looked at him, and nodded. 'I suppose there are. Still, remember what I said. Don't ruin a friendship with sex, no good will come of it.'

'You had me,' Sebastian said.

'True. True,' agreed Rita. 'And I wouldn't be without you. But I lost a friend.'

But if Richard was no longer Rita's friend, he was Sebastian's. They adored one another, phoned at least once a week and never ran out of things to say. When Sebastian had been a boy, he'd spent all his holidays with his father, an elegant, sociable man who, after his affair with Rita, had come out. 'I am,' he'd told her, 'gay.'

'Was it me?' asked Rita. 'Did I do that to you? Put you off women for ever?'

He'd told her no. He'd always preferred, fantasised about men, but hadn't had the courage to admit it, not to anyone. 'Not everything has to do with you, Rita. You're such an egotist.'

Still Rita secretly thought she was so overbearing this was what she did to men.

'Are you gay?' she asked Sebastian now, emerging from her train of thought.

Sebastian was used to his mother's long introverted silences, followed by a probing and usually personal question that seemed to come out of the blue. He told her no. He wasn't.

'Only, your father went off women after me,' said Rita.

'He was never particularly on women,' said Sebastian. 'Not everything has to do with you. You're such an egotist.'

Rita said, 'Hmm. You're not the first person to tell me that.'

'Come and have a cup of tea and stop musing and torturing yourself.' He led her to the living room.

'You do know me, don't you?' said Rita. 'Do you have Earl Grey?'

His living room. Large, spacious, modern. Huge windows looking on to the river. The walls were pale, hung with large abstract paintings. Two black leather sofas, chrome floor lamps. He went into the kitchen to make tea.

Rita watched him. She could never look at him without thinking of the boy he used to be. The child in denim dungarees and striped T-shirt, who'd taken her hand as they walked along the street. The things they'd done together, games they'd played, books they'd read. Back then, when he was very young, they'd been happy together. Then he'd gone to school, met other children, seen lives that were different to his own, and they'd drifted apart.

He'd seen, she decided, other families, children who were allowed to be children. She wanted too much for Sebastian. She wanted him to be strong, well made, educated, erudite, balanced, sociable, well read, a good cook, charming to women, happy. Too much, way, way too much, she thought. But still wondered if the rift was down to a moment, something she'd done, something she'd said. She wanted to apologise for it, whatever it was, but didn't know how.

Sometimes she wished she could have it all back. Make her son a child again, turn back the clock. She'd do it right this time. She'd be a better mother, more understanding, kinder. She would try to make friends with his friends. She wouldn't hand out Kate Millett books to his girlfriends.

Sebastian put a cup of pale tea on the table beside her. 'So what brings you here?'

'I was just thinking about you. I came for a chat.'

'You drove all the way here for a chat? You don't even like to chat.'

'I know,' agreed Rita. 'I'm not good at chatting. It's such a dumbed-down sort of thing. Talk about golf, or the weather, or the route you took to get to the place you happen to be when the chat takes place. It is the stuff of the battery-hen Rita. I prefer the free-range Rita.'

Sebastian said he knew that.

'I was interviewed yesterday by Lily. She found a picture of her mother as a young woman in one of my books, and she stroked it. It was so tender. Nice, I thought. I wondered if she'd be spending Christmas with her family and what it would be like. Would they all mingle and chat, and linger for hours at the table? That sort of thing.'

Sebastian said that as an only child of a single mother, he wouldn't really know. And who the hell was Lily?

'She's a writer, doing a book on lost icons. I, apparently, am one.' She looked at him, raised her eyebrows, mocking herself. 'Lost, I'd agree with. Icon, I'm not so sure about. Anyway, she came to the house yesterday and it got me thinking.'

'What did you think?' asked Sebastian, dreading the answer. It might be lengthy.

'I was thinking that if I had concentrated on one thing – the photography, perhaps – and not drifted off into trying to write books, I might have become an icon. I certainly wouldn't have got lost. I have a cluttered mind.'

Sebastian smiled. 'You should stop beating yourself up. You're getting too old for it.'

'Oh,' said Rita. 'You're never too old for that. I think I'll still be beating myself up about things on my deathbed.'

Sebastian said, 'Probably.'

Rita sighed. 'I read those questionnaires in newspapers, and one of the questions they always ask is how do you relax? People usually say enjoying themselves with family and friends. What does that mean? What do they do? Do they sit about in comfy chairs, in front of a crackling fire, drinking wine, or tea, chatting, joking? Do they, perhaps, play games at a cluttered table, snapping down cards amidst the crumbs and leftovers? I was just sitting there in the room after Lily left, it was getting dark, and I thought to myself that I didn't know how to relax with family and friends. In fact you're my only family and I have very few friends. I just don't know how to enjoy myself.'

Sebastian thought, Typical Rita, completely over-the-top vision of relaxing with family and friends. And he thought, Is she asking my advice? It's happening. The thing that people say happens. That in time you become more knowing than your parent. You grow up, the world you live in is your world, you understand it and she doesn't any more. So she turns to you, and you become the parent. Christ, I don't want that. In fact, help!

Rita thought, If he could tell me what it is I've done wrong. If he could shout at me. Let rip. Tell me, honestly, how much he hates me. He could maybe start to love me.

'I think, perhaps,' Sebastian spoke slowly, rubbed his chin, 'you might try to be less extravagant with the truth. You could – well – tone down your opinions.'

'Tone down! Tone down! I don't think so.'

Sebastian thought, Shouldn't have said that. There she blows.

'You think I should become a faceless nonentity. A nothing. The invisible woman who stands unnoticed at shop counters. Why don't I buy a wall-coloured coat so I can slip through the world unseen? I don't think so.'

Sebastian had, for a little while, thought his mother was mellowing. She seemed almost to doubt herself. But here she was back being the old Rita again, expounding. 'I think,' he said, 'you just have to learn to be a little more trivial. You'd probably have to embrace the battery-hen Rita. Free-range Rita is probably too much for people, especially if they're wanting to relax.'

Rita said, 'You think?'

Sebastian said, 'I think.'

'I always suspect,' said Rita, and she didn't mean to say this, it just spilled out, 'that you don't love me.'

Sebastian hated talking about love. It was all right in moments of intimacy, but love wasn't a word he liked to use in conversations held in the afternoon, in daylight, with his mother. Still, knowing what was expected, and always a dutiful son, he said, 'Of course I love you, you're my mother.'

Rita smiled, but weakly. He'd told her he loved her, but he had qualified it by mentioning their relationship.

And Sebastian added quickly, before this discussion got too heavy, 'I love you. I just wouldn't want to live next door to you.'

Rita sipped her tea. 'Fair enough.'

It was almost six o'clock when Lily finally walked along the street and up the steps to her front door. In this Islington terrace, unlike the terrace where Rita lived, the houses were identical. They all stood back from the pavement behind black railings. They all had basements, were all three storeys high. They all had bay windows on the ground floor. Some had window boxes, some didn't. Some, like Lily's were divided into flats. She and Art owned a double upper. But sneaking peeks into rooms as she passed, Lily could see rooms painted in dark red, or pale blue, or off-white (like her living room); she could see book-lined shelves, huge plants, American shutters. Interesting people lived here, she thought. Though after living in this street for six years, she didn't know any of them.

She opened the front door of her building. Then climbed the wide staircase that led to her flat and went in, shouting, 'It's me. I'm back.'

'Hello,' Art called back. 'I'm in the kitchen.' He was preparing supper.

She dropped her bag in the bedroom, took off her coat and hung it in the wardrobe, built in, glass-fronted doors, floor to ceiling, wall to wall, and kicked off her shoes. Then bent to line them up properly, side by side. She picked up the sweater Art had left lying on the velvet waist-back chair, folded it and put it in its drawer. Plumped the pillows, and gave the duvet a shake. Then she went through to the en-suite to wash, stared at herself in the mirror, thought she looked weary. Sighed, and folded the white towels imported from France which had been hanging untidily on the rail. She rinsed out Art's shaving brush and put it and his razor on to the natty chrome stand where they were meant to be.

Things in these two rooms, at least, sorted, she went to see what Art was making. Down the hall, herringbone sisal, pale grey walls hung with a row of black and white prints. Into the kitchen, big smile. She never could see Art without smiling. The room was large, square, a pale greyish green, pleasantly shiny, fabulously equipped with retro toaster, with a scattering of golden crumbs beside it – Lily fought the urge to wipe them up – retro mixer, dark red, rarely used, and espresso machine. Art was working in the central unit, chopping onions.

He poured her a glass of wine. Came towards her arms spread so that she could wrap herself round him, and he could enfold her.

It was good to have her back. She put her head against him. 'It's great to be home.' Kissed his cheek. Then tossed Mattie's carefully wrapped biscuits on to the kitchen unit. 'Biscuits. Mattie insisted I bring them to you. She said you liked a biscuit.'

'And so I do,' said Art. He took the packet, unwrapped it, sniffed deeply and said, 'Yum. Homemade biscuits.' Then he tossed the package back on to the unit.

Lily watched, and knew Art would never go near these biscuits again. They would lie on the unit till tomorrow morning, when she would throw them out. But there was something in the easy way Art smelled the home baking, and said a wholehearted yum, that stunned her. Why couldn't she do that? Why hadn't she taken the package and said, 'Oh thank you. How kind to think of Art. He loves home baking.' It would have saved her and her mother the slightly messy business of doing an absurd biscuit dance on the pavement. Mattie thrusting forward biscuits in hand, 'Take them.' And her backing off, hands in the air, 'No. No. You keep them.' Art's casual attitude made Lily aware of how much more perfect her perfect life would be if only she could learn to tell very small, very white diplomatic lies. This would help her immeasurably with her pursuit of happiness, the perfect life, and wonderful friends who loved her. Tiny lies, a balm against the truth. Everybody loves a pleasantry.

'So how did it go?' asked Art.

'Rita Boothe is interesting. And home was fine. Mattie has got some sort of cleaning bug and was too busy to give me the look.'

'What look?'

'You know. The swift glance at my stomach to see if there's any swelling, any babies growing in there. Then up to my face with a hopeful expression that says, "Any news? Any interesting developments? A new grandchild, perhaps?" '

'Oh, that look. You get it every time you see her?'

Lily nodded. Took her glass and sat at the kitchen table. 'Yes.'

Art said, 'Never mind.' He put some penne into the seething pot on the hob. He wanted to say that maybe one day she would have news for Mattie. But thought the better of it. Lily was home after a long trip and looked tired. He didn't think she'd react reasonably to the baby conversation right now. So he said, 'Mattie? Cleaning?

I don't believe it.' He put the onions into a pot where garlic was melting. Then added some chillies.

'I know,' said Lily. 'I thought it odd. There's something going on between her and John. There was an atmosphere.'

'They'll be bickering about something.' He added some tinned tomatoes to his mixture.

'It felt like more than bickering. More than an argument. I don't know.' She sipped her wine. White, and not quite chilled enough.

'Everybody argues,' said Art. 'Wouldn't be natural if they didn't.'

'Suppose,' said Lily. She got up and went through to the living room.

Art shaved some Parmesan and smiled. There was a newspaper spread on the sofa, his coat slung over the back of a chair, a cup on the coffee table, several CDs left out of their cases needing to be put back on the rack. Fixing all this, returning the room to its perfect state would keep Lily's mind off the atmosphere at home.

A Kitchen Despot

It was John and Mattie's grandson, Tod, who solved the remote control situation. In the afternoon, after school, he'd flicked open a flush panel at the front of the television set and changed the station by pressing a button. John had watched quietly, hands in pockets. Damn, he thought, if I'd known to do that my wife might be speaking to me, and I might have had a plate of soup for lunch. But he smiled at Tod and said, 'Thanks, son.'

Feeling mellowed now he knew he could change the television station, and slightly repentant at the things he'd said to Mattie last night, he went into the kitchen. He was going to apologise to her. He was going to say he'd been in a foul mood when he found he couldn't watch the football. He was going to ask her to forgive him.

But Mattie was fretting. 'I shouldn't have made a fuss about the biscuits,' she said. 'It was plain as day Lily didn't want them. Why did I insist she take them? What got into me? I mean, biscuits. Art. He doesn't want biscuits. Not where they live, they can buy all sorts . . .'

'Forget it,' said John. 'Art will be pleased to get them. He'll be touched that you were thinking about him.'

'No he won't,' said Mattie. 'He'll toss them aside and laugh at me for sending them down to him. Lily and Art don't eat biscuits, well, certainly not big biscuits like that. Their biscuits will be small and delicate with Belgian chocolate on top.'

'Mattie,' said John. 'Will you stop? Will you forget it?'

Momentarily she stopped fretting, and turned to face him. Scowling. He didn't understand. Men never understood things like this.

'Is there any of that soup left?' said John. 'I'm really hungry.'

'I threw it out,' said Mattie. 'You should have come when you were called.'

John opened the fridge, stared in. He considered the food before him – tomatoes, cucumber, several yoghurts, apricot flavour, a small piece of cheese, steak for stewing, mince, milk, apples. 'There's no food in here.'

'There's plenty of food in there.'

'There's nothing I can eat. I'm bloody hungry.'

'Your tea will be ready in an hour,' said Mattie.

'I'm hungry now. You have no conception of hunger.'

'I do,' said Mattie. 'I have fed a family. I know all about hungry mouths.'

'I'll do some toasted cheese,' said John.

'Not in my kitchen you won't. I'm busy preparing a meal.'

'Your kitchen,' said John. 'This is *your* kitchen?' He was so hungry it hurt. It wasn't doing his temper a lot of good. 'This is your fridge, I suppose. And your cooker. And,' lifting a tea-towel, 'this is your tea-towel. And this is your fork. What are you? A kitchen despot? This is my kitchen, too. This is my house, too. And I am starving.' He took the car keys from the table. 'You think I need you to feed me? You think I'm to sit meekly in the corner waiting for the kind lady to serve me something to eat? I'm not that helpless, Matilda.'

He went into the hall, took his jacket from the hook and left. Mattie heard the car start, went to the window, saw it back out of the drive and roar off down the road. She did not know for sure where John was going, but had the notion food was involved. Betty's All-Day Breakfasts was five minutes away.

Lily phoned Marie. 'I'm worried about John and Mattie,' she said.

'Mum and Dad?' said Marie. 'Why? What's up with them?'

By now, only a few brief words into their exchange, they were both irritated. Lily hated that Marie called their parents Mum and Dad, it sounded so much more affectionate than John and Mattie, as if she were closer to them, more a daughter than Lily was. Marie, on the other hand, hated that Lily called her mum and dad by their first names. It sounded so much more grown-up, as if Lily had moved up in John and Mattie's esteem, and was now more friend than daughter.

'I don't know,' said Lily. 'You see so much more of them than I do. I thought you'd know.'

This irritated Marie even more. What Lily said implied that she, Marie, was the dowdy stay-at-home girl, while Lily was the sophisticated and wise one who got away. And as they talked, Marie pictured Lily sitting on the sofa in her perfect flat in Islington, while she was standing in the draughty hall of her cramped and noisy council house.

It was a beautiful flat, Marie acknowledged this. She would like to live in such a place herself. But much as she loved visiting her sister, she found the experience fraught. It wasn't just that she was prone to leaving things lying around; she had three children, none of whom seemed bent towards tidiness. Well, they're kids, she thought.

Whenever they were at Lily's, Marie thought her children looked out of place. They didn't match the decor. Tod in jeans and football shirt and training shoes that no matter how new always seemed grubby. Agnes, with her passion for wearing as much colour as possible – pink hooded top, green leggings and yellow and purple striped shoes the last time she was there – looked garish, an alarming fusion of hues. Added to that she wore the red velvet hat Lily had bought her constantly, refusing to remove it from her head. Marie could see it had made Lily tense just looking at her. Then there had been Lauren, two at her last visit, and appalling. She'd been teething and fractious, a bright spot of red on her left cheek, her nose running. When the girl wasn't crying, she'd been zipping from room to room, top speed. She'd been able to empty a kitchen cupboard in a trice.

Then again, Lily hadn't anything suitable for anyone under ten to drink out of. Marie remembered sitting on the edge of her chair watching Tod swig Coke from a crystal glass. 'Careful,' she'd said. 'Don't break the glass. Don't spill anything.' Coke on Lily's white sofa. It would never come out.

Still, Lily had tried. She'd spent time with Tod and his PlayStation, and had become expert. She had sat rapt watching Agnes flamboyantly go through the songs and dance routines she and her friends had devised as part of their girl band act. Lauren, though, plainly had bothered her. Marie remembered coming home and taking a week off. 'I need a holiday to recover from my holiday,' she'd told Mattie.

'Mum and Dad seem fine to me,' she said to Lily now.

'I thought things were a little strained when I was there,' said Lily. 'There was an atmosphere. And Mattie's cleaning.'

'So?' said Marie. 'People clean. It's what they do. Unless they have someone to do it for them.' As Lily had.

Lily ignored this small taunt and said, 'Mattie doesn't clean. Not beyond the necessary. The house is immaculate. And John didn't come in for lunch. He always does that. In fact, they're hardly ever apart. You know that.'

Marie thought about this. It was true. John and Mattie appeared inseparable almost on a minute-to-minute basis. It was as if one did not feel complete without the other. 'Where's John?' Mattie would say, after he'd been out of the room for ten minutes without telling her where he was going. And she'd go off to find him. John was the same. He'd come into the kitchen saying, 'There you are,' as if Mattie had been away on some long voyage to the other side of the globe and they hadn't seen each other for months, years even. They'd launch into a catch-up conversation, filling one another in on the long five or so minutes they'd been separated.

'Just emptying the tumble dryer. Then I'll chop some onions, start getting a meal together,' Mattie would say.

'I've just been looking at the television guide, checking what's on tonight,' John would tell her.

These utterly obvious and seemingly pointless exchanges drove Rory, when he was at home, into a muted rage. Behind John and Mattie's backs he'd imitate them, and roll up his eyes. Marie and Lily would laugh, and then pretend not to have noticed him. As everyone in the family knew very well, Rory was not a catch-up conversation kind of guy.

'Now you mention it,' Marie said now, 'it was very odd this morning. Mum was in bed when I arrived and I didn't see her at all. She's always up and busying around. Then when I went to collect the kids at night, Dad wasn't there. Tod said something about them having lost the television remote and not being able to change the station. Then he said Dad and Mum were sort of shouting, well Dad was. He shouted something about not being helpless and he drove off in his car.'

'They've had a row,' said Lily.

'Mum and Dad?' said Marie. 'Never. They bicker and squabble sometimes. But they never row. They've never had a row in their lives. Not a full-blown insult-slinging humdinger. Never.'

'I think they must have now,' said Lily. 'If a television remote is involved, that would be the trigger. I'm convinced the rising divorce rate is linked to the increase in remote-controlled televisions. I think someone should do a survey.'

Marie snorted. 'You're probably right. But not about Mum and Dad. They've had a little tiff. People do. They'll be back to their same old selves tomorrow.'

Plainly she was right. She was, after all, a mother, and the most mature and experienced at people skills. Of the three of them, herself, Lily and Rory, Marie considered that she was the most sensitive.

Lily said, 'Hmm. We'll see. But somehow I doubt it. Something's going on.' She didn't understand why Marie couldn't see it, couldn't read the signs. Perhaps she was too close to them. But she, Lily, knew something was amiss. She was, after all, the oldest of the three children, and perhaps, through age, experience, through helping to bring up her two younger siblings, the wisest. She was definitely the most sensitive.

'Are we taking bets?' she asked Marie, changing the subject.

'Of course, we always take bets. A fiver says it's twenty minutes,' said Marie.

'No,' said Lily. 'It's always during the main course. Time we have starters, then she'll bring out the turkey and the veg and the cranberry sauce and the bread sauce and she'll pour more wine and tell everybody to tuck in, I say more like thirty-five minutes. Will you phone Rory?'

'Yes,' said Marie.

They rang off.

John had always had notions. During Lily and Marie's childhood he had spent a deal of time in his shed constructing things. Sometimes they worked – the indoor swing, the rocking horse which wasn't really a horse, it was more llama-shaped – but usually they didn't. The sledge, for example, that would take the whole family. A mighty wooden sledge brightly painted Christmassy red and green, ornately decorated with stencils, that had two bench seats that would accommodate everyone, including Grandpa.

Snow is not always guaranteed in Edinburgh. But that January, many years ago, nature obliged the White family. For an afternoon and all the following night fat flakes had tumbled down. Next morning they had taken the sledge, that John had been working on since April, to a hill on the outskirts of the city. The other sledgers had watched in awe as the huge boat-like object was hauled to the top of the hill. This took some effort, with the weight of it, and everyone was in a lather by the time they got there. Then they had all clambered, very excitedly, aboard. Mattie and Rory in the front, Lily, Marie and Grandpa behind. John pushed the sledge off, running beside it, intending to leap on as it gathered momentum. Only it didn't gather momentum. It was too large, too heavy, especially with five people on board. It slithered a few yards, then stuck in the soft powdery snow. How the other sledgers, most of whom were eight or nine years old, had laughed and mocked, as the Whites, tricked out in long scarves and matching bobble hats, had sat wedged and immobile on a gaudy gondola on the hillside, plainly visible for miles around.

Now never a family gathering passed without Mattie mentioning it. Affectionate and joking though she was, John was still always slightly humiliated. He often pondered what had gone wrong. They should have gone sledging later in the day when the temperature dropped and the soft snow turned to ice. He should have greased the runners. He always meant to resurrect that sledge and make it work.

Mattie's bringing up of the subject was now so predictable that Lily, Marie and Rory always took bets on how long, after everyone was sitting at the table for Christmas dinner, it would take for her to say, 'Oh, remember that sledge? Sitting wedged in the snow on that hill? I was mortified.'

Lily wondered, perhaps she should have opted for the half-hour? Then again, last year Mattie had mentioned the sledge just before she went to the kitchen for the pudding, and Lily had lost to Rory. She had hated that; winning was very important to her.

'Are you betting on the sledge?' she asked Art.

'Oh yes, put me down for forty-two minutes,' he said. 'How's Marie?'

'Fine,' said Lily. 'She doesn't think there's anything up with Mattie and John.'

'Maybe there isn't,' said Art.

'There is something wrong at home. I know it. I feel it.'

She always thought it strange that she called the house where she was brought up home. She didn't live there any more. This flat she shared with Art was home. But there it was, whenever she was going to visit Mattie and John, she said she was going home. She wondered about this, and wondered if home was beside the ones who taught you to speak, and eat with a knife and fork, and use the lavatory, and tie your shoe laces, and who kissed you goodnight before you went to sleep. Home was Mattie and John.

'Leave it be,' said Art. 'It has nothing to do with you.'

It had, though. Lily was sure of this, and it was up to her to sort it out. Whatever it was.

Grandpa emailed Nina. This argument between John and Mattie, he told her, is getting worse, there is no sign of them making up. He told her that John was saying terrible things to Mattie, and that if they kept on fighting they might never make peace with one another. He said he thought it wrong for a man to be rude to a woman. John should learn to love and protect Mattie. And besides, he said, there was an awful atmosphere in the house. It was giving him indigestion.

Nina replied that men should not think they have to love and protect women. Love has to be earned. And women should not think they have to be protected, they have to make their own way in the world. *This is good training for Mattie*, she said, *it will make her strong when she goes out into the world. She will know how to stand on her own two feet. She should fight back, and John will respect her. For the indigestion, breathe deeply, drink plenty water, chew slowly and think the beautiful thoughts.*

Grandpa didn't think this would help. But he pondered Nina's words. Women should not think they have to be protected. He'd protected his wife, Sylvia. He'd considered it his duty to keep her safe, warm, clothed and fed. He'd cosseted her. In over forty years of marriage they'd hardly exchanged a cross word. For a long time he'd been proud of this gentle harmony. He'd gone out to work. She'd stayed at home, where she cooked, cleaned, and brought up their children. Every morning, at half past eight, he left the house and drove to work. Every evening, at half past six, he came home again. Weekends they took car trips or stayed home and worked in the garden. A routine, and everyone needed routines. This had gone on for years.

Then he retired. He stayed home all day in the house that was Sylvia's house. He got under her feet, he was in the way. His routine had stopped, but hers went on. Rather than argue, fight for his space in the home, he'd found solace in his shed. In time he'd put an old armchair in there, along with a paraffin heater. He'd sit and read his newspaper. He made things – toys for his grandchildren, a chess set, a standard lamp. At first he'd felt ousted from the house he worked to pay for, but then he started to rather enjoy the calm he felt in his own little space. It smelled of wood, he was surrounded by his things, his tools, his golf clubs, his books. He could think out here, away from Sylvia's dusting and wiping. Away from the insistent drone of the vacuum cleaner.

Then Sylvia died. He was a widower. Just as he was settled into his new routine, another started. It took him two years to recover from her loss. Two years to realise he could do what he liked. He moved the horrible bashed armchair out of the shed and into the living room. It was infinitely more comfortable than the three-piece suite Sylvia had chosen. His books came too. He piled them next to the chair. He read, he watched television. He was lonely. He'd never been close to his children, they'd been Sylvia's responsibility. Whenever they'd asked for something he'd said, 'Ask your mother, she's boss.' He wished he'd had more time for them. He wished he'd seen more of them, taken part in their growing up. He missed them.

He started to go to the park, where he'd sit watching children play on the swings. Every day he'd observe them, their games, squabbles, their friendships. Little voices drifting over to where he sat, hands clasped on his knee, made him smile. Being a man who abided by routines, he went to the park every day at the same time. It seemed the rest of the world abided by routines too, for every day in the park the children he took such delight in watching were the same children. Though he did not dream of trying to approach them and speak to them, he felt he was getting to know them, their faces, their personalities. This went on for two months.

One day the police came to his door. One of the mothers had noticed his presence, and assumed he was up to no good.

'This woman thinks I'm a child molester?' he said. He couldn't breathe. He was shocked, pale and trembling. 'I was just watching the children play. Listening to their voices. That's all. It makes me happy.' His arm swept the room. The dust, the alarmingly battered chair that sat in front of the tele-vision, the piles of books, yesterday's plate of bacon and eggs that had been left, half eaten, on the floor beside the chair. It was as if he was indicating that observing children at play gave him pleasure, because nothing else did. 'I'm not a dirty old man,' he cried.

The two policemen said they knew that. They were wise enough to know a lonely old man when they met one, but they told him to stop visiting the park. He was frightening the children.

Grandpa doubted that. He'd been frightening the children's mothers. He'd been quietly enjoying watching little people at play, indulging himself in the dream that he could have been a better father, observing other people's offspring, remembering his own fondly. And all the time he'd been dreaming this dream, he'd had the leading role in someone else's nightmare.

He stopped going to the park. In fact, he almost stopped going out. He only ventured over the front doorstep to go to the corner shop for basic food supplies. He was suspected of being a child molester. Oh, the shame. He hid.

It was Mattie who noticed. 'He's terribly depressed,' she told John. John replied that his father had always been distant and grumpy.

But Mattie, convinced something was wrong, persisted. 'What's up?' she'd ask. He'd tell her nothing. In the world he'd grown up in, and had seen his own children grow up in, you didn't mention things like child molesting. It was rude. It disturbed people, stopped the flow of polite conversation. Nowadays, he thought, people seemed to speak about it and other unmentionable things all the time. Well, he supposed, they would, perhaps to compensate for the years of silence. Or perhaps because they were comfortably removed from unmentionable things and felt they should try to empathise with those who weren't.

In time, Mattie's questioning wore him down. It was her constant concern. Is everything all right? Is something bothering you? You seem so upset these days.

He needed to tell someone. He needed to share this awful accusation. 'I've been accused of being a child molester,' he said.

Mattie said, 'What!'

So he'd told her the whole story. Mattie had looked round, seen the loneliness and depression, felt the old man's shame – though he'd done nothing to be ashamed of – and said, 'That's it. You're coming to live with us.'

Two months later Grandpa had sold his house and gone to live with his son and his wife. He'd seen his grandchildren grow up. He'd loved them, played with them, bought them treats. He became Grandpa. First to his grandchildren, then his grandchildren's friends, then to John and Mattie and their friends and neighbours. He felt he was born to be Grandpa. In fact, he just about forgot his own name. When joining the local library, the librarian behind the counter said, 'Name?' He'd said, 'Grandpa.' Then felt foolish.

John had watched sullenly when his children had chatted to his father about what was happening at school, or why they loved a certain band. And even more sullenly when Grandpa had taken Lily, Marie and Rory to the cinema, and when they all played football in the garden. 'He never did that with me,' he'd said. They still didn't have any real contact. They just lived under the same roof.

'Oh, don't be jealous,' Mattie had said. 'He dotes on them. Let him. We have to scold and nag. But a bit of absolute doting makes them feel special.'

John had snorted. Why couldn't his father have loved him like he loved his grandchildren? Mattie listened, but said nothing. It surprised her that the man she loved, and thought she knew well, could be jealous of his own children.

Grandpa was happy. John and Mattie's house pleased him. It sparkled, but not in the way his old home had sparkled when Sylvia cleaned it. Here the atmosphere was lively with chat and banter, people coming and going. He started to wonder about his marriage. It hadn't been all contentment and gentle harmony at all. It had been a commitment to a life without fuss.

Now he felt people should make a fuss, stand up for themselves, say what they thought. It still shook him, though, when he was standing in the hall outside the kitchen and he heard John shout, 'And this is your fork.' And, 'This is my house, too . . .'

He felt horrified to hear his son speak to his wife so rudely. It just wasn't the thing to do. And he felt, at the same time, proud of John for making what was, after all, a valid point. It *was* his house, and if he was hungry, he should eat. And he felt ashamed of himself. This was what he should have done, demanded his right to live as he wanted to live in the house he'd paid for. He knew if he'd done this he'd have spent a lot less time in the shed. He'd have had some say in his children's upbringing. He might have been closer to them. He might not have gone to the park to drift and dream and listen to little voices. He wouldn't have been suspected of being a child molester.

He could see now that settling for the peaceful life, always acquiescing to his wife's wishes, the no-fuss, yes-dear, no-dear existence could lead to as much despair as making his own wishes known, risking the possibility of a fight. Probably more. But worth it, definitely worth it. So, he decided that only good could come from the conflict between John and Mattie. And anyway, it would all be over by Christmas.

Marie sat in her hall. She'd finished her phone conversation with Lily an hour ago, but still she sat. The children were in bed, in the living room the television was on, a sit-com, raised voices, bursts of canned laughter. But none of that beckoned her to move to a warmer seat, nor did the hilarity do anything to ease the silence that always fell after the children were asleep. A draught swept under the front door, curled round her feet; she went barefoot at home. She lifted them on to the seat of her chair, hugged her knees. On the floor beside her lay a heap of coats that she'd lifted from the chair as she'd answered the phone.

She thought about Andy, her husband, though she didn't want to. Never a day passed but she thought about Andy, and it always had the same effect. She'd bury her face in her hands and curse herself. The language she used was foul, four-lettered. She never forgave herself for her dire deed or even offered herself excuses. For what she'd done had been dreadful. There was no forgiving it.

Four years ago she and Andy had gone to a party. The children, Tod and Agnes, had stayed overnight with John and Mattie. 'You can come home as late as you want, and have a bit of a lie-in next morning,' Mattie had said. Marie had relished the thought; with two young children, a long lie-in never happened. Once she'd dreamed about exotic holidays, designer clothes; now an extra hour in bed was her fantasy.

She had worn, that night, a long deep blue dress, high at the neck and daringly low at the back. She looked sexy, and revelled in it. They had dinner at an Italian restaurant, the room was dimly lit. They sipped wine and spoke in low voices. He said she looked gorgeous, he couldn't wait to get her home and to bed. She slipped off her shoe and rubbed the inside of his thigh under the table and suggested they skip the party. 'Let's just go home,' she said.

But he said no. They had to go, he'd promised. The party was being given by Don, Andy's long-time best friend and fellow mountaineer. Marie had sighed. She knew what it would be like, Andy and Don would drink too much beer and talk mountains. She had a friend who'd told her that no self-respecting woman should marry a mountaineer. All they wanted to do was go up mountains. Climbing, she said, was more addictive than cocaine or nicotine; mountaineers dreamed only of their high.

Marie had sighed. She knew what would happen. Don and Andy would get together and reminisce, and plan their next climb. She would try to look interested, and eventually she would wander off to find someone else to talk to. This would usually be the wife of another mountaineer, and they would chat about their children.

101

Tonight was meant to be special; tonight, just for once, she was what he was meant to be dreaming about.

The party, when they arrived, was humming. The music was loud, and in the centre of the living room, cleared of furniture for the evening, a throng of people danced. Marie, who had fixed ideas about parties, thought this a bad sign. Parties had peaks and troughs. They rose in wildness, dipped into lows where people sat about and chatted. Peaks shouldn't happen before ten o'clock, they should come roundabout midnight. A party that peaked at nine would sink to nothing by eleven. If that happened, it was likely Andy and Don would end up in the kitchen, drinking beer, talking mountains. They'd get home sometime after two in the morning, Andy too beer-weary and tired to do what she wanted him to do. 'Let's leave early,' she whispered.

But the evening went the way Marie had predicted. By eleven the party waned. Don, Andy and several others drifted into the kitchen, started to drink beer and talk mountains. Marie's fantasies about what they'd do in an empty house with no children to overhear their ecstasy faded. She joined Andy for a while, listening to, but not joining in, the jokes, the banter. She started to sip from Andy's can, not a good idea after wine and a liqueur at the restaurant, and several vodkas here at the party. She knew she was already drunk, and now she was getting drunker. She started to flirt with Don. Smiling at him, sipping his beer as well as Andy's.

When the beer took its toll, she went upstairs to the loo. She stared at herself in the mirror, thinking her eyes too bright, her face flushed. She was a bit worse for wear, not a pretty sight, she thought. When she came out, Don was waiting on the landing, smiling. She flirted some more, why not? It was a party, and flirting was what people did. He put his hands on the wall behind her, one either side, imprisoning her. He said he liked her dress.

'It's lovely, isn't it?' she agreed.

'Lovely,' he said. And she knew he didn't mean the dress. 'Andy's a lucky guy.'

'I think,' she said, 'that you are standing too close.' She could feel his breath on her neck, and his eyes were full of intent. Staring at her, she knew what he was determined to do.

'Not close enough,' he said. And slipped his arms round her, kissed her.

At first she didn't respond, then again, she did not tell him to stop. It was the night, the disappointment, the faded fantasies, it was his hands on her back, the way he touched her. It was the drink. She kissed him back.

She knew she had done many wrong things in her time, mostly when she was a teenager. She had been the one who came home reeking of drink, who had been discovered to have a pack of condoms in her handbag, who had phoned at three in the morning stranded and broke after a rock concert, who had stolen money from Mattie's purse, who had been excluded from school for constant unpunctuality and being rude to her teachers, who had been brought by the police to the doorstep after being caught stealing books, who'd smoked dope in her bedroom.

Lily had been the dutiful daughter, always ready to help in the kitchen, to cook if Mattie was sick, to hoover the carpets, dust. She'd done well at school. Rory had been the rebel, always arguing, doubting Mattie and John's parental authority. She'd been the wild one, a handful, and had seen the relief on her mother's face the day she married Andy – that at-last-she's-off-my-hands look.

But Marie had settled down. 'Marriage is good for Marie,' Mattie had said. 'It's been the saving of her. She's so good these days.'

Indeed, she was good. She returned to her studies, going to adult education classes. Then her job with Bartlett, Bartlett and Hogg. Along the way she had two children. And was, at the time of the passionate encounter outside the lavatory upstairs in her husband's best friend's house, four weeks pregnant with a third. Though she did not know it at the time.

And why had she done it? She still did not know. Except that an opportunity presented itself. New and exciting lips were pressed against hers. New and exciting hands were moving over her body. She was aroused. And as Mattie always said, 'Marie's so wilful and headstrong, you just never know what she's going to do next.'

What Marie did next was accept Don's invitation to the bedroom. When he tried to lift her dress up to her waist, she insisted she remove it. It was, after all, a beautiful thing and she didn't want it crushed or stained. When Don said they had to be quick, she agreed: someone would soon realise they were both missing.

They'd hardly started, but their passion was hot – the wrongness of it was thrilling, then a slanting light fell across the bed. She looked over Don's shoulder and saw Andy standing in the doorway. She would always remember his expression, a mix of shock, loathing, jealousy and pain. The scene was fixed in her memory, her on the bed, propped on her elbows, Don on top of her. The room black, save for that searing light pouring through the half-opened door. Andy silhouetted in shadow. It came to her now, that moment, a vivid picture, like the cover of a cheap noir novel. She was an easy lay, a thrill-seeking slut, Don just some man, and Andy the noble cuckold. It had no subtleties. In her mind now, her lipstick is red, though it was pale beige, her hair unaccountably blonde. In fact it is brown. Andy had said nothing. He turned and walked away. He picked up his coat, and left.

She and Don had stopped their naughtiness right away. Andy's look had dowsed their fire.

'Oh Christ,' Don had said, rapidly getting off the bed, hauling up and zipping his trousers. 'Shit.' Then he'd looked at her and she'd seen he felt nothing for her. She hated herself. 'What are you going to say to him?'

What was she going to say? Obviously Don wasn't planning to say anything. He would avoid Andy for the next few months, or years, however long it took for the pain and embarrassment to wane.

'I mean,' said Don, 'it'll be all right, won't it? He'll understand, it's a party. We got drunk. It was only sex.'

'No, it won't be all right,' said Marie. 'And there's no such thing as only sex.'

She was right. When she got home, Andy had packed his things and was gone. He wanted no excuses, no explanations; he would never forgive her.

The last she'd heard of him, he'd moved to Canada. Good mountains, Marie thought. She imagined him walking out of their house, fired with rage and betrayal, walking and walking. Walking all the way to that distant place. Still in her mind he was walking, putting in as much mileage as he could to get away from her. In her mind's eye she saw him moving across a vast wheat plain, carrying his case, headed for the mountains.

In fact he had a job in Toronto, lived in a small modern lakeside flat, and taught physical education. He sent the children presents at Christmas and on their birthdays. He put money into a bank account that each of them would have access to when they were eighteen. He never wanted to see or hear from Marie again.

Marie lived with it. She'd done a dreadful thing. Now her children had no father. She was a disgusting person. If only. If only she had slipped below Don's imprisoning arm, told him, 'Oh yes, too close.' And gone downstairs to her husband. But she hadn't.

After Lauren was born, Marie had written to Andy telling him about her. *You have another daughter. She was born on the 8th of September at half past three in the morning, she weighed seven pounds and she's beautiful.* She enclosed a photograph, and posted it and the letter to Andy's mother, hoping she'd send it on to him.

After that, she sent him letters regularly via his mother. *Tod has been selected for the school football team*, she wrote. And, *Agnes is going to ballet lessons every Tuesday after school.* And, *Lauren has her first tooth.* She sent him photographs of his family, told him what was happening. Their illnesses, their triumphs – *Tod scored two goals* – the silly things they sometimes said, their likes and dislikes. She never mentioned herself. One day a letter from Andy came for Tod; it congratulated him on his goals and contained money for new boots. Soon after there was one for Agnes with money for ballet pumps. And after that Andy wrote to his two older children at least once a month, telling them about his life, reminding them that he loved them

Meantime, Marie told nobody what had happened. She couldn't find the words. Besides, she was too ashamed. How could she say to her mother, 'Andy's left because he found me having sex with his best friend. But it's all right, I'll cope. I'll get by. And I didn't enjoy it. It's not as if I came or anything'?

She vowed to be good. She promised herself she'd never do anything silly or selfish again. She cared for Tod, Agnes and Lauren with love and patience. Never shouted, never lost her temper, made sure they were warm, fed and loved. She dressed down, became dowdy. Mattie, John, Lily and Rory thought she was a saint. Only Grandpa had his doubts. His short-term memory constantly let him down, he could never remember where he'd put his glasses, or what he had for tea last night, but his long-term one worked overtime, and he remembered well the naughty Marie, the handful.

Sitting in the hall, hearing the laughter on television, feeling the chill sweeping under the front door, Marie thought about all this. The shame and guilt still quivered inside her. She thought about her mother and father, and what Lily had said. That something was going on. Had they had a huge row? What could have caused it? Well, not the same thing that had ruined her marriage. Her parents were too loyal, too loving, too conservative for that sort of nonsense. It was nothing, a routine difference of opinion that happened all the time between couples. It would all be over by Christmas.

John came home sometime after eight. Mattie heard him come in and go straight upstairs. She presumed he was still angry with her, and had gone to bed to avoid talking to her. She was wrong. John had discovered that his digestive system could not cope with Betty's breakfasts, no matter what time of day they were served. He'd been greedy, ordered bacon (four thick rashers), eggs fried sunny side up (two), sausages (three), fried tomatoes and mush-rooms, followed by waffles (two) with maple syrup and whipped cream and two cups of coffee. Now he felt ill. A person should know, he told himself, that if he groans every time he heaves himself from an armchair, and if he can no longer comfortably digest a fish supper, and if having a cup of coffee after nine at night keeps him awake and means he needs to get up at three in the morning for a pee, he can no longer eat one of Betty's fry-ups. The days of fatty foods are over. He groaned, removed his clothes and climbed into bed. The feast lay leaden in his stomach. Lying on his back gave him heartburn, lying face down was unthinkable, so he manoeuvred himself into a position that was somewhere between the two. Sleep and bad dreams took him, and as he dozed, the layers of eggs, bacon, sausages and waffles slowly,

slowly worked their way through his system. He belched, he farted, he snored, he dreamed horrible dreams.

Mattie came to bed just before midnight. She did not put on the light, but slipped out of her clothes in the dark, letting them fall on the floor. Under the duvet she reached for John. She'd been wrong. The fight about the remote and the heated exchange this afternoon about how she did not exclusively own the kitchen had both been her fault. Of course John was right, she now thought. If he was hungry, he had a right to eat something.

Filled with remorse, she touched him, put her hand on his thigh, let it move up to his shoulder. John was in pain. Searing indigestion bit into his chest, gnawed round his heart. He felt the food he'd eaten was sweating out of him, through his pores. The tastes that came boiling up through his throat into his mouth were vile. What did Betty use to fry her bacon? He didn't like to think. But he was in no mood to be touched, stroked. He wanted to lie perfectly still till the four o'clock breakfast was digested and gone from him. He shrugged Mattie off, said, 'Don't.' And farted.

Mattie turned over, moved to the edge of the bed, as far from him as possible. And tried not to cry.

Lily and Art lay in bed, holding hands. Art was keen to give Arthur and Lillian an airing. After all, they'd missed a night on account of Lillian being away. But Lily was rigid, unmoving, and paid little attention to Arthur's enthusiastic advances.

'Still thinking about John and Mattie?' he said.

She told him yes. It wasn't like them to behave the way they had. She'd never seen them like that before. 'It's strange,' she said. 'In fact, I'd say unnerving.' What really unnerved her, though, was the little glimmer of glee that nestled somewhere beneath her worry. There was Mattie with her ideal life, her harmonious relationship with her husband, her wild and love-crazed hippie past, her carefree attitude to cleaning, and her lovely grandchildren who came by every day. And now something was going wrong. About time reality caught up with her, Lily thought. But not without a pang of shame.

'It's a normal run-of-the-mill marital tiff,' said Art. 'We have them all the time. What sort of marriage would it be if they didn't disagree? Now *that* would be unnerving.'

Lily said, 'You're right. It's a minor tiff. It's nothing. It'll all be over by Christmas.' And the tiny, nasty worm of jealousy inside hoped not.

Art said, 'Didn't they say that about the First World War?'

Mattie and Rita

Rita drove home. The day was bright and frosty, faraway hilltops dusted with snow reminding her of the Lofty Peak flour packet her mother used to buy. For a while she thought about her mother, who had died several years ago in an old folk's home, Sunny Braes.

Her mother had been a gentle soul, fond of baking. Rita wondered if it was the way of things, a kindly, shy, withdrawn person bringing a loud-mouthed, obstreperous one into the world. Then in time, the loudmouth produced another tender, genial individual, and on, and on. If this was so, then pity the meek always sandwiched between generations of clamorous, vociferous parents and children. Thank goodness they'd inherit the earth, they deserved it. Though she wondered if they'd know what to do with it.

Towards the end of her life, Mamie, Rita's mother, had developed a fondness for sherry, which, she claimed, calmed her nerves. This, as far as Rita knew, had been her only vice. She had enjoyed Sunny Braes, or said she did. She and several other women had formed a sort of gang, playing cards every afternoon, joking quite shockingly about death, refusing to join in the evening sing-a-longs. They'd reminded Rita of the in-crowd at school, and she was glad her mother had done a little rebelling at last, though it was, she thought, a little late. It had taken Mamie an awfully long time not to care what people thought of her. She wondered if her mother had no longer cared what people thought because she considered she didn't matter any more.

Once when Rita arrived to visit bearing gifts, flowers, some of Mamie's favourite Clarins moisturising cream, chocolates and several paperbacks, her mother smiled, accepted a kiss on her cheek, considered Rita's offerings, and sighed. No sherry.

They sat for a couple of hours talking, sometimes about Mamie's new friends. But mostly Mamie spoke about her childhood, which she now remembered vividly. 'I had a pair of red shoes, very shiny. They had buttons on the side. I loved them, I used to watch them as I walked, looking down, seeing the pavement pass beneath me. I wonder what happened to them. I don't remember throwing them out. Some things just fade out of your life.'

She asked after Sebastian.

'He's fine,' Rita said. 'He's at home, studying. Exams in a month.' Sebastian was outside in the car, reading a graphic novel. He'd refused to come in. He'd said he hated the smell.

At ten to five Mamie looked at her watch, which hung on her thin wrist. 'It's time for supper,' she said.

Rita had walked her mother along the corridor, and at the door of the dining room had kissed her goodbye. Mamie's cheek was more than soft now, it was too soft. Then Mamie had gone off into the large, almost cruelly bright room. Long tables laid with white cloths and heavy cutlery. 'Thursday,' the old voice rang out. 'Steak pie tonight.'

Those were the last words Rita ever heard her mother say. Three days later the matron of Sunny Braes phoned to say her mother had died of a heart attack. This haunted her. She wished she'd told her mother she loved her, or at least parted with something more meaningful than a swiftly planted, dutiful kiss. And now she couldn't see a steak pie without thinking of her mother, and feeling guilty.

Last night Sebastian and Rita had gone out to eat. 'Shall we have wine?' she asked him, looking round.

It was a small restaurant, quite busy, even though it was a weekday. There was a comfortable bustle about it – white table linen, glistening glasses, and on each table a small red vase containing a rose. Rita fingered the one at their table, checking if it was silk or real. Real, excellent. Sebastian was known here, they welcomed him. There were smiles from the waitresses, who all looked to Rita as if they were students. Still, she noted the smiles, which were flirtatious, shy, adoring. Sebastian nodded hello to a group of people sitting at a table in the corner. Academics, thought Rita. What other profession would talk so loudly and with such confidence about the deliciousness of smoked wild duck or home-made pea and mint soup? Pristine linen, sparkling glasses, admiring waitresses and a slightly upmarket but not pretentious menu. Yes, she thought, this is the sort of place you take your mother to.

Sebastian said, 'Of course we'll have wine,' considering the question unnecessary since they both always drank it with their evening meal.

'What shall we have? Red or white?' Rita was determined to chat. And hoping he'd say white, which she preferred.

'Red,' he said. 'I'm having the steak and Guiness pie with mushrooms.'

'Excellent,' she said. 'I don't eat steak pies. I'll have the lamb.'

'We don't have to have red. I could order fish, or chicken. They do an excellent wild mushroom risotto here.'

'No, red wine and lamb will be fine. I'm feeling meaty.' Rita thought about this. 'Well, not physically. I feel like eating meat. Vitamin B and all that.'

So they had ordered a bottle of house red, and they'd talked. At least they said things to one another. Both found this easier than eating in silence, which made them acutely aware of how uncomfortable they were with each other. Better to talk than not talk and wrestle with things to say, or worry what the other might be thinking.

Actually, beneath the idle exchange Rita was thinking about pudding. Would she have one? Sebastian was talking about a scheme he'd read about which proposed the damming of the Mediterranean Sea.

Rita said, 'Oh really, why?' She wondered why she rarely ordered pudding. She thought it had become a bit risqué, almost indecent, to eat pudding in public. Yet when reading a menu, she always looked at them first.

'It's getting saltier,' said Sebastian.

'Why is that?' said Rita. Puddings were lovely, she thought. Pudding, what a nice word. So comforting, so full of sweet promise. The best ones were in her childhood. She remembered sitting at the table, five years old, legs swinging because they didn't reach the floor, and a bowl of rhubarb crumble before her.

It would be too sweet and not really crisp enough, because her mother cooked everything slowly on a low heat to save gas, a wartime thing. She'd savour it, study it, carefully selecting which bits to gather up, some topping, a little rhubarb and juice and cream, clumsily wielding a spoon that was too large for her mouth.

That table, the kitchen table, small, wooden, sturdy, perfectly square, had been at the core of her early life. As a baby she'd lain on it while her mother changed her nappies. She had no real recollection of this, but she'd been told about it so often – how she'd kicked, screamed and wriggled – it was printed vividly in her mind. She'd learned to read at that table, spelling out letters, forming words. She'd worked at her colouring books there. Made models that never looked quite right. She'd eaten her mother's bland cooking there, her watery stews, pale fruit crumbles. Listened to her parents' gentle dull conversations: 'Looks like rain.' 'Yes, good for the lawn, though.' In the end, she'd rebelled at that table, accusing her mother and father of being boring, grey, suburban people. She'd refused to do anything her parents wanted her to do, she'd stayed out late, worrying them. And all scoldings for her disobedience had taken place seated at that table.

'Not enough fresh water flowing into it,' said Sebastian. 'From the Nile, mostly.'

Rita said, 'Oh?'

When, at eighteen, she'd left home, she'd left her rucksack in the hall by the front door, and gone into the kitchen to say goodbye. Eleven o'clock on a Sunday morning, they were at the table, reading the papers, drinking coffee. 'Well,' she'd said. 'I'm off.' She'd hoped she sounded nonchalant. She was off, big deal. It was nothing. She said that every time she left the house. Except this time she was off for good, she was going to St Andrews University, and had no intention of coming back. Her mother had come and kissed her and told her to take care. Her father turned in his chair and said, 'Goodbye, then, and good luck.' And that had been that. She'd walked down the hall, picked up her rucksack, opened the door and stepped outside. September, a warm, balmy day, just a hint, a sniff of autumn in the air. An undertow of chill. She'd walked to the bus stop on the corner, stood alone. And when the bus arrived, she'd climbed on, sat at the window and looked at her home as she passed it. Her mother and father would still be sitting at the table.

Had that happened? Had they really not driven her to the station? Maybe in the end they'd been as glad to see the back of her as she'd been to go.

'The water from the Nile is being diverted for irrigation purposes so less of it is reaching the sea.'

'Goes to show,' said Rita. 'We just don't think things through. You'd have thought a bit of irrigation would do nothing but good.'

'Yes,' Sebastian agreed. 'It's not my field, but sometimes something just grabs you.'

Rita agreed. She noticed they'd almost finished the bottle of wine they'd ordered and the food hadn't yet appeared. That must have been her. Sebastian would never overindulge like that. He sipped. She swigged. She thought him charming, well mannered, considerate, and wondered how that came about. It certainly could have nothing to do with her. She was opinionated, rude at times, certainly never charming. He dressed well – black trousers and grey herringbone shirt tonight – and his nails were manicured. He always had a slight tan from time spent outdoors, either working in the field, or walking, which he did at weekends. She noticed women at other tables noticing him. In the background Louis Armstrong sang 'Mack the Knife', which made her smile; Louis Armstrong always made her smile.

'It could cause the next ice age,' he said.

'Goodness,' said Rita. She should have gone back, she thought. She should have made friends with her parents, talked to them, found out what they thought about things, what they'd done in the years before she was born, discovered them. Too late now. She'd been angry with them. For years she'd blamed them for all that went wrong in her life. If they hadn't been so quiet, so unadventurous, maybe she wouldn't have been so emotionally unruly, so hot-headed. It was all their fault, all that table's fault. Then one day, when she was forty-six, she'd realised she was a bit old to go on blaming her mother and father for her failures. She came to the conclusion she was responsible for her own catastrophic life.

Her mother, shy, gentle, couldn't really have been as boring as all that. Give her her due, she made wonderful puddings.

'The currents moving out of the Mediterranean into the Atlantic . . .' Sebastian was saying.

Puddings, thought Rita, are interesting. They move with the times. Perhaps you could identify an era not by the fashion or music of the age, but by the puddings people ate. Baked Alaska, lemon meringue pie in the sixties. Lemon meringue pie, what ever happened to that? You never saw it nowadays. Banana fritters, another thing, gone. Where are you now, banana fritters?

'. . . causing huge climatic changes . . .' said Sebastian.

Little pots of chocolate and sticky toffee pudding and Mississippi mud pie in the eighties, truffle tortes and crème brûlées in the nineties. And now, in an age of ladettes and people in designer outfits who spoke with impassioned insincerity about almost everything, there were an awful lot of puddings made from berries. It must all mean something. Perhaps there was a book. She could start at the Middle Ages and work through to the present day. There would be recipes, and a rundown of events and fashions of the time. Elizabethan puddings, Tudor puddings, puddings from the Middle Ages, Biblical puddings. Puddings favoured by famous people – Mary Queen of Scots, perhaps, Shakespeare, George Washington. She felt herself getting excited at the thought. It definitely had the makings of a Rita Boothe book. A sideways look at things. Like looking at the sixties and celebrity by photographing the groupies who followed bands about. Rita had never felt that kind of passion for someone she didn't actually know, and it had fascinated her. The girls themselves she had loved. Their laughter, their enthusiasm she found endearing. And *The Joy of Filth* had come from wanting to know why certain people cleaned so much. Too much? She remembered asking her mother why she dusted every day. 'It will all still be here tomorrow, you could dust it then,' she'd said. But her mother said that it only took a moment and a clean house was a good house. It had occurred to Rita that it wasn't the cleaning her mother enjoyed. It was the routine, it gave her some kind of security. Maybe that was why she hated routine. Maybe that was why she moved from one thing to another, one place to another, one lover to another. Security scared her. Another bottle of wine had appeared. Sebastian must have ordered it, she certainly hadn't. She filled her glass.

'. . . causing all the rain that at the moment falls on Scotland and Ireland to fall as snow on Baffin Island.'

'Oh, Baffin Island. I love Baffin Island,' said Rita.

'You've been there?' Sebastian was surprised. She'd never mentioned going there.

'No. But I'd like to go. I could tramp about and look at the penguins. If they have penguins there. It's such a wonderful name. Baffin Island. It would be a good name for a pudding. Baffin Island pudding. Chocolate truffle ice cream and maybe some berries.'

Sebastian nodded. 'It is a nice name. Good pudding, too. Anyway . . .'

She'd enjoy the research, she thought. And the business of updating old recipes so that they could be made using modern ingredients. She could photograph her creations. She could write about the trade in spices and sugar. And what did people think when they encountered their first imported banana? There was such a wealth of material. She thrilled at it. She had forgotten how exciting it was to discover new ideas, how passionate they could make her. *The Puddings of Time*, she'd call it.

'That's why there is a theory that damming the Mediterranean might stop the next ice age,' said Sebastian.

'The puddings of time,' said Rita.

'You haven't been listening to a word I've said,' Sebastian accused.

'I *have* been listening,' said Rita. 'Mediterranean too salty. Water from the Nile being diverted. Currents into Atlantic. Scotland's rain falling as snow on Baffin Island. See.' Snow, she thought. I love snow. She thought about it falling on her garden. She thought about home, and how she loved being there, tucked away with her thoughts, opinions and memories.

Their food, at last, arrived. Sebastian started to eat, and looked across at his mother, who was considering her plate, deciding where to start. 'So, what do you mean by puddings of time?' he asked.

She told him.

He said, 'That's quite a good idea.'

Rita nodded. 'If history had puddings attached, people might become more interested in it.'

He smiled and told her he worried about her. 'You should make more friends,' he said. 'You need to see people.'

'I'm seeing you,' she protested. But knew what he said was true. She knew a lot of people, but had few friends, and none that lived anywhere near her. She longed for social contact. She missed voices, all the voices that had once filled her life. Children's voices, voices that whispered across her pillow in the night, the yatter and clack of women's voices gossiping, a voice on the telephone so familiar that all it had to say was 'It's me' and she'd know who it belonged to, a voice at the front door calling, 'I'm home.' Sometimes she thought that any voice would do, as long as it broke the silence. Meantime, she went to the library once a week, she went to exhibitions at the Crawford Centre, concerts at the Younger Hall, and to the cinema, into the early evening showing of films she fancied. She had a life, she had interests, but a few voices would be nice.

When she reached Edinburgh, she didn't take the by-pass, but drove into town to the supermarket. It was busy. She shoved her trolley to the far end, starting at the wines (four bottles, white) and water (six bottles, still), and moved across the store towards the vegetables and fruit, picking up things as she went. She always bought too much, shopping, as ever, for two. She hated, and was slightly ashamed of, the lonely line of goods that trailed past the checkout saying *old woman, lives alone* – one chicken breast, instant microwave meal for one, small can of peas, small loaf of bread – so she lied about her status when she shopped.

She spoke to herself softly, a habit she had. 'Pasta. Parmesan. Do I need a couple of tins of tomatoes?' What would Sebastian be doing now? He'd probably be thinking she'd lost her mind saying she loved Baffin Island, then admitting she'd never been there. And, oh my God, almost shouting, 'The puddings of time.' She cringed remembering this. She must be more abstemious when drinking in public. She'd phone and apologise when she got home.

Then again, maybe not; perhaps the whole thing would be best forgotten.

Sebastian had met a colleague, Tricia, for lunch and had told her over pudding – compote of wild berries – about his mother suddenly saying, apropos of nothing it seemed, 'The puddings of time,' and about how she might write a book about puddings through the ages. Tricia had laughed, and asked about his mother.

'Oh, she's written a few books. And she did some photography for the Sunday supplements back in the sixties and seventies.' He gave her a brief biography of Rita Boothe.

'Goodness,' said Tricia. 'You have an interesting mother. You must be proud.'

Sebastian considered this new thought. And agreed, yes, he was. Now that she mentioned it.

Rita reached the fruit and vegetable stands. She picked out some cabbage, organic carrots, potatoes and onions. Gently squeezed a few aubergines, muttering to herself. She noticed a woman nearby doing the same thing. 'Well, I'm not having you,' the woman was telling a tomato before tossing it back into the red pile it had been lifted from. 'But *you* can come home with me.' She placed a firm but ripe one in her bag. 'Now, who else is up to snuff?'

Rita smiled. There was some comfort in spotting someone who was a little madder, and perhaps even lonelier, than she was. She stared. The woman was familiar. She couldn't quite place her, but had the feeling she'd seen her somewhere recently.

Sensing the stare, the woman turned. Stared back, before colouring slightly, recognition spreading over her face. 'Oh my. You're Rita Boothe.'

Rita lost control of her face and grinned, couldn't help it. Years and years it had been since she'd been recognised. 'Yes, as a matter of fact I am.'

'Oh, I loved your books. That one about not cleaning your house was my bible.'

Rita still smiled, though she'd never really meant to imply, when writing *The Joy of Filth*, that people should stop cleaning; she'd been putting forward the proposition that perhaps some people cleaned too much. That some women got a satisfaction from cleaning that might be more rewarding if found from doing something else. That some women overdid the housework thing out of a sense of guilt, then became over-proprietorial about their homes, so their partners and children found it hard to relax in them. But she acknowledged that in the reviews it had been cited as a call for all women to stop cleaning. She knew she should work harder at her titles. Right now she was working hard at trying to place this woman who was so chattily conversant with tomatoes. 'You seem familiar,' she said.

'I'm Mattie. Mattie White. You took my photograph once, in the back of a limousine. Though I wasn't Mattie White then. My daughter interviewed you the other day.'

'Yes,' said Rita. 'How wonderful to see you after all those years.' She looked at Mattie, piercingly. Yes, it was her; she could just about make out that somewhere beneath this somewhat sad, unmade-up face, unkempt blonde hair and baggy clothes was the child she'd snapped holding a bottle of Jack Daniels, smiling at the camera. All sex and melting enthusiasm. 'It *is* you,' she said. And her heart warmed to this woman, this vegetable whisperer, whose smile, whose whole body language still emitted that charm, that buoyant energy, a puppyish, flamboyant longing to be loved. Something stirred at the core of Rita's solitary being, and she thought, oh please let it be that here, beside the tomatoes and lollo rosso, I may have stumbled across a soul mate.

'Would you like to have a coffee and chat about old times?' she asked.

There are Ways
to Talk to a Woman

John and Grandpa had never really communicated much. A good-morning nod, a shared sigh as they settled on the sofa in the evening to watch *The Simpsons* while Mattie prepared supper. Such comfort, the sound of food in the making, the clatter of pots and crockery, the steady chop chop of Mattie's knife slicing vegetables. John and Grandpa didn't have to say a word; they basked in a mutual contentment, they were about to be fed. This was as close as they got.

They might stand side by side in the garden and debate the best way to light a bonfire, or to prune roses. They could lament the weather on a rainy day, then sit all afternoon watching a Western on television and happily not exchange a word. They could discuss which route to take if they were driving somewhere, and revisit the conversation when they returned home, wondering if there was a better route they could have taken instead. They might exchange a small dialogue on some item in the news. But they never spoke to one another.

It came as a surprise, then, when Grandpa turned to John and said, out of the blue, 'There are ways to talk to a woman.'

John said, 'What?'

'There are ways to talk to a woman,' repeated Grandpa, 'and the way you speak to your wife isn't one of them.'

For a few seconds this stunned John. He didn't know what to say. He was a boy again, getting ticked off by his dad. In those few silent seconds he felt the quiver of fear his father's wrath had at one time sent shooting through him. Years ago, Martin White had been a forceful man, a glowering, authoritarian presence in John's life. He well remembered being terrified of his father, his belt, his bellowing rages. For an instant, John felt that fear again. In that same instant he was fifteen, rebel again.

'Yeah. Like you know how to speak to a woman,' he said. The thick sarcasm in his voice implying that it had been years and years since his father had had a woman, and when he did have one he hadn't really known what to do with her.

'I think I do,' said Grandpa. 'Your mother and I hardly exchanged an angry word in over forty years of marriage.'

It sprang to John's mind to say that if his father had engaged in a few arguments with his wife he'd have been less frustrated and probably less brutal with his children. But he didn't. He said, 'I can never figure out if that's a good thing or not.'

Grandpa said, 'A woman wants to be pampered. She wants you to be gentle with her. If you're lucky enough to have someone like Mattie, you should let her know every day how much she means to you. You should tell her she looks beautiful. You should praise her cooking. You should never laugh at her. And telling her she's stupid and a slut is no way to talk to a woman.'

'Even if she is,' said John. Then, 'Women don't want to be pampered. Well, only if it's a pampering moment, but you won't know that. You'll have to guess. Women want to work, to have the opportunity to get to the top. And they want beautiful homes, and cars, and when it's time, children. And they want their men to earn and to understand them and help clean the house and look after the children. Women want everything.'

Grandpa looked at him and said, 'And you don't? I thought these days everyone wanted everything.'

They left it at that. John went out to the shed to start work. He'd been thinking recently about kites. As a child he'd loved them, but had never owned one. It's time for me to get a little of what I want out of life, he'd thought. Before it's too late. He was going to build a kite. It would be huge, multicoloured. It would take to the sky and soar, shifting through thermals, tugging the long, long cord in the hand of the one who was earthbound, and watching it with envy.

Grandpa went into the living room, switched on the television. The afternoon film today was *The Guns of Navarone*. Which was good. It wouldn't make him cry. Most afternoon films were weepies, which, to Grandpa's surprise, made him weep. This shamed him. He used to scoff at people who cried at movies, but now here he was, one of the weepers, a box of tissues at the ready. And it amazed him. What an odd thing the human body was. He had so many bits that no longer functioned reliably, and some that no longer functioned at all, but he could still smile effortlessly if something came along to cause his face to crease with laughter, and he could still cry at the drop of a hat, it seemed. If, in a film, someone died, or gave birth, or lost a love, or found love, perhaps running along an empty beach at sunset towards their heart's desire, arms spread, then there they would be, the tears. He'd mop them up, and sniff. They'd blur his pale and faded eyes. They felt strange, almost alien, on his face. He thought his cheeks too old for tears.

Lily and Art were shopping. It was part of their Christmas ritual. Lily bought most of their presents over the internet, selecting them with care, and always in November, to make sure they arrived in time. Now they were all tastefully wrapped in matching papers, beribboned, and in a perfect pile below the Christmas tree. But still she loved to see the lights, to mingle with the crowds and to wander round the shops picking up any extra little things that appealed to her. Christmas wouldn't be Christmas without a little throng-battling and over-the-counter buying. So they went to Harrods, then took the bus to Oxford Street and Selfridges. They went to Carluccio's for coffee and to buy some treats: cheeses, chateau-bottled olive oil, truffles.

Then suddenly Lily wanted to go home. This pleased and rather surprised Art. Lily's shopping abilities were legend. She was an Olympian shopper. Could bound effortlessly from shop to shop, examining shirts, skirts, shoes, and often returned to the shop she'd started at to buy the shirt, skirt or shoes she'd tried on first.

Shopping with Lily was the only thing that made Art grumpy. He'd start off sharing her enthusiasm, saying, 'I like it. You look great in it. Buy it.' But how could Lily possibly buy the first thing she looked at when there was so much more out there? You never knew, the ultimate garment, in the perfect colour, the perfect fit might be in some shop waiting for her to come along to claim it.

That was what shopping was about. It was a quest for the holy grail of clothes. By the third shop Art would be saying, 'Terrific,' in a slightly disinterested voice. By the fifth, 'Fantastic,' in a sarcastic voice. By the tenth, 'For God's sake, Lily, buy it and let's go for a drink.' By the twelfth shop he'd have gone for a drink. So he was delighted when Lily wanted to get a bus home. 'Are you sure?'

'Yes,' said Lily. 'I'm really tired.' Actually she wasn't. She was having problems with herself. This new jealousy that had developed over the last few days had unsettled her. She didn't like it. And yet she got a weird satisfaction from it. She indulged herself in allowing herself to feel resentful towards people because of what they had. Her mother's naughty past; her sister's patient goodness, her stylish clutter, her children; Art's good nature, his humour. They seemed so much more worldly, so much more likeable than she was.

More than that, she was beginning to see herself as too controlled. She had an organised life, everything in its place. She planned. She had never done anything on impulse.

She had friends who'd seen a cottage in the Scottish Highlands for sale while they were driving past on a touring holiday. And had bought it, just like that. Then had sold up everything they owned and had gone to live in it. Marie used to do things on impulse all the time. She'd dyed her hair purple once, just because she momentarily thought it would be fun. She'd given up a boyfriend because she didn't like the way he ate kebabs. She'd had a second baby. 'Oh,' she'd said. 'Andy and me were in bed, and, you know, I thought, why not? We were in the right place, we were both willing. I'd stopped taking the pill because it made me feel nauseous. So, well, hey. We did it.'

And there was Agnes, bright little multicoloured person, in the world. If Marie hadn't acted on her impulse there might be no Agnes.

So Lily turned to Art and said, 'Let's go home. And to bed.' She nearly added, 'And make a baby.' But didn't. That would be taking an impulse too far. Some things still needed to be planned.

Art thought they should get a taxi. But no, Lily wanted to take the bus. It was part of her Christmas. Years ago, even though they had a car, Mattie and John would take their children by bus to the theatre to a show. They'd sit on the top deck so they could see the lights. Marie and Lily always counted the Christmas trees in the windows they passed. It was a game they played. The one with most trees was the winner. No prizes, of course, just the ultimate satisfaction of being the person who'd spotted most trees. That, and the gloating glee of bettering a sibling. Lily always won. Lily was competitive, she cheated.

'I saw one,' she'd shout. 'That's ten I've got and you've only got six.' Of course she hadn't seen a Christmas tree, she just said she had. And how could Marie check up on this claim? The bus was trundling on into town, the treeless window far behind them.

'Didn't,' Marie would cry.

'Did. Did. Did,' Lily would say. 'Mum, tell her I did.'

'Liar, liar, pants on fire,' Marie would accuse.

'Am not a liar.' Lily would be incensed. She always managed to convince herself the charge was unjust. 'Am not. Am not. Am not.'

'Now, now, girls,' Mattie would say. 'It's only a tree, don't fight.'

So Lily loved to relive this Yuletide glory. Christmas-tree-counting champion. She'd sit atop a double-decker bus and gaze down at the shops, the lights, the people, and she'd secretly count trees.

It was from the bus that she spotted the car. It was black. It was an Alfa Romeo convertible. 'I like that,' she said to Art.

'I thought you weren't interested in cars,' he said.

'I am in that car. It's lovely.'

Shopping vigour returned to Lily. She stood up, squeezed past Art, who was in the aisle seat, clattered down the stairs and jumped off the bus. This had happened too suddenly for Art. He was left behind, squirming round, watching her go; he leaned over to the window and saw Lily disappear into the car showroom. At the next stop he got off and walked back carrying the shopping.

By the time he reached her, Lily was in the car, in the driving seat, playing with the steering wheel and gearstick. Was she making brooming noises? Or did he just imagine that when he thought about it later? She had attracted two car salesmen, who were standing each side of the Alfa Romeo and explaining its finer points to her.

'How do I work the radio?' Lily wanted to know. 'And is the roof electric? I don't want to have to get out and pull it down. Or up if it rains.'

One of the salesmen assured her that indeed the roof was electric, and started to explain some more of the car's refinements. Not that Lily was interested. For Lily cars needed to be three things – good looking, black and shiny. Art stood in the background, Lily's shopping at his feet. What was the point in saying anything? If Lily wanted something, Lily got it. She was a woman who strove to make her house, her job and her appearance perfect. She was a fool with money.

She left the showroom an hour later with both salesmen's cards in her handbag, and a rundown of what the car would cost, deposit and monthly payments.

'We don't have the money,' said Art.

'Money,' said Lily. 'What's money? Who has money, anyway? Money is hypothetical these days. We are creditworthy; hypothetically we have money.'

'I mean,' said Art, 'we can't afford it.'

'Of course we can,' said Lily. 'We can afford anything. Anybody can afford anything.'

'What are you talking about?' said Art.

'We could afford a Rolls Royce if we wanted. We'd just have to remortgage. Or sell the flat.'

'Then we'd live in the car?' said Art.

For a moment, Lily thought this romantic. 'Yes. Not that I'm suggesting we do. I'm just saying if you want something badly enough there's always a way of getting it.'

'And you're going to get that car?'

'I'm seriously thinking about it.' Which meant yes.

'I thought we agreed we didn't need a car. A car is an encumbrance in the city. A lump of metal you have to find a parking space for. And tax and insure, and it sits by the roadside depreciating.'

'So?' Which meant she agreed with him, that was what she thought about cars until she saw *that* car.

'Isn't that the sort of car your mother wanted?'

Silence. Then, 'I think it might be.' Which meant she knew very well it was the sort of car her mother wanted.

'Don't you think she'll be hurt if you go out and buy something she really wanted?'

A longer silence. 'Of course not. She's far too mature for that sort of thing. And why shouldn't I have something I really want?' Which meant yes, Mattie might be hurt, if she finds out about it. But I have just done something on impulse for the first time in my life, and it was wonderful. Better than sex, she thought.

John and his father avoided one another for most of the afternoon. If, by chance, they met in the kitchen where one was making a cup of tea, the other waiting to make himself one, there was a stiff, sullen silence neither was willing to break. John worked in the shed. At first he'd planned to make a box kite; it would be large, but not so huge it would be cumbersome to carry to some windy place to fly. But angry at his father's intrusion into his disagreement with Mattie, he thought to make something bigger. Something huge, a giant kite, the kite of kites, a vast and magnificent thing that would take its place among the clouds, so big it could be a cloud. And when he stood on the ground, strings tugging his arms, he'd feel the air, know the thermals. He'd join the sky. He would be the kite.

So, draughtsman that he was, he drew up plans. His kite would be six metres wide, three long. A kite needed width to catch the wind. It would be built in lengths, sewn together. He worked out where he would need the holes to put his guide strings, how to strengthen them. Where he would place his six tails, all decorated with ribbons. He planned his colour scheme, scarlet and black. He thought about his life. His children. His work.

Towards the end, he'd hated going to the office so much he'd felt like a reluctant schoolboy, dragging his bag along the ground, head hung. Misery. Going home he'd been the same, and he couldn't quite work out why. He loved Mattie, still did, despite the on-going fight. He loved and was proud of his children, still was. But there was something routine, dull and chillingly predictable about it all. Sometimes he wouldn't go home; he'd drive to the park, sit in his car and watch the swans. At such times he'd contemplate going away. To where he didn't know, just away. Just driving. He'd thought he could live in his car, and tune the radio to some twenty-four-hour jazz station. Not that he knew of one, but in his imaginings he found one. He never did it, though. He'd sit, stare, dream, sigh, pull himself together and drive home.

'Working late again?' Mattie would say.

He'd tell her yes.

'All those times you stay late in the office,' she'd say. 'You'd think they'd pay you overtime.'

John would shrug. 'It's the times we live in. You're hired nine to five. But in reality it's eight to whenever you're finished.'

He leaned over his workbench. This kite would be amazing. He would spend his days, at last, doing something he wanted to do.

The survivors of the Navarone raid sat bobbing in a small boat in the Aegean Sea. They were surrounded by noise, ships' horns, a crescendo of blasts and hoots. Naval applause from the sailors in the gunboats, who were safe from the deadly onslaught of the huge guns that protected the straits. Grandpa blew his nose, and mopped his tears. Damn, he hated this crying thing.

As he watched the film, he'd thought about his children. And in doing this he'd tried to blot out his guilt about how little he'd seen of them when they were growing up, and tried to remember only the happy times. The days at the beach, the trips to the zoo, the games in the park playing football, and, when they were small, pushing them gently on a swing. He thought about birthday parties and balloons he'd blown up. Card games in the evenings when the television wasn't working. And when it was (it had been temperamental), how the whole family would sit watching favourite programmes (he couldn't for the life of him think what any of them were) handing round a crumpled bag of sweets.

He tried to blot from his mind the appalling times, when he'd come home and Sylvia would be in one of her moods. Some child would have been naughty, or simply might not have come up to her expectations – a low mark, a bad school report – and would be being ostracised by her. The mischievous one or the failure would be sitting glumly alone, while Sylvia fumed. She expressed fury by tightening her lips, and moving stiffly about the kitchen, serving the evening meal with a swift, tense, dismissive bustle. Even worse was when a child would have been sent to his room and told to wait till Father got home. A spanking was called for. Grandpa still felt the pain of it. Before he could sit down to his supper he'd have to deal with the child. It had made him angry, so angry his spankings were more vicious than he intended. Why couldn't Sylvia do this? Deal with things when they happened. He'd rage and shout. The atmosphere in the house was horrible, awful, fearful. The trauma would last for days.

He heard John in the kitchen, making himself his third or fourth cup of tea of the afternoon, and thought to go and apologise to him, to explain to him how upsetting he'd found this wait-till-your-father-gets-home business.

But when he entered the room, John said, 'It's just she makes me feel guilty. She wants all these things, and I can't get them for her. I feel useless. And I hate it that she makes me feel like that. I think she has no right to want what we can't afford. I don't want a velvet sofa or a bloody sports car. I never wanted anything like that. I just want to be happy. How the hell do you do that?'

He was wrestling with a packet of biscuits. He gave it a savage wrench so it burst open, spilling its contents over the floor. 'I just wanted a bloody biscuit. I can't even have that. I nearly had one, then it shot out of reach.'

'A bit like happiness,' said Grandpa.

Mattie and Rita were on their third cup of coffee. They had gone through the absurd female paying ritual when they bought their first. Mattie digging in her purse saying, 'Let me.' Rita protesting, 'You put that away. I invited you.' Mattie saying, 'Nonsense, all the pleasure *The Joy of Filth* gave me, I insist. I owe you.' Rita saying, 'If you bought my book, then I owe you.' Considering how few people had bought the book, Rita was convinced of this. So in the end, she paid. A relief for the assistant behind the counter, and the long queue forming behind them.

They found a seat by the window, near the Christmas tree, and settled down. They had, at first, that thing Mattie's son Rory hated so much, a catch-up conversation. Their lives since they'd last met in the limousine where Rita had taken Mattie's photograph. It had been a long time; it took a long time.

'So you married and settled down,' said Rita. 'I didn't. Settling down has always evaded me. I married. It didn't last. Had a fling with Richard and we had a son, Sebastian. Then he announced he was gay. I think I did it to him.'

'Nonsense,' said Mattie, patting Rita's hand. 'People are gay or not gay. It's the way of things. He'd have been gay all the time, but not admitting it. You should be proud he slept with you. Of course,' dipping into one of her many theories about the human condition, 'it always surprises me that this switching is thought of only as a gay thing. It's not just a sexual matter, though that must be hard, sex being so fundamental. I think all sorts of people are all sorts of other things under the surface. A vicar can secretly long to be a plumber. Or a carpenter. And a truly kind person can have a nasty side. Someone who appears balanced and well adjusted can turn out to be hoarding all sorts of wild jealousies. We hide a lot.'

'How very true,' said Rita. 'Still, you must be proud. Three children, all doing well.'

'Well,' said Mattie. 'Marie's marriage broke up. Her husband upped and left her, overnight it seemed to the rest of us. She's changed. She used to be the wild one of the family. Now she's quiet, withdrawn, even. And she's so patient with her children, she's a genuinely good person.'

'Overnight?' said Rita. 'Something must have happened. Maybe he had a drunken one-night stand and she threw him out.'

'That's what I think. But Marie's not saying. So we don't talk about it. Rory lives in Paris. He designs websites, whatever that entails. I don't do computers. He's lovely, full of opinions. I think I get on his nerves. He talks about things I don't understand, and I drift off thinking about my own worries, and he can see it. He gets angry with me. Mind you, Rory's always been angry. He was an angry child. Funny, isn't it, when your children grow up, and you watch them and listen to them and see the person they've become, and you think, you were always like that. Even in the womb Rory was angry. He'd jump about and kick me in the bladder. And he gave me terrible heartburn. Marie used to bounce and wave her arms about, she used to whack me in the ribs and bang her head on my lungs, at least that's what it felt like. Lily was peaceful, the occasional kick, but mostly you felt she was happy in there. The womb suited her. I think she found it tidy.'

'Your Lily is lovely,' said Rita. 'So well dressed, and quite beautiful.'

'Oh yes. I'm proud of Lily. She knows where she's going and what she wants, and just goes out and gets it. She's not impulsive like the other two. She is so thoughtful, always phoning. Actually, in a way she keeps the family together. Sometimes I think she's the perfect human being. I don't know how she turned out like that. Nothing to do with me.'

'Rubbish,' said Rita. 'And they're all coming for Christmas?'

'Yes,' said Mattie. 'Though Rory's partner, Isabel, is going to her own family. They're both independent, Rory and Isabel. She's quite a bit older than him. I used to wonder what they saw in one another. But then I thought, Isabel's a lot like Lily. I think that's what Rory sees in her, but I don't think he realises that. And Isabel loves it that Rory's so reliable. They're not entwined like John and me. They walk parallel paths. But yes, the rest of them are all coming for Christmas.' On an impulse she thought to invite Rita too. But no, a woman like that would have hundreds of friends, a pile of invitations. And she had a son who would no doubt be begging her to come to spend time with him. No, a woman like that wouldn't want to come to her house. 'It's going to be wonderful,' she said.

Then Rita remembered something, and said out of the blue, 'John Lennon?'

Mattie blushed and shook her head. 'The nearest I ever got to him was the front row of the balcony in the Odeon when I went to see *Help!*'

'We agreed,' said Art. 'No car. We said that when we sold the last one. No car.'

'I know,' said Lily. 'But that car's different. It's lovely.'

'What do you want it for?'

'We can drive to Brighton at weekends. Or down to Cornwall. Or Kew. I can take it to work, save me carrying things.'

She imagined herself turning up at work. Roof down, of course. And looking relaxed, totally cool about having a cool car. This black vehicle would give her kudos. She'd drive past groups of students, who'd look casually at her. But she would no longer be considered uptight, distant. She thought about her colleague, Martine, who could walk into a room, sit on the edge of a table and talk quietly about the modern novel, and hold fifty or so students spellbound. Or Professor Robertson, Simon, who regularly wrote reviews in the *Observer*, and appeared on television discussion programmes, and could make people laugh. Such a gift, she wished she could do that. She was remote. She did her job well, but nobody loved her like they loved Martine or Simon.

But this car would say something about her. It would say she wasn't quite the prissy person people thought. Beneath the groomed exterior there lurked a secret woman of fire and passion, who drove a cool car. It would make her distant but desirable.

'You don't understand,' said Lily. 'There's more to me than people think. I'm not just uptight, anally retentive and annoyingly overly tidy. I have passion. I *am* Lillian.'

'I know that,' said Art. 'But you only let her out at night.'

'But in a car like that I'd hint at her during the day. I'd have cachet. And Lillian's such a good driver.'

'I didn't know that about her,' said Art. 'Good job, too, because quite frankly, Lily isn't. Lily dreams. Lily looks at shop windows instead of the road. Lily regularly crashes red lights. Lily shouts rude words at other drivers. Lily can't reverse-park.'

'But apart from all that I'm a good driver. Anyway, none of that matters. This will be Lillian's car.'

Art sighed. He walked across the kitchen and put on the kettle. It was deadlock. He didn't want the car. She did. She'd win, there was no doubt about that. It was one of those moments – a bubblegum moment.

When he was seven Art's mother had bought him a pink sweater. He'd hated it. She'd insisted he wear it. He'd known she held all the trump cards – she made the meals, she dished out the pocket money, she had control of the television, she could keep him in. In the end, she'd win. He'd put on the sweater. He'd stared at her, and was chewing gum at the time. Hands in pockets, eyes fixed on her face, he'd chewed, then flattened the gum against his teeth, and blown a huge pink bubble. It had snapped, burst. He'd slowly gathered in the gum and chewed again. Slowly. Rebellious. Defiant. And it worked, he knew that from the furious smack he got for his efforts. But he wore the sweater.

So here he was again in another bubblegum moment. Only he had no gum. He turned, leaned on the kitchen unit. Hands in pockets, he stared. What was the use in trying to make her see reason? Lily had seen the car and fallen in love, and Lily would do what Lily wanted to do. She always did.

Looking at her now, considering their time together, Art realised there had been many, many bubblegum moments.

A White Christmas

All parties had a high point, Mattie thought. For her it was that moment when people arrived, the air filled with greetings, expectations of a jolly time. The front door open, a rush of fresh air, and guests milling, the smell of outdoors on their coats, cheeks when you kissed them still cold, slightly red from their brush with winter. It was a few fleeting minutes of coming together, of promises, hopes and bonding.

On Christmas Day, however, the only people who would arrive were Marie and her children. Lily, Art and Rory always turned up the day before. She had picked up the first two from the airport, and Rory always insisted on making his own way to the house. Those platform kisses had to be avoided. Though at the airport they would have been concourse kisses. Now they were front-door kisses. So his cheeks did not escape Mattie's lips, but at least it did not happen in public.

He knew when this hatred of the platform kiss started. It was when he'd first come home from Paris, after he'd been living with Isabel for six months. He'd flown to London where he'd had some business, and taken the train to Edinburgh from there. Mattie had met him at the station. She'd been bobbing about watching every face, waiting for his face, the face she loved. And when she saw it, she'd swooned. Hadn't meant to, but the surprise and joy at seeing him had overwhelmed her.

Rory had changed. Of course she already knew that. When he'd first brought Isabel home to meet Mattie and John he'd had his hair cut. But in the intervening months, Isabel had worked her magic; he was lean, tanned and chic. For years Mattie had affectionately called Rory her lumberjack son. For that was how he dressed – jeans, checked shirt over T-shirt and boots. The train had been three-quarters of an hour late, and while waiting, Mattie had got into conversation with another woman, who was waiting for her daughter. They were both excited and proud. Their children were coming home.

The other woman's daughter arrived first. Mattie noted with approval that she was a lumberjack, too. Jeans, checked shirt and boots. As she smiled and said hello, she noticed a beautiful man smiling shyly at her. She noticed almost every other woman on the platform noticing the man too. He was tall, his body gym-toned, his hair short, immaculately cut, his skin tinged with a slight tan. He wore a linen suit, a perfect fit; his shirt was dark blue, open at the collar. An obviously expensive leather bag hung over his left shoulder. For a second Mattie could not understand why this *Vogue*-model-cum-filmstar person was smiling at her. And the moment she realised it was Rory was the moment surprise and joy overwhelmed her.

'RORY!' She called his name, and advanced towards him, arms spread. She did see him pale and take a couple of steps backward, but she was moving forward with too much enthusiasm to stop. 'You look lovely.' And she'd flung those outspread arms round his neck, and kissed him. Not a polite platform peck, but a huge wet smacker. 'It's wonderful to see you.'

Then she'd taken him over to the woman she'd been talking to, telling her life story to, her new and never-to-be-seen-again bosom buddy. 'This is my son. Isn't he handsome?'

Rory had winced. The woman was momentarily drowned in envy, for Mattie was blatantly implying that her son was so much better looking, better dressed and plain all-round better than her daughter. And, quite frankly, thanks to Isabel and her tactful insistence that Rory take a greater interest in his appearance than he had ever done before, he was. But his heart went out to them. And from then on he did not allow anyone in his family to meet him at the airport or station when he came home. He took a taxi to the house.

To give Mattie her due, her joy at seeing her son was heartfelt. When she saw him standing on her doorstep, her emotion was not in the least diminished by the lack of audience. She loved him.

And he, in his way, loved her. But she was embarrassing.

'Mothers are,' Isabel had said. 'Mine is. I expect when we have children I will be also.'

Rory stared at her.

Isabel nodded. 'Yes, four.'

'But not all at once,' said Rory.

Isabel had given him a pained look. 'I want children. Soon.'

So Rory had turned up on the doorstep. He was the only member of the family who didn't ring the bell and come in. He waited for someone to come to the door, open it and invite him into the house.

'You should have come on in,' said Mattie. 'It isn't as if you don't live here.'

'I don't live here,' said Rory.

'But you used to, which is the same thing,' Mattie told him.

There had been a time when Rory would immediately start arguing that no longer living somewhere was not the same thing as actually living somewhere. He had moved away, years ago. But this time he let it go. Maybe he was preoccupied, worried about the four children he was expected to sire. Soon.

Mattie kissed him on the cheek. Then she looked at the tight leather trousers he was wearing and said, 'Goodness.'

'Goodness, what?' said Rory.

'Goodness leather trousers,' said Mattie. 'Very Gene Vincent.'

'Who is Gene Vincent?'

'He's an old rock star. Before your time. He sang "Three Steps to Heaven". Aren't they sweaty?'

John, who was coming up the hall, heard this and said, 'That was Eddie Cochran, "Three Steps to Heaven". Gene Vincent sang "Be Bop A Lula".'

'Are you sure?' said Mattie.

'Positive,' said John.

'I think you'll find Gene Vincent sang "Three Steps to Heaven",' said Mattie.

'I think I won't,' said John.

Rory felt ignored. Only a slight peck on the cheek before his mother had launched into a rock'n'roll altercation with his father. 'No,' he said. 'The trousers aren't sweaty.' He went to the living room, where Lily and Art were seated side by side on the sofa. 'Hi,' he said.

Lily got up and kissed her brother; Art said, 'Hi.'

From the hall they heard Mattie say, 'And I suppose Elvis didn't sing "Jailhouse Rock", and Bob Dylan didn't sing "I'm a Rolling Stone".'

'As a matter of fact he didn't,' said John. 'It's "*Like* a Rolling Stone".'

'It never was,' said Mattie. 'You can fault me on many things, but not my memory. I've got a memory like a wotsit.'

Art and Lily sniggered.

'Elephant,' said John. 'You've got a memory like an elephant.'

Rory rolled his eyes upward. 'They seem to be bickering.'

'I think it's been going on for ages. Weeks,' said Lily.

Rory nodded. Lily would know. Lily would be planning how to sort it out. That was what Lily did. 'Is Marie coming over?' he asked.

Lily said, 'No. She wants to be with the kids. She'll be here tomorrow.'

Rory nodded. He'd look forward to that, Marie was his friend, his favourite sister. He loved Marie.

Mattie bustled into the room carrying a tray with a bottle of champagne and glasses. 'Now we're all here, we can start celebrating.' She was flushed with joy at having her family round her, and triumph after winning the 'Be Bop A Lula' argument. 'And you must tell me all your news, Rory. What have you been up to?'

So here it was, the catch-up conversation. Rory said, 'Nothing much. You know.'

'No, I don't know,' said Mattie. 'You tell me.'

This was what Rory hated about these conversations, the demand that he tell someone – in this case his mother, and it was usually his mother – the details of his life. It seemed to him that as soon as the question *What have you been up to?* was posed, his brain went numb. He could never remember anything he'd been doing.

'The usual,' he said. 'Nothing much.'

His days were filled with work, going to and coming from, and sometimes he worked from home, and the taste of coffee (ten or more cups a day), and the smell of bread from the patisserie along the road, and the music that played in the office or in his small study in the flat, and Isabel. That was it, really. They ate out several times a week, often with friends. They went to the cinema, occasionally a concert, mostly classical though Rory preferred rock. Sundays Isabel cooked. Rory never cooked, Isabel thought his efforts disgusting. Twice a month she visited her parents. He never accompanied her, he wasn't invited. Her mother and father did not approve of their living together, and had decided this was his misdemeanour rather than Isabel's; besides, he wasn't a Catholic.

Isabel was an assured woman, self-confident, poised, totally convinced that her taste was perfect. She seemed unflappable, except for the odd outburst when a bee or wasp flew in the window. She was three inches taller than Rory, and seven years older. In fact, she was not unlike Lily. Despite that, Rory adored her.

That Rory adored Isabel was easy to understand: the woman had a lot going for her. She ran her own company designing theatrical costumes. She was comfortably off, good looking. The mystery that puzzled the family was why Isabel adored Rory.

Lily and Mattie spent a deal of time on the telephone discussing this. Mattie was defensive. 'What do you mean, what does she see in him? He's lovely. So handsome these days. He has a tan and cheekbones. Of course she adores him, he's my Rory.'

Lily had thought: Of course she'd think that. But it doesn't answer the question. 'He has a tan now, and he always had cheekbones but you couldn't see them for hair.'

'Well,' said Mattie, 'Isabel saw his potential. She made him get his hair cut. She revamped him. But he was always good looking.'

'But what made her go for him in the first place? He's seven years younger than her, but that hardly makes him a toyboy. And he can be quite iffy with people sometimes. Curt,' she said.

'I know,' said Mattie. 'I've always worried about that. Maybe he's only like that with us. Maybe he's perfectly friendly with people he isn't related to.'

Lily had said, 'Hmm.' One thing she knew. There was a lot of sex involved. On the few occasions Rory and Isabel had visited her and Art, there had been ardent noises coming from the bedroom every night. And the pair had sat entwined on the sofa, stood entwined in the kitchen, talking quietly, kissing while Lily cooked. She'd found this perturbing. Isabel knew things about Rory that she didn't know. She wanted to say that he was her little brother. And she really, really wanted to know what attracted Isabel to him.

Isabel had first been attracted to his accent. It had reminded her of Sean Connery. Rory had designed her website, and had, on a visit to Paris, dropped in to see if she was having any problems with it. Then she'd fallen in love with his hands as he leaned over her and took control of the mouse on her computer. 'Such hands,' she'd said. 'Long fingers, so creative.'

Rory had smiled, and felt a glow of pride. Then she'd told him he should get his hair cut. 'You shouldn't hide your face. It's a good face.'

By the time he'd finished looking over her system, he'd asked her out to dinner that night. And when he turned up at her office to collect her, his hair was cropped short. 'Ah,' she'd said. 'Excellent.'

What Isabel loved about Rory was his quietness and his reliability. He was always there when she wanted him. She could depend on him, she was sure he'd never let her down.

Of course, Rory wasn't really reliable. He was content. His life with Isabel suited him. Beautiful flat, beautiful woman and plenty of personal space. Isabel worked long hours, so he had the flat to himself. He could come and go as he pleased. He thought he'd landed on his feet.

'How's Isabel?' Mattie asked him now.

'She's fine,' Rory told her. 'In fact, I think I'll go phone her. Tell her I've arrived safely.'

He took his case up to his room. Same old room, he thought. Sisters of Mercy posters on the wall, Tolkein books, a battery-operated toy car on the shelf by the bed, a row of baseball caps hung on the back of the door. When he was sixteen he'd painted one wall purple, the rest white. He wished his mother and father would redecorate. The duvet cover on the bed was red and black. When Isabel had seen it, she'd shuddered.

He sat on the chair by the window and dialled her number. 'Hello, it's me. I'm here.'

'Hello,' she said.

He could hear voices in the background, Isabel's mother and father discussing the seating arrangements at the table for supper. Not a lot to talk about there, he thought, there's only three of them. But formalities had to be observed.

'How are you?' he asked.

'I'm well. I'm as well as I was when you last saw me a few hours ago.'

'Great. I wish you were here. Though I'm sort of glad you're not. They still haven't redecorated my room.'

'It's still terrible?'

'I didn't use to think so. But I can see that my taste at sixteen wasn't anything to be proud of.'

'Ah. When we have children their rooms will all be beautiful.'

'Rooms?' he said. 'We've only got three rooms.'

'We'd have to move. Somewhere bigger.'

He looked out of the window at the garden. It was winter damp, grey. The lilac tree was bare, the grass sodden. It was raining.

'It's raining here,' he said.

'It's always raining there,' she said.

'No it isn't.'

This children thing was starting to bother him. Isabel mentioned it often. At first he'd joked about it, hadn't taken it seriously. He thought Isabel wanted four children in the same way he'd wanted a gleaming white stallion when he was ten. It was a glorious notion. But he was beginning to think she really meant it. He imagined his four children sitting in a row on their sofa, legs dangling, looking at him expectantly. One had glasses. They were of course immaculately turned out. Babies, he didn't want to imagine. Babies scared him. He thought he'd drop them. 'If we have four children,' he said, 'I mean, what with your folks being so straight and that, wouldn't we have to be married?'

He was seeking a way out. They weren't married so they couldn't have children; they'd all be bastards, unthinkable for

Isabel's parents and, therefore for Isabel. And he was trying to map out the pros and cons of the situation.

'Yes, we would,' said Isabel. 'I thought you'd never ask. I suppose you find it easier to do on the phone, so you wouldn't see me if I refused. That's so sweet. Of course I don't refuse. I accept, I will marry you. Oh, thank you. *Merci.*'

He heard her tell her mother and father that he'd just asked her to marry him. And he heard their joy. He was sure there was clapping. Cries of glee. And sounds of kissing.

'Thank you. Thank you,' said Isabel. 'I love you.'

'I love you too,' said Rory.

'We'll get the ring when you get back?'

'Oh yes,' he said. Then he told her once more that he loved her, and that they'd talk when he returned to Paris, and rang off. He sat and started into the gathering dark in the room. Rain spat on the window pane. It appeared he was getting married. He didn't quite know how it had happened. It wasn't as if she'd tricked him; she'd simply misunderstood what he was trying to say, had decided he was saying what she longed for him to say. Now his life was slipping out of control. No, it wasn't slipping, it was spinning into a wild, unbridled skid.

He went downstairs where Mattie, having finished her glass of champagne, and sneaked a second from the bottle in the kitchen, was setting the table for supper. 'So how's Isabel?' she asked.

'Still fine,' said Rory.

'I still want to hear all your news,' said Mattie.

'There is no news. Life just ticks along.' He knew his mother thought his life exciting now that he lived in Paris. But he thought that in fact nothing much had changed. Yes, the food was better, and yes, he was better dressed, and now he did everything in French, and that rather amazed him. Though Isabel told him he'd never be truly French till he made love in French. Thus far, he always cried out in English. But apart from that he felt he was the same messy, confused, scared-of-committing person he'd been since he was sixteen.

Still, though, he lied to his mother. He *did* have some news. He was getting married. He had just, it appeared, proposed to Isabel. How had that happened? But he wasn't going to tell anybody about it. If he ignored it it might go away. Or something might happen to stop this precarious skid into matrimony and father-hood. Maybe Isabel would go off him – though he'd miss her if she did. Maybe she'd discover what an absurd, indecisive, secretly childish person he really was, and decide he would make an unfit husband, not at all the sort of chap she wanted to sire one child, far less four.

Anyway, he didn't have to put up with more interrogation from Mattie because John appeared waving some ancient LPs he'd unearthed from a box at the back of the shed.

'See,' he shoved the first under Mattie's nose, 'Gene Vincent, "Be Bop A Lula".' He whipped this LP away, and pushed a second in front of her, 'Eddie Cochran, "Three Steps to Heaven". AND, Bob Dylan, "*Like* a Rolling Stone". WHICH I also happen to have on CD, so nyah.'

Mattie said, 'Pathetic.' And went back to the kitchen, where she topped up her glass. Swigged and thought, Utterly, utterly pathetic.

So dinner passed with Lily, Art, Rory and Grandpa struggling to make pleasant conversation against the seething undertow of John's gloating 'Be Bop A Lula' triumph, and Mattie's scorn at someone who'd take a minor mistake about who sang a silly pop song almost fifty years ago to such absurd lengths. There was, Lily said to Art when they retired to bed at eleven o'clock (early for them), a distinct frisson in the air.

'Lil,' said Art, 'your middle-class knack of understating things never ceases to amaze me. Your mother and your father are at war.'

Next day Mattie got her Christmas high spot. Marie arrived with the three children in tow, all dressed in their Sunday best. Into the house they came, bringing with them the scents of the icy morning. The hall was filled with the chime of greetings and good wishes; there were kisses. 'Merry Christmas,' Mattie called as she battered down the hall, her arms wide, ready to embrace whoever came near.

'Merry Christmas, Mum,' said Marie, moving into the open arms, staying there a moment, held close, breathing in her mother's smell.

And there was milling: though there was only Marie and three children to mill, they did it well enough to satisfy Mattie. 'Come in, come in,' she cried, almost weeping with happiness at seeing them. It was as if she hadn't seen them all for years, though it had been yesterday, when they'd all dropped by at lunchtime with the turkey Marie had picked up from the butcher's.

The aroma of that turkey, stuffed with chestnuts, filled the house. The lights on the tree gleamed; beneath it lay a spreading of gifts still wrapped; in the living room a log fire crackled. It was Christmas.

Marie kissed John. 'Merry Christmas, Dad.'

She flung her arms round Art's neck. 'Hi, Art. How're you doing? Merry Christmas.' Smacked a huge kiss on his cheek.

She threw herself at Rory. 'Rory! Merry Christmas.' He swept her up, twirled her round, still clinging to him. Laughing.

Once she'd landed, and let Rory go, she crossed to Lily. 'Merry Christmas, Lily,' she said, and gave her a polite, impersonal air kiss.

Lily felt unloved. Everyone else got a huge greeting, but she'd only got the sort of thing one gave to people you didn't know very well. Wasn't it always the way? When she was growing up it had always been, 'Look after your sister and brother, Lily.' And she hadn't been allowed to play on her own, or go off with her friends, because she'd had to take care of Marie and Rory. She'd helped them dress, taken them to the park, overseen their homework. When they'd been watching television, she'd had to help with supper, peeling potatoes, making the salad, setting the table. 'Lily's so good,' Mattie would say. 'Quite the helper around the house. And so serious.'

Huh, she thought, she'd been middle-aged from the age of eight. No youth for her. She'd worked at school, gone to university, studied hard, stayed at university, got her PhD, written academic books, well, easy-to-read academic books, married, and that was that. Sensible Lily. No juicy past like Mattie. Or Marie and Rory, come to that.

She'd been to only two rock concerts in her life. How many had Rory and Marie been to? Hundreds, she thought. And who had driven into town to pick them up afterwards, when they'd phoned to say they were stuck in some out-of-the-way place and had spent all their money, often at two or three in the morning? She had. Who had lied to Mattie about how drunk they'd been? She had. When Marie got pregnant and decided to get married, who had chipped in to help pay for the wedding because John and Mattie had no savings? She had. And what thanks did she get? A polite air kiss.

'You look absolutely washed out,' she said to Marie.

'I've been up since before six,' said Marie. 'It's Christmas. Tod and Agnes were charging around at dawn. They had to see if Santa had been. And I couldn't get them to go to bed last night.'

Tod and Agnes had been too excited to sleep; they'd been high. Eventually Marie had phoned their next-door neighbour to ask for help. Then she'd taken her children out into their small back garden to watch the sky and listen for sleigh bells. The neighbour, Mrs McMann, had leaned out of her window, jingling her cat's collar.

'It's him. It's him,' Marie had squealed. 'Better get to bed. He doesn't come if you're awake.'

That had done it. They'd all rushed inside, and upstairs to their bedrooms. Put on their pyjamas in a flurry and leapt into bed. Though Tod was a sceptic when it came to Santa Claus. 'That was Mrs McMann with Tibby's collar, wasn't it?' he said.

'Never,' lied Marie. And they'd both agreed on that. Tod was willing to suspend his disbelief at nine thirty on Christmas Eve, just in case.

'God,' said Rory now. 'Remember we used to do that? Shouting, "Has he been yet?" at six in the morning. Then we'd run downstairs, and rip open our presents, and drag them all upstairs to Mum and Dad's room. Remember I got a bike, and couldn't wait to ride it. So I cycled along the street at half past six in the morning in my pyjamas.'

And I had to go after you with your coat, so you wouldn't catch your death, thought Lily. But that part seemed to have been edited out of the memory. Everyone was laughing fondly, remembering Rory disappearing along the street on his brand-new red Chopper wearing his Star Wars pyjamas. In the vision Lily wasn't running behind him, her duffle coat over her pink nightdress, her pink slippers slapping on the pavement, yelling at him to stop and put on his anorak.

'Great days,' said John. He looked at Agnes, Tod and Lauren, who were standing by the Christmas tree, fingering the presents. 'Shall we open them now?' he said.

'Oooh, yes,' said Rory. He and Marie started to dish them out. Mattie helped.

'Perhaps we should wait till after the meal,' suggested Lily. 'It would be so nice in the evening, and there's all that anticipating what's beneath the wrapping. It's sort of sophisticated.'

Everyone turned to look at her in horror. Wait? They didn't think so.

Lily squirmed. 'It was just a suggestion.'

'Champagne,' said Mattie. 'We must have champagne as we open our gifts. I'll get it, and don't start without me.' She hurried to the kitchen, where she gave the turkey a swift baste and fetched a bottle from the fridge.

She poured a glass for everyone, Coke for the children, and hoisted her drink in the air. 'Merry Christmas, everyone. Best ever.'

And they all agreed. And chorused her wish. 'Best ever.'

Within minutes, the floor was covered in wrapping, Mattie trying to take charge. 'No, wait. We should open a present one person at a time, so we can see the receiver's face. The way it lights up. That's what presents are about.'

Lily was thinking it was a waste of her good Harrods paper, the way it was being torn apart and tossed aside. Nobody had remarked on how tasteful it was.

Grandpa got: two bottles of malt whisky, a copy of *Billy Budd*, a jumper with a zip at the neck. 'Very trendy, Grandpa,' said Marie. A box of butterscotch sweets, a video of *The Seekers*, his favourite Western, a denim shirt, a pair of Calvin Klein boxer shorts and four pairs of socks.

Mattie got: three bottles of perfume, Joanna Trollope's latest novel (signed), a silk shirt, a pair of leather gloves, a Tony Bennett CD, Dior nail varnish, a box of pralines, a box of chocolate truffles, a bottle of liqueur, framed photos of her grandchildren and a drawing done by Lauren.

143

Art got: three pairs of socks, a tie, a video of *Crouching Tiger, Hidden Dragon*, a book by Toby Litt, a shirt, a jar of chutney with a fancy label and a bar of expensive dark chocolate.

Rory got: much the same.

Marie got: two bottles of perfume, a bottle of Chardonnay, a jumper with a high polo neck, a Nigella Lawson cookery book, a box of liqueur chocolates, and from Rory a long dark blue cashmere scarf, which Lily seriously envied.

Lily got: a book about yoga, no chocolates, no perfume, a Dido CD, a CD of Pablo Casals playing Bach, a book on the cheeses of France, a book on the life of Samuel Pepys, a book about meditation, and a beautiful copper bain-marie that had a white ceramic inset.

John got: an expensive black sweatshirt, two pairs of boxer shorts, three pairs of socks, a video of *Fitzcarraldo* (his favourite film, or what everyone thought was his favourite film), a box of chocolate gingers, a bottle of Plymouth Gin, and a book about kite-making from Marie.

'Kite-making?' said Mattie. 'I didn't know you were interested in that.'

'Dad's making a kite,' said Marie. 'Didn't you know?'

'No,' said Mattie. She looked across at John, 'No, I didn't.' She was hurt that he had told Marie and not her. Why hadn't he told her? Did he think she'd laugh at him? It was just a little bump in the excitement. A little glitch, but it was there.

'Oh, it's going to be huge,' said Marie, not noticing the looks her mother and father were exchanging (champagne on an empty stomach probably affected her judgement), 'en-or-mous.' She spread her arms, indicating the proposed enormity of the kite, 'and all bright colours. He's going to put a slogan on it, only he can't think of one.'

'I see,' said Mattie. 'I'm sure we'll all look forward to that. I better go check on the turkey.'

She went to the kitchen, opened the oven door. The bird was golden brown, and ready. She removed it from the oven, drained off the fat and set about making some gravy. She'd already prepared bread sauce and cranberry sauce. She sniffed. Dabbed a tear that had run down her cheek. John had told Marie all his kite plans, but hadn't told her. Well, two could play at that game. The little bump, the little glitch had grown. Mattie was no longer hurt, she was wounded.

Still, the Christmas dinner went well. The smoked salmon was moist, the turkey tender, the roast potatoes crisp on the outside, soft within. The Brussels sprouts glistened and were served in a dish with chestnuts, the sauces were appreciated, the stuffing a treat. The conversation sparkled.

Just as she'd started to eat her turkey, Mattie looked round, moist-eyed. 'Do you remember that sledge John built. It was so huge it stuck in the snow, and we were all on it. I was mortified.'

Lily, Rory, Art and Marie all looked at their watches. Thirty-six minutes. 'Yes,' said Lily. She'd won. The others smiled. Mattie had mentioned the sledge, and Lily had won the bet. Same old, same old. Lily nearly always won.

Lily had, for the first time ever in the White Christmas tradition, forgotten to bring the bowl for the trifle, so Mattie had put it in her baking bowl. The children had a choice of that or ice cream. There was, of course, Christmas pudding, which Mattie doused in brandy and lit, and everyone said, 'Oooh.' She offered rum butter or brandy cream to go with it.

Then Rory said, 'Isabel would have a fit at all this rich food. The cholesterol.' The champagne, the selection of wines with each course had probably affected *his* judgement.

Mattie said, 'It's Christmas. You're allowed a treat. Diet tomorrow.'

Grandpa said, 'Cholesterol has changed the world. Ever since it was discovered, things have changed. Once people ate it all the time, and they were happy. Nobody swore. But now people eat low-fat this and low-fat that and sushi which wouldn't fill a flea, and they swear all the time. "Fuck," they say. On the telly, in the street, in the papers, it's all fuck, fuck, fuck.'

There was silence. Nobody had ever heard Grandpa swear. The children stopped eating and stared at him.

'Grandpa!' Mattie said. 'The children . . .'

'Oh, it's all right,' said Tod. 'Mum says that all the time.'

Marie flushed. And shrugged.

Then, to change the subject, Lily started to talk about their planned holiday in August next year. 'We're thinking of touring Italy.'

'Oh,' said Mattie, eager to hurry on with this subject and leave cholesterol and swearing behind. 'Will you travel by train? Or take buses everywhere?'

'Driving,' said Art.

'Hiring a car when you're over there?' asked John.

'Nah,' said Art, unaware that the kicks on his shin under the table were from Lily and not Agnes, who'd been swinging her legs during the meal. 'Taking our own car. Got a new one.'

'Really?' said John. 'What is it?'

'Alfa Romeo,' said Art. 'Just got it the other day. Nice car, high mileage, though. Looking forward to motoring about with the roof down.'

'You've bought an Alfa Romeo *convertible*?' said Mattie. 'Oh.' The wound from the kite discovery had deepened, the pain was almost physical. It was as if everything stopped. There was only this aching knowledge that someone she loved had gone out and bought for herself something that she, too, longed to own. She sipped her wine, but could hardly swallow. She fought back tears. She felt hollow inside. There was only deep, deep hurt.

'What colour?' she asked. Trying to sound bright and interested.

'Black,' said Lily.

'Very sleek,' said Rory. 'Very Lily.'

Lily shrugged and returned to her trifle.

Marie said, 'You knew that's what Mum wanted. And you went out and got one when she couldn't. What a shitty thing to do. You shit, Lily.'

'Marie,' said Mattie. 'We're at the table. It's Christmas. Don't speak to your sister like that.'

Marie ignored her. 'You always were sneaky, Lily. You always had to best everyone. I knew one day you'd get found out.'

Lauren, sensing acrimony, started to cry. Agnes and Tod had stopped eating again, though Tod still had his spoon in his mouth, and were staring at their mother, who was swearing at their Auntie Lily. Goodness, this was interesting.

'Marie,' said Mattie sharply, 'if Lily wants to have an Alfa Romeo convertible, then she had a perfect right to one. Just because I wanted one too is no reason she has to buy something else. We could buy one, nothing stopping us. Only we don't have the money, but apart from that we could have one. Now let's hear no more about it.'

Marie said something like 'Humph.' And pulled the sobbing Lauren on to her knee to comfort her.

Lily looked down at her plate. She'd gone right off her trifle now, and she'd been enjoying it. Damn Art and his big mouth. Now she felt awful. She was a horrible person, a shit, a sneak, and everyone in her family knew it.

They had coffee and worked at some cheery small talk, but the festive mood had gone. Then Art said, why didn't he take Agnes and Tod for a walk? It would do them all good, some exercise after such a huge blow-out. Marie and Rory said they'd go too. Mattie said she'd stay home and look after Lauren, who'd fallen asleep on her mother's lap. Then Lily said she'd enjoy a walk as well, before it got dark. In fact she didn't want to go at all, but she really didn't want to be left alone with Mattie. John said he'd help Mattie clear up, and Grandpa had fallen asleep, his paper hat askew and slipping over his eyes.

When they'd gone, Mattie started to cry. John took her in his arms. 'It's all right,' he said.

'My daughter,' said Mattie. 'She knew I wanted a car like that. And she knew I couldn't afford it. So she went and got one, just to hurt me. Lily did that to me. My good and perfect Lily. She betrayed me, John.'

John stroked her back. Put his cheek on her head. 'I know,' he said. 'I know.' It was the closest they'd been in weeks.

At the park, Art raced ahead with Agnes and Tod. They'd brought Tod's new leather football, and the three were kicking it between them, Art shouting a commentary. 'Agnes has got the ball, she's not going to pass. This could be dangerous for Chelsea . . .'

'Hibs,' corrected Tod.

Rory and Marie wandered along together. Lily trailed behind, watching them. Marie had her hands in her pockets, her coat open; she had a long scarf (not the new Christmas cashmere, she was saving that for good, though when that would come, she didn't know) draped under her collar. Lily liked the way her sister's coat swung lightly as she moved, and the easy way she strolled with her hands in her pockets, holding the coat round her. It was long, black, nicely cut. And though her own coat had cost more than Marie earned in a month, and though Marie had worn her coat for over three winters, Lily couldn't help envying it. Also the scarf, which was long, striped brown and black, and had come from Oxfam.

Rory was making Marie laugh. Lily couldn't quite hear what they were talking about. She tortured herself it was her. They were laughing at her.

'C'mon, Marie,' Rory was saying. 'Tell me why Andy left. You haven't told anyone. Tell me, I need to know. I'm your brother. You used to tell me everything.'

'No,' said Marie.

'Go on. Go on,' said Rory. 'Did you come home and find him in bed with someone else? Was that it? Did you throw him out?'

Marie shook her head, hands still in pockets, head down, watching her feet. 'No. It was worse than that.'

'Worse?' said Rory. 'He was in bed with two women?'

Marie laughed. 'No. No.'

'Three?' said Rory. 'Three and a cocker spaniel.'

'Stop it,' said Marie. 'Andy didn't do anything. It was me.'

'You? You were in bed with a cocker spaniel?'

'No, Rory. He found me in bed with his best mate.'

'Never!' said Rory. 'Oh, Marie.'

'Don't,' said Marie. 'Don't say anything. I feel bad enough about it as it is. I can't bear to hear what you have to say. I have ruined everything. I wrecked Andy's life, the children's lives. I even wrecked my own life.' She looked at him, her face white, about to crumple out of control, her eyes blurred with tears. God help me.

'What did he say?' asked Rory.

'He didn't say anything. We were at a party. He'd *promised* we'd go home early, but he got caught up with his friends, talking mountains. Don came upstairs and started kissing me. And it was so nice just to be wanted, you know, when you've had two kids, and you're thinking you're past it. One thing led to another. Andy found us and walked out. He came home, packed his stuff and left. He hasn't spoken to me since. He sends the kids Christmas presents and birthday presents and that. But that's all.'

'He won't forgive you? To err is human and all that.'

'When it comes to erring and forgiveness, all I can say is I did well with the human bit, but Andy is not now, and never will be divine. I don't think he'll ever forgive me, and I don't blame him.' Marie hung her head, bit her lip. And when she looked up, she was crying.

Rory put his arm round her. 'It'll be all right. You haven't told anybody?'

'No,' said Marie. 'I couldn't tell Mum I'd been caught with another man. I couldn't tell *Lily*, you know what she's like. So perfect, so censorious.'

Coming along behind, slowly, Lily heard her name. They *were* talking about her.

'I'm a bitch,' said Marie. 'A shit. I hate me.'

Bitch, shit, hate, Lily heard all that. Guilt and self-loathing spread through her. That was what they thought of her. No wonder, it was true. She turned and walked back to the house, alone.

John and Mattie cleared up together. He scraped the leftovers from the plates, she rinsed and stacked the dishwasher. There was a harmony, the rhythm of working together.

'If you want an Alfa Romeo, we'll get one. We'd manage.'

'No,' said Mattie. 'I don't want one. Not now. It wouldn't be the same. Besides, it was just a notion, it doesn't really matter. What hurts is Lily. I think she did it just to get at me. Getting a car, any car, won't fix that. Actually, I've gone right off that car.'

John was glad. He'd never been on it. He said that he was in a way relieved to see this side of Lily. 'She's always been so good. Too good, if you ask me.' There was something comforting in seeing her doing something so human. 'It's like I'm thinking, I'm not so bad after all.'

'Of course you're not bad, John. What a thing to say.'

This brought them even closer. They smiled, and carried on with their scraping, rinsing, stacking routine.

Spurred on by their new closeness, Mattie said, 'Perhaps I could help you with your kite.'

Silence. She turned. John was examining a plate. He didn't return her gaze.

'Oh, I see. You don't want me to help you. It's your project, and you want to do it alone. That's fine.' She wanted to say she'd get her own project. But thought that a bit childish. Still, she was hurt. Hurt by Lily, hurt by John. Just plain all-round hurt. 'It's really, really fine,' she said. 'I completely understand.'

Lily arrived home. She fetched her new books from the living room, where Grandpa still slept, despite the James Bond film roaring on the telly, and took them upstairs to her room. The same room she'd had since she was a girl and lived here. Only now it had a double bed. John and Mattie had bought it not long after she and Art married. 'Just so you know how much we want you both to come visit,' Mattie had said.

Lily switched on the lamp, lay down and started to leaf through her books. She realised that this was exactly what she'd done every Christmas when she was a child. She'd brought her presents here so she could play with them alone, while Marie and Rory watched television, or played with their new toys in the living room. There was something pleasant about it. Outside, it started to rain. It splattered against the window. The comfort of rain, Lily thought. Especially when you are in the warmth, and the light is on, and you know for certain there are people out there, getting soaked and running for shelter.

John went out to his shed. He put on the light, and spread his kite-making book on his workbench. There were new things to learn. He felt bad about not letting Mattie help. He knew she thought he was shutting her out. But his dream was fragile, and he knew Mattie: she'd be full of suggestions, criticism, wild enthusiasm that would sweep away his patient plans about his enormous kite that would fill the sky.

❀　❀　❀

Mattie finished packing the dishwasher, and left the next load soaking in the sink. Christmas, she thought, who needs it? Always the same, people talking out of turn, feelings getting hurt. She poured some champagne from the half-finished bottle on the kitchen unit, and sipped. First Marie saying John was making a kite, meaning she knew and Mattie didn't. Then Lily getting that car. And she tried so hard. She'd been up since half past six, which was when she'd had to put the turkey on. Still in her dressing gown, struggling to heave it into the oven. She poured another glass. She'd tried the Pickwickian Christmas, all roast chestnuts, merriment and games in the parlour, even though they didn't have a parlour. Then it had been the Marks and Spencer Christmas, luxury puddings, cakes with glazed nuts, specially boxed treats – Italian chocolates, little presents at every plate. Now she was on the Delia Smith Christmas, up at dawn wrestling with the turkey, which had a different stuffing at either end, making pudding weeks in advance, making alternative desserts for those who didn't like plum pudding, Brussels sprouts, roast potatoes, all the trimmings. It was hard work. And nobody said thank you. Nobody appreciated the effort she'd put in. In the end, what did you get? A decimated carcass, a pile of uneaten veg, a vast array of leftovers and a mountain of washing-up. Christmas just wasn't worth it, she decided. Next year she wouldn't invite the family; it would be John, Grandpa and herself. They'd have something simple, a microwave curry, perhaps. But then, she remembered, she'd vowed to do that this time last year.

Bookmarks

Marie went home shortly after six o'clock on Christmas Day; Rory went with her, carrying Lauren. They chatted comfortably about their lives, walking along in the easy silence of people who know each other well. Rory thought this would be the perfect time to tell Marie of his recent engagement to Isabel, but though the words formed in his head, he said nothing. He wasn't keeping it a secret, it was just his habit not to address matters that bothered him. He preferred to ignore his problems, and hope they would go away.

The streets were wet after the rain, and Christmas quiet. Yet in the short distance from John and Mattie's house to Marie's they met three acquaintances – two old friends of Rory's and one mother of an old friend – who all asked what Rory had been up to since they last saw him.

Rory stood, clutching Lauren, swaying slightly to keep her lulled and sleepy, and hummed and hawed, said, 'Nothing much,' and 'You know, rubbing along. Same old, same old.'

Marie wanted to know why he didn't tell people he was a website designer and lived in Paris.

'People don't want to hear that,' he told her. 'They want to hear that you're a bit down, having money troubles, out of work. It makes them feel awful to know someone from their past is happy and doing well.'

'Does it?' said Marie. 'I thought they'd be glad for you.'

'Your understanding of human nature is worryingly lacking,' said Rory. 'Nobody wants to be told I'm living in Paris. They imagine idle strolls by the Seine, accordion music drifting through the air, sitting in small cafés sipping Pernod. They suppose you to be living some sort of idyll, where you are permanently on holiday. This would depress them terribly. Why do that? It's Christmas.'

'How kind you are,' said Marie. 'But I know you, and when you rant in your over-the-top way about something trivial like being asked how you are doing, it means you've got something on your mind.'

'Does it?'

'Yes.'

Rory said nothing. Marie shrugged. His silence affirmed her suspicions. He had a problem, but she knew that if it ever got too much for him to cope with alone, he'd phone her to chat about it. He always did. And if his problem got really bad, he'd turn up on Lily's doorstep looking to her to help sort things out. He always did that, too.

It was late when Rory got back. John and Mattie and Art and Lily were watching television. He stuck his head round the living room door and wished them goodnight, but Lily summoned him in. 'Come talk to us. It's ages since we've seen you.'

He sighed, came into the room and sat down, and worked at not saying, 'What will we talk about?'

'Been a good Christmas,' he said. 'Great meal.' And waited for his mother to say, 'That's it over for another year.'

'Oh well,' said Mattie. 'That's it over for another year.' This always saddened her. This season, with its good wishes, secrets, hopes and festivities, never quite lived up to her expectations. 'Still,' she said, 'it'll be my birthday soon.'

'Your birthday isn't till April,' said John.

'Well, that's soonish, anyway,' said Mattie.

She loved birthdays. She thought them a good idea, everyone ought to have a special day. Rory hated them, they disrupted his routine. The easy coming and going that he enjoyed.

'Birthdays,' he said. His tone was disparaging.

'What's wrong with birthdays?' said Mattie.

'You never know with them. Someone might arrange a surprise party.' Isabel had done this once, when they'd only been together for six months. He had never quite recovered from the shock of arriving home that night. The flat had seemed empty, silent, dark. But there was something about this silence, this dark. It was heated, lively. He thought he heard whispering, muffled laughter. There was someone here. He called Isabel's name. His heart beat against his ribs. 'Who's there?' He switched on the light. In the sudden dazzle, he saw everyone he knew, and they were all shouting his name. For a fleeting moment he couldn't imagine why they were there. But Isabel had emerged from the throng wishing him happy birthday. She was like that: she sparkled, she had zest, she loved frivolity. He didn't. Sometimes he wondered what he saw in her. He liked a certain constancy, a routine. He liked that his days all followed a similar pattern. He supposed he was dull. Mostly he wondered what Isabel saw in him.

'People think you should *do* something on your birthday. It's a strain,' he said.

'It's not a strain. It's lovely. A break from routine.'

'I love my routine,' said Rory. 'I love waking in the morning and hearing the city just beyond my window. I love the coffee I drink. And going to work, I can walk by the river. I love the smell of Paris, and the sound of it. I like my life the way it is and I hate when it's disrupted by things like birthdays . . .'

Birthdays, Mattie thought. I love birthdays. When I was little I'd get cards with money slipped inside, and the postman would shout, 'Happy birthday,' when he was delivering them. I'd get to have whatever I wanted for tea. I could have a picnic this year, if it's sunny. I love picnics. We could take sandwiches, maybe a quiche, though John hates them, and wine, fruit juice for the kids. We could play games . . .

'I just want to carry on my life exactly as it is now. I love it,' said Rory. 'I love listening to music when I get home, I love my work, I love the internet. I don't want to get married. And I don't want to have to go out for dinner if I don't feel like it just because it's my birthday, or have the flat filled up with people I don't want to see . . .'

It will be April, thought Mattie. There will be daffodils, and crocuses, the first bluebell. Too early for swallows, probably. But the birds will be singing. I might even hear a cuckoo, though you don't hear cuckoos that often these days. In fact, it's years since I heard a cuckoo . . .

'Why do people always want to change things? Why do they keep moving the goalposts?' said Rory.

'Wait a minute,' said Lily. 'Rewind that speech a bit. Married? Are you getting married?'

'No,' said Rory. 'I said I didn't want to get married.'

'But why mention it?' said Lily.

Rory felt a prickle of anger. How like Lily to pick away at what he'd said and just *know* what was bothering him.

'Because . . .' he said.

Then Mattie, who'd daydreamed through everything Rory had said, turned to John. 'You know, I was just thinking, it's years since I heard a cuckoo.'

It really was a relief to Rory that he didn't have to answer Lily's marriage question, but that didn't occur to him till he was halfway up the stairs. After Mattie's cuckoo remark he'd stamped out of the room, saying, 'For God's sake, don't you ever listen to people?'

In his room, he threw himself on to his chair. What was his mother on about, talking about cuckoos? He sighed. He'd said too much downstairs, and wished he hadn't. He opened the window and breathed in the night, cold, wet. Then he took one of his *Judge Dredd* comics from the pile in his bedside cabinet. Each copy had been carefully kept in a polythene freezer bag. As he opened it, his youth came flooding back, and then he smiled, for he remembered something.

In the living room, Mattie said, 'Is Rory getting married?' The word lingered in her mind, something Lily had been saying before she chipped in with her silly remark about cuckoos.

'No,' said John. 'He has just told us he doesn't want to get married.'

'I think he protests too much,' said Lily. 'I have a suspicion Isabel has been putting the pressure on. She told me last time she was over in London that she wants children, four to be exact.'

'Four,' said Mattie. 'How ambitious. But they'd be French. I couldn't spoil them in English.'

'They'd be bilingual,' said Art.

'Bilingual, how lovely.' Mattie dreamed. She'd have seven grandchildren, far more than any of her friends. She imagined introducing her four French ones around. 'They're bilingual,' she'd boast, but only slightly. She wouldn't be too smug.

Upstairs, Rory rummaged through what used to be his sock drawer. It contained a couple of pairs he'd left behind, and some T-shirts that now embarrassed him. But he was sure he'd had some dope in here. It was in a plastic carton that once held a camera film. He found it, held it up. Excellent. The dope was still inside, wrapped in tin foil. He wondered how potent it would be; it had been hidden in that drawer for almost ten years. He rummaged some more and found a pack of Rizla papers. He got out a packet of Gauloise and rolled his first spliff in years. He found it wasn't like riding a bicycle or sex, it was a skill that once neglected slipped away. It was a leaky thing he rolled. Never mind, it would do the trick. He looked through the tapes he hadn't taken with him when he left home for good, after returning several times for prolonged stays, during terms of unemployment, and once when a relationship had broken up. He found *Screamadelica* and wondered why he'd left it here. But put it on, sat in his chair, opened the window and lit up. Brilliant. He was a boy again, no worries (or none that he cared to remember); marriage and children were not on the agenda.

Mattie, going to bed, stood on the landing at the top of the stairs, sniffing wildly. 'I know that smell. Marijuana. Rory's smoking dope, in our house. That's not very nice.'

'How do you know it's Rory?' said John.

'It's hardly likely to be Grandpa.'

'True,' said John. He sniffed. 'Ah, me. It's quite like old times. Rory in there smoking away thinking we don't know, and that music blaring out. I could get all nostalgic.'

Mattie went into the bedroom, started to undress. 'It's not nice him doing that. We could get raided by the cops.'

'Raided by the cops?' said John, sitting on the bed untying his shoelaces. 'You watch too much television.'

'Still,' said Mattie, sitting at the dressing table, putting on her night cream, 'he shouldn't be doing it. You should go and talk to him.'

'Me?' said John, taking off his trousers. 'Why me? You go talk to him. You're his mother.'

'But,' said Mattie, removing her bra, 'he prefers you. They all prefer you.'

'Nonsense,' said John, taking off his shirt. 'I'd say they prefer you.' He got into bed.

'I hate that you keep on the boxers you've been wearing all day when you get into bed,' said Mattie, climbing in beside him. 'You should put on a fresh pair.'

'They're comfy. I put on a new pair in the morning. I've worn these ones in.'

Mattie said, 'Hmm. And another thing, I've noticed you keep leaving the lavatory seat up these days.'

'Yes,' said John. 'I know. It's a habit I've been encouraging in myself. Post-feminism and all that.' He switched off his bedside light, turned on to his side, heaved the duvet over his shoulder, and made a flamboyant show of going to sleep.

Mattie lay in the dark. She thought about John, the man he was when she first met him. He'd worn a corduroy jacket, jeans and desert boots. He had wild curly hair, and when he saw her coming towards him, he'd spread his arms and shout her name. He was the first person in her life who'd made her feel wanted. The things they'd done, the fun they'd had. Her life had turned into an adventure. She remembered the first time they'd gone to bed together. Naked, she'd turned to him, the thrill of it; she'd thought she might stop breathing. She remembered how they'd kissed, and the feel of his skin against hers. The warmth, the passion as her flatmates chattered and played Eric Clapton records only yards away in the living room. We should have bookmarks for our lives, she thought, so we can easily turn back to the precious moments, the ones we wish we could live again.

Letters to Daddy

The next day everyone left. Rory went back to Paris. Lily and Art went to visit Marie to say goodbye, before leaving for the airport. The house was quiet again. Mattie complained about that. 'I don't know, you miss them when they're not here. Then they're here and it's all noisy and bustle, and you long for a bit of peace. Then they go away again and you start missing them again. You just can't win with family. And nobody ate any mince pies.'

John would have said she shouldn't have bought them, but he knew what she'd say. It was Christmas and you had to have them. It was the rule. So he kept his mouth shut. After breakfast he went out to the shed to reconsider his kite plans in the light of his new book.

Mattie sat at the kitchen table, wondering what to do. She'd cleaned a bit, stripped the beds, opened the window in Rory's room and sprayed it with air freshener to get rid of all the illegal smells. Now what?

She'd wanted to phone Rita Boothe ever since they'd met in the supermarket, but was too shy. She imagined a woman like that would have hundreds of people calling all the time. It was probable Rita wouldn't even remember who she was. So she thought no, she wouldn't do that. She would look at the television guide and see if there were any Katharine Hepburn films on.

The space Marie occupied at home was her own. Once it had been hers and Andy's. But in the time he'd been away from her, she'd redecorated. Not that she'd sought to expunge all memory of her husband – in fact, she still thought of him fondly. It was her guilt she wanted to get rid of. Coming across anything that reminded her of Andy brought it on. So she'd gathered everything he'd left behind, packed it all in a box that she'd put at the back of the cupboard under the stairs. She had left one framed photograph of Andy hanging in the hall by the front door. She felt she had no right to remove all trace of him from his children. She had by now mastered the art of passing it without looking at it every time she entered and left the house. But Tod and Agnes were sometimes to be found gazing at it, and then the questions would come. Where is he? Why did he go? Is he coming back? Marie would say that he was in Canada, and he'd gone because he had a good job there, and she was sure he'd come back one day. She knew how unsatisfactory this was. But it was the best she could do, considering how racked with guilt she was.

She missed him. His presence in the house. His laughter. His body beside her in bed. But felt she had no right to miss him, and knew he would never miss her.

He deserved better than a life without his children. He had been a wonderful father and had adored both Agnes and Tod. They had adored him in turn. It would all come to grief, Marie thought. One day her children would discover the truth, and then they would blame her for their fatherless childhood. The fury was yet to come. She dreaded the day.

Her house had four rooms, two up, two down, with kitchen and bathroom. A small place, but warm, comfortable, messy. There was a constant pile of books on the table in front of the sofa. Marie read. It kept her guilt at bay. She visited the library with her children every Saturday morning. But what people saw when they came into Marie's house was a home, tenderly, lovingly decorated. It was Marie's, it reflected the person she'd become, and the taste she'd discovered when she'd made decisions about colour schemes on her own. Marie, as Lily and Mattie both agreed, had an eye. Matisse prints round the walls, a dark indigo carpet, throws over the ageing sofa. This was a comforting place to be.

This morning had been particularly bad. Andy had, as always, been generous with his gifts to his children. There had not been as much as a card for Marie. But Tod had received a bike, Agnes a huge doll's house, Lauren a five-foot-tall pink furry rabbit, and as well as all this, he had sent an eight-foot-long bright yellow play tunnel for the three to share. Three of these extremely large objects were now in the living room, leaving little space for anything, or anybody, else. In order to escape from all this (though another thing Marie realised was that in time you stopped noticing the garish plastic clutter; you just manoeuvred your way round it, and the only time you really saw the reality of the mess was when someone who didn't have children came into your house and looked at it in unrestrained horror), Marie had taken the three children to the park. It was nine o'clock in the morning and Tod had been nagging to go since seven. He wanted to learn to ride his bike.

As the PA to an architect, every time Marie stepped out of her front door and looked round, she could see in her mind's eye how this housing scheme had looked in its planning stage. And this always made her smile. It would have been drawn as a street of matching houses with a huge area of green in front of them, and perhaps a tree or two. She wondered what whoever had designed the estate would make of it now. If only people hadn't come to live in the houses and spoil the perfect plan. But people will be people; they had to make their mark, they had to have their individuality.

Some had bought their council houses, and to stamp their ownership had painted the exterior, blue or, in one case, pink. Some had built porches, or extended upwards, adding a couple of rooms in the loft. Some people, like Marie's neighbour, had dug up their allotted area of green and concreted it over as an off-road parking place for the car. Others had planted roses. Marie had clematis growing round her front door, delphiniums, poppies and lupins from Mattie's garden in her patch of green, and, like Mattie, a huge tub of winter pansies.

The back gardens, which had been designed as open plan, had been divided up and were now a patchwork of individual plots, separated by small fences and hedges. Some were cultivated; some weren't and were just scrubby play areas where children ran, skipped or kicked footballs about. And where cats wandered. Marie preferred it this way. She liked what people did to mark out their territories. 'That's what gives the place life,' she said. After years of living here she knew all of her neighbours, and could not walk down the street without waving hello and smiling to familiar faces. She liked it here. Today, as she walked down the path, Tod leading the way pushing his bike, she noticed a new Saab parked a few doors down, and since she knew everybody, and their regular visitors, she wondered who it belonged to. Places like this, huge windows looking out on to huge windows opposite, make you nosy, she thought.

Neither Agnes or Lauren had wanted to go out. But Marie was a great believer in bribery. She'd promised Agnes a bar of chocolate and pointed out that since Tod was going to be riding his bike she would probably have the swings and the merry-go-round to herself. Lauren had succumbed when she discovered that they could take the five-foot pink rabbit, now named, inexplicably, Mavis, and he could ride in Lauren's buggy.

Of course, this meant Lauren had to walk, and as she wanted to push the buggy herself, gripping the handle halfway down, plunging ahead, not looking where she was going, the ten-minute walk to the park took half an hour.

On the way, Agnes pointed out that a trip to the park would be a lot more fun if they had a dog.

'We're not getting a dog,' said Marie. 'Who'd look after it when we're all out all day?'

'Grandma and Gramps. They look after Lauren. They could look after a dog. We could call it William, and have a lead for it and everything.'

'I don't think they'd like that,' said Marie, grabbing the handle of the buggy, and steering it back on course. Lauren had been heading for the road. 'It's very kind of them to look after Lauren; that's enough to ask.'

'But,' said Agnes, 'I want a dog. Tod's got a bike. I want a dog with a lead.'

'Maybe one day,' said Marie. Along with bribery, Marie had found that avoiding confrontation was a good thing. If she delayed the dog decision, Agnes might forget she wanted one, and might start wanting something else, which Marie could avoid buying by saying, 'Maybe one day.'

The park was an open space, with a walkway running through it. This led from the houses to the main shopping area and library. There was a football pitch, muddy all winter, at the far end, trees evenly spaced along the public path, a play park with swings, a merry-go-round and climbing frame, and a paddling pool that was drained for the winter and strewn with leaves. When they got there, Tod insisted on going on his bike, which he couldn't ride. Marie had to run along beside him holding the thing up while Tod pedalled. Plainly, in order for Tod to get the hang of bike-riding, he and Marie would have to go further than round and round the small play area. Marie put Lauren and Mavis on the merry-go-round, and told Agnes to look after them. 'Just for a few minutes,' she said. 'While I help Tod.'

Agnes had nodded solemnly. So, holding the bike, Marie had set off across the park. It was not long before Tod could manage to hold the handlebars steady, and stopped wobbling as he travelled along. Now all Marie had to do was hold the saddle as Tod cycled. This meant running, bent double, but, hey, she was used to that. Only she lost track of how far she'd come.

She stopped when she heard Agnes shouting, 'Mummy! Mummy! Mummy!'

She turned, realised her other two children were some distance away. Agnes was jumping up and down, pointing. 'A puppy,' she yelled.

And sure enough, as Marie was running bent double, helping Tod to ride his Christmas bike, on the other side of the park, beyond the play area, a woman had appeared, walking what was obviously a Christmas puppy, a small, energetic golden cocker spaniel. It was too tempting for Agnes, who abandoned her sister-minding duties and took off to see the dog close up, and pat it.

This left Lauren alone. The child knew an opportunity when she saw one. Mavis flopped over on the roundabout as Lauren climbed off and, little legs going like pistons, headed across the park in the opposite direction from Agnes, towards the road.

Screaming for Lauren to stop, Marie let go the bike. Tod fell off, and started to cry. But Marie did not notice; she was sprinting over the ground, yelling at her daughter. Except Lauren loved to be chased, and started to laugh, a gleeful childish chuckle. And run faster. Marie caught up with her as she reached the edge of the grass and was about to flee across the pavement and on to the road in front of the Saab that had been parked in the street where they lived.

As she picked Lauren up and tucked her under her arm, Marie paused a moment to watch it go, and had the vague feeling she was being watched. I'm going nuts, she thought. All guilt and neurosis; soon I'll be talking to myself. Then she thought: I do talk to myself. I am nuts.

Meantime, at the other side of the park, Agnes was down on her hands and knees in the football pitch mud playing with the Christmas puppy. Marie turned and yelled to Tod at throat-bruising volume, 'Stay there. Don't move.' Then, gripping the squealing and wriggling Lauren, ran over to get Agnes.

Young things are attracted to other young things, she thought. Agnes and the puppy seemed to have found one another. They were rolling and cuddling. The cocker spaniel was in ecstasy, licking every available part of Agnes. They were both encrusted with mud. Marie might have laughed, but she was red and breathless. She had a stitch in her side from the sprint across the park, and bent over panting to relieve it.

The puppy owner was obviously disgusted at Agnes and told her to go away. 'You've got my dog all muddy,' she said.

Agnes started to cry.

'Look at him,' crowed the puppy owner. 'I'll have to give you a bath now, won't I, Julius?'

Marie said she was sorry, but her daughter was somewhat muddy too, the words coming out in short gasps, as she fought to regain her breath. As she straightened up, the pain of the stitch diminishing, she caught the other woman's look. A swift, sweeping and dismissive glance from foot to head. Marie realised she was red, sweaty and breathless, her hair was sticking out and up, her boots were old, worn for comfort rather than style. There was a fraying hole in the knee of her jeans, which she had till this moment rather liked. She thought it casually stylish. The look demoralised her.

The puppy woman was wearing her designer dog-walking outfit. Armani jeans, long leather coat. 'You should keep your children under control,' she said.

Belittled, feeling small and irresponsible, Marie grabbed Agnes's hand and pulled her away.

Agnes tripped after her mother. 'That woman told me to go away.'

Marie said she knew. She'd heard. 'You shouldn't bother people. You shouldn't pat strange dogs.'

Under her arm, Lauren was wriggling, drumming her fists against Marie's side, and screaming to be put down.

Agnes said, 'I want a puppy like that. With a lead.'

Marie put Lauren down and told Agnes, 'Maybe one day.'

They all went to collect Tod, who was still standing by his bike. Marie brushed him down after his fall and said, 'No harm done. Let's go home.'

Lauren was secured in her pushchair, Mavis was tucked under Marie's arm. And all the way back through the streets Agnes asked, 'Why can't we have a puppy now?'

Marie only answered, 'Because I said so.'

After that they walked in silence. It hadn't been a good outing.

When she was expecting Tod, Marie had passionate views on how children ought to be brought up and had always vowed she'd never say this. But now she had three, and was exhausted most of the time, she said it regularly.

Once home, she put Lauren, who had fallen asleep in her pushchair, to bed, and bathed Agnes. Then she made herself a cup of coffee, and as she waited for the kettle to boil, she sat Agnes and Tod at the kitchen table with a glass of orange juice apiece, pencils and paper, and told them to write a lovely thank-you letter to their daddy. 'Tell him how pleased you are with your beautiful presents, and do some drawings to show him what you've been up to, and don't forget to put lots of kisses at the end,' she said, willing some enthusiasm into her voice.

Everything done, children warm, safe, fed, she could, at last, sit down and have her cup of coffee and, for a few moments, let her mind wander, imagining the things she ought to have said to the puppy woman. Of course, to do that in proper comfort she would have to sit on the sofa, which meant clambering over the enormous yellow tunnel, shoving aside the outsize doll's house, and accepting the violently pink and now somewhat grubby rabbit on the seat beside her.

She was doing this when the doorbell rang, the front door opened and someone called, 'Marie, yoohoo. It's us.'

Lily and Art, come to say goodbye before they returned to

London. Lily's idea. Marie had called her a shit when Art let slip about the car. After they'd come back from their walk Marie had been shooting her vicious glances. They were silently fighting. Lily needed to look into Marie's eyes to see how much hate was there.

Marie heard Lily and Art squeeze past the bike, which was standing in the hall (Tod wouldn't consider keeping it anywhere else, it was far too beautiful to live outside in the shed). She stood watching the door, waiting for Lily's entrance, the swift critical look round, eyeing the mess, the gaudy toys. But when Lily did come in and cast her eyes about her, what Marie saw on her sister's face was not horror. It was envy. Surely not, she thought. Shock, I'd expect. Pity, I'd accept. But envy? Who could be jealous of this?

What Lily saw was a homey room. A lived-in clutter. A person could relax here, hide here. She could feel the tension ease in her shoulders as the wave of warmth hit her, and the lingering smell of the bacon Marie had cooked earlier for breakfast enfolded her. It was undemanding, this home. It required nothing of the people who lived in it, other than they love one another.

Lily's home, on the other hand, was very demanding. It required to be kept immaculate at all times, and that the people who lived in it maintained a certain standard of fashionable dress and taste in food, books and music. There was something about Marie's home that made Lily feel safe. She thought she could easily curl up on the sofa beside that hideous giant pink rabbit and fall into a happy sleep.

Instead of congratulating Marie on the comfort her home brought, Lily said, 'Goodness, the toys. A huge yellow tunnel cluttering up the place.' The words didn't come out as she'd intended. She had simply wanted to mention the huge yellow tunnel. Not having any children, it surprised her.

'A present from the childrens' father,' said Marie. Sounding defensive. Why shouldn't she have a huge yellow tunnel in her living room if she wanted?

'You didn't get anything like this in my day,' said Lily. Sounding resentful and a little disapproving.

'Nor mine,' said Marie. 'It's fun. Do you want a shot in it? You can crawl through to get to the sofa. Easier than climbing over it.' Sounding sarcastic.

Art listened to this bemused. He was listening to a displacement argument. Lily and Marie were exchanging sharp words about a yellow tunnel when they were actually fighting about the fact that Lily had hurt her mother's feelings by buying herself the car Mattie dreamed about. Why didn't they say what they meant? Get it out in the open? Clear the air?

So he said, 'Oh, stop all this stuff. This is about the car, isn't it? Lily bought the damn thing on an impulse. She was on the bus, saw it in a showroom window. Got off and bought it.'

Lily and Marie turned and glared at him. This was their dispute, it had nothing to do with him. He sat down and said, 'OK. OK. It's your fight. Get on with it.' In fact, he rather liked the tunnel. He thought he and Lily could do with it in their living room. It would add a certain whimsy which he felt his life lacked.

Marie said, 'You bought a *car*? On an *impulse*?'

Lily looked at her feet, shamed. She felt disgustingly extravagant.

'If you've got that much money to throw about, you should give it to the poor and needy,' said Marie. Like me, she thought.

'I know,' said Lily.

'Have you any idea how hurt Mum was?' said Marie.

Lily said she had, and she would make it up to her.

'How?' said Marie.

Lily shrugged. She didn't know. It occurred to her to give the car to Mattie. But contrite as she was, she wasn't that contrite. Besides, it seemed a little grandiose. 'I've come to hate impulses. I'm never going to do anything like that again.'

She and Marie stared at one another. Then, when the silence was becoming awkward, Marie said, 'Coffee?' And without waiting for a reply she clambered towards the kitchen, leaving Lily to stare with childish longing at the doll's house.

Lily was imagining the fun she would have with it. She could decorate the rooms. Well, that wallpaper in the tiny living room was horrendous. A pale off-white would be good, and she'd certainly do something about the floor covering. But the bedroom was perfect.

'I always wanted a doll's house,' she said. And sighed.

Marie came to the door of the kitchen and looked at her. 'Play with it if you want.'

Lily smiled weakly, and shook her head. Even though she did want. She looked round. 'Where's Lauren?' She'd been looking forward to seeing her little niece. She'd hoped she could pick her up and cuddle her, and perhaps play little games with her.

'She's upstairs, sleeping. She's tired after going to the park this morning.'

'Oh,' said Lily. 'So what have you been up to?'

'I only saw you yesterday, so there have been no big developments in my life to report. Like I said, we went to the park. Came home. The kids are writing thank-you letters to their dad.'

Lily followed her into the kitchen. 'Does Andy always send such big presents?' she asked.

Marie told her he did.

'Doesn't he remember how small your house is? I mean, there's hardly room in here for everything.'

Marie handed a mug of coffee to Lily, and took one to Art. 'He did live here. I'm sure he remembers what it's like.'

'Do you think he's doing it deliberately? To annoy you?'

'I think he just doesn't want his children to forget him. It's been a while since they've seen him.' But the notion struck home. Marie ran through the gifts Andy had sent – a drum kit for Tod's birthday a few months ago – the noise had been excruciating – a trumpet for Agnes, a battery-operated car that had whined up and down the hall banging into the skirting board, a chemistry set. She shook her head. No, Andy wouldn't be so bitchy. That was the sort of thing she would do.

Lily lingered in the kitchen. She sat at the table, watching Tod write, and asked what he was doing.

'Writing a thank-you letter to Dad,' he said. Then returned to the task.

The way he curved one arm round his notepad, and wrote head down, lips tight, concentrating, reminded Lily of Rory. It embarrassed her now when she thought of how she'd treated her brother when he was little. She'd dressed him up, carried him about, and had taken him with her wherever she went, clutching his hand and telling everyone she met that he was her little brother, without ever mentioning his name. 'She treats him like a doll,' Mattie had said. Naturally, Rory had reached five and rebelled. He'd run away from her, and taken tantrums when she tried to brush his hair. She sighed. Sometimes she thought it would be good to have a child. A little girl, a bit like Lauren. But she would never allow a plastic yellow tunnel in her living room.

'Are you writing to Daddy too?' she asked Agnes.

'Yes,' she said. 'But I don't know what to say.'

'Have you said thank you?' asked Lily.

'Of course I've said that,' said Agnes. 'But that only takes up a line. I need to fill up the whole page.'

'Well, tell him what you've been doing. What have you been doing today?'

'We went to the park so's Tod could ride his bike. And Lauren ran away and nearly went on the road, she could have been run over by a car. And I saw a puppy. And played with it. I want a puppy.'

'Well,' said Lily. 'That's lots. Tell him all that. You've had an exciting morning.'

Agnes brightened. 'OK.'

Lily left them to it, and went through to join Art and Marie. 'You never did say why Andy left,' she said.

'Didn't I?' said Marie, and jerked her head in the direction of Tod and Agnes in the kitchen. Now was not the time to talk about this, the children were listening. She changed the subject. 'I hope your new car isn't being vandalised. I presume it's sitting outside your flat.'

'It'll be fine,' said Lily.

There was a thick silence, full of Marie's disapproval and Lily's guilt. Neither of which Lily could bear. She stared into her mug. Sighed. Looked up and caught Marie's censure. 'What?' she said.

'You know what,' said Marie. 'That car.'

'I thought we'd discussed that. Why shouldn't I have a car that I want? It's fun. I've never had fun. You did. All our lives you and Rory had fun, you did things. I didn't, I was good. I helped in the house, I was always looking after you two. Remember yesterday we were laughing about Rory cycling down the road in his pyjamas when he got a bike for Christmas. Nobody remembers me running down the road behind him with his anorak. I was *told* to do that.'

Marie shook her head. 'No you weren't. I was there. You just grabbed his anorak, put on your duffle coat and took off after him. Nobody told you to do it. Mum said it was because you were naturally good. A good person.'

'I don't remember it like that,' said Lily. 'What I remember is always having to do the washing up, always having to help cook and clean when you and Rory got to play. You had all the fun. You went to rock concerts. I hardly ever did. Now look at you. You've got this lovely snug home and three terrific kids. What have I got?'

'A good job,' said Marie. 'Money. A super husband.'

'Absolutely,' said Art.'

'A beautiful flat,' continued Marie. 'Fantastic clothes. Fabulous holidays. And a car that broke your mother's heart on Christmas Day. That's a lot, Lily.' The sarcasm flowed.

Reviewing Marie's list, however, Lily thought she was right. After a long, stiff silence, she said, 'Well, that's me told.'

She and Art left not long after that. There wasn't much anyone wanted to talk about. When they went Lily took Agnes and Tod's thank-you letters, addressed to Andy's mother as Marie still did not have an address for him in Canada, and promised to post them.

Marie stood at the door, watching them go, then went inside. Lauren was up, coming slowly down the stairs, backwards. Her preferred method. Marie hoped she'd grow out of it before she was forty. She ran up to meet her, and picked the child up, touched the hot, sleepy little face, said, 'Do you want some juice? You missed your Auntie Lily and Uncle Art, they came to see you.'

This seemed of little importance to Lauren, who simply said, 'Juice.'

As she poured orange juice into a plastic cup, Marie asked Agnes and Tod what they'd said in their letters to their daddy.

Agnes said, 'Auntie Lily said we should tell him what we'd been doing today so I said we'd gone to the park and Lauren had nearly got run over, 'cos you weren't looking after her, and I got all muddy playing with a puppy.'

Marie thought: Thank you, Lily.

169

Tod said, 'I told him thanks for the bike. It's brilliant. And Lauren ran away, and you had to let go of the bike to run after her, and I fell off.'

'Well, I think I come out of these letters very well,' said Marie. 'The perfect mother.'

'Also,' said Agnes, 'I told him I wanted a puppy with a lead, and you said we'd get one soon, one day soon.'

'That is *not* what I said,' said Marie. 'As you know very well, I said, "Maybe one day," which is a totally different thing.'

'But I want a dog,' said Agnes. 'Why can't I have a dog? And why doesn't Daddy come home?'

It was going to be a long, long day. Marie sighed, and worried that what Lily had said about Andy sending cumbersome presents that filled the house to annoy her might be true. In which case a puppy might seem a wonderful idea to him. It occurred to her that one day very soon, a small, eagerly friendly but seriously incontinent animal might be joining her household.

Everybody Hurts

For several weeks Mattie contemplated phoning Rita Boothe, but always shyness got the better of her. She'd pick up the receiver, start dialling the number, then her mind would flood with images. Rita's busy life. Rita working at her computer, tutting as she was interrupted by a stream of important calls. Rita chatting wittily to friends, fellow writers, artists, actors. Rita throwing a huge and lively dinner party, where guests talked, laughed and drank wine well into the night. How could such a high-powered, dynamic person possibly be bothered with her, Mattie White, housewife and mother?

It was early March, then, after losing her courage many times, before Mattie finally dialled Rita's number, waited for an answer, and said, 'Hello. Is that Rita Boothe?'

'It is. Who is this?'

'Um,' said Mattie. 'You won't remember me, but I'm Mattie White.'

'The old groupie. Of course I remember you. We met in the supermarket. How lovely to hear from you. How are you?'

'Oh, I'm fine. How are you?' Mattie thought this was going well.

'Well as can be expected considering the weather,' said Rita. 'This damp goes for my knees.'

'Oh, mine too,' said Mattie. 'Inside me I still feel young, but my knees are really old.'

And that was all it took. They were off, chatting.

'Did you have a good Christmas?' asked Mattie. 'I know it's a while back now.'

'Very quiet,' said Rita.

Mattie imagined Rita sitting by a crackling log fire with a few select and precious friends, who were all dressed in velvet. They'd be sipping a very fine brandy from large balloon glasses; they'd probably have had pheasant washed down with an excellent claret, and laughed merrily when the pudding was lit.

In fact, Rita had spent Christmas alone. Sebastian had phoned before he went out to have dinner with friends, and said that he'd be up in Scotland in the spring and would drop in to see her. She'd eaten a baked potato with tuna in front of the television and gone to bed early.

'We had the family round. The usual thing,' said Mattie.

Rita imagined a house decorated with boughs of holly, a gleaming tree, and a huge family, joshing one another, teasing, joking, exchanging fond memories of Christmases past, energetic-ally playing games – charades, or maybe hide and seek, running up and down the stairs. An only child and single mother of her own only child, she had no idea what large families were like.

'Thing is,' said Mattie, 'the reason why I phoned. It's my birthday next month and we're planning a party, well, not really a party. Just a get-together with the family, and I wondered if you'd like to join us. We'd thought if the weather was fine we'd have a picnic.' Of course she won't come, thought Mattie. A family picnic, ants, soggy sandwiches, coffee from paper cups – a woman like that. I don't think so.

'How lovely,' said Rita. 'And how nice of you to think of me. I'd love to come.' Picnics, she thought, I love picnics. A creaking wicker hamper, a checked cloth spread on a grassy meadow, decked with home-made fruit cake, cucumber sandwiches, lemon-ade and wine chilled in some nearby spring, and perhaps a game of rounders afterwards. What fun.

'You would?' said Mattie. 'That's wonderful. I'll look forward to seeing you. It's on the twenty-eighth of April. Fingers crossed for some sunshine.'

After she'd rung off, Mattie went to tell John her good news. He was in his shed wrestling with his kite, which was proving trickier than he'd originally thought. He was making a parafoil, which involved sewing, using Mattie's extremely old Singer machine, layers and layers of material into one huge parachute thing that would with some expert hauling on the strategically placed strings lift into the air.

'Rita Boothe is coming to my birthday picnic,' Mattie said.
'Who?' said John.
'*Rita Boothe*,' said Mattie. 'You know, Rita Boothe.'
'No, I don't know,' said John. 'Who the hell is she?'
'Rita Boothe.' Mattie was exasperated. 'Remember I met her in
the supermarket just before Christmas. She wrote *The Joy of Filth*.
I loved that book. Lily interviewed her, remember?'
John nodded, 'Oh, yes. And why is she coming for your
birthday?'
'I invited her,' said Mattie. 'I plucked up my courage and phoned
her up and invited her. I'm so excited. I mean, Rita Boothe. *The*
Rita Boothe. Here, in our house. And at my birthday picnic. We
can't just have cheese and ham sandwiches. It'll have to be smoked
salmon, at least.'
John stopped sewing, and stared up at her. Every single thing
she ever did cost money. Why was that? And why did she think
that just because some damn woman had written a book she was
somehow above eating cheese sandwiches? You couldn't beat a
good cheese and pickle sandwich.
'And I'll make some almond pastries,' said Mattie. 'I think I'll
do some crayfish sandwiches, too. And Belgian chocolate biscuits.
Wine, of course. Though I think Rory and Art would prefer beer.
What do you think?'
'I think you're off your head,' said John.

Lily had developed a love-hate relationship with her car. On the
one hand it was a lovely-looking thing; on the other, it was
the cause of a certain rift between herself and her mother.
On the phone – and Lily was a person who liked to keep in
touch, it was her duty – Mattie sounded stiff, distant. In fact, she
was hurt. When Mattie heard Lily's voice on the line, she thought,
All those years I prided myself on my good daughter. And now I
find she is secretly trying to get back at me for being a dreadful
mother to her, sending her out to the shops for things I'd
forgotten, making her help in the house. It's revenge, that's what
that car is.
Lily would flop down on the sofa after she'd rung off. 'It's no
use, she'll never forgive me. I don't know why I did it.'

'I'm quite impressed,' Art told her. 'It's the first really impulsive thing I've ever seen you do.'

'It will also be the last. If this is where impulsive gets you, I want nothing to do with it. One greedy moment and my family have ostracised me. It was the tattoos that did it, I think. When I saw the photo of Mattie in that book, I saw she had a tattoo of a dragonfly on one thigh. Right up here.' Lily pointed to her knicker line. 'And on the other was written *Kama Sutra – Harley Davidson Position.*'

'Mattie?' said Art. 'On her thigh? Goodness. I'll never look at her in the same light again. I think you've just told me more than I need to know about your mother.'

'What's the Harley Davidson position?' said Lily, thinking Art more worldly than her, and, therefore, likely to know.

He shook his head. 'Can you do it on a Harley Davidson? Or any motorbike come to that? I don't suppose the actual manufacturer matters.'

They both contemplated the possibilities of the Harley Davidson position, and smiled.

Art said, 'It would have been a lot cheaper if you'd satisfied your impulses by getting a tattoo, instead of that car.'

Lily wished she'd thought of that. Still, thanks to Mattie, Arthur and Lillian might have some fun with the Harley Davidson position tonight.

The call came at two in the afternoon. A Sunday. Marie was watching an afternoon movie on television. The fire was on, and the room was slightly too hot, and the volume on the set was slightly too loud. But that aside, it was pretty near blissful. She certainly had no intention of moving to fix anything. Tod and Agnes were also watching the film, and were enraptured. Lauren was sprawled on her knee, sleeping. Marie looked at her. She thought children slept beautifully. Lauren's face was smooth and perfect, eyes shut, a small sweat beaded on her forehead. Life had not yet made any mark on that face, no sorrow, no grief, no disappointment or bitterness. It was a lovely face.

When the phone rang, Marie eased Lauren from her knee, laid her on the sofa, and went to answer it.

'Marie?' A man's voice. Her heart quickened. That voice was familiar. She had waited four years to hear it. She'd always known he'd have to get in touch one day.

'Speaking,' she said.

'It's Andy.'

'I know,' she said. 'I recognised the voice. How are you?' How strange it was to engage in this polite, almost disinterested conversational formality with someone she'd once been so intimate with. He'd only said three words, yet she could hear his anger. So, she hadn't been forgiven. And this was the man who'd shared her bed, who had seen her red-faced and swearing, giving birth.

'Fine. How are you?' he said. 'How're the kids?'

'We're all fine. Lauren's sleeping at the moment. Tod and Agnes are watching television. Do you want to speak to them?'

'No, I want to talk to you about the children. I want them.'

'What do you mean, you want them?'

'I want them to come and live with me.'

At that, knowing a serious conversation was coming, Marie got up and quietly closed the door to the living room. Returning to the phone, she told Andy she wasn't going to let that happen.

'I'm their father. I have a right to them. I want them.'

'I can understand that. But I've looked after them till now, I've managed. I'm not giving them up. They're settled and happy. I'm not going to let anything upset them.'

'It's your fault that I don't see them. If you hadn't done what you did, I'd still be there with them. I miss them. I want to be around to see them grow up,' Andy said.

'I know it's my fault. I don't blame you for leaving and I understand how you must miss them, and want them. And it must be awful to think they are growing up without you. I'd hate that. But they're mine. I love them, and you're not going to take them.'

'I'll fight you. I'll take you to court. I have a good lawyer.'

So, it had come to this. Lawyers. It had started so sweetly, too. He'd walked her home after meeting her at a club in town. A long walk, after midnight. Endless streetlights stretching in front of them, rows and rows of houses. She remembered she'd talked too much, she always did when she was excited or nervous, but couldn't remember what they'd talked about. She did remember that he'd kissed her, at the front door with its art deco glass pane, and the front door bell that went ding-dong. A little kiss, and she'd stayed in his arms; then, face slightly tilted, a bigger kiss that moved, flowed almost, into a full kiss, the warmth and softness of it. The meeting of lips she remembered as thrilling. She also remembered hoping, praying he'd want to see her again.

'Well, I'll get a good lawyer too,' she said heatedly. Though how she was going to do that, she didn't know.

'You can't afford it,' said Andy.

'I know I can't afford it. But I'll have to find a way to afford it. You're not taking my children away to Canada. I'd never see them.'

Andy sighed. 'I'm not in Canada any more. I'm back in town. I have a job here, and I'm with someone. She says she'll be happy to have Tod and Agnes. I don't know about Lauren, though I'll take her if you don't want to separate them. But it's Tod and Agnes I want.'

Marie was incensed. 'What's wrong with Lauren? Why don't you want her?'

'She's little. She doesn't know me. I think moving in with me would be traumatic for her.'

'It would be traumatic for us all. You may want them, but as far as I'm concerned you can want away. Like I said, it's not going to happen. They're mine. I'm happy for you to see them and to have them for weekends and holidays. But they'll live with me. And you are never going to split them up.'

For a few moments neither of them spoke. Then Andy said, 'I don't think you are managing. You have to take them to your mother's every day. And look at that fiasco in the park – Lauren ran away. Agnes went and rolled in the mud with a strange dog licking her face. She could have caught something. And Tod was left to fall off his bike.'

'Did Agnes tell you that in her letter?'

'Yes,' said Andy. 'But she didn't need to. I saw it all. She also said she wanted a puppy. Which I'm thinking of getting her.'

'You've been watching me,' said Marie. 'You've been spying.'

'No, not spying. Just checking up on my kids. I want to look after them, and it's the nearest I can get, for the moment.'

'Oh, you can get nearer than that,' said Marie. 'You have a right to see them, to get to know them. Just tell me when.'

'I want more than that,' said Andy. 'I think you're going to be hearing from my lawyer.'

'Please, Andy,' said Marie, 'don't do this. Can't we meet and sort something out?'

But he didn't want to meet, and she didn't blame him for that. She had started to dislike herself so much that she didn't really trust anyone who treated her reasonably; she thought they must have some glitch in their judgement. On that basis, Andy's refusal to get together, and his obvious bitterness towards her, earned him her respect. So she happily agreed that he should call her to arrange a day when he could pick up Agnes and Tod, and start to get to know them again. And they would take it from there.

'But I still want them to live with me permanently,' he said.

'I realise that,' she said. 'I just won't let it happen.'

A week after his return to Paris, Rory bought Isabel an engagement ring. It was a beautiful and costly thing. Diamonds in a platinum setting. Isabel walked from the shop holding her hand in front of her, fingers spread, admiring it. Seeing this, Rory realised he should have taken her somewhere romantic, and proposed properly, before slipping the ring on her finger.

Only he didn't want to propose, and more than that, he didn't want to go where the proposal would take him. He didn't want to get married. He wanted things to remain exactly as they were. Still, Isabel's delight surprised him. He hadn't known how important a ring was to her. He'd always considered Isabel to be relaxed, untethered by convention, a free spirit who would scoff at social formalities – engagement, marriage. He'd rather imagined them both drifting through life, hand in hand, free spirits together. A few yards from the shop, Isabel started to cry, and he took her in his arms, heard her whisper that she loved him, and thank you, thank you for wanting to marry her. After that there was something about her mother and father which he couldn't quite make out because her head was buried in his neck, which was getting wet, and her voice was choked with sobs.

But he held her head, softly patted her back, and stared bleakly over her shoulder into the distance. He felt he was getting sucked into a huge morass of relatives that included his mother and father, Lily, Marie and Grandpa, Marie's children, Isabel, Isabel's mother and father and the four children as yet unnamed, indeed, unconceived. It was an awful lot of people to be associated with and concerned about. It was a huge crowd in his head that diminished his own significance. It was also rather a lot of birthdays to remember.

Lily decided to have her bottom tattooed in Soho. It seemed the most suitable area, for the bodily part selected. She had thought of going to an upmarket shop that now boasted a body-decorating department, but thought, no. Getting a tattoo was more a Lillian thing than a Lily thing, and Lillian was definitely a Soho lurker. Though only in a nice way; she wouldn't pick up loose men, or anything like that. She'd only be there to soak up the night.

The parlour was intriguing, and was a Lillian sort of place. Lily had problems with it. And found, when actually in there, she did not want to remove her clothing and reveal the bit of her she wanted engraved for eternity.

'Not dead centre,' she said. 'I want it on the cusp of my bum, where it slopes up from my back.'

It hurt. It hurt more than Lily had imagined it would. In fact, the whole experience was horrible. The persistent grind of the tattooer's needle, the little curtained room, and the pain. She wanted to scream, to get up and run out of there. But instead she lay still, nails biting into the palm of her hand, face twisted in a silent scream. And when it was done, she had a small red and black Harley Davidson etched permanently on her left buttock. With the aid of mirrors, she saw the handiwork. It looked awful, raw. 'I think I'd have preferred the blue,' she said.

'A bit late now,' said the woman who'd just desecrated her backside.

'I've changed my mind. I don't want it,' said Lily. 'Take it off.'

'I can't,' said the woman. She'd known the second she'd clapped eyes on Lily that she'd hate her tattoo, and she'd be trouble.

'I hate it. I hate it,' said Lily, and there were tears now. 'Please, please do something about it.'

'I can't,' said the woman. 'That's it. I could add a bit if you like. But you'll need laser treatment to get it off. We only put them on. You can pay at the counter.'

So Lily paid, and went back out into the day to move stiffly into the swim of tourists and production company runners and other Saturday-afternoon people. She found a taxi, sat leaning to the right, to keep the weight off her left and, she now considered, vandalised buttock. She wept.

At home, Art was watching television. He watched as Lily came into the room, and gingerly sat down. He noted the red eyes, the running mascara, the woeful look. 'What now, Lily?'

Things hadn't been going well for Art and Lily. Though Arthur and Lillian still hit it off, if a little less often these days. Since Christmas there had been a vein of angst running through their relationship – Lily's worry that her mother and Marie now hated her haunted her, kept her awake at night. She'd lie staring into the darkness, body weary, mind afire, refusing to rest. She'd torture herself with memories, words spoken in haste, heated scornful looks. The fleeting pain that had scorched Mattie's face when she learned that Lily had bought *that car*. Marie's icy disapproval. Lily revisited it all, and cursed herself. She wished she was back on that bus, and this time, when she spotted *that car* in the showroom window, she'd just notice it, think it was rather splendid, but stay in her seat as the bus moved on. By the time she and Art reached their stop, she'd have forgotten about it. But she hadn't. She'd jumped out of her seat, run off the bus and into the car showroom. So now she was plagued by wishes and vile imaginings, the horrible things her family thought of her.

All this was dumped on Art, who was expected to offer sympathy, be supportive, caring, banish Lily's woes with jocular banter. After months of effort, he'd run out of steam. So seeing Lily across the room, tear-stained, snivelling and looking for reassurance that she really wasn't a despicable person, he was too weary to say anything other than, 'What now, Lily?'

'I got a tattoo,' she said.

'A tattoo,' he said. 'Whereabouts?'

'On my bum. Well, not exactly *on* it. More on the cusp of it.'
Then she cried. The slight sobbing turned into a full-blown howl.
'I hate it. I've ruined my body. I'll never let anybody see it.'

'I want to see it.'

Lily got up. Turned round and lowered her jeans. Because not
letting anybody see it had been a lie. She needed Art to look at the
damage, and sympathise. The tattoo was covered with a large
Elastoplast. Art slowly peeled it off, and viewed the damage. The
area was red raw, bleeding slightly, but the Harley Davidson was
easily made out.

He took a moment, working at finding something appropriate
to say. 'Why, Lily?'

'It's in keeping with my mother's.'

'You wanted to be the same as your mother?'

'No, you don't understand. I wanted to suffer what she suffered.
I wanted something suitable, sort of sympatico.' She was still
bending over, letting Art see the damage. 'I did it for the pain. I
wanted to hurt physically.'

Art said, 'Oh, Lily.' It was all he could think of. Then he told
her she was a fool.

'I don't think I need to be told that right now,' she said.

He told her he thought she did. 'You pass your days torturing
yourself. The only thing you think about is you. What do people
think of you? Pack it in. To quote a phrase I hate, get a life, Lily.'

'I've got a life. I've got friends. A job. A home.'

'A home! A home! This isn't a home. It's a picture from a
magazine. A home is where you live. Put your feet up. Shut the
door, pull the curtains and relax. You're too busy keeping the
place perfect to do that.'

'I'm in pain. I have wrecked my body. I don't want to hear this
right now.'

'And when do you want to hear it? Do I have to make an
appointment?'

'I don't want to argue. I hate arguing.'

'I know. But it's what people do. They kiss, they love, they
fight, they lose things, they forget things, they make messes. You
don't. You only want the good things, the kisses. You're afraid of
the rest. It's time you stopped standing looking at your life, and

started joining in. Leap off the cliff screaming, Lily. Quit sighing and dreaming and get grubby like the rest of us.'

Lily left the room. 'I'm not going to listen to this.'

Art followed her up the hall to the bedroom. 'Do you suppose Marie tortures herself like you do? She's got three kids, she hasn't got time.'

'I'm not going to have the children argument. I know you want children.'

'I want children, yes. And if you didn't want them I could live with that. Come to terms with it. But you're scared of having children. You think they'd mess up your home, there would be toys scattered everywhere, they'd be sick on you, they'd throw food about, spill stuff. And so they would. But they'd be fun. We'd love them. Watch them grow. A child would be your child, and my child. It would be ours.'

Lily picked up her coat. 'I'm going out.'

Art took the coat and threw it on the bed. 'No you're not. I'm going out. To the pub, for a drink. To breathe some air that hasn't been freshened and mix with people who have got on with the business of being alive, who are getting by, whose lives are grubbied up by not having enough money, kids who don't do what they're told, crumbs on their kitchen units, sofas that aren't constantly perfectly plumped.'

She watched him put on his jacket. Then said, 'Do you want a divorce?'

'No, Lily, I don't. We're having a fight. It's what people do. They fight. It isn't nice. But then things often aren't nice. People sometimes aren't nice. It's how life is. Deal with it.'

And he left. Lily sat on the bed and cried.

The Perfect Sandwich
and Reading the Hush

All three of Mattie's children had painful secrets. Though Rory's secret was double-edged. He hadn't told his family he was engaged to Isabel, and he hadn't told Isabel that he hadn't told his family. When Mattie phoned to make sure Rory was coming to her birthday picnic, and Isabel answered and said of course he was coming, and she was coming too, Rory could see he had a few awkward moments ahead. Not that he was free of awkward moments now. Isabel was hurt that nobody in his family had phoned or sent a card to congratulate them on their engagement. She kept asking if they disapproved of her or disliked her.

'It's rude of them not to get in touch,' she said. 'Even if they do think I'm too old for you, they should say how happy they are for us.'

'It's how they are,' Rory told her. 'Easy-going. They don't really show their emotions. But they are delighted really.'

Isabel snorted. 'They don't like me. But they still should welcome me into the family.'

Rory said he knew. But they had each other, they didn't need a family. As the day of the party grew closer and closer, he worried. He knew how insulted Isabel would be that he hadn't told Mattie and John of his impending marriage. 'Are you ashamed of me?' she'd say. 'Is it because I'm older than you?'

'Why didn't you tell us?' Mattie would say. 'You always shut us out of your life. Do you think I'm interfering? Do you think we don't like Isabel?'

He ran through these scenarios, and fretted. Yet did nothing about the situation. He hid from it. He vainly hoped that when it came to the crunch, he would be able to wing it. He didn't think it would go down well if he simply said he didn't want any fuss, he hated his mother's enthusiasm, and furthermore, he didn't really want to get married. He wanted everything to stay just as it was now. Living in Paris, which was still new and exciting to him, with Isabel, and no serious binding commitments.

Marie hadn't told anybody about Andy wanting Tod and Agnes to come live with him. It might mean she'd have to explain why he left her in the first place. She kept it to herself, and worried.

Lily wasn't going to tell anyone *ever* about the damage to her bum.

It was, as Mattie had hoped, a beautiful day. 'Sort of like an Easter card,' she said to John. 'Blue sky, yellow sun. Just perfect. You couldn't wish for better.'

John gazed out of the window. 'As days go, this is a good one. But cold. Too cold for a picnic.'

Nothing could dampen Mattie's enthusiasm. 'We've got jumpers. We've got coats. I'll take coffee and soup. It will be perfect.'

'Nothing is ever perfect. And especially nothing we do is perfect. I cannot bring to mind a single perfect outing. Something always happens. It rains, or somebody falls into a river or the sea or gets stung by a bee or is sick or catches a chill or . . .'

'You're such a pessimist, John.'

'Damn right I'm a pessimist. It's the only way forward. Pessimists are never disappointed.'

Mattie continued to make her smoked salmon sandwiches. Their very presence in the kitchen displeased John. They were sandwiches of sycophancy. Only on the menu because Rita Boothe was coming along on the family outing. Without Rita they would be having cheese and tomato or cheese and pickle or plain old ham. And what was wrong with that?

'I wouldn't like to live in your head,' said Mattie. 'The sun never shines there.'

'It is always easy to please a pessimist,' said John. 'We have low expectations. Optimists, like you, are butterflies fluttering into a thunderstorm. About to get swamped, but smiling about it.' He took a sandwich, which was a delicate, crustless thing, and stuffed it whole into his mouth. It was small enough to eat effortlessly. He declared, sending a small shower of crumbs into the air in front of him, that it barely needed chewing, and wasn't proper food at all.

But this stealing of food and eating it indoors in the kitchen before the allotted time, which was outdoors at the picnic, angered Mattie. She slapped the thieving hand. 'Stop that. These are for Rita Boothe.'

Mattie was, by nature, an outgoing and openly friendly person. New people in her life were usually called by their first name as soon as she'd met them. Rita Boothe was different. Rita Boothe had once been a hero, and Mattie found it hard to call her simply Rita. It didn't seem right. It somehow brought her down to Mattie's level. And goodness knows, Mattie thought, she's got to be better than that. So, in her absence, Rita Boothe always got her full name.

'So,' said John, 'some decrepit old numpty is going to eat all these sandwiches. And are you going to throw us common folk a few scraps? A bowl of thin gruel, perhaps, as you and her sit and grandly chat about art and literature and life?'

'It's not like that at all. And let me tell you, John White, Rita Boothe is no decrepit numpty. She is a tour de force, she's full of joie de vivre. She is opinionated, articulate and wonderful.'

'And she eats mountains of sandwiches while us simpletons stand with a single cold sausage and our trousers flapping in the breeze.'

'You're going to spoil it, aren't you? My lovely day, my special picnic, you're going to spoil it by saying things. Just for one day could you please keep your mouth shut and be polite to my guest?'

Their dispute was interrupted by a sigh. A slipping of sad air from the mouth of Grandpa, who had come into the room and was standing in the doorway, looking upset. 'Can I have one of those? Please?'

'Of course you can,' said Mattie. She took a plate from the cupboard, placed two sandwiches on it, along with a paper napkin. 'There you are.'

'Oh,' said John. 'He gets two sandwiches, and a plate. I get my hand slapped. I know how things stand now.' He stamped out of the room.

'He asked nicely,' Mattie shouted after him. 'He said please.'

'So, I've got to say please. Are there any other rules, O great sandwich despot?' Damn, he thought, I'm shouting again. He'd been seriously trying to stop.

This morning, over breakfast, he'd given Mattie a new rose, a climber for the garden called Peace, and an amethyst ring. Amethysts, he knew, were meant to bring harmony and peace of mind to those wearing them. He thought all this appropriate. But since he'd removed the label from the rose as the market garden's price tag had been stuck on to it, and since Mattie knew nothing of the relevance of gem stones, all this was lost on her. Still, she thought her gifts lovely and gave John a kiss to tell him so.

He hoped that this was the end of the acrimony that had been passing between them. He blamed himself for it. He'd been grumpy for months, and this grumpiness had been heightened every time he saw Mattie. Considering they were married, shared a house and, indeed, a bed, John had been grumpy a lot. There was something about Mattie, her cheeriness, her softness, her hunger for comfort and security, that had angered him. He wished she was less home-loving, and shared his notion to do things. He admitted she had wanted to travel across America, but his longings were for lesser things. He wanted them to, perhaps, go out more often to the cinema or to a small restaurant to eat and chat, or to go on trips here and there and stop overnight at a bed and breakfast.

He fancied a gentle coming together, an easy drift back to the times they'd had before they were married. He wanted someone to talk to. It was that realisation that made him aware he was missing work. Not the job, exactly: the companionship, the banter. He looked to Mattie to be his wife, lover, companion, cook and colleague. Perhaps it was asking too much. He was, with the roses and the amethyst, seeking a truce.

He returned to the kitchen to apologise. After all, it was her birthday. He slid his arms round her waist and said, 'Sorry.'

'It's OK,' said Mattie. 'I'm sorry too. You can have as many sandwiches as you like.'

He took one, though he didn't really want it. This was a smoked salmon sandwich of contrition. Now, as part of the apology, he had to say how delicious it was and what a talented sandwich-maker she was.

'It's a gift,' said Mattie. A little flattery was always welcome.

John noticed she was now constructing a large cheese doorstep sandwich, something he was particularly fond of. He loved cheese. 'For me?' he hoped.

'Yes,' said Mattie. 'One of my specials. Just for you. But you're not getting it till we're on the picnic. You have to wait.'

'I'll wait. I'll look forward to it all the way to the picnic spot.' He kissed her cheek. 'Thank you.'

By midday everyone, except Rita, had arrived. Mattie had her arrival moment, the peals of greetings at the door, the bustle. There were kisses, and catch-up conversations that Rory dealt with manfully and even joined in. 'What have you been up to, Rory?'

'Working, eating, sleeping. Same old, same old.' He didn't mention getting engaged. So far nobody had noticed the ring on Isabel's left hand. 'And you, Lily?'

'Same. Work, eat, sleep. Busy, busy.' She didn't mention the tattoo. 'Marie?'

'Same. Work, eat, feed the kids, bath the kids, put the kids to bed.' She shrugged. 'You know.' She didn't mention Andy wanting her two older children. They all just smiled, and looked delighted to see one another.

They sat in the living room waiting for Rita Boothe to arrive. Isabel, next to Rory on the sofa, lifted her left hand to move hair from her forehead. And Mattie noticed the ring, as she was meant to do.

'You're engaged,' she said.

Isabel smiled.

Unthinkingly Mattie said, 'Who to?' Not Rory, surely. He would have said.

'To Rory,' said Isabel, quite hurt that Mattie would think there would be someone else.

Rory lifted his hand and gave Mattie a tiny wave.

'Why would I be here with Rory if I was engaged to another man?' Isabel asked.

'True,' said Mattie. 'When did this happen then?'

'Just after Christmas,' said Rory. He smiled. It seemed the right thing to do.

'Why didn't you tell us?' said Mattie.

The doorbell rang.

'That'll be Rita Boothe. I can't believe you didn't call us so we could congratulate you, and send a card or a little something. That's so rude, Rory.' She got up and went out of the room. Everyone could hear her disappearing disgruntled voice saying, 'When I got engaged the very first person I told was my mother.' Then, with a clearly noticeable uplift in tone, 'Hello, Rita. How lovely to see you, and how good of you to come.'

They heard someone say, 'Thank you for inviting me. I've been so looking forward to this. I love picnics. This is Sebastian, my son. I hope you don't mind my bringing him along. He turned up last night. We have a habit of turning up on each other's doorsteps.'

Sebastian had arrived last night. He'd been with a group of students studying rock formations in the Grampians. And when the trip was over had debated with himself whether he should go straight back home, or visit his mother. In the end, he went to see Rita; her cooking lured him.

'I'm visiting some new friends tomorrow. We're going on a picnic. You could come too.' She'd told him.

'A picnic, I don't think so,' he'd said.

'Please,' she said. She wanted to show him off.

He'd shrugged. 'OK.' He was curious to see what kind of new friends his mother had.

'The more the merrier. Hello, Sebastian.' Mattie's voice floated through to the group in the living room now.

'Hello.' A male voice.

In the room the family exchanged glances. 'Who is Rita Boothe?' asked Marie.

'I didn't know she was coming,' said Lily. 'I didn't know they were in touch.'

Isabel turned to Rory. 'You didn't tell anyone about us?' This hurt. It removed her to a confused and lonely place. The room was buzzing, new people arriving, but Isabel was no longer part of it. She desperately needed to get Rory on his own so she could talk to him about his not telling anybody about their engagement. Though that, at least, explained why nobody in his family had phoned to congratulate them.

Then Mattie appeared at the door. 'Everyone, this is Rita Boothe and Sebastian.'

Sebastian saw a roomful of new faces, every one looking in his direction. They were all doing the meeting-a-stranger routine, smiling, being friendly while sizing him up.

Mattie skimmed through the new names. 'Sebastian, Rita, this is Marie, and her children, Agnes, Tod and Lauren, and that's Grandpa.'

That one's easy to remember, thought Sebastian. Though he knew he'd have difficulty calling a total stranger Grandpa.

'Then there's John, Rory and Isabel, Art and Lily. Though you know Lily already, don't you, Rita?'

Rita said, 'Indeed I do. Hello, Lily.'

Lily nodded and said, 'Hello,' back. Recently, she'd been feeling guilty about Rita Boothe. She had interviewed the woman, sat in her living room eating her cake, drinking her tea, she had accepted a gift copy of Rita's cookbook, she had a notebook filled with observations, jottings and quotes, but she had written nothing. She would switch on her computer, bring up the Rita Boothe file, consult her copious notes. Then, nothing. Her mind would fill with indulgent thoughts: I'm not a very nice person, nobody likes me. Then it would be time for a cup of coffee and a biscuit.

Coffee made, she'd return to her computer, stare at the blank screen. *Rita Boothe is one of the enigmas of the late twentieth century.* Rubbish, she'd think. And press delete. She'd swing in her chair, check her emails, surf the net. Then return to Rita and her blank screen. *It would be wrong to categorise Rita Boothe as a has-been; she isn't even a might-have-been. Meeting her, looking through her books, you have to conclude that she is an ought-to-have-been. Blah blah blah. I think everybody hates me. Definitely my mother doesn't love me any more. I'm a fool*, Lily wrote. Then thought about her mother and her mother's young thighs and the decorations she'd seen on them. And how she'd had her own bum hideously tattooed so she could experience what Mattie had experienced, and to escape from this painful thinking she'd decide to have another cup of coffee, and a biscuit too. She was putting on weight, and it was Rita Boothe's fault.

And now here she was confronted by the woman in person. 'Nice to see you again, Lily,' said Rita. 'How's it all going?'

Well, thought Lily, my family hates me, I'm arguing a lot with my husband, I can't write a word, and I've got a hideous tattoo on my arse. 'Fine,' she said.

Mattie meantime had swung into action. 'Time to go, everybody,' she called. 'Let's get picnicking before we miss the best of the sunshine.'

Sebastian, the only child of an only child, watched the ensuing bustle with horror and fascination. He wanted to press himself against the wall to keep out of the way as people jostled round him, gathering coats, jackets, scarves, umbrellas, rugs to sit on, and took these things along with baskets and bags packed with boxes full of sandwiches, a quiche, cakes, bottles (wine, lemonade and water) out to the car. The rush and movement amazed him. The stream of banter and mild bickering seemed too much for him, a current of voices his could never join. Rita, however, was filled with joy. She watched the whirling activity and thought the family like starlings.

They drove, in convoy, to Gullane. Rory and Isabel in Mattie and John's car, Lily, Art and Sebastian behind them in Rita's and Marie with her children and Grandpa bringing up the rear. Mattie was fond of seaside picnics, the air, the ozone, the sound of the sea. John hated them, the wind, the chill, the sand in his food. But this was Mattie's day, so he'd decided to put up with grainy sandwiches and a runny nose.

It took about half an hour to reach Gullane. All the way, as they drove along the coast, past golf courses, cresting small hills, catching a glimpse of the sea then losing it as they dipped back down again, John thought about his sandwich. The giant doorstep, a man-size sandwich, the sandwich of sandwiches. He anticipated it, relished the idea of sinking his teeth into it, the soft bread, the cheese and the after-tang of pickle. They parked, and, like starlings again – a whoosh of chattering milling people, a swarm of relatives, Rita thought – made their way over the wooden bridge and down to the dunes. They found a spot out of the wind, and set about the serious business of picnicking.

Mattie spread out a tartan rug and insisted Rita sit on it. Patting the area she thought to be the comfiest. Marie, meantime, was sprinting to the shore behind Agnes and Tod, who had seen the sea and announced they were going in. It seemed to Marie that they intended to do this fully clothed. She was hurtling down a huge dune, running faster, caught in the momentum of the steep slope, than she wanted to. So she was squealing and shouting, 'Come back here!'

Rory and Isabel, watching this, had temporarily forgotten they weren't speaking and were laughing. As was Sebastian. He remembered that feeling, arriving at the seaside and needing to plunge in immediately, drawn towards waves and an endless stretch of blue, the lure of water. He, too, hadn't been able to see it without wanting to join it. Overhead, gulls called, and fresh salty air hit their city faces.

'Isn't this lovely,' said Rita. 'What a wonderful place. I've never been here before.'

She felt the openness, the ozone on her cheeks, smelled sea and warm sand and had the sensation of uncurling, letting go of her tired winter self. She embraced the day. 'I'm going to have a wonderful time.'

At this Mattie glowed. It was going just as she'd rehearsed it in her mind. And John was being friendly too. This was a relief.

They unfolded a canvas chair for Grandpa, who'd said he didn't mind sitting down on the rug. It was getting up again he worried about. It was an old chestnut from his repertoire of jokes; everyone had heard it many times before, but laughed anyway.

Lily helped Mattie unpack the food. She'd insisted that she and Art supply the wine, which she brought in a large cooler, part of Mattie's birthday present. Something she would add to her collection of picnic accessories. Mattie claimed to be a picnic person and had a fair selection of things to make the al fresco meal perfect – two wicker hampers, three thermos flasks of various sizes, folding chairs, a wind-up radio, a portable barbecue, rugs, cushions, a parasol, three wind-breaks, and more. Despite this, she only ever managed to have one picnic a year, though always at midnight on the thirty-first of December she made the same vows. 1. Do more things, get out more. 2. Get up earlier in the morning and read the newspaper instead of just doing the crossword. 3. Have more picnics.

They were all only notions, she never did any of them. She still only managed one picnic a year, her birthday.

Lily opened a bottle of champagne, poured everyone a glass (Mattie wouldn't consider plastic cups, not when Rita Boothe was coming) and proposed a toast to her mother. 'Happy birthday. And lots of them.' Art, John, Grandpa and Rita joined in. The others were still cheering Marie in her race to stop the children rushing into the sea. This was a minor irritation to Mattie, who liked everyone to be there for the traditional birthday toast, but she overlooked it. It was the cheese sandwich that started the row.

The food was spread out, a selection of cold meats and salami, salads and sandwiches – smoked salmon (for Rita), roast beef and mustard, still warm (for Grandpa, Rory and Art), tomato and crayfish (for Lily, Marie and Isabel), tuna and mayonnaise (for the children), avocado, bacon, tomato and lettuce (Mattie showing off to Rita that she was a sandwich sophisticate), and one extremely large cheese doorstep heavy with grated Keen's cheddar and pickle for John.

He'd been looking forward to this. Had only taken a sip of champagne so he could have some cold beer as he ate it. One beer was his allowance, since he was driving. But he'd been anticipating this sandwich since the smoked salmon spat earlier, when he had seen Mattie making it.

He'd smiled and given her a friendly hug. The rose and the amethyst were doing the trick. There was a new peace between them.

Mattie made a show of producing the doorstep. The thick slices of home-made bread, softly white, crisp crusts, the fat layer of cheese, the tangy pickle. John planned to climb to the top of the dune and savour the treat, sipping beer, watching the sea. It would a little bit of quality time just for himself – the sparkle of water, the salt air and the sandwich.

Mattie laid it on a plate, put a little salad beside it (but only a little, John was not a salad person) and raised it towards him.

He saw it coming, licked his lips. Then Rita said, 'Oh my, a lovely cheese doorstep. Fantastic.'

The sandwich, on its journey to John, stopped. He held his breath.

'You like cheese doorsteps?' said Mattie. 'There's smoked salmon.'

'Not really keen on smoked salmon,' said Rita. 'But yes, I do absolutely adore big, fat cheese sandwiches. Don't have them very often, though.'

The sandwich moved into reverse, started retreating away from John's outstretched hand.

'Well go on,' said Mattie. 'Have this one. A treat.'

The sandwich swung left, towards Rita, who reached out and took it.

John watched it go. The thing that was to make his afternoon tolerable, the thing he'd been looking forward to, savouring, was slipping away from him. He watched Rita take a bite, some stray bits of grated cheese, squeezed out by the force of her descending teeth, spilling out on to her chin, and with her fingers she scooped them up and put them into her mouth. Her eyes were shut, the pleasure of this. And John hated her. He also, for a few scalding minutes, hated his wife for giving *that woman* his sandwich. He stood, watched Rita eat, and he breathed. It was all he could do.

Mattie glanced at him, checking the extent of his rage. Saw that it was boundless, and said nothing. She bit into her own sandwich, stared at the ground and waited for the onslaught.

It didn't come. John collected some food on to a plate, said he would eat his lunch in a higher place, and climbed the dune behind them to sit atop it, stare out at the horizon and the distant waves and mourn his cheese sandwich. He chewed his roast beef. He felt betrayed. It wasn't the sandwich, it was the eager way Mattie had handed it over to someone else that hurt him. That doorstep had been special in different ways. Not just that he wanted it, that it was one of his favourite things to eat; it had been a symbol of the truce between them, it was a love sandwich. He'd kissed Mattie as she made it. Now she had, without a second thought, given it to a woman she wanted to impress. It grieved him deeply that Rita's approval meant more to her than his friendship, companionship, love. Sitting high on the dune, wind shifting through his hair, sand creeping into his shoes, he stopped being angry. He felt deeply, utterly wretched.

Mattie looked anxiously up at him. She saw Rita follow her gaze.

'Oh, don't mind John,' Mattie said. 'He likes to sit alone and ponder things. He's always coming up with notions. He's making an enormous kite at the moment. Huge.'

Marie arrived back at the picnic spot, red-faced and breathless. She flopped on to the rug, and lamented missing the birthday toast. 'You didn't wait for me, that's not very nice.' She didn't wait for an apology, but started to eat. 'Great sandwiches.' She turned to Rita. 'You should come more often. My mother usually only does ham and cheese, she's obviously out to impress you.'

'Marie,' said Mattie. 'That's not true.' She prickled indignation. 'How could you say such a thing?' She turned to Rita. 'I always make splendid sandwiches.' She caught Rita's amused expression, realised Marie had been joking and joined in the laughter.

The sound of mirth, the group below sharing a joke, drifted up to John. He rose, indicated to the rest of the party that he was off for a stroll, and set out to walk along the shore. He wasn't in the mood for laughter.

Sebastian watched Marie tease her mother. The intricacy of insults, he thought. This was a jibe that wasn't a jibe at all, it was a declaration of affection. Now there was something he and his mother didn't indulge in – the gentle jest, loving ridicule. Perhaps they should. It was certainly a lot easier than saying I love you. Obviously, since neither of them ever said it.

He put his glass down on the rug, picked up a sandwich and said he thought he'd go for a bit of a wander, see what he could find. Tod followed him. 'What are you looking for?'

'Stones. Fossils. You never know on beaches.'

'What sort of stones?' said Tod.

'Gems,' said Sebastian. Not really looking at the boy.

'Precious gems? Worth millions of pounds?'

Sebastian shook his head. 'Doubtful. We might find some agates.'

'Are they worth millions?' Tod was full of hope.

'No,' Sebastian told him.

'I'd like to find something worth a million pounds,' said Tod. 'What wouldn't I do with a million pounds?'

Sebastian looked at him and smiled. The child in front of him was dark-haired, thin. He had large brown eyes, thick lashes, a dusting of freckles across his face. He seemed to be filled with worry and longing and a desperate, innocent sincerity. 'What would you do with a million pounds?' he asked.

'Well,' said Tod. 'The car's on its last legs. We could get a new one. And the washing machine's on the blink. And we could have a nice big sofa to spread out on.'

Sebastian smiled. Tod was speaking, but he was hearing Tod's mother. He remembered when he was like that. He'd been, so he was told, an exquisite child. Utterly beautiful, his mother said. 'Blond, fair skin, lips like a bruised strawberry,' she'd sighed. Sebastian didn't like to think about this.

Yet there had been a time when he had sat at his mother's kitchen table, as Tod obviously had, taking in thoughts, opinions and facts that were of no importance or use to him. They'd taken up a lot of space in his young mind, these facts – Janis Joplin was misunderstood, Margaret Thatcher was a disgrace to her sex, there was no cure for wrinkles, you couldn't beat a good robust red wine. There were many, many more: Rita was an opinionated woman. He thought now that if information could rattle, his brain would have clunked, all the stuff that had been banging about inside it.

He'd lived in solitude. In two worlds – inside and outside. Outside had been the world of play, where local boys kicked footballs in the park, and he never could join in. Always the last to be picked for the team. Inside there had been Rita in her kitchen with her opinions. The room had been full of her words, and he had hardly understood any of them. This solitude of his had been burst apart by his father and his partner, who'd taken him to the cinema, to restaurants, told him funny stories about their colleagues, bought him books and toys, and had always let him be

SECRETS OF A FAMILY ALBUM

part of their lives, asking what he thought, telling him he looked cool in his 501 Levi's, choosing T-shirts and training shoes for him, appreciating his jokes.

Rita could only ever dip her hand into the pool of loneliness he lived in, reach out to him, touch his cheek and tell him he was beautiful, beautiful. In time he'd realised this touching his cheek, running her fingers over his head had also been something she did when her own loneliness started to hurt a little too much.

He smiled down at Tod. 'Shall we go looking for fossils and gem stones?'

Tod nodded. 'Yes.'

They set off along the beach.

'If we find something worth a million pounds, we'll share it,' enthused Tod.

Sebastian smiled. He thought to say he doubted they'd find anything that valuable, but realised that would be patronising. You can have it all, he might say. But no, that wasn't the deal, that wasn't companionship. 'Half each,' he said.

'Excellent,' said Tod.

Rory and Isabel, having eaten, had gone off alone to find a secluded spot where they could argue. Mattie and Rita could, to Mattie's horror, hear Isabel's voice shrill above the sound of the waves and gulls. 'You didn't tell them. You're ashamed of me. It's because I'm older than you.' Then Rory said, 'No. No. You don't understand. It isn't that. I love that you're older than me. At least when I think about it. I hardly think about it. It doesn't matter to me.'

'Why? Tell me why you didn't tell them.'

'Because . . .' Then his voice dropped. Mattie strained to hear more. But couldn't.

Marie took Agnes and Lauren to paddle in the sea. Lily and Art went with them. Grandpa fell asleep in his chair. Rita and Mattie stayed with him so he wouldn't find himself alone when he woke up. Rita raised her glass. 'Here's to you, Mattie. Happy birthday, and many more of them.'

'Don't say that. The many more of them thing. People always say that when you're getting old. I'm getting older, and it's not stopping. Older and older, every minute.'

'Well, you could say that of all of us, even little Lauren.'

'Yes, but I haven't done anything. Look at me, a housewife. What have I done? Nothing, nothing at all.'

'Rubbish. Look at what you've got. Your family all here, come from far and wide to be with you on your birthday. You are very lucky.'

'My life,' said Mattie. 'The list. Mattie White, four lovers, then one husband, three children, three grandchildren. In my time I have had, I think, something like twenty winter coats, don't know how many pairs of shoes, shirts, skirts too many to mention. There have been seven cars – though not all at the same time, that's trade-ins and not one of them was brand new – four washing machines, four televisions, one dishwasher, two videos, two stereo systems, one small record player when I was fifteen, three sofas, the first two did not survive children jumping on them. Then there are rugs, lamps, sheets, towels . . . I feel that I am at the centre of things to be maintained, and people to be kept in touch with. And in doing that, I have lost touch with me. I know, people would just say, "Get a life, Mattie." But I've got a life, I just don't seem right now to be able to lay my hands on it. I've forgotten where I put it.'

'Don't be silly,' said Rita. 'You have a wonderful life. You can't dismiss it in a list of possessions past and present. There are memories – it's more a collage of moments than a collection of consumer goods.'

'I can't seem to separate them,' said Mattie. 'If I recall a moment it seems to come along with whatever I owned at the time. Like when Lily was fifteen she came home and told me she'd won the school essay prize. She burst into the living room, full of her news. She was so excited. But I was unblocking the vacuum at the time. All I said was, "That's nice." I should have left the vacuum and given Lily a hug. Now when that moment comes back to me, I have a huge pang of guilt, and the vacuum has a leading role in the memory. It was blue, that vacuum, and had a little light at the front that shone on to the carpet you were cleaning.'

'That sounds entertaining, for a vacuum anyway,' said Rita. 'I don't think you should worry. I think you must have been a wonderful mother. I wasn't. Mothering took me by surprise. I always knew Sebastian preferred staying with his father to being with me. Richard had time for him. I was regarded as second best. And children are so demanding. The only way, when they are little anyway, they can express their need is to cry. It used to haunt me, that if our relationship had been anything other than mother and son, with all its in-built love, I'd have left him. You certainly wouldn't put up with all that crying and demanding from someone you'd met in a bar and ended up sharing your life with.'

'You can't compare relationships,' said Mattie. 'Your relationship with your child is all bound up with love and guilt. Love makes the world go round? I don't think so. Love and guilt make the world go round.'

Rita nodded. 'Maybe that's the difference between loving someone and being *in* love. When you're in love it's all euphoria. But love, without the little *in* before it, is bound up with guilt and responsibility and loyalty.'

'Absolutely,' said Mattie. 'Taking that to its proper conclusion, you'd have to say that infatuation is best of all. It is an exquisite thing to be infatuated, all sighs and longing and no commitment.'

'Oh yes,' said Rita. 'I think it beats unrequited love. You can be physically involved with someone you are infatuated with, and that can be exhilarating.'

'Yes,' enthused Mattie. 'I love kissing. Long, deep kisses are especially good for taking your mind off things. If you are sharing a lovely kiss, soft lips, inner mouth, contemplating taking things a bit further, you absolutely never worry about what you'll make for supper, or how you'll pay the gas bill, or if the car needs new brake pads. You just kiss, and the kiss is the only thing going on in the world. Oh, my.' She sighed, remembering such kisses.

'Yes,' agreed Rita. She also sighed, remembering such kisses. It was a bonding moment.

Grandpa shifted in his seat. He'd been awake for some time, and had pretended to sleep so he could eavesdrop – women's conversation fascinated him. Though he thought they were talking nonsense. But it was amazing how women chatting could shift the topic of discourse so swiftly, in seconds it seemed, from vacuum cleaners to kisses.

Mattie noticed his flickering eyelids, knew he was awake and had been listening to her conversation, felt embarrassed at him hearing some of her innermost thoughts, and suggested she and Rita take a stroll along the shore. She leaned over, patted Grandpa on the knee, and told him they'd be back in a minute. Thus letting him know she knew he was awake, and feigning sleep so he could listen to a private conversation.

Rita, who didn't realise her conversation had been overheard, and thought Grandpa had just woken up, also patted the old man's knee. 'See you soon, Grandpa.'

Grandpa said, 'Herrumph.' He wasn't her grandpa. In fact, he thought he might even be too young to be her father. Which was a comfort. It had been a long time since he'd come across something he was too young to qualify for.

The day had mellowed. Figures on the shore were silhouetted black against the dazzle, sun on water. A soft breeze was pushing up from the sea. Mattie said that it would be getting cold soon. It was April after all. She could see Marie holding Lauren's hand as they walked in the shallows, skipping over tiny ripples that rushed inland. Lily and Art were playing with Agnes, throwing a ball. Sebastian and Tod were further along, crouched, heads close, examining life in rock pools. Far, far away there was John, a distant outline against the shimmer, skimming stones across the surface of the sea. She didn't know where Rory and Isabel had got to. They had been silent for some time now.

John was selecting flat stones and hefting them across the surface of the sea, watching them hop, bounce away from him. He threw with effort, a small grunt escaping from the back of his throat as each stone left his hand. 'Sodding woman,' he said. Grunt. Throw. 'Effing picnics.' Grunt. Throw. This outing had cost him dearly, and it wasn't just his bank account that was suffering (he was dreading his credit card bill). The way his wife had thrown herself at *that woman*, smiling at her instead of smiling at him, slavishly trying to impress her instead of wanting to please him, giving her his sandwich, which had broken his heart.

He saw Mattie and Rita heading towards the shore together, saw them laughing and confiding, sharing jokes, and thought: Bugger them. Then, knowing Grandpa would be sitting alone, he headed back to the picnic spot to be with him. He climbed up the dunes, feet digging deep in the soft sand. He would walk back along the top of them, avoiding Mattie and Rita.

Dunes undulated round the bay. Dips and valleys, small secret places behind thick grasses. But walking along the crest that swept down to the shore afforded a splendid view. Though, in fact, John heard Rory and Isabel before he saw them. He'd always fancied Isabel might be a noisy lover. It was one of his theories that stylish, seemingly aloof women often were. And now he knew he was right. In fact, it was such a quiet afternoon, it was surprising her moans hadn't carried further and stopped the routine seaside activities the rest of his family seemed engrossed in.

He wasn't prying. He certainly didn't mean to follow the noise. He just happened to take a track towards the picnic area, and on hearing a particularly loud cry, turned to look in its direction. Below him, nestled in a sandy hollow out of the wind, Rory and Isabel were making love. Consummating her forgiving him for not telling his family about their engagement.

John did not mean to linger and stare. But he did. Their passion, for a few seconds, absorbed him. What he felt was not disgust, or horror. He was caught in a wave of nostalgia – he and Mattie used to do that. The couple below him were engaging in reconciliatory sex, post-fight coitus, the sweetest sex of all, thought John. Isabel's legs were in the air, her hands clutched Rory's bum, her knickers were wrapped round her left ankle. She was in raptures. Just before he felt like a dirty old man, spying on young lovers, John, standing hands in pockets, observing his son in action, had a burst of pride. Rory was doing well. That's my boy, thought John.

Then the sun slipped from behind a cloud and John's shadow was cast in front of him, spreading long over the ground and over the two entwined below him. Rory sensed it, and sensed he and Isabel were not alone. He looked up, saw his father and reacted. 'Jesus Christ, Dad. Fuck off.'

John mumbled, 'Sorry.' He felt his face turn red, as he stumbled off dizzy with mortification. He heard Isabel's expletive as Rory told her what had happened. He didn't speak French, but profanities explode across language barriers. He knew exactly what she was saying.

He broke into a run, as if movement might ease his embarrassment. And arrived back beside Grandpa before he had really calmed down. 'Hello, Grandpa,' he shouted, too loudly. 'How're you doin'? On your own, I see.'

'I'm not deaf,' said Grandpa.

'I know. I know,' said John. 'Would you like to take a little walk? Would you like to have a look at the sea? Dip your toes in the briny, Grandpa, eh?'

'I'll tell you what I'd like.'

'What?' said John.

'I'd like you and Mattie and everyone who isn't one of my grandchildren to stop calling me Grandpa. My name is Martin.'

'I thought you liked being called Grandpa,' said John. 'Part of the family and all that.'

'I am part of the family anyway,' said Grandpa. 'I started it. I am the founder member of this family. And I think it would be nice to be called by my name.'

John helped his father to his feet, and put a steadying hand under his elbow as they started towards the sea.

'I'm perfectly capable of walking on my own,' said Grandpa. 'I don't need help.'

John walked beside his father. Their pace was painful.

'Bloody woman patted my knee and called me Grandpa. I'm not her grandfather. How dare she? Patronising cow.'

John didn't need to be told who his father was talking about. He agreed wholeheartedly. 'Bloody woman.'

They looked at one another, nodding in mutual dislike of Rita Boothe. It was their first bonding moment in decades.

Lily paused in her ball game to watch Marie. She thought her sister beautiful in every way she wasn't. Marie was bent over Lauren, holding the child, then lifting her over the edges of the waves as they broke and scattered on the shore. 'Big jump,' she'd say, hoisting Lauren above the water. Then she'd hold her close, kiss her soft round cheek. And they'd do it all again. Something about the gentleness of this activity touched Lily. She wished she could do that, she wished she could fill a child with such delight. She felt she was awkward with children, a little frightened of their honesty. Even her body, which was thin, angular, unlike Marie's which was rounded, soft. And Marie's face was wise, wide-lipped, full of the kind of knowing only experience brings. Lily thought Marie to be like a sensuous foreign film star, mature and utterly sexy.

Further along the beach, Mattie and Rita walked side by side. Lily could see they were chatting vigorously. Occasionally a gesturing arm would be raised, or waved. Now and then one of them would stop and turn to face the other as if agreeing whole-heartedly with something that had been said. Looking at them, Lily was filled with a yearning so deep it almost hurt. The lives these women had led. Her mother, the wild hippie of yesteryear, lying on strange floors smoking dope, guitars playing somewhere. Her mother had known many lovers, Lily imagined, and had known the joys of tuning in and dropping out, whatever that was. Lily didn't really know.

And Rita. Lily wondered if the woman was multi-talented or simply someone who couldn't decide what she wanted to do when she grew up. Lily had read the gifted cookbook cover to cover, not for the recipes but for the outpourings of, often absurd, culinary advice, which amazed her.

Music to cook by, Rita had written. *Mozart is excellent for sorbets and soufflés. I do like a bit of Verdi when making a cassoulet. Beethoven goes well with roasts. The Rolling Stones are excellent with a steak done rare, and Neil Young's more lyrical, thoughtful songs are a splendid accompaniment to soup. On no account should anyone cook to Wagner.*

And Rita on sex while cooking. *Can be wonderful. But not when the cook is preparing a meal to be shared with invited guests. This could lead to you having to answer the door in a rumpled state, not having had time to go fix make-up, etc., or could lead to a certain angst about food burning while you are pursuing your pleasure. Inevitably this will lead to both food and sex coming to an unsatisfactory conclusion.*

Lily marvelled. Was Rita writing from experience or specu-
lation? In her time with Art, they'd had many dinner parties, and
never once had it occurred to her to stop cooking and snip to bed
with him.

She stared along the beach at Mattie and Rita. There they were,
two ladies, strolling, gesticulating, talking. Lily realised she had
never bonded like that with anyone. This sad, lonely thought made
her want to run. To run away from this spot, this emotion. She
kicked off her shoes and ran, fully clothed, into the sea. It was icy.
But she laughed. 'Come on in,' she called to Art. 'The water's
lovely.'

Art shouted at her to come out, she would catch her death.

Lily splashed back to the shore. When Art asked what had got
into her, Lily said it was an impulse.

Art said he thought she'd given them up.

But Lily, feeling momentarily invigorated, turned to Agnes and
said, 'Race you.'

'Oh,' said Art. 'Don't race Lily. She runs every morning. She'll
beat you.'

'No she won't,' said Agnes. 'I'm a fast runner.' Then, impressed
at her auntie, said, 'Do you? How far do you run? A hundred
miles?'

Lily looked embarrassed, said, 'Hardly.'

This mention of her keep-fit programme, running every morning, gave Lily a stab of filthy guilt. Her running exploits had
started with a trip to Selfridges to buy the proper outfit. She
figured she might sweat and heave and go red in the face, but at
least she'd look smart while she was doing it.

On the morning of her first run, she'd left her building at six
thirty. The air was clean, almost unleaded. The streets empty. She
jogged on the spot, did a few stretches, and started at an easy,
even pace towards the corner. She encountered a bejewelled
woman in a fur coat but didn't say hello. They didn't know each
other yet. She jogged round the corner and up the next street,
then the next, and stopped. She leaned forward, hands on her
knees, breathing, panting. She'd hardly gone any distance and
already her heart was pounding and she was exhausted. I'm out of
condition, she told herself.

Must run, she told herself as she walked the length of the street. She turned the corner at the end and was into the main drag. Morning traffic was gathering; it wasn't quite busy, but it was busier than Lily had imagined it would be. She noticed a café, tables spread on the pavement, that was serving breakfast. Oh, the alluring smell of bacon. Soon Lily was a well-known morning customer at this breakfast place. They'd greet her, 'Morning, you want the usual?' And she'd nod. Then take her thick bacon roll, with an ample spreading of brown sauce, and a cup of coffee to a table and sit watching the world go by as she munched.

'Good run?' Art would ask when she returned home, feigning exhaustion.

'Excellent,' she said. 'I really think it's doing me good. I'm getting into the rhythm of it.'

This, she thought, wasn't a total lie. The run to the café for a bacon roll was getting easier, and taking less time than it had on her first morning. And she was now on nodding terms with the bejewelled lady in the fur coat.

Still, it pricked her conscience when Art proudly boasted to Agnes about her morning runs. She didn't think it proper to deceive someone so young.

Agnes looked at her now. 'I bet I win,' she said.

'Bet you don't,' said Lily.

Agnes had no scruples about cheating. 'Right,' she said. 'Ready, steady, go.' And took off before Lily had a chance to prepare herself for the race.

'Hey,' shouted Lily. 'That's not fair.' And thought, I have a right to say what's fair? I don't think so.

She chased after Agnes. Then slowed as she caught up with the child. Pretended to pant. 'You're too fast for me,' she said.

Agnes, realising that the boundaries of the race hadn't been set before it was started, put on a spurt to the nearest rock. Face red, hell-bent on winning, she streaked ahead. Lily paced herself behind her. She knew she mustn't look as if she was trying to lose. As soon as Agnes reached the rock, she declared the race over. She stopped, lifted her hands in the air and shouted, 'I won. I won.'

Lily arrived seconds behind her. 'You're too fast for me.' And she lifted Agnes in the air, whirled her round. 'The winner.'

It was a good moment for Lily. She felt the child's triumph almost as a physical thing; the glee of victory throbbed through them both. She kissed Agnes, held her, and twirled round and round with her in her arms. She felt how good it was to make other people feel proud.

Watching, Marie turned to Art and said, 'My God, she let her win. She's beginning to understand children.'

Art nodded. 'At last,' he said. 'I do believe she's mellowing.' He knew Marie would be astonished if she knew how hot and passionate her sister was in bed.

An Abundant Life

At four o'clock they packed up and went home. Lauren was crying, well, howling, lower jaw juddering alarmingly, because she was cold. Grandpa seemed to be in a bad mood. Isabel and Rory insisted they travel in Marie's car as neither of them felt comfortable around John. John was grumpy. Lily was feeling a bit queasy as, to relieve her worry that Rita might ask her about the *Lost Icons* article she was having problems writing, she'd eaten too many smoked salmon sandwiches, and drunk more wine than she'd admit to. Added to that, her jeans were soaked, she was shivering; she'd caught a chill that would, she knew, go straight to her stomach. Tod complained that they hadn't had their usual game of football – a family tradition which they all, including Grandpa, joined in. He said Mattie was chatting too much to the new lady and hadn't bothered to organise it. Agnes's nose was running; she looked as if she was coming down with something.

Mattie declared the afternoon a huge success. 'Best picnic ever,' she said.

Rita agreed. 'It's been wonderful. Next time you must all come to me. I'll cook.'

Mattie clapped her hands, so filled with glee was she. 'Excellent. We'd all love to.'

Neither of them noticed the momentary look of horror that flitted over the faces of the rest of the gathering. They were both too delighted with the new friendship.

Back at the house, Mattie bustled into the kitchen to make coffee and open wine. Isabel said she absolutely had to have a bath, she was covered with sand, and disappeared upstairs. Rory went with her. Lily said she felt a little under the weather and thought she'd have a lie-down. Grandpa went to his room to check his emails. Marie said she ought to get the children home, they were worn out. Rita said that she and Sebastian better get on up the road, they had a long drive ahead of them.

John went to the kitchen to tell Mattie they were going. Found her filling dishes with Twiglets and stuffed olives. 'What the hell are you doing?'

'Putting out a few nibbles,' said Mattie.

'Nibbles! Nibbles! Who the hell wants nibbles, we've just eaten a huge picnic. Put them away.'

'I thought people might be a little peckish.' Mattie was hurt.

'People are all going home,' said John. 'Come and say goodbye, and put these effing embarrassing things away.'

'I thought we'd all like a nice glass of wine or a cup of coffee to round off the day. We've had such a lovely time,' whined Mattie.

'Some of us have had a lovely time,' said John. 'Some of us haven't.'

Mattie saw the glint of anger in his eyes, and knew the cheese sandwich argument was looming. She had her defence worked out. 'Rita was our guest,' she would say. 'We have to be considerate to those we invite to eat with us.' She bustled out of the kitchen to the front door, wiping her hands on her apron as she went.

'Oh, must you go?' she said to Rita. 'I'd hoped you might stay for a little wine, or perhaps some coffee since you are driving.'

She did not notice Marie and her family climbing into their old VW Golf. Rita filled her eyes. Lovely, witty, wonderful Rita. Marie looked at her father and shrugged. 'See you soon, Dad,' she told John.

John said, 'Of course.' Kissed Marie on the cheek and helped Lauren clamber into the back of the car, fastened her into her safety seat.

'I'll phone,' Mattie told Rita. 'Tomorrow, to check you got home in one piece. And thank you so much for bothering to come.'

'It was a pleasure,' cooed Rita. Their voices seemed to be getting louder and louder. They rattled through the suburban spring silence, drowning the evening blackbird calls. Neighbours' heads popped up at windows, peering politely out. People wondering what was going on. 'We must get together again soon,' called Rita.

'Absolutely,' said Mattie.

Marie said she was going. The noise that Mattie and Rita were making was bothersome. She started the engine, and drove off, waving to her father. Mattie didn't turn round; she was too busy saying goodbye to Rita.

As Marie's car disappeared down the street, Rita's followed, her hand stretched out of the car window, waving goodbye. Mattie jumped up and down on the pavement, arm up, waving, shouting. 'Bye-eee.'

When both cars had slipped from view, John came up to Mattie. 'Marie's gone. You didn't say goodbye to her.'

'I'll see her soon enough,' said Mattie. She sighed. 'Isn't Rita wonderful?'

They walked back indoors. 'You might think so. I'm as yet undecided on her wonderfulness.'

'Oh, that's because she ate your cheese sandwich,' said Mattie. She'd decided to take the offensive in the argument.

'It isn't her eating of the sandwich that I object to. It's your giving it to her that I find hurtful.'

'It was just a sandwich, John. And she was our guest. You have to respect the wishes of people you invite to eat with you.'

They shut the front door and went into the kitchen.

'You think this is about a sandwich,' said John. 'And men are meant to be the insensitive ones.'

'If it's not about a sandwich, what is it about?' Mattie wanted to know.

'It's about you throwing yourself at that woman. It's about your perceived pecking order. It's about who you care about.'

'I care about you.' Mattie was on the defensive.

'Do you? You didn't seem to this afternoon. You gave the sandwich you had made specially for me, the sandwich I had been looking forward to, relishing, to a complete stranger.'

'Our special guest,' argued Mattie. 'For heaven's sakes. It was a sandwich, a simple bloody sandwich. You stupid, stupid . . .' she searched for an insult, '. . . man.'

'That's it, isn't it? That's me. A stupid man. You think men are stupid, simple souls. Give them a sandwich and football on telly and let them be. I happen to be very fond of a cheese sandwich with pickle. A good one makes me happy. Doesn't take much when you think of it. Simple soul, me. I don't want a flash car, I don't ask you to dress up in black stockings, which I find very alluring, I was just looking forward to a sandwich that I was charmed you'd made for me, specially for me. I have worked for years at a job I hate, I haven't come home drunk, I haven't looked at another woman, I haven't squandered any money on nights out or gambling or drink. I have loved you. I have given you all I have. And I was thinking, stupidly it turns out, that you loved me too, but when it came to the bit, you didn't say, "Sorry, Rita, this is for John." You just handed my sandwich over to someone you hardly know. That's what you think of me.' He walked out of the room. Mattie waited for the door to slam, but he closed it quietly and went to his shed to find solace in his kite.

Mattie carefully put all the Twiglets back in their box, and the stuffed olives back in their jar. She washed the dishes, put the cups and glasses away. Made herself a cup of tea, and went to sit alone in the living room. She sat on the edge of the rose-coloured armchair (that would have had to go had she acquired the longed-for red velvet sofa; they clashed), clutching her cup in both hands. Nerves stung inside her stomach.

John didn't understand. That was plain to her. What a fuss to make over a sandwich, she thought. It should have pleased him that Rita had enjoyed it so much. Thing was, she wanted a friend. How could he not see that? Ever since she'd married, she and John had mixed with other couples who were at the same stage in life as they were – newly-weds, married with a baby, married with toddlers, and on, till now the people they knew were married with children who'd left home, empty-nesters. They had known the Heywoods across the road for over twenty-five years now, the couples had dinner together once a month or so. Others they had known had moved away and either disappeared from Mattie and John's life, or become names on their Christmas card list.

And now here was someone new, someone who had come into Mattie's life not as another mother at the school gates, or as the wife of one of John's colleagues, but someone completely separate who had a unique life of her own, quite different to Mattie's. She was exciting, and Mattie had no intention of letting her slip away to the world of trite, empty – must get together someday, hope you're keeping well, thinking of you – yearly greetings at Christmas time.

Driving home, speeding north, Rita asked Sebastian what he thought of her new friends.

'Loved Marie, didn't know what to make of Lily, hardly saw Rory and Isabel, they went off on their own.'

'But what about Mattie?'

'What about her? She's mumsy.'

'Oh Sebastian, what a horrible thing to say about somebody. Mattie is never mumsy. She's lovely, warm. She has a wonderful life filled with people. An abundant life, I'd say. Only she seems to have lost her way. She can't see the point of it any more. But I like her enormously.'

Sebastian said, 'Good.' And returned to thinking about Marie.

He had been drawn to her, her face, full-lipped and pale, dark eyes like her son Tod. Her hair was fair, tumbled over her face. Halfway through the afternoon, she had gathered it casually in her hands and pinned it to the top of her head, revealing her neck. Though that hadn't stopped it falling in careless curls over her face.

But it was her expressions Sebastian noticed. Every now and then she'd gaze into the distance, worrying, he thought. There was depth there, and a certain sensuousness. He loved the way she cared for her children, picking up the little one, carrying her on her hip. Looking at Tod's shoreline findings with genuine interest. 'Oh, what lovely shells. We'll look them up when we get home.' Rubbing her daughter's feet after she'd been in the sea. Such tenderness. He wished Marie would rub his feet too.

Two years ago, the woman he'd been living with, Suzanne, had left him. She'd been offered a job in America that had been too juicy to resist. Though they'd both sworn the split was temporary, and just a matter of distance – 'You'll only be an ocean away,' he'd said – they had both known it was over. Six months after she'd left, Suzanne wrote to tell him she'd found someone else. He'd sold the house they'd shared and used his part of the profit to put down the deposit on the flat he now lived in.

He'd taken up the bachelor life, and had secretly decided he didn't really like it. He enjoyed companionship – a shared meal in the evening, chat. He didn't like the round of first dates. He wanted a pal he could sleep with.

Marie was definitely sexual. Sebastian imagined some might say she looked like she'd been round the block a few times. And maybe that was true, he didn't know. But he felt comforted and intrigued to think that if she had been around the block, she certainly would have stopped on the way to look at the view. He thought he might phone her, if he could work up the courage and face rejection.

'Could you ask Mattie for Marie's number?' he asked.

'Why?' said Rita.

'I'd like to phone her.'

'Why?' said Rita.

'Why do you think? She might like to come out with me.'

Rita said, 'Oh.' She switched on her old Bob Dylan tape and they hurtled north, motorway rumbling beneath them, landscape whooshing past. Sebastian worried about what he'd say to Marie, and what he'd say to his mother if she turned him down. He couldn't lie and say he hadn't managed to get hold of her, because if he knew women, though he didn't think he did, Marie would tell her mother she'd refused his offer of dinner, and her mother would tell his mother. That was the way women were.

Rita, meantime, dreamed. If Sebastian asked Marie on a date, and Marie accepted, and they got along, then there might be another date, and another. Till, well, wedding bells; then she would be the grandmother of three children, or step-grandmother if there was such a thing. They might come visit, perhaps, even stay overnight. She could decorate the spare room for them. They would all go for walks together. Perhaps the children would come alone when Marie and Sebastian went for a quiet weekend together to Amsterdam, perhaps, or to Paris to see Rory and Isabel. That would be fun. They might even go pony trekking and have trips to the cinema. She would read them stories, bake cakes. They might all play games by the fire in the evening. Yes, she could enjoy being a grandmother.

'I'll phone Mattie tomorrow,' she said, hoping she sounded nonchalant.

Rory and Isabel sat either end of the bath. The water was getting cold, but neither of them felt inclined to move. Locked in here, they were safe from the rest of the family, especially John.

'You have to speak to him,' said Isabel.

'I can't do that,' said Rory. 'He's my dad. He saw us having it off. Christ, that's embarrassing enough without talking to him about it.'

'Don't you talk to your father about sex?'

'Sex generally, occasionally. Sex specific, as in me doing it, never.'

She looked appalled. 'Terrible. Uncivilised.'

'Normal,' said Rory.

'Didn't your father explain about sex to you? Didn't he tell you how to do it?'

'No way.'

'Then how did you find out?'

'A bit of initial groping. Lily's *Cosmopolitan*, which she got every month. Very instructive. And we had a talk at school.'

'You Scots are uncivilised.'

'We are not. I'll have you know we are the most civilised nation on earth. We invented television, the bicycle, tarmacadam, the pneumatic tyre, the postage stamp, the fountain pen, golf . . .' He was beginning to run out of inventions. 'That's a lot.'

'If you all spoke about sex more, you wouldn't have to distract yourselves inventing things. Or if you weren't so busy inventing things, you might have better sex lives.'

'Rubbish. We have wonderful sex lives. Look at us, fabulous complexions, orgasmic eyes. First love bite, here in Scotland, Angus Macgregor and Fiona Wallace, in the heather somewhere outside Inverness, fourteen thirty-two.'

Isabel shifted up the bath, causing a small tidal wave, to lie with Rory. Putting herself between his legs, head on his chest. 'First love bite, outside St Tropez, Mimi and Jacque le Grande, long, long before fourteen thirty-two.'

'Oh oh,' said Rory. He turned on the hot tap to heat up the water. Then folded his arms round her, kissed her neck.

'You should speak to your father,' said Isabel.

'Do I have to?' said Rory. 'I mean, if it had been your mother watching us doing it, would you speak to her?'

'Of course. I do speak to her, all the time.'

'But not about sex,' said Rory, hopefully. 'I mean not about *our* sex. Not about me, how I do it.'

'Of course I do. We're both women. We talk.'

'I don't know about that,' said Rory. 'That's a bit much. I wish you hadn't told me. Next time I see your mother I won't be able to look her in the face.'

'Why? She's a woman of the world. Who do you think taught me all the little tricks I do?'

'Shut up, Isabel.'

She kissed him.

Lily's nausea was swimming through her. 'You shouldn't have let me eat so much,' she said to Art. 'You saw me. You should have stopped me.'

'You'd have paid no attention to me,' said Art. 'You never do.'

'I was upset at seeing Rita Boothe, I was worried she'd ask me about the article. Eating helped.'

'State you're in, it doesn't seem to have helped much.'

'Also,' said Lily, 'I got chilled after being in the sea. My jeans were soaked and all sandy. I don't feel well.'

'No wonder,' said Art. 'You ate too much. You ran into the sea. At home, you tidy up. You wipe and clean. You plump cushions. You play at being Lillian. Lily, when are you going to give up on the distraction activities and come out to play properly. It's fun out here in the world.'

He lay on the bed beside her, stared up at the ceiling. Lily said nothing. And the silence between them deepened into a thick hush. Lily hated that. In relationships she considered herself fine as long as there were words to play with, mete out. Silences disturbed her. She never could interpret them properly. Some were peaceful, when mutual emotions didn't need to be expressed. Some were deep, where feelings went beyond words. Some were a respite when two people were gathering strength before declaring deeper love, or, in an argument, before hurling more insults. Silences could be so sweet. Or they could be turbulent. And some, like this, were an enigma. Lily couldn't imagine what Art was thinking. She thought that in the end, when people parted, it was the silence, more than the words, that caused the rift. Silence could be such a bitch.

Reading the hush, Lily decided that Art was growing tired of her. He wanted more from her than she could give. He wanted her to relax, enjoy herself. Enjoy yourself, she thought, how do you do that when you've an article to write and your family despise you for hurting your mother? And Art wanted children, and she still couldn't decide if she did or not. Reading this hush, Lily concluded that Art was considering leaving her.

Art wasn't bothered by this silence. He was shutting his eyes, pleasantly drowsy after time in the open air; he was drifting into sleep. But, thinking he ought to say something reassuring to Lily before hitting oblivion, he patted her stomach. 'There, there. Never mind, you'll feel better soon.'

It was a sympathy pat Lily didn't need. It seemed to land exactly where her over-indulgent picnic lunch was lying waiting to be digested. She leapt from the bed, hand clutching her mouth, and ran to the bathroom, which was locked. There were sounds of carnal enjoyment coming from within. Rory giving Isabel thrills her mother had never dreamed of – he hoped.

This enraged Lily. She banged on the door, shouting, 'Rory, you bastard. Let me in. What are you doing in there?'

Mattie at the foot of the stairs heard this. The nostalgia of it eased her worry about the cheese sandwich row with John. It's quite like old times, she thought.

In his room, Grandpa wrote to Nina. He told her he'd hoped the animosity between John and Mattie was over, but now she'd ruined everything by giving away his sandwich. And that the house was crowded and noisy, with Lily battering on the bathroom door demanding Rory let her in. *John's doing the right thing*, he said. *He's locked himself away in the shed making his kite.*

Nina replied immediately, telling him that he should scold

Mattie severely for giving away John's sandwich and send her to bed without any supper. It might only be a sandwich but it was the principle of the thing that mattered. Then she asked who Lily and Rory were.

Grandpa was about to reply that Lily and Rory were his grandchildren, but realised that since she thought he was forty-two and that John and Mattie were his young children, he was hardly likely to have any. He switched off his computer while he thought about this. Really, he decided, the fiction he'd created was getting out of hand; also, he was getting too old to lie.

On his desk beside the computer was a framed photograph of his wife, Sylvia. She was standing in the garden of their old house beside the lilac tree, which was in bloom. It was one of his favourite photos of Sylvia. Her face was relaxed, not quite smiling, but she'd plainly been enjoying herself. There was a touch of colour in her cheeks, her hair was tousled. It was usually immaculate. She was wearing a green and white floral dress, belted at the waist. He'd cut the grass earlier and that new-mown smell still lingered. They'd not long eaten lunch, their first meal of the year outdoors. Salmon quiche, he remembered, with salad and a glass of sparkling apple juice. She had made a rhubarb crumble for pudding, and they'd had it warm with cream. They'd both been charmed when a blackbird, almost tame, hopped under the table on the patio and pecked at the crumbs he'd thrown down for it. Sunday, they shared a newspaper; he had the Review section, she the colour supplement. 'There's a lovely recipe for a rhubarb pavlova in here,' she'd said. 'I think I'll try it when the Harrowers come for dinner next Saturday.'

He'd said that was a good idea. And had she noticed the delphiniums were coming up? And why didn't he make the coffee?

'That would be lovely, dear,' she'd said, and smiled. The cancer that would kill her was already growing in her ovaries, but neither of them knew that then.

He'd gone inside through the French windows, and seen his camera, a Minolta, on the sideboard, a new acquisition, G-Plan.

He wondered, now, where it was. Nearly all of his furniture had been sent to auction when he moved in here.

The camera was next to a framed photograph of his children; next to that was an arrangement of daffodils and lilac Sylvia had put in the crystal vase they'd got as a wedding present from his Uncle Jim and Aunt Margaret.

They were both dead now.

The room smelled of the air spray Sylvia used every morning, and every evening before they went to bed. The radio was playing; somebody called Janis Joplin, who had not long died, was singing a song about somebody called Bobby McGee. He'd never heard of her.

He made the coffee. The day was so clear to him, he remembered he popped the top of a new jar, jabbed his finger through the seal, always a satisfying thing to do. He got two cups from the cupboard, where they hung in a perfect row on the white plastic hooks he'd put in. The cups were white, patterned with red and yellow flowers. He never liked them, would have preferred a mug. But Sylvia hated mugs, she thought them common.

On the way back to the patio, he'd stopped by the sideboard and placed the camera on the tray with the coffee cups. He would take Sylvia's photograph. John had returned the camera yesterday after borrowing it when he'd gone to some festival or other on the Isle of Wight. He'd brought a girl with him, Mattie. She'd been thin, too thin, Sylvia said. She'd had long blonde hair, blue eyes, and wore a pair of jeans with huge wide bell bottoms.

Grandpa remembered watching John and Mattie. How they'd walked along the street so entwined he'd thought one of them would trip the other up. John's arm round Mattie's shoulders, her arm round his waist. In the house they'd sat together on the sofa, John's arm round her. Her leaning into him. Several times Grandpa had walked into a room and found them locked in a kiss. They'd move apart, only slightly embarrassed. At dinner they'd spoken about a film they'd seen by someone called Jean Luc Goddard, and had laughed when Grandpa revealed he'd thought that was a girl.

'He's French, Dad,' John had said. Patronisingly, Grandpa thought.

Later John had asked what he thought of his new girlfriend.

'Seems like a nice lass,' he'd said.

'I'm going to marry her,' John told him. He'd been studying to be an architect at the time. Grandpa had said best wait till he graduated and had a job. At that, John had glowed impetuosity, bristled with it. He'd fallen in love, he was young, he'd manage.

Grandpa took the tray outside, placed both cups and the camera on the table. 'I'm going to take your photograph later.'

'Please don't. I hate having my photo taken.'

'But you're looking lovely today.'

He sat. He sipped. 'What about going to the cinema to see that film by Jean whosit that John and his new girlfriend were talking about?'

Sylvia said, 'I don't think so. One thing I know – anything a girl like that likes, I don't. And anything that I like, she doesn't. It's an age thing.' She looked down the garden. 'The roses are in bud already. It's going to be a good year for them.' Then she'd smiled at him. 'John and his girlfriend are young and full of themselves. They'll grow out of it.' She'd paused, taken a sip of her coffee. 'Unfortunately . . .' Her voice trailed away.

It was the first time Grandpa had seen any kind of regret in his wife. She was changing. It was only a small thing, an insidious whisper of something different inside her. Was it the disease that in several years' time was to take her? Had she known? He didn't think so. But it had been the beginning of the end of their life together. As if she'd accepted that the mothering was over. She and Grandpa had drifted into a sweeter, gentler, more tender time together, reliving, almost, the people they'd been, the relationship they'd had at the start of their marriage. But she still always called him dear.

He thought it strange. Here he was, sitting in this room, and he could remember with vivid clarity a day over thirty-five years ago, every detail of it: the crumbs on the kitchen unit, his green cardigan, which was draped over the back of an armchair, the way Sylvia had sliced the salmon quiche, everything. Yet he was damned if he could recall what he did yesterday.

He got up and went to his chest of drawers, and fetched out his camera, the same Minolta he'd used to photograph Sylvia all those years ago. He took it downstairs.

Mattie was in the living room, reading a magazine.

'We forgot to take a camera,' he said to her. 'We should have taken some photographs.'

'We always forget something,' said Mattie.

'I'd like to take your photograph now,' he said. 'Just to remember today.'

'I hate having my photograph taken,' said Mattie.

Grandpa said women always said that. She looked away as he awkwardly fiddled with the camera, adjusting the speed for the darkening room, and as he held it to his face and tried to focus. He moved towards her, then back, working the lens. He did this very slowly.

Mattie smiled mildly, and remained patient. His harmlessness charmed her, but watching him now, she realised how unhappy it made him. When John had first introduced them, Grandpa had been head of the family, tall, a bit overpowering. A man who'd lived by his own rules – he was rarely, for example, seen without a tie. He even mowed the lawn in formal dress more suited for going to the office. After she and John married, she hadn't known what to call her in-laws. They weren't the sort of people who discussed such things, they wouldn't dream of saying, 'Just call us Martin and Sylvia, you're one of the family now.' So they'd been Mr and Mrs White until Lily was born, then shyly, shyly, Mattie had called them Grandma and Grandpa.

She smiled to think of this. How silly they all were. They'd eaten meals together, shared Christmases, talked about politics and religion (but never sex). Mattie remembered she and John had once joined her in-laws on holiday in the Lake District, but still she'd called them Mr and Mrs White. And, if she remembered correctly, they'd been perfectly happy with that. Weren't people the strangest things?

Click. 'Got it,' said Grandpa. He'd captured Mattie looking slightly bemused, and slightly amused, sitting forward in her chair, so lost in her musings she'd forgotten she was having her photograph taken. Later, John was to say it was one of the best snaps of his wife he'd ever seen. 'Essence of Mattie.' She was a bit bewildered, smiling at some thought or other, and (though he never mentioned this) a tad vacant.

'I never knew what to call you until we had Lily,' Mattie told Grandpa. 'I didn't like to say your first name without you telling me to. It was a relief when I could just say "Grandpa".'

'I wish people would call me Martin,' said Grandpa. 'That's my name. Even that woman today called me Grandpa. I'm not her grandpa. I'm Martin. It's years since I heard anyone say my name.'

'Well, we'll call you Martin then,' said Mattie.

He looked at her. Even that small mention of his name touched him. It almost took him by surprise to hear the word spoken out loud. And Mattie worried. She didn't think she could call Grandpa by his name. He'd been Grandpa for so long. He *was* Grandpa. 'I've got a few things to do in the kitchen,' she said, though she hadn't.

She stood busily folding the tea towel, though it had been perfectly folded in the first place. She wondered what everyone was up to. Lily and Art were upstairs, Lily was feeling ill. No wonder, the amount she'd eaten, then running into the sea like that. Mattie wondered what had got into her. John was working on his kite in the shed. And Rory and Isabel, what were they up to? Well, she knew perfectly well what they were doing, only she didn't like to think about it. Did they have to be so noisy about it? She didn't know where they got the energy. Then again, she remembered once she had had that energy. And she secretly wished she still had.

Middle-Age Fury
and Sibling Rivalry

Sunday morning, Lily and Art went to see Marie. The yellow tunnel had been, in the months since Lily was last here, removed upstairs. It now lay along the landing between the top of the stairs and the bathroom, making the journey to the bath interesting, Marie claimed. Though she didn't use it. Well, she had once when her friend Connie, who was also a single mum, came round for the evening and they'd drunk too much vodka, and had crawled through the tunnel every time they went to the loo, which was often. They'd giggled hugely at this. But they didn't use the tunnel in the morning, after Connie stayed the night on the sofa, her kids sleeping in Marie's kids' rooms. It wasn't any fun with a hangover.

The same feeling of lazy comfort that always seeped through Lily when she came to Marie's house ran through her today. She wanted to settle down on the sofa, old and battered though it was, and sleep. The room was painted a pastel green, the carpet was deep blue and the sofa was covered in Indian throws. There was a black and white Man Ray framed photograph on the wall behind it. Today it was unusually tidy and quiet.

'Where are Tod and Agnes?' asked Lily.

'Playing at a friend's house,' said Marie. A lie: they were with Andy, their father.

He'd come for them over an hour ago. Marie had them pressed, polished and drilled in what they could and could not tell him. The picnic for Mattie's birthday was on the can-tell list, the vodka and tunnel into the bathroom escapade was on the can't-tell.

The resilience of her children always amazed Marie. They seemed almost to accept that their dad had been away and was now back, and wanted to take them out. Not that there hadn't been questions. Where had he been? Why wasn't he at home with them? Why wasn't Lauren going too?

'He's been away in another country,' Marie said. 'He isn't going to live with us any more, he has a new lady in his life, and you have to be kind to her.' Though she privately hoped they wouldn't be. And, 'Lauren's too little to go.'

They seemed to take all that on board, and when Andy turned up at the door they went with him without a murmur. Though Tod did say he wanted to stay home and watch his *Simpsons* videos. And Agnes insisted on taking her toy dog, William, with her. William had been consigned to the bottom of her toy box some time ago, but in moments of despair, need and doubt (a pending trip to the dentist, a bout of chickenpox, a scolding for spraying the bathroom with Marie's best Armani cologne after Tod had been in and made it smelly), he was retrieved and cuddled. William offered constant, silent, uncritical comfort, and sometimes Marie wished she too had a William in her life.

She'd dreaded seeing Andy again. Waited on edge for his arrival. Would he walk in, or ring the bell? He rang, and stood waiting for her to open the door. There he was, looking exactly as he had done four years ago when she'd last seen him standing in the doorway of his best friend's bedroom, watching her misbehave with his best friend in his best friend's bed. Except he'd grown a beard, short and stubbly.

He was tall, his hair was swept to the left with some stray strands falling over his forehead. He was wearing jeans with a white shirt open at the neck, brown shoes. She said, 'Hello. Agnes and Tod are ready. Do you want to come in?'

He said, 'No. Lucy's waiting in the car.'

Marie peered round him, saw a woman, younger than she was, bobbed hair, black jacket over red T-shirt, sitting at the wheel of a new Saab. She recognised the car. It was the one that had been in the street when she'd taken her children to the park on the day after Christmas. In fact, she realised, she'd seen that car quite a lot. Hadn't it been outside Mattie and John's house once or twice? She couldn't be sure.

She felt a stab of loathing. The woman in that car was not getting her children, Andy was not getting her children. But remembering her sins of that night four years ago, she felt flushed with embarrassment and self-doubt. A red rash throbbed on her throat. A sign of fear and nerves, and Andy had seen it.

Marie touched her chin, indicating the beard. 'Suits you.'

He smiled. Looked past her into the house. 'You've redecorated. Looks nice.'

They stood looking at one another, politely formal. Then Marie had said, 'Well, have a nice time.'

He said, 'We will.'

Marie wanted to say, 'Please, please don't tell the children what I did.'

He'd smiled stiffly and gone down the path to the car.

She watched Agnes and Tod walk down the path with their dad. Watched them climb into the back of the car. Watched the car disappear down the road and round the corner. She'd waved. 'Have them home by six o'clock,' she'd said. 'They have school tomorrow. I don't want them to be up too late. And Tod still has some homework to do.'

Then she'd gone indoors, picked up Lauren, and held her close. It helped ease the turmoil. She imagined Andy telling Tod and Agnes, 'Your mummy did a very naughty thing. That's why I went away.' She rocked Lauren, swayed back and forward. The child offered willing comfort, at three, and still ready to accept unasked-for kisses and cuddles, she was the nearest thing to William Marie had.

Now she made coffee for Lily, Art and herself and brought it through to the living room. The radio in the kitchen was on, a disc jockey's cheery banter drifted through, then the Eagles sang 'Hotel California'. Lily said that she wished Mattie and John would sort themselves out, there was an atmosphere in that house.

Marie said she was sure they'd sort themselves out, even though they'd been at odds with each other for months now. She shrugged. Right now, she didn't really care. It was almost ten o'clock, eight hours before Tod and Agnes returned and she could quiz them about Andy's flat and Andy's girlfriend. What would they be doing at this moment? She wished she'd asked where he was intending to take them. And she should have reminded him not to fill them up with sweets and fizzy drinks. They'll be high as kites when they get back, she thought. I'll never get them to bed. 'You shouldn't worry about Mum and Dad,' she said.

'I just hate to see them like that,' said Lily. 'They used to be so happy, sort of entwined. It was lovely.'

'They're still entwined,' said Marie. 'Beneath the hostilities, they're still in love.'

'You think?' said Lily.

'Yeah,' said Marie. 'Definitely.' But in fact, she didn't really care. Right now, she just wanted Tod and Agnes back home here with her. 'Actually,' she said, for she needed to talk about this to someone, 'Tod and Agnes aren't playing at a friend's house. They are out for the day with Andy.'

'Andy?' said Lily. 'He's back?'

'Not with me, he isn't. He's got a new girlfriend. He wants to see his children.'

Lily thought about this. 'Well, he has a right. He is their father. It's probably better for Tod and Agnes to have contact with their father, rather than think he just walked out on them. You don't want them imagining the split was their fault or anything like that.'

'Of course it wasn't their fault. It had nothing to do with them. It was . . .' About to say, 'It was me,' Marie stopped. 'You know,' she said. 'One of these things that happen.'

Lily reached forward, took Marie's hand and squeezed it gently. 'I know,' she said. 'But children are so vulnerable emotionally. They can think all sorts of things and never let you into their fears and doubts.'

'I don't want them to be with him,' said Marie. 'I want them here with me. I don't want him coming back into my life, interfering. I was doing fine.'

Lily said she knew that. She told Marie that the children would be fine, and their outing with Andy would be fine and when they got home they'd all be just fine. She noticed she'd said fine rather a lot, and hoped this didn't sound as if she was being a little over-placatory.

Marie smiled, and said, 'I know.' She wished she could be like Lily. Lily's hair hung smooth, black, to just above her shoulders, and was always immaculate. It shone. Lily's clothes were perfect, stylish, expensive. Lily cared about everybody. Lily the good.

Except that she'd bought *that* car, and hurt her mother deeply. Maybe Lily wasn't so good after all, but who was she to criticise after what she'd done?

Lily, on the other hand, wished she was like Marie. Had tumbling hair, looked good in casual clothes, and could wave her hands about as she spoke in the animated way Marie did. Rita, Marie, Mattie – how Lily envied them. They were flawed, Lily realised that. But they were darkly flawed, interestingly flawed. She, on the other hand, was boringly flawed. She was neat, tidy, organised – boring, boring, boring. Rita, Marie and Mattie were women of mystery and intrigue. Their faces filled with secret sexual wisdom. Things they did in the night. It never crossed her mind that the things she did in the night with Art – Lillian and Arthur – were a lot more interesting and exciting than anything any of the three people she fantasised about had ever done.

They finished their coffee. It was time for Lily and Art to leave, they had a plane to catch and planned to share a taxi to the airport with Rory and Isabel. On the short trip from the sofa to the front door, Lily reassured Marie that the children would be fine, and Marie would be fine and everything would be fine. She wished she would stop saying that, she thought she sounded fussy and a bit neurotic. Marie, however, found her words heartening.

After everyone had left, Mattie phoned Rita. 'Just checking you got home all right.'

'Oh yes,' said Rita. 'No problem. And thank you again for the invitation. I really enjoyed myself.'

'Oh no,' said Mattie. 'The pleasure was ours. We so enjoyed having you.'

'Oh,' said Rita. 'Sebastian wanted to know if you could let him have Marie's phone number.'

'Oh my,' said Mattie. 'Really? How intriguing.'

Rita said, 'Yes, maybe a little romance brewing.'

'Wouldn't that be lovely?' said Mattie.

John, sitting at the kitchen table, listening to this, heard his wife's voice rise an octave as she spoke, noticed she was so enthused about telling *that woman* how lovely it was to have her on their picnic, she was elevating herself, standing on tiptoe. It was more than he could bear. He went out into the garden to burn his spring clippings, prunings and loppings.

Grandpa saw him gather the rubbish together and thought he'd join him. He liked bonfires. They were, he shyly admitted to himself, manly. He never said this to Mattie, however; she seemed to disapprove of manly things. In fact there were areas of John and Mattie's relationship that Grandpa disapproved of. Mattie, for instance, did all the fuse fixing and plug changing, busily fetching her favourite screwdriver from the kitchen drawer. This was bad enough. But John, who was infinitely more artistic than his wife, did all the flower arranging. There was something about this that deeply unnerved the old man. Though he could see at a glance that whilst Mattie just dumped flowers in a vase and said, 'That'll do,' John would carefully mix long stems with short stems, and create something of real visual appeal. Furthermore, John would sometimes bake scones, since Mattie said, 'I can't do scones. They come out like bricks.' But Mattie would wield the plunger should drains get blocked. He couldn't help but think there was something not quite right about this. So he was pleased to see John building a fire. Some things were still as they should be.

He could accept that his new bank manager was a woman, as was his lawyer ever since his original lawyer, Mr Stewart, retired fifteen years ago. But there were still some things a woman shouldn't do. Lighting bonfires was one of them. Other things Grandpa thought women shouldn't do were drive long-distance lorries, drink pints of beer and play wind instruments, except for the flute. 'Women do not look right playing the trombone,' he'd said to Mattie once.

'Why ever not?' said Mattie. 'Women can do anything they want to do just as well as men.'

Grandpa could see this conversation might get heated and left it at that. For even though he knew his bank manager and his lawyer were both charming and more than competent, he couldn't help but feel that the monstrous regiment had arrived, and were taking over his world.

He went out to help John with the bonfire. They stood watching flames curl over the starter pile of dried twigs. Grandpa said he liked a good fire. John agreed. They surveyed the pending pile to select what they'd burn next. 'Nothing too green,' said Grandpa. 'Not yet.' John agreed. They threw on the clippings from the newly pruned rose bushes, and turned round to warm their bums.

'Fine day for it. Not hot. Not cold.'

John agreed. 'Fine,' he said.

'You're a bit grumpy these days,' said Grandpa.

John said he knew. 'Can't seem to help it. I'm just angry all the time. I swear inside my head. These words going round and round.'

Grandpa said he knew. 'I used to do that. Just bloody furious.'

'Furious,' John agreed.

They turned round again, and added some more clippings to the blaze.

'Is it the money thing?' asked Grandpa. 'The pension not coming up to snuff?'

'Probably,' said John. 'I'm angry at Mattie for insisting I bought the pension scheme. But mostly I'm angry at myself for not cashing it in when I saw what was happening. It was there in the financial pages for everyone to read.'

Grandpa nodded his head. 'I don't know why I was so angry. It just swept over me. I wanted to bang on the horn at the slightest thing when I was driving. People turning without signalling, I wanted to give them a good blast.'

'Yes,' said John. 'I remember. It was like being driven about by the Incredible Hulk.'

They turned again, almost in unison.

'It was work. Endless days coming and going. Then it was over. I didn't go in any more. I went back to see them and it was like they'd forgotten who I was. I was furious. Not at them, at me for putting up with it all those years.'

John agreed. 'Bloody stupid.'

Mattie paused at the living room window to look out at them. She was smiling. Wouldn't it be wonderful if Sebastian and Marie got together? Then she and Rita would be related in some vague sort of way. What if they had a baby? That would be four for Marie, she'd have to move to a bigger house. Still, someone like Sebastian must earn enough for them to buy something with enough rooms for all six of them.

'You've got a good one there,' said Grandpa, nodding in Mattie's direction.

'Certainly do,' agreed John. He agreed with himself, he certainly did. Even if they were going through some sort of bickering phase. He found he loved her more when he was not with her these days.

'I had a good one too,' said Grandpa. 'Though I didn't deserve her.'

'Oh, I wouldn't say that,' said John.

'I would.' Grandpa moved some stray embers back into the fire with his foot. 'I was never faithful.'

This stunned John. He was, after all, talking to his father, and this confession conjured up images he didn't want in his brain. His dad having sex with another woman. Then again, he didn't want to think about his father having sex with any woman. He wished the pictures in his head weren't so graphic. 'You?' he said. There was something adolescent about this; it implied, who'd want to have sex with you? You're my dad.

'Me,' said Grandpa. 'I wasn't always this old. I like to think I cut a dash in my younger days. I only mention it because it was when I was your age, during my angry period. I met her on the golf course. Lindsay. I used to go out on my own every Saturday morning, early. Loved it. Me and the grass and the sky. Air, space. Whack the ball and walk after it. I was never any good. But I could think, that was the thing, alone with your thoughts. Anyway, one day the greenkeeper asked if I would mind playing with somebody. This Lindsay Barclay was an early-bird player, like me, and was looking for a partner. Never crossed my mind it would be a woman. So I said yes.'

It was time to turn round and face the fire once more.

'But there she was the next Saturday morning. And she was something. Not beautiful, but full of life, banter, laughter. She teased me about my awful game.' He was smiling, lost in memories. 'She called me Martin. That was what did it. Hearing my name. I'd been dear to your mother for years. I was Mr White at work – that's what it was like back then, none of your first-names stuff. We called people we'd known as colleagues for fifteen years Mr this and Mr that. She called me Martin, and it touched me.'

It had gone right to the heart of him. He wasn't a husband or father or colleague to this woman, he was Martin, who golfed alone, and badly, on Saturday mornings.

'A fortnight later, after two matches together, she invited me to her place for lunch. She was divorced, lived alone. That was it. Lasted three years. I told Sylvia I'd joined the office golf team and that we all played three times a week. I didn't play golf, I was with Lindsay. Lovely woman. But she wanted me to leave Sylvia, and I wouldn't do that.'

'What happened?' asked John.

'It fizzled out. Lindsay married a bloke she met at some conference or other. She was a dentist. Gave me some lovely bridge work. Still have it, as a matter of fact.'

They stared down at the fire.

'Think you could put some of that greener stuff on now,' said Grandpa.

John did as he was told. 'Did Mum know?'

Grandpa shook his head. 'Nah. She had no idea. I'm sure of that.'

'Just as well,' said John.

'Just as well,' said Grandpa. 'The day Lindsay left me, told me it was over, you and Mattie were there in the house when I got home. Next day, it was spring, just like this. Sylvia and me had lunch outside. Salmon quiche. Apple juice to drink. I made the coffee. I took her photo by the lilac tree. She looked lovely that day. She wasn't ill, but the cancer must have been there. Just as well she didn't know.'

John heaped more clippings on to the fire, 'Just as well,' he agreed.

They served salmon quiche on the plane. It was soggy, tasted of nothing really and had small green bits in it that might or might not have been chives, but Lily ate it anyway. She drank sauvignon blanc from a clear plastic cup. Turned to Art and said, 'It was Marie.'

'What was Marie?' Art said.

'Who cheated on Andy, and that's why he left.'

'How do you know that? You don't know that,' said Art.

'I know it,' said Lily. She tidily dissected her slab of plastic food and popped a morsel into her mouth. 'This is truly awful.'

'Then why are you eating it?' asked Art.

'Because it's there,' said Lily. 'I know Marie. The way she looked when she talked about Andy having the children. Shifting in her seat like that. Not meeting my eye. She's guilty as hell about something. It has to be Andy. It was her, I tell you, she slept with someone else.'

'She might be guilty about some other thing.'

'What other thing? There is no other thing. She has been saintly since Andy left. Looking after the kids, cooking for them, playing with them, taking them on outings at the weekends. She hasn't had a date or anything.'

'You don't know she hasn't had a date,' said Art. 'You are just presuming that.'

'Don't be silly, Art, of course I know she hasn't had a date. If she had she'd need a baby-sitter, and most of her friends are single mums like her who couldn't come unless they brought their children too. She'd have asked Mattie. And she hasn't asked Mattie.'

'How do you know that?'

'Mattie would have told me. She'd have phoned up to discuss it. Who Marie's date was, and was he suitable and would he get along with the kids? All that sort of thing.'

'Christ, I'm glad I'm an only child.'

'You're missing a lot. This quiche is vile.'

'Well don't eat it.'

'Somehow that seems impossibly sensible.'

The business of having a brother or sister puzzled Art. The sibling rivalry thing left him perplexed and weary. Only a few days ago, Lily had been serving supper – baked salmon with a crumble topping of Parmesan cheese and cayenne, that she loved and he didn't. She'd boiled potatoes, tossed them in olive oil and mint and parsley, steamed broccoli and tossed salad. She laid out two plates on the unit beside the gas hob. Lifted a portion of salmon on to one plate, 'Art.' Then the other, 'Me.' A helping of potatoes on to the first plate, 'Art.' Then the other, 'Me.' She went through the same routine with the broccoli and salad.

Then Art had come into the kitchen and said, 'Great. I'm starving.' And he'd picked up a plate – Lily's plate.

'That's mine,' said Lily. 'This one's yours.' Pointing to the plate remaining on the kitchen unit.

'They're both the same,' said Art.

'I know that,' said Lily. 'But still that one's mine and this one's yours.'

'What difference does it make?' said Art.

'A lot of difference. I served up that one for you and this one for me, and I was looking forward to eating it.'

'Eat that one.' Art pointed to the plate on the unit.

'No.' Lily took the plate he was holding. 'I'll eat this one. You eat that one.'

'Why can't you eat that one?'

'Because,' said Lily, 'this one's mine.' And she took her plate over to the table, sat down and started to eat.

Art took his plate and did the same. But he could not help feeling there was something more appetising about Lily's food. He asked if she had done something to her salmon to make it better than his, perhaps it had more topping?

Lily told him of course it didn't. It was just that as she was serving up, she'd designated this plate for herself and that plate for him, and to eat the wrong one would be upsetting. He left it at that. But felt it had something to do with Lily having to share her meals with a brother and sister in her youth. Definitely her obsession with exact measures had. She would, when pouring wine, make sure they both had the same amount in their individual glasses. Would lean down till her eyes were level with the liquid, and pour the tiniest drop into the glass with less to make sure they were the same. 'Eeksie peeksie,' she'd say.

'What?' Art would say.

'Eeksie peeksie,' Lily would explain slowly, as if talking to someone with severe learning difficulties. 'Equals. Sames.'

Art had once, when thoroughly sick of this passion for perfect sharing, taken his glass, drained it in a single gulp, then, before she could protest, done the same with Lily's. 'Sibling rivalry, get over it.' Then he'd felt a bit queasy.

Still, Lily was vindicated about her theory of Marie's dates. Not long after they arrived home, Mattie phoned. 'Rita's Sebastian has asked for Marie's phone number.'

'Really?' said Lily. 'Do you think he's going to ask her out?'

'Definitely,' said Mattie. 'I'll have to baby-sit. Though he hasn't asked her yet, so she hasn't asked me.'

'But she will,' said Lily.

'I should imagine so,' said Mattie. 'It will be good for Marie. She could do with a night out.'

'Yes,' agreed Lily. Though this was worrying. If Marie started to see Sebastian regularly, he might start turning up at family get-togethers. Then Rita might start turning up too. Eventually there might be some sort of confrontation about the matter of the interview and the article Lily was struggling to write.

'It will be lovely,' said Mattie. She did not mention Marie and Sebastian getting married and having a child. Another boy, Mattie thought, would even up the family nicely. She thought Lily would say she was jumping the gun a bit. And such overbearing maternal enthusiasm would surely put Sebastian off.

Marie, unaware of the matchmaking that was going on, was trying to get her children to tell her about Andy and his girlfriend. She'd planned this carefully, knowing the dangers of having the children feel they'd returned from a day out to face the Spanish Inquisition.

Both Agnes and Tod had come home bearing gifts, Tod a skateboard and Agnes a watch. Quizzing them was tricky, since Tod wanted to go out into the garden to play with the skateboard, and Agnes kept telling her the time.

They'd gone to the Dynamic Earth exhibition, had lunch at Lucy's flat – spaghetti, and Coca-Cola to drink, followed by strawberry cheesecake ice cream, which Agnes declared was lovely and they should get some – and it was now twenty-two minutes past six. Tod was noncommittal on the subject of Lucy's flat except it had a huge bath and the kitchen had a microwave and a thing for making fruit shakes which he thought cool. Agnes said the walls were a funny pink colour.

'Plum?' asked Marie, eagerly.

'Yes, the colour of plums when they're going squishy. And we had to take our shoes off because of the carpet. It's twenty-eight minutes past six.'

Marie was piecing together a lifestyle – a spacious flat, dark walls, light carpet, a Magimix, probably chrome, a new Saab with, she'd noticed, leather seats. Money, she thought. This did not bode well for the custody case. Andy could afford a top-class lawyer. She'd be looking for legal aid.

A Bare Tummy and
Miles Armstrong's Dilemma

By the time Mattie, Rita and Lily had confirmation of Sebastian's intentions towards Marie, the pair had been living together at weekends for over a month.

Sebastian was a quiet, gentle man, never prone to rushing into anything. Watching his mother move from personal and professional catastrophe to personal and professional catastrophe had taught him that rushing into things could lead to heartache, frustration and the word *overdrawn* on the bank statement. And to sitting at the kitchen table at three in the morning cursing your folly. Rita had also taught him the joys of conversation, music, books and food. Still, he'd waited a week before calling Marie.

'Hello, this is Sebastian Boothe, remember me? We met at your mother's picnic.'

'Of course I remember you,' said Marie. 'You are my son's new hero. He wants to be a geologist when he grows up.'

'Excellent,' said Sebastian. 'He's a great kid, your boy.'

'I know,' said Marie. 'I brought him up.'

'So,' said Sebastian, 'would you like to go out to dinner sometime?'

Marie said she'd love to, but had a baby-sitter problem.

'Can't your mother do it?' he asked.

'She could, but it would be tricky,' said Marie.

'In what way tricky?' said Sebastian.

'I don't think I want to tell you that.'

'Oh go on,' he pleaded.

'Well, if I ask her, she'll phone Lily and they'll gossip and speculate and in no time we'll be married with a child, probably a boy, on the way and moving to a bigger house because this one is

232

too small. And my mother will start nagging me about not moving to Newcastle as soon as she gets through the door. I can't face it.'

'Neither can I when you put it like that.'

He asked if there wasn't someone else. In the end, Marie called her friend Connie, and Connie's mother baby-sat Connie's children while Connie baby-sat Marie's.

'Where do you want to go?' Sebastian asked the first time he picked her up.

'Anywhere where they don't ask if you want fries with that and offer you a happy hat. And I'd prefer if I could order alcohol rather than a shake.'

He nodded. 'Italian? Though your happy hat place sounds fun. My mother never took me to any dens of cholesterol when I was young.'

'Well, they're out there, thousands of them. The world in a bun. You can go to one any time I'm not with you.'

They ate Italian. They spoke about their childhoods, found they'd shared a fondness for Scooby Doo. They'd both read *To Kill a Mockingbird* when they were twelve. And both had seen *Back to the Future* three times. 'Excellent,' said Sebastian. 'We've a lot in common.'

'Back then,' said Marie. 'But I think you've left me behind.'

Sebastian said, 'Rubbish. I bet you still love Jaffa Cakes.'

Marie said, 'Ooh, Jaffa Cakes. Yes.'

Their first date was a swim through the time they'd been through before they got to this moment of being together. They spoke about their families, their hopes, dreams, but neither of them mentioned past loves. Marie worried about the children. Had Connie managed to get Tod and Agnes to bed at a reasonable time? Had Lauren woken up, found her gone and taken a tantrum? She didn't like to mention this concern to Sebastian.

On the Tuesday after their dinner together, Sebastian phoned Marie to thank her for coming out with him. He told her he thought her lovely.

'Don't flatter me,' she said. 'I can't cope with it. Insults, bad news are my routine fare. Flattery is unnerving.'

He told her she deserved a little flattery. But he wasn't trying to flatter her, he was telling her what he thought to be true.

On the Thursday he phoned again and asked if she'd like to come out with him the following Saturday. She said she'd love to but would have to check on the baby-sitting situation.

Connie's mother was still willing. This time they ate Thai. This time they just spoke. Marie couldn't remember what about. But did recall how easy it was to just chat. This time when Marie worried about the children she asked if he would mind if she phoned home. He gave her his mobile.

'I should get one of these,' she said, dialling the number. 'But they cost, and . . .'

'The washing machine's on the blink. And you need a new car,' said Sebastian.

She looked at him.

'Tod probably talks too much,' he said.

'Tod definitely talks too much,' she said. 'I don't think my car likes me. Probably because I don't look after it. I take it to the car wash now and then, and it usually goes when I want it to. But I can't really afford its upkeep, you know, tax, insurance, new tyres.'

'Don't drive on bald tyres. Please. I'll worry about you now.'

It was said with such concern that something within Marie stirred. She'd forgotten what it was like to be cared about by someone she wasn't related to. She phoned home, and was assured everything and everyone was fine. She relaxed enough to want to stay with Sebastian when the meal was over.

They walked. First to Princes Street, then along the shopless side, looking down into the Gardens and up at the Castle, which was floodlit. Sebastian remarked on how busy it was, even at night. 'It's humming.'

They walked up The Mound, stood a moment leaning on the railings, staring across the city. Old rooftops, spires, and the river beyond. 'It's lovely,' said Sebastian. 'I should come and live here.'

Marie said she'd like that. He took her hand. Up till now they'd been walking slightly apart, him with his hands in his pockets. Their palms pressed together, their first real physical intimacy made them smile. He lifted the entwined fingers and looked at them, admiring them, then smiled at her again. He thought taking someone's hand for the first time almost more romantic than the first kiss.

They walked on into the High Street, and down into the Grassmarket, where they bought a drink, and sat at the tables outside, people-watching.

'Isn't it strange how you forget about the night when you've been away from it for a few years,' said Marie. 'I stay home because of the kids. But all this is going on when I'm away from it. People, cars, taxis, noise, music. This used to be my old stamping ground.'

'Where you prowled in your teenage years looking for kicks.'

'Yeah,' said Marie. 'Looking for kicks, hoping to meet someone new and nice.' She smiled.

He said they should get back to the car, it was a long walk.

She agreed. But no, the car wasn't far away. They'd come in a circle. It was only a short walk along King's Stables Road to the car park.

He was disappointed. He wanted to walk and hold her hand.

He phoned her the next day, knowing she'd be feeling low. Her children were with Andy. 'I had a great time,' he said. 'So did I,' she agreed. He asked what she was doing. 'Sitting in the hall, talking on the phone to you. Then I'll probably take Lauren to the park.' He wished he could come with her.

He phoned again on Monday and asked what she was wearing.

'I've changed out of my good working skirt and shirt and have on an ancient pair of baggy pull-on pants and an old sweatshirt with number one written on it.'

'Sounds wonderful,' he said.

On Tuesday she lingered by the phone, willing it to ring. She left the door of the living room open lest she miss his call. She wondered if she should call him. Why not? He was a friend, people phoned their friends. Then again, she didn't want to appear forward. And what if he was busy, or didn't want to speak to her? Or, oh please no, with someone else. When her children were in bed, she finally plucked up the courage.

'Hello, it's me,' she said. 'I just wondered how you were.'

'Hello,' he said. 'I was just going to call you. I've been out with friends.'

Friends, she thought. He's got friends. 'Who are they?'

'Just people I work with. I'll introduce you.'

He'll introduce me, she thought. So he'll see me again, and one day I'll meet his friends.

On Wednesday he phoned her. 'I was thinking about you.'

'I was thinking about you,' she said.

And they both stood in their separate homes holding a receiver to their ear, smiling.

On Thursday, Marie's boss asked if she was all right. 'You're not coming down with something, are you? You seem distracted. And you were singing.'

'Was I?' Marie said. 'I'm not coming down with anything. I'm fine.' And she smiled dreamily.

'Well,' said her boss. 'This is a modern office. We have an image to maintain. I'd appreciate it if you refrained from singing songs as old as "It's Almost Like Being in Love" and do something a bit more appropriate to your surroundings. What about "Satisfaction"?'

'That's pretty old,' said Marie. 'You're showing your age now.'

'And you are showing your emotions. Very dangerous.'

Marie agreed, indeed it was.

On Friday she phoned Sebastian to tell him her baby-sitting arrangement had fallen apart, Connie's mother was having people to dinner, and Connie's oldest child had flu. 'Sorry,' she said.

Sebastian suggested they stay in. He would bring some take-away food, some videos and a couple of bottles of something special. Marie said, 'Sounds promising.' And worried that her children might not like him, or let her down by asking awkward questions and squabbling.

Sebastian also worried. What sort of takeaway food did children eat. Pizzas? No. They were good, but didn't really feel like a meal. Unless Marie made salad, but if she didn't know what he was bringing she might not have anything in the fridge. Indian? Too hot, and maybe the children wouldn't like that sort of thing.

In desperation, he did something he'd never done in his life before. He called his mother.

'I have this friend,' he told her, 'who is sort of seeing a woman who has a couple of kids.' He thought he would disguise identities by lying about the number of children. 'Anyway, they have a baby-sitter situation. They can't get one. So he's offered to bring along some takeaway food to her house only he doesn't know what sort. What do children eat? Burgers?'

'Burgers?' said Rita. 'Burgers? I don't think so. All those E numbers. The kids will get high, and they'll get no peace to do what they plan to do when the children are sleeping.'

Sebastian said, 'Oh.' And had a flashback to his youth. His mother standing at the freezer compartment in the supermarket, sounding off about global marketing and the corporate companies whose produce polluted the bodies of young children. He shuddered.

'I'd say,' said Rita, 'Chinese. You used to love Chinese when you were little. There is the MSG factor. But lots of dishes, fried rice, dumplings, noodles, prawns, duck, sweet and sour. Kids love all that. And the sharing helps break the ice. Yes, definitely tell your friend Chinese.'

Sebastian said, 'Excellent. Thanks. I'll tell my friend.'

'Who is your friend?' asked Rita.

'Um,' said Sebastian. His mind went blank. 'Miles.' He knew no Miles, other than the one who was playing on the stereo.

'Miles what?' asked Rita.

'Um,' said Sebastian, not wanting to say Davis. The CD stopped, another started. 'Armstrong,' he said.

'Well, you tell Miles Armstrong Chinese. Your mother says so.'

Sebastian said, 'Thanks, Ma.' And he would.

Rita put down the phone, and walked through to the kitchen feeling proud. He son had phoned and asked for her advice. How wonderful. It was as if she was a real mother. Then she thought: Miles Armstrong? He hasn't mentioned him before. She thought about the music she'd heard in the background. She reached for the kettle, and it struck her. There is no Miles Armstrong. It's him. He's seeing a woman who has children. It's Mattie's Marie; Sebastian is lying about the number of offspring to throw me off the scent. Sebastian is seeing Marie. Wonderful.

She turned and ran back to the phone. She had news, she had gossip. She simply *had* to phone Mattie. She picked up the receiver, and thought: Hold your horses, Rita. You don't know for sure. Wait till he tells you, wait till he wants people to know. Let him get to know her. It's time you stopped bloody shooting your bloody mouth off. This is your son, let him be.

She replaced the receiver, feeling mature, and a little big smug. Mature, she thought. A first, and at your age. You should be ashamed.

Sebastian phoned the Edinburgh Tourist Office to find the best Chinese restaurant in town, and then phoned it to ask if they'd fax him a menu. That done, he ordered a vast selection of dishes, enough, in fact, to feed about twelve people. He bought videos of Harry Potter, *Shrek* and *The Hours*. And from Oddbins bought two bottles of Australian chardonnay, one bottle of Chilean merlot and a bottle of champagne. In the end, he thought he'd overdone things.

Marie was stunned. 'How much do you think we eat?'

'I don't know,' said Sebastian. 'I needed to cover all the possibilities. What if nobody liked prawns? I got chicken just in case. And duck and beef and pork. And noodles in case nobody wanted rice, and prawn crackers and . . . well . . . everything.'

She led him into the hall, away from her children. Held his face, kissed him. 'You're such a fool. You could have just asked me what to bring.'

He said he hadn't thought of that.

That was the first time he stayed overnight. Then he always stayed over, but left on Saturday evening. Marie didn't want him around on Sunday morning when Andy collected Agnes and Tod.

'It isn't that I want you to go,' Marie told him. 'It's just I don't want anyone to know you've been here. My husband is threatening to take me to court, he wants custody of Tod and Agnes, and I want to appear to be an exemplary mother.'

'I think you are,' Sebastian said.

'No,' said Marie. 'I'm not. Believe me, I'm not.'

Sebastian said that sounded interesting.

'It's shameful and I'm never going to tell you about it. Please go. And know I am starting to like you. I wouldn't normally say that; affection is known to put men off because they mistake it for a need for commitment. Don't worry about that from me. I like you, I truly wish you could stay, but please go.'

So he went. He didn't mind at all really. Driving home to Newcastle in the early summer evening when the roads were relatively empty was pleasant. Besides, he was used to women who spoke their minds. When it came to speaking directly, Marie was an amateur compared to his mother.

But the deceit was doomed, as all deceits are.

He woke at eight o'clock one Saturday morning. Lauren, who had crawled into bed in the middle of the night to be with her mother, was lying next to him. A small face on the pillow, staring thoughtfully.

'Hello,' said Sebastian.

Lauren continued to stare. Then she started to cry. This wasn't her usual routine, what was he doing here? She cried harder. Sebastian put a tentative hand on her shoulder, said an ineffectual, 'Ssshhhh.' And the volume of Lauren's howls increased.

So Sebastian called on Marie, who was in the bathroom. 'Help.'

Marie appeared in the doorway, mouth foaming, toothbrush in hand. 'Pick her up. She's little, she needs reassuring.'

'What about?'

'I don't fully know, it's been a while since I was three. Maybe she needs to know there really is a God, or that we're not about to be made homeless. Whatever, all it takes is a cuddle.'

'Works for me, too,' said Sebastian. He leaned over and gingerly picked Lauren up. Which surprised her enough to silence her for a few seconds.

Marie disappeared back into the bathroom and continued brushing her teeth. Lauren, finding herself held at arm's length by a strange man, resumed her defence – howling.

Marie reappeared. 'That's not a cuddle, hold her close. Pat her. Sing her a little song.'

Sebastian did the first two, but the third defeated him. He rarely if ever sang, and right at this moment, when he needed one, all the songs he knew had vanished from his brain. He stared into space, thinking. Then, a flash of inspiration. A Human League number from his distant youth. '*Don't you want me baby,*' he sang. It stopped Lauren crying, but Marie came through and begged him to stop.

'Just talk to her,' she said.

He looked down at the little face that was looking up at him, wiped Lauren's nose and eyes with the sheet and said, 'Bet you didn't know that Isaac Newton discovered gravity. And he devised calculus . . .'

Marie came through and took Lauren from him. 'She's three, Sebastian. We're still on the grass being green, and cows going moo.'

'She looked interested,' said Sebastian.

'She'll grow out of it. We're all mathematically challenged in this household.'

Sebastian got out of bed, and pulled on his jeans. He took Lauren from Marie. 'We're just beginning to bond here. You butt out.'

'She needs her breakfast,' said Marie. 'You have to keep children topped up or they become insufferable.'

Sebastian insisted he was perfectly capable of making a three year old breakfast. 'Egg in a cup,' he said. 'I am master of the fine art of egg in a cup. Want some?'

Marie shook her head. 'You could make me some coffee, though.' Then, 'What in the hell is egg in a cup?'

'Boiled egg, peeled, then mashed up with a spot of butter, served with toast. Excellent. My mother used to make it for me. You can't whack egg in a cup.'

He went downstairs, Lauren bouncing in his arms. He started preparing breakfast. Laid out cereal for Agnes and Tod, filled a pan with water and put it on the hob, fetched eggs from the fridge, put the kettle on. Marie came down, sat at the table and said she could get used to this. Sebastian put a mug of coffee in front of her and told her not to, she was on the dishes. Tod and Agnes appeared, both in pyjamas, both still numb from sleep. Sebastian gave them both some orange juice. Agnes said she didn't want Rice Krispies, she wanted what Sebastian was making for Lauren. And Tod said he did too.

Sebastian said, 'More eggs.' Took them from the fridge and put them in the pot.

The doorbell rang. Marie said it would be the postman. Sebastian told her to drink her coffee, he'd get it.

'You should have a T-shirt on,' said Marie.

Sebastian told her he would, but she was wearing it. Marie apologised, she'd put on the first thing that came to hand and would give it back when she'd drunk her coffee. So, wearing only his jeans, barefoot and carrying Lauren, Sebastian answered the doorbell. Only it wasn't the postman. It was Mattie.

She stared, wrestling with reasons why this bare-chested man was standing in the doorway holding her granddaughter. She wasn't ready to embrace the obvious – he'd been there all night. 'Is Marie in?' she said.

'Sure,' said Sebastian. 'Come in.'

He shut the door behind her and followed her down the hall. He was, like Art, unaware of the shifting intricacies of family life – the tiny power moves, the small sways of affections, the momentary favouring of one relation over another, the absolute importance of telling your mother what you'd been up to recently. And the dire consequences of her finding out that one of her daughters had been seeing someone for several weeks without telling her about it.

Mattie liked to think that in her own quiet, tactful and superbly diplomatic way she was in control of her family. 'I see I've caught you at an awkward moment,' she said as she entered the kitchen.

'Not at all,' said Sebastian. 'It's great to see you. Have a seat.'

Mattie sat. Though she'd rather have stood.

'Just making egg in a cup,' Sebastian continued. 'Want some?'

'No thank you,' said Mattie. 'I've had breakfast. Egg in a cup? It's years since I made that.'

'You'll have coffee, though,' said Sebastian. He flicked the switch on the kettle. Settled Lauren in her high chair, put some slices of bread into the toaster, and set about removing the cooked eggs from their shells.

Behind his back, Mattie glared at Marie. Marie switched her gaze between the window and the tabletop. Then put her hand on her chin, and made apologetic eyebrow movements at her mother.

'Coming up,' said Sebastian. 'Egg in a cup prepared by a maestro.' He placed three cups on the kitchen unit, put an egg into each one and mashed them with butter. The toast popped up.

Mattie glared. Marie made her eyebrow movements. Tod and Agnes said nothing. They had lived all their tender years in this

241

extended family, and knew an atmosphere when they encountered one. They were wise when it came to navigating an emotional undertow; the thing to do was be good and say nothing. Lauren, however, was still naive when it came to such matters and banged the table with her spoon.

Sebastian buttered the toast. 'Toast soldiers,' he said. 'Just the thing.'

He served the breakfast, and made Mattie a cup of coffee, which he put in front of her. She thanked him stiffly. He made himself a cup, and because there were no chairs left to sit on, leaned against the sink. Then, noticing Lauren struggling with her food, and fearing it might all end up on the floor, he started to help her eat, popping spoonfuls into her mouth. Tod and Agnes kept quiet, ate diligently, not looking at anybody. Glad of having something to do.

Finally Mattie looked at Marie and said, 'Is that a new T-shirt?'

Marie pointed at Sebastian. 'It's his.'

He looked up and smiled. 'Suits you, though.'

Then Marie asked Mattie if this was just a flying visit, or did she want something?

'That book of summer recipes. Remember you borrowed it last year and never gave it back.'

'Right,' said Marie. 'I'll get it.' She didn't move.

Sebastian fed Lauren. Tod finished his egg and asked to be excused. As did Agnes.

Mattie sneaked a look at Sebastian. That's Rita Boothe's son, she thought, here in Marie's kitchen. Goodness me. He had a beautiful body, quietly muscular. Not overly bound with bumps and ripples. An interesting line of black hair stretching down from his belly button to his . . . Well, she didn't like to think of where that interesting line of hair went. He had lovely hands, long fingers. These hands had . . . She shook her head slightly, she didn't like to think of what these hands had done to Marie.

'So,' she said, 'how long has this been going on?'

'Oh, ages,' said Sebastian. He did not know that sometimes it is better to lie.

'Ages, and you didn't tell me.' Mattie turned on Marie.

And now Sebastian knew it was better to lie. He should have said, 'It's a new thing. Just happened.'

Marie shrugged.

Now that the children were out of the room, Sebastian felt free to talk.

'We thought it best to keep it to ourselves for the moment.'

Marie stood up, fearing Sebastian was about to talk about the custody case, shot him a fierce keep-quiet look over the top of Mattie's head, and said, 'I'll get your book.'

'It definitely seemed the thing to do,' said Sebastian. He was waving the spoon about as he spoke. Lauren was following it, mouth open wide.

'Does your mother know?' said Mattie.

'Good heavens, no,' said Sebastian. 'I don't tell Rita about my love life. And I certainly don't want to hear about hers.'

'Why ever not?'

'Too much angst. And analysing people and relationships and what he said and what he really meant by what he said. Can't be doing with it. Mind you, she's getting too old for all that now.'

'You're never too old,' said Mattie. 'Does Lily know?' She had to find out if she'd been left out of the loop.

'Don't think so,' Sebastian told her.

Marie came back with the book. Mattie took it. She was anxious to leave. She had news to spread. She absolutely had to phone Lily.

When Mattie got home, she parked the car in the drive and beetled into the house. 'You'll never guess,' she said to John and Grandpa, who were at the kitchen table.

'What?' said John.

'That Sebastian Boothe, Rita Boothe's boy, is at Marie's. And he's been staying the night. And it's been going on for ages and ages. And she never told me. And he's cooking breakfast, egg in a cup. And he's half-naked.'

John said, 'Which half?'

Grandpa said, 'Egg in a cup. With toast soldiers. I used to love that when I was a boy. Don't hear about it these days.'

'He made toast soldiers,' said Mattie. Then she looked at John scathingly. 'Which half do you think. Marie was wearing his T-shirt. That's a sign.'

'A sign of what?' asked John.

'A sign of deep intimacy. You don't wear the T-shirt of a man you hardly know. You'd have to have spent a few nights together before you wear his clothes.'

Grandpa and John exchanged surprised looks. This was new to them.

'I must phone Lily,' said Mattie. 'She won't know. And if she does know I'll want to know why she hasn't told me.' She bustled out to the hall.

John looked at Grandpa. 'Egg in a cup.'

'With toast soldiers,' said Grandpa.

'You do the toast,' said John. 'I'll get the eggs together, and tea, I think.'

'Yes,' said Grandpa. 'A cup of tea.'

When Lily picked up the phone, Mattie didn't bother with hello, or it's Mattie. She said, 'Did you know about Marie and Sebastian?'

'No,' said Lily. 'What about them?'

'They are only living together. I was just round there. And Sebastian was half-naked feeding Lauren egg in a cup.'

'Egg in a cup,' said Lily. 'It's years since I had that. You used to make it when I was little.'

'Never mind that,' said Mattie. 'Marie and Sebastian, and they never told us.'

'Well, you don't, do you? When you're sleeping with someone.' For a second Lily forgot who she was speaking to. 'I mean, I didn't tell my mother who I was sleeping with.'

'Why not? Who did you sleep with?'

'Nobody,' said Lily. Then, 'Did you tell your mother who you slept with?'

'I don't think that's got anything to do with you,' said Mattie. 'Anyway, Marie and Sebastian can't have known one another very long, but it all seems very intimate to me. She was wearing his T-shirt.'

'A good sign,' said Lily.

'You might think so, but if you rush at relationships they can come to grief. In my day you were advised not to kiss till the third date.'

'Did you wait till date three before you kissed John?' said Lily. Mattie didn't answer this.

'How long before you slept with him?' asked Lily.

Mattie didn't answer this either. It had been on their first date. It had all seemed so natural, the thing to do. They could tell there was something special going on between them. Furthermore, Mattie remembered, they'd sort of run out of things to say. But she wasn't going to mention any of this to Lily. 'I just thought you should know about Marie and Sebastian,' she said. 'And how hurt I am that Marie didn't confide in me.'

After she put the phone down, she thought she'd phone Rita Boothe (she still couldn't quite bring herself to call her by her Christian name alone); there might be a proper adult response from her. She picked up the receiver, and was about to dial, then doubted herself. She put it back, and went through to the living room to sit on the edge of an armchair, hands folded in her lap, and torment herself with her new knowledge. Nobody liked her. She was an irritating, interfering fool. She was a busybody with a big bum in pull-on pants. She replayed inside her head the scene of her arrival at Marie's house.

She hadn't combed her hair properly this morning. She had people coming for dinner tomorrow and had thought she'd make rhubarb pavlova for pudding, then remembered her summer cookbook was at Marie's. Without having a look at herself in the mirror, she'd picked up the car keys and driven over there, and had, therefore, arrived at Marie's door in rumpled pants, hair dishevelled and face shiny. She thought her cheeks fat, and she always had a puppyish, eager-to-please expression, slightly shy, slightly unsure of herself. And she had stood gawping at Sebastian, at his naked chest, the ridge of dark hair, the child in his arms, her grandchild, who'd squealed recognition that she'd been too astonished to acknowledge.

In her mind, she imagined herself barging past Sebastian, and stamping down the hall, through the living room into the kitchen. He followed. He'd have been watching her vast ungirdled bum sway, two enormous buttocks jostling inside her dreadful pull-on pants. Then she'd sat in that small, over-heated kitchen, arms folded, looking at her daughter as if she was a hussy. 'A shameless hussy,' said Mattie. 'Which she's not. She's a lovely girl who deserves someone to love her.'

Then Marie had sat looking at her, elbow on the table, hand over her mouth. To hide her laughter? Had she been mocking her? No wonder, fat-bummed glowering mother that she was. And there had been the eyebrow movements. What did they mean? Was Marie telling her that Sebastian's presence in her kitchen making egg in a cup was none of her business? And neither was it.

She went up to the bathroom, stared in the mirror at the object of her loathing. There she was, unkempt hair, fading blonde, fat cheeks, a network of crinkles round the eyes, full, wide lips, ideal for smiling and kissing, but she rarely used them for these things nowadays. They curved downwards in a desperately glum and disapproving look. Plainly Mattie loathed the person she was staring at – herself. She put her hands on her cheeks and pulled them upwards. Too much cheek here, she told herself, I could do with a facelift. She stared to make faces in the mirror, jutting out her chin to tighten the skin below her jaw. I've let myself go, she thought. I should do facial exercises. I should work out. I should get my hair done. I meddle in other people's business. I'm a horrible interfering old bag. She pulled her mouth down, widened her eyes. Revolting person, she thought. Get a life, Mattie. Then she told herself what she'd told Rita weeks ago. But I've got a life, I just don't know what I've done with it. It seems to have slipped away from me.

She ran a bath. Climbed in and lay back. She would change. She would stop fretting about her family. In fact, from now on she would stop advising and fussing, she would never phone any of her children again, she'd wait for them to phone her. She thought she might have to wait a long time for that to happen.

Lily thought about Marie, and what Marie was going through. A romance, the wonderfulness of it, when life becomes a waltz. The thrill of those first few weeks, phone calls filled with passion, wonder, longing and the bittersweetness of not wanting to ring off. Rushing to meet one another, recognising the face you have been aching to see moving towards you through the crowd. Thinking of the loved one when they are not with you, sighing, pondering what they might be doing now. All that, Lily realised, drifted away in time. The preciousness of being together mellowed to a quiet acceptance of each other's company and then mellowed some more into taking one another for granted. Not that she took Art for granted, or he her; she just worried that one day they might.

Recently she had stopped cursing herself for being good, dutiful, and had started to wonder why she sought this organised life she lived. She picked through her distant past, but it only came back to her in a series of moments – winning the essay prize at school, running after Rory on his bike that Christmas morning. There wasn't anything she could put her finger on, an instant, a twinkling even, that could have been the turning point when she'd decided to be the Lily she was.

And why was she so boringly good? In her pursuit of happiness she'd decided that goodness was safe. Or perhaps someone had whispered that notion into her childhood. She feared insecurity. And what did she want? Mystery and intrigue? How childish. She wanted her face to show the quiet and intimately seasoned wisdom of someone who pursued joy and wonder and had weathered the heartaches and sorrows that brought.

Everything flows, she thought. Everything in me, everything that happens to me happens because I'm the dutiful daughter. Everything that happens to Marie happens because she follows her heart. If I had not gone to see Rita Boothe, Mattie would not have been thinking about her, and might not have recognised her in the supermarket. They would have passed in an aisle without one noticing the other was there. Rita would not have been invited to Mattie's picnic. She would not have eaten John's special sandwich. John and Mattie would be living in harmony. Marie would not have met Sebastian. But I did, and everything flows.

Still, an affair, she thought, would be wonderful, an emotional pick-me-up. How odd, though, that while she could not bear to be unfaithful to Art, she could also long for the tingle of a new romance. Of course she couldn't just whistle such a thing up from nowhere. She had to meet someone, she had to fall head over heels for him, there had to be chemistry. Then again, she'd hurt Art. The thought of Art being filled with despair almost made her cry. She imagined him leaving her, sitting alone in a bedsit scanning the property pages for a new flat, drinking beer. He hadn't shaved in days in this vision, he was wearing jeans and an old T-shirt. He no longer cared about anything, including, or rather especially, himself. He ate tomato soup straight from the pot, while staring out of the window. He was drinking too much and that was affecting his work. His company was facing bankruptcy. He was in misery and it was all her fault.

'I'm sorry, Art,' she said.

Art, it being Sunday, was sitting at the kitchen table eating toast, reading the *Observer*.

'What for?' he said.

'Nothing,' she said.

'You're sorry for nothing? C'mon, Lily what are you thinking about now?'

'I was imagining what you'd do if I left you. And I thought you might go to pieces.'

'Did you? Well perhaps I'm not as fragile as you imagine. Perhaps I'd be fine.'

'You wouldn't miss me? You wouldn't let yourself go? You wouldn't be heartbroken. Well that's not very nice of you.'

'You left me, remember. You're the one that's not very nice. Who did you leave me for? Are you having an affair?'

'No. I was thinking, that's all. I was just thinking how wonderful it is at the start of an affair, the kisses, the phone calls, the longing.'

'We kiss. We phone each other. I long,' said Art. 'Sometimes I think about you when you're not there, and I'm sitting smiling.'

'Do you?' said Lily. 'That's so nice.'

'Don't you think about me when I'm not here?'

'Yes, of course I do.'

The conversation was getting heated.

'So who were you having an affair with in your imaginings?' said Art.

248

'Nobody. There is nobody. I was just inventing a scenario, that's all.'

Art said that he didn't come out of this scenario very well. 'How do you know I wouldn't find another woman, and it would break your heart to see me with her when your cheap little toyboy had abandoned you for someone else?'

'Toyboy? Me? I'm not old enough to have a toyboy. It's your bit of fluff would go off with some rich bloke. Women like that do, you know.'

'Who says I'll fall for some bit of fluff? I'll have a sexy, intelligent, funny woman, who wears a thong as she goes about the house. We'll live in Hampstead and probably have a golden retriever. So fuck you with your toyboy.'

'I wouldn't dream of having a toyboy. I'll have a wonderful man who wears Paul Smith suits and works in the media at something or other. We'll live in Primrose Hill and have a Siamese cat.'

'Sounds a bit girly to me,' said Art.

'Your woman is too easily swayed by fashion,' said Lily. 'I don't like her at all.'

Art said, 'Neither do I. I think I'll leave her and come back to you, if you give up the girly bloke with the Siamese cat.'

Lily said she would. They both said, 'Fine.' Then drifted into a strange, disquieting silence. Till Art said, 'What was that about?'

Lily said she didn't really know.

'Do you want to have an affair?' he asked.

Lily said, 'No. Of course not.'

'Then what's up with you these days? You've gone all weird and into yourself. And what's with the tattoo, and the car? You hardly ever drive it.'

'I hate it. I bought it in a fit of pique. I was pissed off at my mother for having a misspent youth, and making me into a dutiful daughter. The family goody-goody. I want to be like Marie, she's so sexy and full of some sort of secret knowing. I'm so organised and neat, there's nothing interesting about me. I want mystery and intrigue.'

'You can't buy mystery and intrigue or have it stamped on your arse.'

'So tell me. I know.'

Art said, 'Oh Lily, what are we going to do with you?'

He thought she did have mystery and intrigue. He thought Marie and Mattie and even Rita Boothe would be surprised at the things Lily did in the dark. When the lights were out and she slipped between the sheets she became the extravagantly naughty Lillian. Though Lillian hadn't been around much recently. Art missed her.

'This is the stupidest argument we've ever had,' said Lily.

'I was thinking that,' said Art. 'But I was hurt that you thought I was such a loser I'd fall apart without you – ruin myself with drink.'

'I was hurt that you wouldn't,' said Lily.

Art said, 'I love you, Lily. I think you ought to remember that.'

And Lily said, 'Have you ever had egg in a cup?'

The Letter

It was a new thing, Agnes slipping her hand into her father's. For their first few outings she had refused to let him touch her. When he'd tried to help her zip up her jacket, she'd turned adamantly away from him, telling him she could do it herself. Once, when he'd put his hand on her shoulder, guiding her across the road, Agnes had wrestled it off. She was a big girl now and didn't need help crossing the road. Taking her hand had been impossible; she'd pressed her arms hard into her sides and looked straight ahead. So, to Andy, this small palm touching his brought joy.

He had found the meetings with his children thus far a strain. Neither Agnes or Tod spoke much, and they were both unnervingly good. He imagined Marie had told them to be. When in Lucy's flat they sat neatly side by side on the sofa, and did not pick anything up – an ornament, a framed photograph, a CD – turn it over, examining it closely. Andy envisioned Marie lecturing her children, 'Be good and for heaven's sake don't *touch* anything.'

On their first date he'd taken his children to the Dynamic Earth exhibition. On their second they'd gone to the cinema, and he decided afterwards that this hadn't worked. They'd sat in darkness, looking ahead at the screen, and hadn't exchanged a word. He knew he needed to talk to his kids, he needed eye contact. They had to get to know one another again. So he'd taken them swimming, and to the park to play football or to toss a frisbee about. He believed in all things physical. Exercise, he thought lifts the spirits, frees the mind. When his children were exhilarated from running and playing, they'd come to him, be at ease with him, and he'd start healing the rift.

It was happening. Tod and Agnes were beginning to open

251

up, ask questions. Where had he been? Why didn't he live with them any more? He answered as best he could. He'd been in Canada, but he'd missed them both too much so he came home. And he'd always sent presents for Christmas and birthdays. He didn't live with them any more because he lived with Lucy. He'd paused then, considering the wisdom of asking Tod and Agnes if they'd like to live with him and Lucy too. But thought it too early in the new relationship to propose drastic changes in their lives. Best wait. Meantime, he'd filed for divorce, and when that came through he'd marry Lucy. Then he would fight for custody of his children. And win, he was sure of that.

He and Agnes had been playing tennis – it being tennis time of year – in the park near the flat he and Lucy shared. They'd been standing not very far apart, and he'd hit gentle balls to her, that, in time, she could return. 'Excellent,' he cried. 'A little Navratilova in the making.'

Agnes had no idea who Navratilova was, but knew a compliment when she heard one, and glowed. Across the park Tod and Lucy were also playing tennis – part of Andy's plan that Lucy should befriend his children.

'Get to know them. And let them get to know you,' he'd said. 'This is vital when it comes to the court hearing. They must want to come to live with us.'

Lucy had agreed on the importance of this. But children were difficult. She wasn't used to them, and she'd noticed they couldn't sustain long conversations about Bergman films – which she loved – or books by Anita Brookner. She considered this to be a flaw in anybody she met, even if they were only nine, or, in Agnes's case, six going on seven. And children were hard to figure out; you never knew what they were thinking. They had small faces that life had yet to make a mark on. Still, she was trying, for Andy's sake. He desperately wanted Agnes and Tod to come and live with them.

'To be a family,' he'd said. 'Then, when we have a couple of kids of our own, we'll be a big happy crowd.' Then he'd said, 'They're mine. Part of me. I miss them. I love them. I want them here in my life.'

Lucy didn't know what to make of that. She liked things the way they were, but didn't like to mention it. He'd sounded so impassioned. She knew he was still suffering from finding his wife in bed with his best friend. He'd been very depressed when she first met him in Canada over a year ago. But slowly slowly he'd emerged from his gloom, and asked her to return to Scotland with him, and to marry him. Contact with his children had cheered him. She'd seen a side of him she hadn't known about. He was a caring, loving father. Still, sometimes she thought he'd never wholly trust anyone ever again.

Andy and Agnes finished their game, and walked over to Lucy and Tod. It was a warm day, four o'clock, time to go home and start making something to eat before the children went back to Marie. There were other people about; sounds of their games and laughter drifted over to Andy and Agnes. Dogs were being walked, children played on the swings. It was the sort of afternoon Andy had dreamed about. Birds hopping on the grass, an aeroplane far, far above them, a couple of boys riding their bikes, someone over there flying a kite. It looked, he thought, like something from a picture book.

Then, oh joy, Agnes had slipped her hand into his. He looked down and smiled at her. She was lovely. Small, blonde, full-lipped, dark eyes, like Marie, he couldn't deny that. But she wasn't Marie, she was Agnes, a small person in the making. He liked the way Marie dressed her, dark red and blue striped T-shirt and jeans. He felt proud to be walking with her small hand enclosed in his. He felt the tug at his arm as she skipped along beside him, three little hops to his one step.

'I don't think our grandma likes Sebastian,' she said, out of the blue.

Andy looked at her. 'Who is Sebastian?'

'Mummy's friend. He was there yesterday when Grandma came round for her cookbook.'

Andy's mind raced. What to ask next?

'So why doesn't Grandma like him?'

'She never said anything to him, she just stared. He was giving Lauren egg in a cup. We got some too. He's very good at that.'

'That sounds very nice of him,' said Andy. 'Why did Grandma stare?'

'I think it was because he had nothing on. She was looking at his tummy. It's quite hairy.'

'He was naked?' said Andy.

Agnes nodded. 'Nothing on. He didn't have anything to wear, Mummy had on his T-shirt.'

'Does Sebastian stay all night?'

'Oh yes,' said Agnes. 'He sleeps in Mummy's bed, and in the morning he makes us breakfast, and yesterday he had nothing on.'

Andy abandoned his carefully planned scheme. He would not wait for his divorce, nor would he wait to marry Lucy. He had evidence of naughty doings. He knew deep within himself that what Agnes was saying was unlikely to be true. It would be a strange person indeed who served breakfast to his lover's children in the nude. And he did not see Marie cohabiting with anyone so inclined, or, indeed, allowing anyone who wanted to flaunt his unclothed body before her children to cross her threshold. But he did not want to acknowledge this glimmer of logic whispering in the depth of him. He'd found an excuse for demanding custody of Agnes and Tod right now, and he'd use it.

For weeks after he'd returned from Canada, Andy had watched his children. He'd parked across the road from Marie's house and observed her leave in the morning. The four of them, Marie, Tod, Agnes and Lauren, would, it seemed to him, tumble out of the front door and into her car. Lauren would be strapped into her safety seat. Tod and Agnes climbed into the back seat and bobbed about, constantly chattering. Andy would follow them to Mattie and John's house, and wait. Always, half an hour after going in, Marie would come out alone. Then, not long after that, Mattie would leave with Agnes and Tod and drive them to school. He would follow, and park some way behind Mattie. He'd watch his children running from the car into the playground and getting lost in the throng of kids waiting for the bell to ring and the school day to begin. At half past three he'd be there again, watching as Agnes and Tod emerged and climbed into Mattie's car. She would drive them back to her house. Andy always parked a few doors down, and waited. At around six o'clock Marie would arrive to pick up her children and take them home.

Andy knew his family's routine, and more. He had watched Tod play football in the park, he'd been there to see his son learning to ride his bike. He'd been outside the sports shop when Marie bought him a safety helmet, and in the viewing gallery when she'd taken all three children to the swimming baths, and there in the cinema, three rows behind Marie, Tod and Agnes, when they'd gone to see a Harry Potter film. Lauren had stayed with Mattie that afternoon.

He felt he was getting to know his children again. It was Lucy who pointed out that that was fine, but they didn't know him. And furthermore, his watching them was becoming obsessive, and it wouldn't be long before someone spotted him following Marie and Tod and Agnes. He could find himself under suspicion of stalking. It was true, Andy agreed. He would approach Marie for visiting rights, and take it from there.

He loved his kids, he wanted them in his home. He wanted to see them fresh-faced and full of the morning first thing every day, and watch them slip into sleep when he put them to bed every night. And when they shouted out in the dark seeking comfort for a sore tummy or dragons and demons that visited in bad dreams, he wanted it to be his name they called.

Three days later Marie received a letter from Andy's lawyer telling her, formally, that her husband wanted residency of their children. There would be, at Andrew Hampton's insistence, a court hearing following a social worker's assessment of the family situation. This would probably mean a visit to her home, and interviews with her children Tod Hampton and Agnes Hampton. She was advised to seek legal representation.

Standing in the hallway in her dressing gown, Marie read and reread the letter. Then shoved it into her handbag so she could read it over and over again at lunchtime. She went through the motions of morning, waking her children, getting them washed and dressed for school, then drove them to her mother's. She had a cup of coffee, then left, saying she had to get into work early. In fact, she wanted, in the quiet of an empty early-morning office, to read the letter again. Maybe in a different location it wouldn't seem so troublesome. It did.

Nor did it seem any better when she read it four more times over lunch, a tuna sandwich and a bottle of mineral water at her desk. Reviewing it again as she had a cup of tea and a chocolate digestive biscuit at half past three in the afternoon didn't help. It was still dire. It remained dire when, at home in the evening after the children were in bed, she read it again.

Then she put it away in her underwear drawer, which was on the top left-hand side of the chest in her bedroom. She decided she would not think about it, and it might just go away. This was the best way to deal with bad things, ignore them. In the depths of her, an undertow of logic told her this was not a good plan. But right now she was not thinking, she was reacting to what she felt in her stomach, in her throat, in her heart.

She walked through her days, battling a gnawing dread that something awful was about to happen. She worked at hiding her apprehension. She smiled, she played with her kids, she made love to Sebastian. She applied to the bank for a loan to cover her divorce and court case costs.

'What is the loan for?' she was asked. And not wanting to admit the truth, she said she needed a new car. Her bank loans manager had brought her statements on to his computer screen, noted she had been overdrawn for the past two years and was making no inroads on her overdraft, and told her he didn't think making repayments on a loan would do anything for her present situation. She was refused.

So she went back to ignoring her problem. Except that she noticed that her silent prayers, that had, since Sebastian came into her life, almost disappeared, had returned. 'God help me,' she whispered in the evenings while standing at the kitchen sink, in her bath, in traffic jams, at night in the dark before she went to sleep, and again at three in the morning when she woke and went downstairs to make herself a cup of tea, and sit drinking it in the silence of a sleeping house. 'God help me, because nobody else will.'

'You're sighing a lot these days,' said Mattie.

Marie was sitting at the kitchen table, Friday morning, sunny, the last day of school before the summer break. Tod and Agnes were out in the shed with John, inspecting the kite, which was still, after six months, under construction. Time had dampened the children's initial enthusiasm, but they still took a little interest and dreamed and speculated about the maiden flight. They both wanted to hold the strings.

John had gone off the whole notion, but persisted doggedly. He didn't want the kite to join the heap of discarded objects that had once been great notions at the back of the shed. The biggest of these was the sledge. There would be no such failure this time. The kite was going to be amazing.

Inside, Mattie sat opposite Marie, and said, 'Yes, sighing. I've noticed that lately.'

'Am I?' said Marie. 'I hadn't noticed.'

'Well I have,' said Mattie. 'Is anything wrong?'

Marie shook her head. 'Probably just the prospect of the school holidays. Six weeks of Tod and Agnes complaining of having nothing to do. And I can't afford a holiday.'

'It isn't you has to cope with them. They'll spend most of their time over here.'

'I know. Don't think I'm not grateful,' said Marie. 'I don't know what I'd do without you.'

'Oh, it's a pleasure to have them around,' said Mattie. 'In fact, John and I were thinking of going to Holyrood Park to watch the kites this Sunday; we thought Tod and Agnes and Lauren might like to come along.'

'Oh, they can't on Sunday. Andy takes them.'

This was news to Mattie. 'What do you mean, Andy takes them?'

'I mean,' said Marie, looking at her watch, 'Andy takes them.' She stood up, collected her handbag. 'I have to go. I'll be late.'

'I don't care if you're late. How long has this been going on?'

'He phoned a while back and said he wanted to see his kids.'

'And you said he could, just like that? He walks out then he walks back in again, and wants to see his children. As if he had a right.'

'He *has* a right. He's their father. And I thought it would be good for Tod and Agnes to get to know him again.'

'What about Lauren?'

'She's little. It's Tod and Agnes he wants to see right now.' Marie headed for the front door.

Mattie followed. 'That's terrible. I'm shocked. You are letting him trample all over you. He can't disappear then reappear and want to pick up where he left off.'

'He doesn't. He's got a new girlfriend. He just wants to see his kids.'

'A new girlfriend? Who is she? And why haven't you told me any of this before? Why am I always the last person in this family to know what's going on? Does Lily know?'

'No,' lied Marie. She was tired of this. She wanted to get away. She opened the door and started down the path towards her car.

'Does Rory know?' Mattie was still on her heels. 'Do you think I'm too old and too stupid to understand? I'm your mother, I have a right to know what's going on. It's about respect, you know.'

Marie got into her car, started the engine, rolled open the window, leaned out, said, 'I know. Respect. I've told you now. See, I respect you.' She drove off before she broke down and confessed about Andy wanting residency. This was her secret, and she was good at secrets.

Mattie stood in the middle of the road watching the car go. Nobody bloody tells me anything, she thought. None of them. I'm their mother, and they keep secrets from me. Things I ought to know. I could help, it's good to know someone cares. I could make them a cup of tea and listen. It's what I do best.

She took Agnes and Tod to school. And when she returned she went to find John and tell him about Andy seeing his children on Sundays.

'And Marie never even told me,' she said. 'What's that about? I'm her mother, she should tell me things.'

'Maybe she needs her own space. Room to make her own decisions.'

'I'm not treading on her space. I just like to know what's going on. It's as if all I'm good for is looking after the children when she's at work. It's hurtful she doesn't tell me things. She didn't tell me about Sebastian, and she didn't tell me about Andy. Does she think I'm too old to understand?'

John shrugged.

'I love them, all three of them,' said Mattie. 'I can't help it. Sometimes I really wish I didn't. I didn't want this. I remember, I wanted babies. But babies don't last very long. A year top whack. Then they are children, and children go on for ever. Nobody told me that.'

Running

'The thing to do when you are down,' said Lily, 'is buy knickers.'

She laid four new silky pairs on the sofa, admiring them. Feeling the silkiness. Enjoying the soft slip of material against her fingers.

'So the level of your depression is four pairs of knickers. You must be feeling pretty down then,' said Art.

'Not so much down,' said Lily, 'as not up.'

'How much did this cost?'

'Not telling,' said Lily. 'There was a sale on,' she lied.

'Not telling and a sale on means a lot,' said Art, knowing that Lily's knickers would not have come from Marks and Spencer. 'Why can't you just drink, it's cheaper. A couple of vodkas. I wish you'd discover beer. A swig of beer, a chat, another swig, more chat. That's the thing to do – go down the pub, mingle, get drunk. A tenner'd do it. Knickers? How many pairs of knickers do you need?'

'A woman can never have too many pairs of knickers. You never know when you'll need them.'

He stared at her, puzzling over this. 'Like there might be a knicker emergency one day?'

'You don't understand,' she said.

'So tell me.'

But Lily couldn't. She knew he would have no sympathy with her passion for extortionately expensive underwear. He'd mock her need to be special all the way down to her skin, to have, beneath her designer clothes, designer knickers and bra. Art could never comprehend the secret upmanship of luxurious lingerie.

Mornings, these days, she ran. It was a new thing, this padding early pavements and park. She saw people and lives she never knew existed, yet they were only yards down the road.

She met other runners. And as they pounded along they would

acknowledge her in their city way. They would break from their private reverie to look at her as she passed, a simple acceptance that she was in the same place doing the same thing as they were.

The old bejewelled lady in the fur coat who Lily had seen on her first outing, however, came to recognise her, and would smile and say, 'Good morning.' This daily greeting cheered Lily. Slowly the thick wall she felt she was living behind disintegrated, and she felt that all that separated her from the rest of the world was a thin membrane that was easily broken with a smile or a nod, and all she had done to earn these things was be in the same place at the same time every morning, be a face other faces had seen before.

The movement, the rhythm of it unleashed her thoughts. At first she'd tried to organise her thinking, as she organised everything in her life. Today, she'd tell herself, I am going to think about my Rita Boothe article as I run. But soon her thoughts would turn into ideas, notions, speculations, and then, running more, running further every day, she found she was not thinking at all. There was only the sound of her feet on the pavement, or on the path in the park, the beat and thwack of rubber sole on concrete, and her breath in her throat. There were pigeons and starlings that scattered reluctantly as she approached, and squirrels, and there was wind in the trees. She was flying, mind devoid of everything but the nowness and the sweetness of the moment. It was the happiest she'd been in years.

It was worth the humiliation and shame she'd felt when Art had discovered her initial deceit. He'd suspected she wasn't actually going running – the faint whiff of bacon when she got home, the slight trace of grease round her mouth. One day, going in to work early, he'd passed the café where she sat every morning reading a newspaper, drinking a latte, eating her regular morning roll, and had caught a glimpse of her sitting looking content, and a little smug.

Next day, a few minutes, after Lily had left, he followed her. He watched her run, smoothly, elegantly, the short and hardly taxing route to the café.

'Good run?' he asked when she returned home, feigning exhaustion.

'Excellent,' she said. 'I really think it's doing me good. I'm getting into the rhythm of it.'

'Liar,' he said.

'What do you mean?' She looked wide-eyed, innocent, hurt even.

'I mean you haven't been running at all. Lily, you have spent over two hundred quid to buy an outfit to run to a breakfast café up the road and run home again. What's that about?'

In truth, she couldn't tell him. But thinking about it, she saw his point. The next day, she skipped the bacon roll stop-off and ran. She had been running every morning since.

Marie, too, was running. But not like Lily. Marie was running madly. Escaping her demon – the letter in her underwear drawer. At work, in quiet moments, she'd remember it and her fears would fly. She confronted herself with a series of dire what ifs. What if her children were removed from her home?

She imagined the scene, burly social workers and policemen carting her screaming offspring out of the house, and she too would be screaming, running down the garden path after them, beating the invaders with puny fists, weeping and wailing, trying to clutch Tod or Agnes and drag them back indoors. She imagined neighbours coming out of their houses to watch. And when the car that would transport the two offspring to Andy's house drove off, she would collapse on the ground shouting their names. 'Come back, come back,' she would cry.

What if there was a court case, and Andy's lawyer told the judge in a loud, censorious voice that Andy, poor fellow, had come across her frolicking and laughing and having noisy sex with his best friend, and had been a broken man? Now he wanted to remove his children from this brazen hussy and give them a decent, warm, secure and loving upbringing. 'I need hear no more,' the judge in her imagination said. 'I award the husband residency of his children. And you,' turning to point at her, indignant finger rigid, 'you, despicable harlot, will pay costs.' She winced at this.

What if Andy moved back to Canada, taking Agnes and Tod with him, and she never saw them again? She and Lauren would eke out lives of loneliness and penury paying off the prohibitive court costs. She imagined herself wearing a shabby dress, a desolate creature, standing in the downstairs bedroom, now a shrine to her missing children, with framed photographs round the walls and their few remaining toys on the shelves, weeping over a bashed training shoe Tod had left behind.

Her eyes would fill with tears, it was too much to bear. She had to get away, and if she could not escape her actual dread imaginings, she could remove herself from the place where she'd thought them up. She'd take a file from the top of her desk (to give her mission the appearance, at least, of importance), leave the room, walk at a quickening pace to the stairs, run down the three flights to the reception foyer, turn around and run back up again. In some small way this helped. But after a few hours the waking nightmares would return, and she would have to leave the room again, run down the stairs, and up them again.

At five o'clock she would run across the car park, and if she had to shop before picking up her kids from her mother's, she'd steam round the supermarket, trolley skidding before her.

Once, when making spaghetti bolognese for supper, she discovered she was out of garlic, and told her children to sit still while she went to Mattie's to borrow some. She did not take the car, but instead ran the ten-minute distance it took to get there. She'd burst in, found her mother in the kitchen and said, 'Quick, quick, do you have any garlic?' Mattie had fetched some from her vegetable basket, said it was a lovely evening and they were about to have a gin and tonic outside in the garden, and why didn't she join them? By now, Marie was worried about Tod, Agnes and Lauren. They were alone in the house, and though they knew where she was, and could easily use the phone, Marie had convinced herself that something dire had happened. They'd put on the cooker and flames were leaping up the wall and across the ceiling. A team of social workers were banging on the door, and, on discovering the children left unattended, would take them away to foster homes.

'I can't, I can't,' she said. 'I must get back. I've left the kids on their own and I think they're on to me.'

'Who?' said Mattie.

'Never mind,' said Marie. And she left at the same speed she'd arrived, rushing out of the front door and down the path, Mattie at her heels.

'What do you mean, they're on to you? What are you talking about?'

'Nobody,' said Marie. 'Forget it.' She raced away along the street.

Mattie went in and told John the oddest thing had happened. Marie had burst in, borrowed some garlic and rushed out again saying someone was on to her.

John had puzzled over this. 'Perhaps you should phone,' he said.

'I'm not phoning,' said Mattie. 'I promised myself I'd stop phoning and wait till I'm phoned.'

'You'll wait long enough for that,' said John.

'Lily phones,' said Mattie. 'She's good.'

John agreed that Lily was indeed good, but right now they were worried about Marie, and if Mattie wasn't going to phone, he would.

Marie ran through the streets, heart pounding. This was stupid, she should have taken the car, she should have phoned Mattie and asked her to bring some garlic round, she should have cooked the pasta sauce without garlic, her kids, she was sure, would not have noticed the difference. Home, she stood at the front door, listening. Silence. She went in, down the hall and into the living room. Her children were on the sofa watching the television programme they'd been watching when she left, all sitting exactly where they'd been twenty-five minutes ago.

She leaned against the wall, gasping for breath. 'Everything all right?'

They looked at her in mild surprise and nodded. She went into the kitchen, sat at the table and slumped forward.

Agnes came through and patted her. 'You shouldn't run, Mummy. You're too old.'

'I am not too old,' said Marie. 'I'm just not as fit as I used to be.'

'Aunty Lily's fit. She runs every morning. She runs a hundred miles.'

Marie was about protest that Auntie Lily did no such thing, but said instead, 'She would.'

❉ ❉ ❉

Mattie had taken to drink. Not that she was sinking into an alcoholic abyss, but she was pursuing happiness and found that two gin and tonics helped. In fact, they helped so much Mattie wished she'd thought of it before.

'We'll sit in the living room by the fire and have a small G and T before supper and chat about what sort of day we've had,' she said to John.

'Why?'

'Because it's what people do,' said Mattie.

'What people?'

'People,' she said, frustrated at being questioned. 'Real people. Civilised people.'

'And we are not real, or civilised?'

'Ye-es,' a sing-song reply, giving the word extra syllables. 'But really civilised people contemplate the end of the day with a coming together over a drink, they don't go about flapping their arms, complaining and bickering like we do. They are in control.'

'What do you mean, in control?'

'I mean they have nice lives, and in the evening they have a gin and tonic and talk about them.'

John's mind crowded with things he could say about this, but the thought of a gin and tonic every evening by the fire was pleasing, so he agreed. This made Mattie happy; she felt she was a step nearer joining the real, civilised people who were out there. People who seemed to have, in her imagining of them, pleasant faces that never showed pain or anger. Maybe they didn't have any emotions. Maybe, if they had, they could cope with them better then she did. Anyway, she was sure that these people had a gin and tonic before supper and sat talking cordially about nice things in a nice way, and she wanted to be like them. They would talk about what they'd done, or maybe what was in the news. They would not talk about the children who did not really stay in touch.

'Let them go,' John had said to her. 'Let them be. Live your own life and stop being a spectator in your children's.'

Good tip, Mattie had thought. So they would gather in the evening, the three of them – Mattie, John, and Grandpa, who she still couldn't bring herself to call Martin. Two drinks, she told herself, a reasonable amount, not too much. But she didn't quite stick to that. She cheated.

Three long glasses on the kitchen unit. Ice, gin, tonic, a slice of lemon. Then she'd sip from each glass, checking, she convinced herself, that they were all the perfect mix. Then she'd top them all up, and sip again from each one, making sure she hadn't spoiled the cocktail. After that, she'd carry them through, and they'd all sit and drink and stare at the fire and hardly speak at all, because none of them had really done very much.

'I finished my library book,' Mattie might say. 'I must go and get another.'

John would say his kite was coming along and the lawn needed mowing. Grandpa would watch the news and say hardly anything at all. Soon it would be time for a refill. Mattie would take the glasses back to the kitchen, set them in a row on the unit. Ice, gin, tonic, lemon. Then the checking the mix, a serious routine. This in fact meant that Mattie was drinking a deal more than she admitted. If the sips were counted, she'd have been discovered to be having three drinks to everyone else's two.

Still, it made her, well, not quite happy, but momentarily jolly.

Rory smoked dope. Evenings he sat beside the open window of the living room, drifting, dreaming, and not speaking to Isabel. He wasn't quite aware of ignoring her, he was just seeking to be in a happy place where his quiet contentment was not about to be shattered by marriage and the arrival of four children.

But Isabel knew very well what he was doing. For years, before she'd met Rory, she'd lived with and nurtured a black musician, Tobias. At first the affair had been hectic, glorious, filled with wine and dance. She'd gone to gigs and stood proud, she was the lead guitar's girl. The thrill she'd felt when he stepped from the stage and put his arm round her, she'd basked in the envy of every girl in the room. She'd travelled with him the length and breadth of France, Italy, Belgium and Spain. These had been her wonder years. They were followed, unfortunately, by what she called her nursing years. Tobias's addiction had taken over both their lives. Isabel had suffered, tending him through sweats, wiping up vomit.

She'd driven across town to bring him home, semi-conscious, from bars and parties. She'd fooled herself she was doing *a good thing*. She was, in her way, contributing to his art. She was helping to keep him alive. One day she'd looked in the mirror: she was twenty-seven and looked forty. The worry, the abuse she'd suffered – his arguments, his insults. Hurting her feelings was something she could understand, forgive, even. She was a woman, passionately aware of her body under her clothes. Naked it was perfect. She was proud of her beauty, carried that pride everywhere she went. Ruining her looks was contemptible. She left him and went home to her mother.

When she'd met Rory, she'd decided he was her soulmate, her destiny. He was calm, humorous, affable. He was charming. Reliable. He was good in bed, always willing. He was happy to shop with her on Saturdays. He adored her. And he was comfortable with older women. He relaxed with her friends. In fact, she'd noticed he was a lot more at ease with women about ten years older than he was. She decided he just liked their maturity.

Now this. He was smoking dope, seeking oblivion. Was this what she did to men? She asked her mother when they met for lunch, a regular Thursday thing.

Her mother, a tall, severely elegant woman, had sipped from a demi-tasse and said, '*Non*. You should not have told him of your intentions. Marriage, he'd do that in time. But babies, you shouldn't have mentioned them. Men don't like babies, I have come to think. They are scared of them. The noise, the mess, the smell and all the attention they take away from them. Children they love. Children they can play with, and children adore their fathers. You should just have presented him with a baby. "I'm pregnant," you tell him. Then here is it, your child. In time he'd have come to love it. Then you present him with another. Don't give him time to think about it.'

'You think?' said Isabel.

'I know,' her mother told her.

'He just sits and stares, he is lost in his own head,' said Isabel.

'Throw him out,' said her mother.

But Isabel doubted she could do this.

Her mother leaned over and gripped Isabel's hand. 'Throw him out, and he'll come back, and he will give you babies. I know this.'

Isabel sighed. How she wanted a baby; the longing consumed her. It seemed it was all she could think about. And now she wanted one, they were everywhere. Until recently she hadn't noticed this. But now she just had to turn around and there was a pregnant woman, cheeks blooming, belly swollen, sailing along the pavement in front of her. And there were babies, being carried in slings, pushed in prams, in cafés, in shops, on the streets – babies everywhere. And, oh, she wanted one.

Rory blamed Lily for his new habit. It was her mention of having an epiphany while running. 'The joy of movement,' she'd said. 'I get high on it. I see myself and my life anew, like having an epiphany.'

He and Marie had discussed this on the phone a few days later.

'What does she mean?' Rory had asked. 'Is it like a sudden glowing light from above? And she suddenly loves herself and everyone about her?' He'd gone for the heavens opening and a hand descending pointing to Lily and showing her the way ahead description.

Marie had dismissed this. She imagined something more orgasmic. A pulsating and thoroughly, almost heart-stoppingly, enjoyable moment of truth.

In fact, Lily, at the time, had been running only as far as the café a couple of streets away, and the only epiphany she might have had was to discover that eating a hot bacon roll, at a table outside on a sunny day, or inside in the steamy warmth when the weather was dull, was a lot better fun than pounding alone through the dawn.

Seeking enlightenment and the meaning of his life, Rory wandered the seedier quarters of the city. He figured he was more likely to find inner understanding when observing people less fortunate than himself. Not that he ever saw anybody who really fitted into that category; everyone seemed relatively happy and busy.

He'd always been fascinated by narrow streets, alleys, wynds. Lanes that led from one main thoroughfare to another. The danker the better. He could not really explain the allure, except perhaps to say that if anything interesting was going to happen to him, he was sure it would be in one of those confined, claustrophobic, dark places. The one he walked up on the day of his finding the dealer in the finest cannabis he'd ever bought was challengingly long, frighteningly dark. But standing at the edges of it, Rory smelled Turkish coffee, spices, tempting things. A few steps in, these scents had been replaced by piss and stale Gauloise. There were long fire escapes, bins, boarded windows, and there was a small café.

When he stepped inside, all conversation stopped as the patrons turned to stare at him. He felt his heart shrink. He was too close-shaven, too neatly dressed, too British for this place. Two old men with gnarled faces were drinking cognac, though it was only nine in the morning. He ordered a coffee, and took it to a corner table. Drink swiftly and go, he told himself. But he didn't. He sat, looking about him, feeling that his presence disrupted the seedy flow of the place.

He wasn't surprised when he was approached. A youngish man sat opposite him and asked if he wanted anything. Rory shrugged. A self-seal polythene bag was placed on the table. Rory opened it, examined the contents: the best cannabis he'd ever been in contact with.

This was what he'd dreamed about when he was a student, it was the stuff of fables and tall tales about seeing God. He bought. He emptied his wallet, and left the café a happy man. In the weeks to come he was to empty his wallet many times, and when Marie eventually plucked up the courage to phone him and ask for help, Rory could offer nothing more than genuine sympathy. He couldn't give her any money, he had very little left.

The Magic Words

It was inevitable that Marie would eventually break down and tell somebody about the solicitor's letter hidden in her underwear drawer. Her out of sight, out-of-mind policy wasn't working. The more she tried to banish it from her brain, the more she worried about it. Now this anxiety was a constant hum within her. She was fretful, abstracted, snappish all the time.

'What's up with you these days?' said Sebastian. 'You're always in a bad mood.'

'Am I?'

'Yes,' he said. 'Is something bothering you?'

'No,' she said. But squeakily and not meeting his eye, because it was a lie.

They were sitting on the sofa watching a film he'd hired from the video shop. Ten o'clock, the children were all in bed. It was warm outside, the windows open, sounds of summer drifting in – the swish of cars passing, the thump of music from nearby houses, calls from gardens. Someone somewhere was having a barbecue.

'Well, you seem distant. It's like you're not here half the time,' he said.

'I'm here,' she said.

They both stared silently ahead for a while, looking at the film. An old man was in a hot tub when a large lady climbed in beside him; it was meant to be funny, but neither Sebastian or Marie laughed. They were too preoccupied with their own thoughts.

'Is it me?' said Sebastian. 'Are you fed up of me? You want to stop seeing me?'

'No,' said Marie. 'It's not that. I'm not fed up of you. I . . .' She nearly said *I love you*. But stopped herself. Not that. Not now. She didn't have time to fall in love at the moment, she had too much to worry about.

'Well, what then?' he asked.

'Nothing.'

They continued to look at, but not actually watch the film. There was an atmosphere, thick with unspoken thoughts: Marie's worry, Sebastian's speculations. Then she blurted out, 'They're going to take my children away.'

He looked at her. 'Who is going to take your children away?'

'Them,' she said. 'The courts. Andy has got a lawyer and he is suing me for custody of Tod and Agnes.'

'Not Lauren?'

'I can keep her,' said Marie.

'So what does your lawyer say?' Sebastian asked.

'I don't have one.'

'Why not?' he said. 'Are you going to fight it on your own?'

'No.'

'So why don't you have a lawyer? What are you going to do?'

'I don't know. I don't know. I don't know. Stop asking me questions.'

'OK. But you can't just sit about waiting for something awful to happen. You must do something.'

'What?'

'Get a lawyer. Fight back.'

'How can I? I can't afford a lawyer.'

'No, babe, wrong. With what's at stake, you can't afford not to have a lawyer.'

'That's all right for you to say. Have you any idea what these people charge?'

'No, what do they charge?'

'I don't know, I haven't asked. But at the moment I have thirteen pounds in the bank. I'm assuming this won't cover it.'

'So deal with that when the bill comes in. You may not have to pay anything at all if Andy loses and is ordered to pay costs. You should proceed with that in mind.'

'How clear-headed and logical you are,' said Marie.

'I find that in seriously important matters logic helps,' said Sebastian.

'I find that in worrying matters logic stops my flow. You can't have a really good worry when somebody keeps coming up with logical things to do.'

'It clears the mind,' Sebastian told her. 'It wins arguments.'

'Pah,' said Marie. 'That's so like a man. It's underhand and downright sneaky to use logic in an argument. If you're quarrelling you should scream at each other, hysterical nonsense, say things you regret, then cry, then go to bed and shag each other witless. That's an argument. Logic ruins it all.'

'No passion,' said Sebastian.

'Exactly,' said Marie.

He got up and went into the hall. She heard him dialling a number on the phone, and went to find out who he was calling.

'My mother,' said Sebastian. 'If you want passionate persuasion about what to do, Rita's your man. She knows everything, gives wonderful advice, and I've never once heard her use logic.'

They heard the phone at the other end of the line ring, then Rita's voice, 'Hello.'

Marie backed out of the hall, waving her hands in front of her, shaking her head. 'No, no. I don't want to speak to her.'

Sebastian said, 'Hello, Rita. How are you?'

'Fine, how are you?'

'Fine. I've got Marie here. She needs to speak to you.'

'How intriguing,' said Rita. 'Put her on.'

By now Marie had backed into the living room. Sebastian ran after her, and dragged her to the phone, stuck the receiver in her hand. 'Speak to Rita.'

'Hello,' said Marie.

'Marie,' said Rita. 'How wonderful to speak to you. So what's all this, then?'

'I have a problem,' said Marie. 'My husband is filing for divorce, and he wants custody of my children.'

'My goodness,' said Rita. 'What does your lawyer say?'

'I haven't got one.'

'Well you must get one right away.'

'I can't afford it.'

'Who can?' said Rita. 'I have known many, many people who have had to turn to a lawyer at one time or another, and not one of them could afford it. And may I say, I know many, many lawyers, and not one of them looks as if they haven't ever been paid. They are all quite disgustingly rich. There are ways. Instalments, some lawyers will accept payment by the month.'

'Will they?'

'Oh yes.'

'But I don't want to go to court. Everything will come out.'

'What's everything?' said Rita. She was sitting by the phone and wished she had a cup of tea beside her. This sounded like it was going to be a long conversation.

'What I did,' said Marie. 'I did a terrible thing.'

'What?' said Rita. She'd known many women who'd done terrible things; indeed, she had done terrible things herself. Frankly, she thought, Marie didn't seem the type.

'I slept with another man,' said Marie.

'A bit of adultery may not be a superbly humanitarian thing to do. It may even be terrible, but it shouldn't affect the outcome of your case.'

'You think?'

'I more than think,' said Rita. 'I know.'

'But my husband caught me in bed with another man. It was meant to be a special night, and he got talking. We were at a party, and I went upstairs to the loo, and his friend came after me. And he kissed me, he lured me, he enticed me. I was so delighted someone was interested in me, I just gave in to him. I am a terrible person.'

'Hardly. A moment's weakness is all. It doesn't make you terrible. For heaven's sake, I once gave a speech to a hall full of three hundred businesswomen with my skirt tucked into my knickers. And it was reported in the press, with photographs.'

'Good heavens,' said Marie. 'But that's not so much terrible as stupid.'

'True,' said Rita. She paused, considered which of her many, many embarrassing moments she should confess to Marie. She trawled through what she thought of as her ludicrous life, her absurd decisions, tricky situations. It wasn't an activity she relished. Too much to squirm about, she thought. 'Well,' she said, at last, 'if it makes you feel better, I once went to a rather upmarket garden party. It was a refined occasion, the women wore hats. I got a little worse for wear on champagne, which always has an effect on me. I should avoid it, but I don't. Tired and emotional is the expression. Only tired didn't come into it. I got frisky and emotional with my hostess's seventeen-year-old son. We were in the library, it was that sort of house. And I must say, I was enjoying myself immensely, when the door opened and in came – I shall give you the list – my hostess and her husband, my then partner, an editor whom I had been trying to interest in a book I wanted to write about the matriarchal society – he didn't even read my synopsis – several ladies from the local bridge club, the vicar, and my mother. They had been getting a tour of the house, which my hostess was extremely proud of. So you see, no matter how terrible you think you are, there is always someone worse. I don't know why this should be, but I know it's a comfort. I was on top, by the way, so I got a good view of their entrance, and of their astonishment.'

'Goodness,' said Marie. 'What did they say?'

'My dear,' said Rita. 'They were middle class, they didn't say anything. Well, not to my face. I have no doubt they said a great deal behind my back, though. My partner left me, and my mother didn't speak to me for two years, though she did send me a Christmas card. My hostess, who is still a friend, suggested it might make for a more convivial atmosphere if I left, which I did as soon as I was dressed. We laugh about it now; well, she does, I squirm. But at no time did anyone think to remove Sebastian from my care. The only thing that matters in terms of who your children live with is who they want to live with, and are they being cared for properly at the moment. It seems to me yours are being well looked after. You seem to be a wonderful mother. Infinitely better than me.'

'Oh, I'm sure that's not true,' said Marie.

'But it is true. I was an appalling mother, and I'm sure that if Sebastian had been given the choice of who he'd rather have lived with he'd have picked his father.'

'No,' said Marie. 'That can't be true.'

'It is,' said Rita. 'I have no illusions about that. You can fool most of the people most of the time, I have found. But, unfortunately, as I have also found as I get older, you cannot fool yourself at all.'

Marie said nothing.

'You must by now know that too,' Rita continued. 'You have been trying to fool yourself that this pending law suit won't happen, that it will, somehow, magically go away. But deep inside you know it won't, so you've been worrying and worrying. Stop that and go to see Claire Bradley.'

'Who is that?' asked Marie.

'A friend. A lawyer, and she's formidable. I'll give her a ring tomorrow to tell her to get in touch.'

When she finally put down the phone, Marie went through to the living room and sat beside Sebastian. She felt strangely enlightened, as if someone had briefly pulled aside a curtain and given her a glimpse of a new way of living. There was Rita Boothe, occasionally brilliant, more often extravagantly absurd, living, breathing, telling deeply embarrassing stories about herself. You'd think, Marie thought, that someone who'd done such things would have to spend what was left of her life hiding, lying down in some darkened room with a blanket over her head. But no, she got up every morning and carried on with her life. Who would think when they saw the nattily turned-out seventy-ish lady that she had once been caught starkers and whooping with joy straddling a strapping lad of seventeen in the library of a country house? You just never knew about people.

She turned to Sebastian. 'Your mother, gosh.'

Sebastian said, 'I know. Appalling. But you have to love her.'

And it was a comfort to know that somebody had done worse things than she'd done and survived. All those years with Andy, when they'd both worked hard at being the perfect couple, holding hands in public, arms round each other at parties and family gatherings, and she'd blown it in a matter of ten minutes. It was bound to happen, she now realised: she'd held her tongue too often, buttoned her lip, kept her own counsel at moments when she should have let go, spoken her mind. The perfect couple, she thought, would not be so dishonest. The perfect couple would know that the truth of love, the safety of it, means you can shout, rage and argue without everything falling apart.

She thought all this, then swallowed hard. Then tears came. It was the relief of having told Sebastian her troubles and having heard Rita tell her she wasn't as terrible as she imagined and of, perhaps, having the formidable Claire Bradley, whoever she was, on her side.

Sebastian looked at her. Held her face, wiped the tears with his thumb, then pulled her to him. Kissed the top of her head and said the magic words of comfort, 'There, there. Never mind.'

Rita Boothe's cookbook had been on the shelf in Lily's kitchen for months. Every so often she would take it down and read a few recipes, fascinated. She knew that some people cooked by following a rigid formula, and others by intuitively throwing things together. But this was the first time she'd come across a book that tried to put simple culinary instinct into words. Measurements were haphazard: some of this, a spot of that, two or three glugs of wine. Timings were vague: cook for a couple of songs on the radio, leave in a moderate oven for as long as it takes to go to the bedroom, make love, sigh and stretch, have a cigarette and a little post-coital chat, that should do it nicely. A slow casserole can be left to cook for as long as it takes to phone your mother. That long. *Omelettes*, Rita had written, *take up a small slice of your life. They demand your total attention, unlike other dishes you can ignore for a while while you kiss the one you love, or banter with your friends or read a chapter of Jane Austen. However, since they cook up quickly, your absence from the rest of your life is fleeting, and probably worth it. And, like life, they should not be overfilled.*

Throughout the book were references to love, sex, affairs, relationships and kissing. It made Lily sigh that someone could cook with such abandon. She cooked carefully, constantly returning to her recipe, checking that she was doing things properly.

It was inevitable, then, that one day she would try some of Rita's dishes. Not that the actual food really interested Lily, it was the suggested method of producing it that caught her fancy.

She started with the Welsh rarebit, insisting that Art come into the kitchen with her since it was to stay under the grill for as long as a lingering kiss.

'How long is a lingering kiss?' said Art. 'One man's lingering kiss may be another man's snog.'

'Don't be silly,' said Lily. 'A lingering kiss is poetic and gentle, a snog is lustier and can be lengthy as it usually leads to more snogging, and things beyond snogging.' It struck her that this was more or less what Rita had written in her book. 'I think I'm getting the hang of this,' she said.

'A wodge of bread,' Art said, reading the recipe.

Lily placed her bread knife on top of the loaf. 'Is this a wodge? Or this?' Putting the knife further along, indicating a thicker slice.

'That one,' said Art. 'We don't want to skimp.'

Lily agreed. 'Skimping isn't Rita's thing at all. I don't think she'd even know the meaning.' She cut two fat wodges of bread. Then started to grate cheese as Art put them under the grill. She carefully scooped up a tablespoonful of cheese and dropped in into a bowl.

'No,' said Art. 'This is hearty, hands-on cooking. Take a fistful and slap it down.'

Lily complied. Heaped cheese in the bowl and mixed in the other ingredients with her hands. Finally she took a bottle of beer from the fridge, opened it, and poured some into the bowl. 'A hefty glug,' she said.

Art took the bottle, and added another. 'That glug wasn't hefty. It was girly.'

Lily heaped the mixture on to the untoasted side of the bread, and put it under the grill. She turned to Art. 'Now for the best bit.'

They kissed, Lily's arms spread wide so her cheesy fingers would not mess Art's shirt. After a minute she pulled away. 'No tongues; that's snogging, not a lingering kiss like it says in the recipe.'

'The recipe's not seriously specific about quantities, it isn't totally specific about the kiss either. It could include tongues; then again, it might not. Depends on the kissers.' They kissed again, enjoying it more now that tongues were allowed. And lost themselves, mouths, lips, the smell of each other's skin and the enfolding aroma of cheese browning. When they stopped, eating was no longer on their minds. They stared at one another for a moment, slightly breathless.

Then Lily said, 'The cheese.'

It was golden, melted, slightly singed at the edges. They took their slices across to the table to eat.

'Good,' said Lily. 'I think I could get the hang of this sort of cooking. I think I know what Rita Boothe is saying – enjoy everything, the cooking, the smell of it, the feel of the ingredients.'

'She's telling you to enjoy your life, make it hearty, a glug of wine and a kiss.'

'I enjoy all that. But I've got too many worries to enjoy it all the time. I'm always waiting for the worrying to be over before I let myself enjoy everything all the time. It's like I'm waiting for my worrying to be done with, then my real life will start.'

'Worrying is life. Solving problems is life. It won't ever be over. You have predicaments, but you still glug wine, make love, that's how life is,' said Art, taking a swig from the bottle of beer.

'How very profound of you,' said Lily, taking the bottle from him and drinking. 'Have you been reading Aristotle again?'

'I'm just naturally wise,' taking the bottle back.

'So what is love, o wise one? I think love is like this cheese,' taking a bite, 'all melty and golden.'

'Love is like cheese,' Art scoffed as he chewed. 'I think love is knowledge. You only love someone once you know them. Then the more you know them the more you love them.'

'Sometimes the more you know somebody the less you love them.' Lily took the bottle.

'Then you didn't really love them in the first place.' He leaned over and kissed her.

He tasted of cheese and beer, but then so did Lily. He took her hand, led her out of the kitchen. They were just entering the bedroom when the doorbell rang.

'Ignore it,' said Art.

Lily looked down the hall. She found it hard to spurn the insistent calls of the telephone or the front door bell. But she let Art lead her towards the bed.

The bell rang again. Lily stiffened. 'What if it's someone we know? It might be important.'

'It'll be Jehovah's Witnesses or some sort of survey. C'mon, Lily.'

The bell rang and rang. Lily let go of Art's hand. He sighed. She went to open the door, and find out who was so insistently ringing the bell. It was Rory.

❊   ❊   ❊

It was inevitable that Isabel would tire of Rory's silence. Though it was a surprise to him that he'd been uncommunicative, there was such a lot going on inside his head. But mostly it was too dreamy and intangible to put into words. Still, he was mildly perturbed when Isabel told him he'd hardly spoken a word to her in three weeks.

'You just sit there, staring. You seem happy, but I'm not,' she said.

He stared, said he was sorry, and continued to stare. It was hard to share what was inside his head, the vividness of the things he saw. And Isabel's voice was cracking the surface of his contentment; he felt himself getting irritated, almost fearful of demons within.

'I think,' Isabel said, 'that you do not want to marry me. But I also think you do not want to marry anybody. You want things to stay as they are.'

He put his hands over his face, he needed to shut her out. But Isabel was not to be ignored.

'Everything changes. Nothing stays the same.'

Rory put his hands over his ears. It wasn't really what she was saying, it was the insistency of her voice that he had to stop. 'Shut up,' he said.

'I won't shut up. How dare you tell me to shut up. This is my flat, I will not shut up in my own home.'

'You don't understand,' said Rory. 'I need you to stop talking. I can't cope with your voice droning on like this. Shut up. Shut up. Shut up.'

'No,' said Isabel. 'You don't understand. I want a baby. I need to have a baby.' She started to cry with longing.

Rory got out of his chair and ran to the door. 'Stop speaking at me. I can't take it. You have to stop.'

'I won't stop,' cried Isabel. 'We are not going on like this. You sitting staring, me tiptoeing round you. I want a baby.'

Rory ran out of the door, stood in the hallway pressed to the wall, breathing. He heard Isabel turn the key in the lock behind him. It was a sobering sound.

He walked, hauling air into his lungs, blinking against the sunlight. There were sounds, traffic, people talking, an aeroplane overhead, but they did not disturb the silence in his head, he could handle this. As he moved through Saturday crowds he felt the encroaching nightmare fade away, he came to himself. He slowly realised that he had clamped his hands over his ears and yelled at Isabel to shut up, and he had also run from the flat. Now he was locked out. He sat down at a café and ordered black coffee and a glass of water. He was a fool.

A family came by, and sat at a table across from him. The mother and father seemed to be about his age; their daughter, Rory thought, must have been about three or four. She had black hair, brown eyes, and when her father leaned down to lift her on to his knee, she smiled. It was dazzling. It was wholehearted. Rory wondered what it would be like to be bathed in such total and unquestioning love. The girl was dressed in a dark blue hooded top and shorts that reached almost to her knees, on her feet scarlet shoes, obviously new, for every now and then she would stretch her legs out in front of her and admire them. Rory could tell that neither mother or father were as enamoured with the shoes as their daughter. But her pleasure delighted them.

Rory thought that Isabel's daughters would be like that. Mischievous, headstrong and utterly beautiful. Suddenly he wanted his unborn, indeed yet to be conceived, daughter to be here with him. To be clambering on to his knee, winning his heart, knowing he would spoil her, give her everything she wanted – scarlet shoes. He thought: Isabel's right, we should have children. Not babies, but who would want babies, messy, noisy, toothless, bald, incontinent? But they grew into such exquisite creatures. He wanted one too.

He would go to Isabel, now. He would beg her to let him in, he would plead and grovel if must be. He would tell her how wrong he'd been. She would take him in her arms, and they would make babies. He stopped. The thing to do was take her a gift – flowers, champagne, perfume, that sort of thing. But for that, he would need money.

On his way home, he took a detour to the bank, climbed the steps to the cash machine and withdrew enough money to buy goodies to enthral Isabel. He put it in his pocket, and, as he was replacing the card in his wallet, turned to run back down the steps. He was excited by his enlightenment – children were OK – and whirled round too quickly, lost his footing and fell, tumbling over and over down to the pavement. He lay, stunned, feeling a wet trickle of blood where his head had hit the edge of a step. His wallet was on the ground, several feet away from him. For a few minutes the shock of falling stunned him, he did not move. Someone passed by, looked at him, assessed the situation, moved on and with one deft sweep picked up the wallet and walked away. Rory was stupefied, he did not call out, he did not even move; all he saw of the thief was a pair of swiftly retreating Nike shoes.

He got up, and nursing his wounded forehead limped home. The door was still locked; he rang the bell. He heard the key turn, and there was Isabel. He'd imagined she would see him, the state he was in, and take him in her arms, cooing sympathetic words. She would bathe and bandage his cuts and bring him comforting things to drink.

But Isabel was done with her nursing years. Seeing Rory, knowing what he'd been doing, buying dope, she concluded he'd been mugged in some seedy, smoky bar, she knew such places well. Enough, she thought. Never again. She shut the door.

Rory rang the bell over and over. He beat with his fists on the black painted wood, calling on Isabel to let him in. When she finally appeared in front of him again, it was to hand him his suitcase and stiffly tell him goodbye.

He knocked on the door again, politely this time. Isabel answered, looked icy.

'My passport,' he said.

Isabel shut the door, returned after a few minutes, opened the door and handed over the red document. Then she shut the door again, went to sit on the sofa, smiling. His passport, now she knew where he was going. To Lily. He always turned to Lily when things got dire. He spoke to Marie, but when life got rough he went to Lily. Her eyes widened. Lily. That was what Rory saw in her: she reminded him of Lily.

She got up, went through to the bathroom to stare at herself in the mirror. She looked nothing like Lily. She was better looking than Lily, had a wider mouth than Lily, darker eyes. But she was bossy like Lily. She loved expensive things like Lily. She went to the kitchen and made coffee; she needed to think about this.

As she sat by the window, looking at the geraniums on the small balcony outside, it came to her. Rory had been brought up in the company of women, a boy with no brothers and a father who went away early in the morning, returned late. He might seek the companionship, the camaraderie of men, but he'd always love the comfort of women. Ah, she thought, now I understand. He's mine. He'll come back, and never go away again.

Rory walked slowly away. He had enough money to get to the airport, buy a ticket for a cheap flight to Heathrow, then a tube ride to King's Cross, and the Northern Line to Angel. After that he walked till he reached Lily's flat.

'Rory,' she said. And let him in.

He thought she smelled of beer and cheese. She led him to the kitchen, told him to sit at the table while she fetched some TCP and Elastoplast. She washed the wound on his head, dabbed it with the disinfectant and covered it with strip of pink plaster. She brought him a glass of whisky. Listened as he told her what had happened.

'I'd been doing a lot of dope,' he said. 'She threw me out.'

'I'll phone Isabel and explain,' said Lily. 'I'll see if she will cancel your credit cards, it'll be easier for her to do over there, probably. The bed's made up in the spare room, if you want to dump your things.'

Rory sat on the bed in Lily's spare room, and phoned Marie.

Lily spoke to Isabel: she told her about Rory's enlightenment, about how he was getting money to buy her some gifts to win back her favour. About the child he'd seen and how he'd thought he'd like one too. She asked Isabel to please cancel Rory's credit cards, 'Though it may already be too late,' she said. 'I think you ought to talk to him,' she added.

'Tomorrow, when we both have had some sleep,' said Isabel. Now she had him, she'd make him suffer a little more before taking him back.

Rory told Marie everything.

'What did Lily say?' asked Marie. 'Did you get a lecture about smoking dope and facing up to your responsibilities?'

'She never said anything,' Rory told her.

'Yeah,' said Marie. 'I remember she never says anything. She picked me up at four in the morning once, I'd got stuck on the other side of town without any money, and it was December and I was freezing. I rang home from a phone box and reversed the charges. She came right away. Took me home, ran me a bath to heat me up. Made me coffee, never said a word about it. She's like that.'

'Yeah,' said Rory. 'Makes you feel really guilty, doesn't it?'

'I know,' said Marie. 'You wish she'd scream and rage. But she doesn't. She's so good, you feel bloody awful.'

'What am I going to do about Isabel?' said Rory.

'Go back to her. Beg her to forgive you. Tell her you want to have babies with her. Beautiful plump babies. Then she'll cry and say she's sorry she threw you out. And you take her in your arms and say the magic words.'

'And what are the magic words?' said Rory.

'There, there. Never mind,' Marie told him.

'What!' said Rory. 'I can't say that. That's a crap thing to say. That's the sort of thing your mum says.'

'Worked for me,' said Marie.

Grandpa's Death,
Another Non-Event

The tall windows of Claire Bradley's office looked on to the private gardens of Herriot Row in Edinburgh's new town.

Herriot Row, thought Marie. Too expensive. It costs a bomb to even park here. If they charged for it, I wouldn't even be able to walk along the pavement here.

The room, painted pale blue with white cornices, was not what Marie had imagined. It was airy, spacious, modern paintings on the wall. Marie had thought it would be browner – an old desk, covered with piles of mouldering files, a row of cabinets containing the legal histories of divorces, wills, litigations. She'd thought, or rather hoped, Claire Bradley would be small, rotund, motherly. With her hair in a bun, perhaps, and tiny wire-framed glasses and a tender smile. In her dreams, Claire Bradley had offered her a cup of milky tea and patted her shoulder and said the magic words of comfort, 'There, there. Never mind.'

But no. Claire Bradley was in her mid-forties, tall, dressed in black skirt and jacket, hair in a bob and no spectacles. She was crisp and efficient, and Marie had the impression she had never said the magic words of comfort to anyone, ever. Still, there was comfort to be gained from the fact that Claire Bradley seemed to know exactly what to do about Andy's claim to have custody of his children.

As she wrote down salient points and read Andy's solicitor's letter, Marie stared out of the window. In the private gardens a woman sat reading a book and shoving a pram to and fro in front of her while her baby slept. A blackbird sat on the branch of a tree, beady eye alert for dangers. Squirrels ran, bouncing, across the grass. Marie liked squirrels, though some people thought them

284

vermin. But they gave her hope. When rounding a city corner and coming across one sitting, say, on a parking meter, or a litter bin, it made her look again at man-made urban spaces and the things that furnished them, and see them the way other species saw them.

'Your children are how old?' said Claire.

'Tod's nine. Agnes turned seven last week. We were going to give her a party, but she wanted a trip to the cinema for her and her friends. Then we went to McDonald's.'

Claire nodded.

More than she needs to know, thought Marie. I should have said somewhere more upmarket than McDonald's.

'Right,' said Claire. 'And what have you granted your husband since he returned from Canada?'

'Sorry,' said Marie. 'What do you mean by that? I haven't been sleeping with him, if that's what you think.'

'No, it isn't what I think. I mean have you granted your husband visiting rights with Tod and Agnes?'

'Oh. Yes.' Marie squirmed.

'Pity,' said Claire. 'We could have bargained with that. Don't give him anything else. If he wants the children to stay over for a weekend, for example, get him to have his solicitor write to me.'

'Why?'

'We can bargain. He can have Tod and Agnes to stay certain weekends and holidays if he forfeits the right to have them permanently.'

Marie brightened. 'Will that work?'

'Doubt it, but we always try. Your husband left four years ago – why?'

'He walked out,' said Marie. 'He just left.'

'Was the marriage under some strain?' Claire asked.

'Not until the night he left. Not until the moment he left, actually.'

Claire looked quizzical.

'He found me in bed with his best friend at a party. He turned and walked away, and just kept on walking. I didn't mean it. I don't know what got into me. Well, alcohol got into me. And I was tempted. It's so nice when you think someone wants you; well, someone you might want back wants you. It's flattering. I was flattered. I was drunk. I have been guilty for four years.' Stop talking, she told herself.

Claire was looking at her. She was thinking something, Marie suspected it was something derogatory. She'd told this woman too much, and it made her want to ask personal questions of her. Where did she live? Did she have a nice house? Was she married? Did she have children? A dog, or a cat, perhaps? Had she ever committed adultery?

'Until he got in touch telling you he wanted his children to come live with him, you had heard nothing?'

'Nothing,' said Marie.

'No phone calls, no letters. Nothing.'

'I wrote to him every so often telling him about the kids, how they were doing at school, their hobbies, if they'd been ill. He'd write back to Tod or Agnes, sending them money. But he never wrote to me,' said Marie.

'He didn't send *you* any money?' said Claire.

'No,' said Marie.

And Claire smiled. 'Excellent. I do believe the Child Support Agency will be interested in that.'

'That's not very nice, reporting him. After all, it was all my fault. Everything was my fault.'

'Marie,' said Claire, 'your adultery will have very little bearing on the case. What the court will be interested in is your children's welfare. Are they cared for? Secure? Happy? Whatever the reason your husband left, he has a duty to help care for Tod and Agnes, and Lauren too. That's the law.' She stood up. 'I think we're through for today. I'll be in touch soon.'

'Um . . .' said Marie. 'How much is all this going to cost?'

'It may not cost you anything if the court finds in your favour. Then again, I charge one hundred and forty pounds an hour. My fees depend on how much I have to do. A recent case cost my client fifteen thousand pounds. I have another client who has just been charged two hundred pounds, and will shortly be receiving a bill for a further two thousand. I doubt it will end there.'

'What?' said Marie. 'I have been refused legal aid. They said I earned too much. But I can barely manage on what I get. They did say I might get some help with the payment, but they wouldn't cover it all.'

'I suspected you would be refused legal aid. Your fee might also include a charge for a lawyer for Tod. At his age, the court might decide he needs his own representation.'

'He's nine, for heaven's sake. What does he need a lawyer for?'

'He's old enough to have his own opinion about who he wants to stay with, therefore he might need someone to put his case across for him.'

'My God,' said Marie. 'This is awful. I never knew any of this.'

'It can get messy, I'm afraid,' said Claire. 'Hopefully it won't come to that.'

Driving back across town, all Marie could think was, My God. My God. Then, one hundred and forty pounds an hour, that's about five and a half grand a week. That's almost three hundred thousand a year. Of course she'll have overheads. But, my God. I should have stuck in at school. My mother was right.

She had decided, it being half past four, that it wasn't worth returning to work. She headed for Mattie and John's instead. She had asked for the afternoon off, and had decided to tell the truth – she had to see a lawyer, her husband wanted permanent custody of her children – rather than opting for her usual gynaecological excuses.

As she drove through the thickening pre-rush-hour traffic, she thought about her meeting with Claire Bradley. Apart from being stunned at the estimated cost of the impending court case, she was also amazed to find that Tod might need a lawyer. She thought children and lawyers a diabolical mix.

She stopped at traffic lights, pulled down the sun visor to shade her eyes from the afternoon glare. It was hot. What if Tod starts considering the possibilities of having a lawyer and sues me for making him eat vegetables? she thought. What if he decides to stay with Andy because he lets him watch all the television he wants? And I can't see either Andy or his girlfriend insisting he eat broccoli. I can see issues developing here. As she drove, her worrying became frenzied.

She was not, then, in any mood to deal calmly with the grim

atmosphere that greeted her when she arrived at Mattie and John's house.

Marie rang the bell and went in, shouting, as she always shouted – as indeed everyone in the family shouted – 'Hello. It's me.' The silence was awful. The thick, heavy silence.

Mattie was in the kitchen. 'We found Grandpa lying on the lawn.'

'No,' said Marie. 'A heart attack? Is he dead?'

'Looks like it,' sobbed Mattie. 'I've called the doctor. And Lily, of course.' She'd called Lily first, and it had been she who had told Mattie to get in touch with Dr Collie. 'He's on his way.'

'He was pretty old. We all knew it was going to happen some time,' said Marie.

'I know. I know. But I'm not ready for it. He was a grumpy old soul at times, but I loved him. The children are really upset. You must talk to them.'

Marie went through to the living room. She gathered Tod and Agnes to her, kissed them. 'Grandpa was really old,' she said.

'Has he gone to heaven?' asked Agnes.

'Oh yes,' said Marie. 'No doubt about that. Let's make some tea.'

She picked up Lauren, hugged and kissed her. Made calming noises, and with the child perched on her hip, led the other two through to the kitchen. 'People die when they get old,' she said.

Agnes was clinging to her, and she stroked the child's head. 'Sometimes they get so tired, their heart just stops beating.'

Mattie was making tea. She looked pale, fraught. Her mind raced with things to do. Call an undertaker. Register the death. Put an obituary in the paper. Beloved grandfather of Lily, Marie and Rory. Great-grandfather to Agnes, Tod and Lauren. There would have to be a funeral, they'd have to decide on hymns, someone would give a eulogy – Lily.

She poured a cup for Marie. 'I looked out of the window. And there he was, lying on the lawn. John's with him. I brought the children indoors.'

Marie said she'd go and see how John was coping. When she got outside, John was sitting on the grass next to Grandpa, who was sitting up, waving his arms about, talking animatedly about something.

Marie went back inside. 'I thought Grandpa was dead.'

'He is,' said Mattie. 'I saw him lying out there, spread out, just gazing up. Totally still.'

'Well, he doesn't look very dead to me.'

The pair went back into the garden. Mattie saw Grandpa sitting up, chatting. 'I can assure you he was dead ten minutes ago.'

Grandpa had been in the garden, strolling the lawn, admiring the flower beds. It had been a good year for the delphiniums, and the roses, his favourite, were blooming. The air round them was heavy with scent. He touched their heads, ran his thumb over the petals. Glamis Castle, Rob Roy, Abraham Derby – he knew them all, helped tend them, feeding them Top Rose in spring and then again after flowering.

He remembered when he was a boy, an old man came down his street selling vegetables from a horse-pulled cart. It wasn't the vegetables that excited the householders, it was the horse, or to be exact what came out of the horse's rear end. People would run into the road carrying shovels, battling and shoving to scoop up the steaming manure. Best thing for roses, and organic too, he thought.

He saw a snail clinging to a delphinium stem, and tutted. Damn things. He picked it off, held it in his palm, examining it. Normally, he surreptitiously popped them over the wall into the neighbour's garden, though Mattie and John knew nothing about this. But for the moment he gazed at it. It was a beautiful thing. Its shell, dark yellows and browns. Pity they ate delphiniums; if they didn't, you could almost like them. He bent down and put it on the grass, then knelt to watch it inch back to the flower bed.

When he was a boy, he and his friends used to gather snails and race them. God, he thought, we must have had time on our hands. He remembered idle summers, barefoot days, endless sun. He remembered sitting on the back doorstep of his home eating bread and jam, the jam freshly made, still warm and very sticky. They don't make jam like that any more. Apple scrumping. Running away, pockets heavy with tiny, tart stolen apples, which he'd eat, and then feel sick. But he swore that they tasted wonderful, because no apple tasted better than a stolen apple.

He remembered his mother used to make apple jelly. A huge muslin bag hung on a pole that was laid across the backs of two chairs. The bag filled with the mush of apples, the golden jelly dripping through the bottom into a heavy bowl. The house filled with the smell of apples.

He remembered he could pass happy hours lying on the grass in the fields beyond his house, staring at the sky. The smell of grass, and the blue above, clouds drifting: you could imagine you were on the curve of the world, feeling it spin through the universe.

He lay down, looked up, felt the sun on his face and wondered why we left such small childish pleasures behind. If it was compulsory for people to lie on the grass, weather permitting, once a day and watch the sky, he thought, we'd all be happier. There would be less stress, less back stabbing, less grabbing and snatching and lusting for material possessions. There ought to be a law, he told himself. And shut his eyes, so there would only be the scents and sounds of the day. Roses, the thick greeny smell of nasturtiums, a bee humming, a bird in the lilac tree, the rustle of leaves . . . He drifted off.

Movements round him, people, whispers, filtered through his sleep. He heard John say, 'Take the kids inside. Call the doctor.'

Grandpa slowly raised one eyelid, and looked up. Mattie was standing a few yards away. Her hands were on her face, she looked shocked. He shut his eye again. Stupid woman. He heard her walking swiftly away. That was right, he'd forgotten, you could hear the thud of steps, the slight tremble of the ground as someone approached, or departed. When he was a boy, he pressed his ear to the earth so he might hear the distant hoofs of galloping marauders on the attack.

John leaned over him. 'God,' he said.

Grandpa thought he might continue to lie here a moment or two and find out what John might do when he did die.

'Keep Tod and Agnes indoors,' John shouted. 'I don't want them seeing this.'

'Has he had a heart attack?' said Mattie, her voice slightly distant now.

If I had had a heart attack I would be dead by now, thought Grandpa, the time it's taking you to call the doctor. And if I had had one I wouldn't be lying like this on my back, stretched out, I'd be more slumped to one side.

Mattie ran into the living room where Tod and Agnes and Lauren were watching television. 'Just keep quiet,' she said. 'Grandpa's had a bit of a turn. I'm going to call the doctor.'

But she called Lily. 'Grandpa's died,' she said. 'I'm sorry to tell you like this. But I don't know how else to put it. He's lying on the lawn.'

'Is the doctor there?' said Lily.

'I'm just going to phone him now,' said Mattie.

'Get off the phone then, call him. I'll be there as soon as I can.'

She had immediately called a minicab, gathered her handbag, told Rory, who had not yet returned to Paris, where she was going. 'Grandpa's died,' she said. 'Stay here and tell Art, then go back to Isabel, for heaven's sake. I'll let you know about the funeral.'

She went to her bedroom, packed a bag.

Rory followed her. 'I should come with you.'

'No,' said Lily. 'You go sort out things with Isabel. I'll let you know what's happening.'

'Grandpa,' said Rory.

Lily turned to him. 'I know. But he was old. We all knew this was going to happen one day.' She held his face. 'It happened quickly. I don't think he felt a thing.' She kissed him. 'Everything will be fine.'

He held her. He hadn't known he'd feel like this when his grandpa died. The doorbell rang.

'That's my cab,' said Lily. 'I must go. You take care, babe.'

Babe, he thought. It had been years since she called him that. He used to hate it. Funny how comforting it was now.

On the way to the airport Lily thought about the funeral. No doubt, she thought, I'll have to arrange it, and say some sort of eulogy. She called the university to say she wouldn't be able to take her lecture tomorrow. She'd probably be away for at least a week. Her grandfather had just died.

❊   ❊   ❊

John put his hand on Grandpa's throat, to see if there was a pulse. He'd seen this in the movies, though he didn't really know which bit of the throat to check. Then he gently opened his father's mouth, took a deep breath, thought, Christ, I don't want to do this.

'It's a bit damn late to be thinking about giving me the kiss of life,' said Grandpa. He sat up.

'What the hell are you doing?' said John. 'We thought you were dead.'

'So I heard. But I'm not, am I? I was just lying here enjoying the day, feeling the sun on my face, smelling the grass.'

'Why didn't you say? We got a shock.'

'Well, I was going to,' said Grandpa. 'Then I thought I'd lie a bit and see what you'd do. Sort of a run-through for the real thing. Can't say I'm impressed. Time it took Mattie to call the doctor, I'd have been dead for real.'

'Jesus,' said John. 'Do you realise the trouble you've caused? Mattie will have phoned the doctor now.'

'Well, she'll just have to call him back and tell him I'm fine,' said Grandpa. 'I was lying here enjoying myself; you disturbed me.'

This was when Marie came out and saw Grandpa, and considering the way he was gesticulating, he was very much alive and kicking. Marie went back inside to tell Mattie it was a false alarm. John followed.

Inside, Mattie said she'd phoned the doctor and told him not to bother coming. 'He was on his way, they had to call him on his mobile. He wasn't very pleased.'

John said nothing. He opened a bottle of Chianti, poured three glasses and they all drank.

'Such a shock,' said Mattie. 'I'm not quite over it.'

Marie and the children stayed for supper. It was Mattie's opinion they could all do with something nice to eat to recover. 'Roast chicken and rice pudding.'

They were eating their dessert when Lily arrived. 'Hello, it's me,' she called as she came in the door.

Mattie put her hand to her mouth. 'I forgot to tell her it was a false alarm.'

Lily came into the kitchen. She was serious, prepared for grief. It took her a moment to come to terms with the sight of Grandpa sitting at the table eating a second helping of Mattie's pudding.

'I thought you were dead,' Lily said to him. 'And there you are eating rice pudding.'

'I know,' said Grandpa. 'It's very good. Got cardamoms in.'

'You might have told me,' said Lily. 'You could have phoned me on my mobile. I've come all this way for nothing.' It was now the full consequences of her flight north hit her. 'Do you realise I cancelled a lecture. I told them I wouldn't be back for a week. They'll be sorting all that out, getting someone to take my place. Is anyone aware of the trouble I could be in? Does anyone care?'

Everyone stared. Then Mattie said she was sorry. What with Grandpa not being dead and all, she hadn't thought to phone her and tell her everything was all right. 'Sorry.' She looked sheepish. Exchanged a raised eyebrow with Marie – oops.

'Bloody hell,' said Lily. 'All the way here my heart was pounding. I was in a state. All sweaty. Then I get here and you're all sitting round the table, eating and drinking. You didn't give me a second thought. That's not very nice.'

John, seeing that Lily was working herself up into a rage, got up and went to her. He put his arm round her. 'You've been put upon,' he said. 'We should have phoned you. We're all really sorry about that. But not absolutely sorry. You're here. And it's lovely to see you.' He took her jacket, pulled out a chair, sat her down. 'Have some wine.'

Lily poured herself a glass, and looked round at the guilty faces. She was still disgruntled, though her father had stopped her flow of rhetoric, and she still had a lot to say about running out of her home in a panic, buying a stand-by ticket at the airport, and taking a taxi here. She sipped, and glared.

John filled a plate with what was left of the roast chicken, potatoes and salad. And when Lily had eaten that, told her to help herself to rice pudding. She did, then had a second helping, which helped soothe her temper. 'Almost worth the trip,' she said.

She took her coffee outside and sat on the old swing that hung from the pear tree at the bottom of the garden. This had been a favourite haunt in her childhood, a place of comfort after being scolded, or when she felt that life was unfair, that her siblings were more favoured than she was. It was an ideal spot for sulking.

Marie joined her, sat on the grass beside the swing. 'Sorry about that. You must be pissed off.'

'You could say that,' said Lily. 'I was in the middle of something when Mattie phoned, she was pretty hysterical. I picked up my handbag and ran out of the flat.' She thought about this, how absurd it was. And sniggered.

'You used to always come here when you were cross,' said Marie. 'Even if it was freezing cold. You'd sit and sulk, hoping someone would feel sorry for you and beg you to come inside.'

'I know,' said Lily. 'But nobody ever did.'

'Dad used to grow peas down here. Over there.' Marie pointed to the vegetable patch, where John's broad beans, onions and garlic were shooting up.

'We used to sneak down and eat them. We'd hide in between the rows, and pluck off the pods. I loved doing that.'

'Used to drive Mum mad, she was always complaining there were none left to cook.'

They smiled, remembering, bonding with small childhood memories.

Lily was mellowing. Her fury at arriving to find Grandpa alive and eating rice pudding had waned. Perhaps, thought Marie, this would be a good moment to feel out her sister's generosity. 'Um . . .' she said. 'Have you got any money?'

'Sure,' said Lily. 'I've a couple of pounds in my jacket pocket.' Thinking Marie needed to buy some milk or something, and had forgotten her purse. 'How much do you need?'

'About fifteen thousand pounds,' said Marie.

Later, thinking about how she would have reacted had someone asked her for that amount of money, Marie had to admire Lily's cool.

'Why?' Lily said quietly. 'Are you in trouble?'

'Andy's back. He wants the children. He's gone to a lawyer to file for custody. I need a lawyer, to fight for my kids. I've been told that's what it might cost.'

'You poor thing,' said Lily. 'I'll write you a cheque.'

'You have that much money?' said Marie. She was impressed.

'Not on me at the moment. I'll get it.'

Marie lay back, propped herself on her elbows. 'How?' she asked, thinking that maybe Lily knew something about the acquisition of money that she didn't.

'I'll sell the car. Hate it anyway,' said Lily.

'It's a lovely car. You can't sell it.'

'You haven't seen it, how do you know it's lovely? Anyway, it's a pest. I can never find anywhere to park it. And if I get it near the flat, I don't want to move it because I'll lose the space. So I take the bus, which is fine, I can see about me. Actually, I prefer it. So what's the point of the damn thing sitting there depreciating? I'll sell it.' I'll sell it and give Marie the money, she thought. But I'll have to keep up the payments with the loan company. Is that legal?

Marie said nothing. Lily's explanation did not assuage her guilt. They watched Agnes and Tod playing with a frisbee.

'What will I do if I lose them?' said Marie. 'I couldn't live, I couldn't cope.'

'Won't happen,' said Lily. 'How could it? Your kids are fine. Cared for, secure. They've got all those people who love them, Mattie, John, Grandpa, me and Art. Besides, in these sort of cases they nearly always find for the mother. There is still the firm belief that mothers should bring up the children.'

Marie looked at Lily, who had her arms round the ropes of the swing, feet on the ground, gently shoving back and forward. She had always thought herself in some way smarter than Lily. Oh, she knew Lily had a degree, was well read, held down a job, but Marie always thought that of the two of them, she was the one with the real knowledge: she'd had kids, she'd given birth, she'd done all sorts of things Lily hadn't. She was street smart, she knew about life, Lily got it all out of book. Still, Lily's words comforted her; she needed all the reassurance she could get.

But there was a niggle of resentment. What does she know? Marie thought. She has a pristine life, everything in its place. She has never suffered any real pain. She looked at her sister's face, narrow, high cheekbones. Huh, she thought, a pristine life, beautiful things, and cheekbones, not fair. But she hasn't got kids, she doesn't know what she's missing. She knew she wasn't being at all gracious, but that made it easier to accept fifteen thousand pounds. 'I'll pay you back,' she said.

'Of course you will,' said Lily. How, she did not know. 'Does Mattie know?'

Marie shook her head. 'I should tell her, but somehow I haven't got round to it.'

'She's bound to find out,' said Lily. 'She'll be really hurt when she does.'

'I know,' said Marie. 'I just have to find the right moment.'

'Do you want me to tell her?' said Lily.

'Would you?' said Marie. 'I just don't think I'm up to one of her emotional outbursts right now.'

'No problem,' said Lily. 'I'll tell her tonight.'

She got up from the swing, and as she heaved herself up, her jeans slid down, revealing the top of her bum, revealing the tattoo.

'Is that a tattoo?' said Marie. 'You've never got a tattoo. When did you get that?' She assumed it would have been during Lily's student years. A foolish decision made on a drunken night out. Though she couldn't imagine Lily having a drunken night out.

'No,' said Lily in the sing-song tone of a liar.

'It is too,' said Marie, getting up, wrenching at Lily's jeans before she had a chance to stop her. 'It's a Harley Davidson. For goodness' sake, a motorbike. Why that?'

Lily sighed. 'I wanted to be like Mattie. I wanted to feel some sort of pain for her after I bought that car. I was guilty. It was an act of penance, I was ashamed of myself.'

Marie said, 'Oh, Lily.'

'So I went and got tattooed to be the same as her.'

'But Mum doesn't have a tattoo,' said Marie. 'Does she?'

'Yes. Up here,' indicating the top of her thigh. 'She has a dragonfly and *Kama Sutra – Harley Davidson Position* written on.'

'Never,' said Marie. 'I've never seen that.'

'Well she does. I've seen it.'

'When?'

'When I was interviewing Rita Boothe she showed me a book she'd done about groupies, and there was this amazing photograph of a young woman in the back of a limousine wearing fishnet stockings and a feather boa and holding a bottle of Jack Daniels.

She looked exquisite and orgasmically happy. And she had these tattoos and it was our mother.'

'Never,' said Marie. 'Really. I must see it. I must get Sebastian to get a copy of that book. My God, our mother.' She was jumping at the juiciness of it. Best gossip in years.

Lily got caught up in her enthusiasm. 'I couldn't believe it,' she said. 'In a limo, with Jack Daniels, and tattoos.'

They looked like two over-excited schoolgirls. Squealing. Then Marie said, 'Tattoos, I'm telling.' And she ran back to the house. 'I'm telling. I'm telling.'

'No you're not,' said Lily, and took off after her. It was as if they were kids again. Running, shouting, goading, teasing.

'I'm telling, I'm telling.'

'No. No. Please.'

Marie burst into the kitchen, too excited to notice that John and Mattie were arguing. John was angry at Mattie for forgetting to phone Lily and tell her everything was all right. Mattie was saying it was lovely she was here, and she was sorry she'd forgotten. She'd been busy making supper, and had been so relieved Grandpa was fine. They both turned to stare at Marie.

'Lily's got a tattoo,' she cried.

Lily burst in. 'No I haven't.'

'Of course Lily hasn't got a tattoo,' said Mattie. 'She wouldn't be so silly.'

'She has,' said Marie. 'I've seen it. It's on her bum.'

Lily was silenced. Looked guilty, embarrassed.

'Have you got a tattoo?' said Mattie. 'Show me.'

'No,' said Lily.

'Go on,' said Marie. 'Show them.'

Lily turned. Heaved down her jeans so the top of her buttock was showing. And there, indeed, was the tattoo.

'Goodness,' said Mattie. 'When did you get that?'

'A couple of months ago,' said Lily. 'I wanted to be like you.'

'I don't have a tattoo,' said Mattie. Quite insulted that someone thought she had. 'Where did you get that idea?'

'You have got a tattoo,' said Lily. 'I saw it in that photo in Rita Boothe's book. A dragonfly, and *Kama Sutra – Harley Davidson Position*.'

John looked at Mattie. Here was the woman he'd been married to for decades, here was a body he knew well, every inch of it. He'd never seen a tattoo.

But Mattie's hands were on her cheeks. The shock of remembering something that had vanished from her mind years and years ago. 'Oh,' she said. 'Lily. Those weren't tattoos, those were those transfer stick-on things that wash off. I bought them, I thought they made me look cool. *Kama Sutra – Harley Davidson Position*, those were two separate ones, I just put them together. I thought it was funny.'

Lily went pale.

'I mean,' said Mattie, 'I don't think there even is a Harley Davidson position in the *Kama Sutra*. No, there can't be.'

It perturbed Marie that the next question was aimed at her.

'You can't even do it on a motorbike, can you?'

'How would I know?' said Marie. 'I certainly haven't ever.'

This was the first real sexual conversation the family had ever had.

'Can you?' Mattie turned to John.

He shrugged.

It rather hurt Lily that Mattie didn't bother to ask her.

'I suppose you could,' said Mattie. 'If the bike was on its stand and firmly placed and the man sat on it, then the woman . . .'

'Mattie, shut up,' said John. Then, to Lily, 'It's so unlike you. Why did you do it?'

'Like I said. I wanted to be like Mattie. I wanted to feel some pain after I'd hurt her buying that Alfa Romeo.'

'For me,' said Mattie. 'That's the nicest thing anyone's ever done for me. Thank you, Lily.'

A Fine Figure of a Man and a
Very Good Flower Arranger Too

In the morning Lily sat at the kitchen table. She felt only a little foolish about the tattoo, it was done now. A stupid act in a demented moment when she'd thought she was losing her family. She'd hurt only herself. What did it matter? It's behind me now, ha, ha.

Last night, she'd heard Mattie and John argue in their bedroom. Muffled voices, she couldn't make out what they were saying, but knew it was about Mattie forgetting to call after she'd discovered Grandpa was fine. Later, she'd been woken by the sound of someone moving about downstairs in the kitchen making a cup of tea. Mattie worrying. That was what she did herself when she worried, made tea, sat at the kitchen table, and, even in the middle of winter, never bothered to put the heating on. Worrying was somehow heightened when you did it alone in the middle of the night, in the cold.

Sometimes she'd look out of the window and see other lights on in other buildings. Were the people in these flats also up, also sitting at the kitchen table, in the cold, worrying?

She hadn't gone down to join her mother, but had lain in the dark planning how to tell her about Marie's troubles. It would be tricky only in that she had to make Mattie feel she wasn't the last to be told. She knew Mattie hated to feel left out, and she mustn't be allowed to believe that Marie had left the job to Lily because she couldn't do it herself. Diplomacy, she thought.

Mattie put a cup of coffee and some toast in front of her. Lily spread the toast with butter, then honey, took a bite. She sipped her coffee and said, 'There's something Marie's been trying to tell you, but she never gets the chance. The kids are always there. She doesn't want them to know.'

Mattie thought her heart had stopped. Marie? What? Some dreadful illness? Her mind filled with possibilities. What would happen if Marie had to spend time in hospital? Well, she and John could take the children in. What if the illness was so terrible Marie couldn't work? They'd all have to come and live here. They'd manage.

Lily saw her mother's mind racing. What's the worst that could happen? Ask Mattie, she knows. She imagines it all the time.

Lily reached over and touched Mattie's hand. She didn't know what Mattie was imagining, but knew it was worse than what she was about to tell her. 'It isn't that bad. Andy's back.'

'I know that,' said Mattie.

'He's found someone else. He's filling for divorce, and he wants the children.'

'What do you mean, he wants the children?'

'He's been to a lawyer and he is taking Marie to court so that they can come and live with him.'

'He can't do that, it's absurd. He has no right. How dare he?'

'He's their father. He probably misses them,' said Lily.

'Then he shouldn't have left them,' said Mattie. Then she thought about this. 'Why did he go? Marie never said. Did she tell you?'

Lily shook her head.

'It was her, wasn't it? She did something to make him leave. Something terrible, and he couldn't forgive her.'

'That's what I think,' said Lily. 'She was always impetuous.'

'What could it have been?' said Mattie.

Lily shrugged. She figured Marie had slept with someone else, but wasn't going to say.

Mattie let her worries flow. 'What if he takes them back to Canada and we never see them again? What if he gets some-one else to look after them when he's at work? And they stop coming over, and just grow up and drift away and forget about us?'

Lily shook her head. 'Won't happen.'

'You don't know that,' said Mattie.

'No, I don't know it. But I suspect it won't happen. What court would take children out of a loving home? Marie's their mother; mothers usually win these battles.'

'Has Marie got a lawyer?' asked Mattie.

'She's been to see somebody.'

'How is she going to afford it? We haven't much money. I suppose we could remortgage.'

'I'll give her the money,' said Lily. 'I'll sell the damn car.'

'Do you mind? It's a lovely car.'

Lily repeated what she'd said to Marie. 'It's a pest having it. Besides, what else can I do? She's my sister.' She took another bite of her toast. Gave Mattie a look that said that was that. The end of it, nothing more to say. But she could tell that Mattie had many nights ahead of her, sitting alone here in this kitchen, drinking tea, worrying in the cold.

Eventually she went out to see John, who was in the shed, working on his kite. Over the last few weeks the kite had been set aside as he planted the garden. He had decided to grow more vegetables to cut down on the supermarket bills.

'Money's tight these days,' he said.

'So,' said Lily, 'why don't you go to work again?'

'At my age? Who'd employ me?'

'You can employ yourself. Work the hours you want. Take on jobs you want. It doesn't have to be a big business. Just something to bring in a little extra. People are always needing plans drawn up. New houses, extensions, conservatories, loft conversions. You could do that. Mattie could keep the books.'

John looked at her and said, 'Hmmph.' But something had clanged within him.

'It would be good for her to have something to do. It would take her mind off things. She worries too much. I heard her roaming about in the middle of the night, making tea and fretting about something. When did this start?' said Lily.

'About the time of her menopause. She gets all sweaty in bed, lies awake, starts worrying, then gets up to have a more in-depth worry downstairs.'

'What does she worry about?' Lily wanted to know.

'I don't know,' said John. 'She's got nothing really to bother her. We may be a bit strapped for cash, but we own the house. We can get by. Look, she's a worrier. Even if everything is fine, she'll find something to worry about. In fact, I think if she's got nothing to worry about, she'll worry about that. She'll think that it's very worrying that everything is fine, and start fretting about what might be about to happen, or what she might have overlooked. She worries.'

'Well make her stop,' said Lily. 'Get her doing something. Take her out. Have more sex.'

John looked at her. 'My sex life is none of your business, young lady. Cheek of you. You're not too old for me to take you across my knee.'

Lily said, 'Ha, ha. That'll be right.' Kissed him on the top of his head and left.

Rory arrived home. He rang the bell. Isabel opened the door, and Rory said, 'Hi.'

She stood aside so he could come in. They stood looking at one another for a few heavy moments before Rory said, 'I'm sorry.'

Isabel said, 'I know.'

'I wanted to buy you something,' he said. 'And I fell down the steps, somebody stole my wallet.'

'Lily told me,' she said.

He threw down his bag and sat on the sofa. He hadn't known coming back would be this awkward. He'd imagined her running into his arms, some kisses, then bed. But now he didn't really know what to do.

Isabel sat beside him. He took her hand. She told him he was a fool. He said he knew that. So they kissed.

The sex was dizzyingly passionate. The thrill of making up. Woes and heartache sweated out. Afterwards Isabel made them both an omelette. They ate in the kitchen, window open, sounds of the world outside floating up. She told him it was wonderful to see him.

'I thought you weren't going to have me back,' he said.

She nodded. She'd always known he would return. It was what she'd planned. 'Let's go back to bed,' she said.

This time the sex was gentler. A tenderness as they soothed the pain they'd been through. Rory watched her face. A wonderful face, he thought. Beautiful and knowing. He told her he loved her and he would never again do anything to hurt her.

Later she lay sprawled, on her stomach, head on his shoulder, arm spread over him. 'I missed you. It was empty here without you.'

He ran his fingers through her hair.

'I was lonely,' she said. She meant it, she had been. She cried a little.

Rory remembered Marie's advice, the words of comfort. 'There, there,' he said. 'Never mind.'

He felt her stiffen. She pulled away from him, sat up. 'What the hell do you mean by that? "There, there, never mind"?'

'I was trying to comfort you.'

'Comfort me? What a patronising thing to say. It's the sort of thing you say when you don't know what to say.'

'No it's not. It's the sort of thing you say when you are being sympathetic.'

'It's what you say to a child that's lost his favourite toy or fallen and cut his knee. You don't say it to a woman who's been alone and worried and lonely. And broken-hearted.' She got out of bed, put on her robe saying, 'Stupid. Stupid. Stupid.'

'Marie said it worked for her.'

'Marie? What's this got to do with her? You spoke about me to Marie. She told you what to say? Lily phones me to explain what happened to you. Isn't it time you took responsibility for yourself?'

'I do.'

'It doesn't sound like it to me. Don't you ever talk about me to your sisters. And don't you ever say "There, there, never mind" to me. Not ever. I hate that.' She stormed out of the room.

Rory heard her slam the bathroom door, then the rush of water filling the bath, her fury as she clattered about pouring in oils, getting fresh towels from the airing cupboard. The flat filled with the scent of Aveda. He lay back and thought: Thank you, Marie.

The next time Andy picked up Tod and Agnes, he sent them on to the car while he spoke to Marie. She was standing at the door, looking at him, as he watched the two children run down the path. He had a good face, she thought, the muscles in his jaw stood out when he spoke. He was lean. There was no doubt he was handsome, but she was no longer attracted to him. In fact, he wasn't her type at all, and she wondered if he ever had been. She could feel his tension as he stood next to her, and knew he still hadn't got over coming into that bedroom that night and finding her in bed with his best friend. She didn't think she would get over such a thing either. She didn't really blame him for hating her. She was just learning to stop hating herself.

His presence on her doorstep disturbed her, though she now believed they wouldn't have stayed together anyway. They'd worked hard at being the perfect couple; she decided that eventually they'd have been too tired to keep up the act. Besides, she was no longer the person she'd been four years ago. She was quieter, more tolerant. And now she had Sebastian, who made no demands on her other than she be Marie. He didn't want to change her, and his only criticism of her so far was that she always burned the toast in the morning.

If it wasn't for the looming court case, Marie thought she might even be happy. She didn't know what she thought of that. She wasn't quite ready to relax and trust Sebastian not to leave her, or start saying hurtful things to her. Or perhaps just get fed up of her, and go looking for someone who was more available, who didn't have children and could devote more time to him. She wasn't quite ready to let go and trust Sebastian, but she was considering it. Then again, loving someone wasn't something you planned. Sometimes it just happened whether you wanted it or not.

'I want the kids to come for the weekend next week,' said Andy.

'Sorry,' said Marie. 'Can't do that.'

'Why not?'

'It's a lawyer thing. If you want them to stay over you must get your lawyer to write to my lawyer and they'll work it out between them.'

'For crying out loud, Marie. You said they could stay whenever I wanted. Now I want. I think they know me well enough.'

'Well, get your lawyer to fix it up.'

'Why?'

'They'll haggle. It's what they do.'

'Why can't Agnes and Tod just come and stay? I want them to.'

Marie shrugged. In fact it would suit her if Tod and Agnes stayed with Andy for the weekend. Lauren could stay with Mattie, and she and Sebastian would have some time alone.

'You're being unreasonable,' said Andy.

'I admit it seems absurd. But there you go. That's what my lawyer wants. You can't complain. You started it.'

He looked at her coldly. 'No,' he said. 'You did.'

Chastised, she stuck her hands in her pocket, stared at her feet and said, 'I know. I'm sorry.'

For a few moments he was silent. Then, 'I shouldn't have left you alone. We should have gone home early.'

Marie said she knew that, she'd thought about that often. 'Why didn't you get in touch? We could have talked.'

'I did get in touch with Tod and Agnes. It was you I didn't want to communicate with. Then time passed, then too much time passed. I didn't know what to say.'

'Something would have been better than nothing,' said Marie. 'We might have been able to sort things out. We might not have been fighting over custody. We could have found a way . . .'

'Marie,' he said. 'You broke my heart.' He repeated it, so broken had his heart been. 'You broke my heart. I didn't know there could be such pain, I thought I'd never get over it. But I have. I thought, Why should you do that to me, then end up with everything? The house, the kids. So I want what's mine. Agnes and Tod. I miss them, I need them. I'm going to win this. I know I am.'

'What makes you so sure of that?'

'I know all about you, Marie. I saw you in the park. You nearly let Lauren get run over. Agnes ran away, and Tod was left to fall off his bike. You let a strange man into your house and the children saw him virtually naked.'

'It wasn't like that,' said Marie.

'Tell that to the judge. It isn't nice, Marie. You have been behaving in some lewd manner when they were in the next room. In fact, Agnes told me, Lauren is often in your bed when that man is there too. Put that with the fact you slept with another man at a party, and you don't seem like a very suitable person to mother my children. My lawyer thinks we've got a good case. And we've got a social worker coming to assess you, she'll be told all about your behaviour.'

Marie said, 'But . . .'

'You're not managing, are you? Your mother has to take the kids to school, and pick them up. I'd get an au pair, they could come home properly at the end of the day. And I've got a new job teaching physical education. I finish at about the same time they do. I could be there for them after school. I'd give them security. Proper holidays. A decent education. Face it, Marie, you haven't a hope.'

Shocked, in turmoil, Marie went indoors to sit in the kitchen, clutch her stomach and cry. Andy walked down the path, jingling his keys. His lawyer was building a sound case. This time next year his children would be living with him, and it would be Marie who had to fight for visiting rights.

John lay on his back in bed. It was hot, so he had his left leg sticking out from beneath the duvet to cool himself down. 'Do you know how long it's been since we had sexual intercourse?' he said.

'I wish you wouldn't call it that,' said Mattie, who was also on her back.

'Why, that's what it is. What would you like me to call it?'

'Something nicer. Making love.'

'Do you know how long it's been since we made love?' said John.

'Quite a while,' said Mattie. 'Not since we lost the television remote, that was before Christmas.'

'A while, then,' said John.

'Yes. I wonder where that remote went? How can you just lose something like that? Mind you, I've got used to not having it. In fact, I think it's healthier not to have a remote control for the television. You have to get up and walk across the room to change channels. And you look up the guide to see what's on, rather than just idly flicking from station to station.'

'You do tend to discuss what you want to watch instead of just hoping you come across something good. You are very good at changing the subject, Mattie.'

'It's a gift,' she said.

He smiled. Though in the dark she didn't see this.

'We haven't exactly been getting on,' she said.

'We could have sex at night and argue during the day,' suggested John. 'We could declare the bedroom a truce area.'

'You have been saying some very unpleasant things to me,' said Mattie.

'And you to me,' said John. 'At least I didn't give away your sandwich to a complete stranger.'

'Rita Boothe is not a stranger. My God, are you still going on about that?'

'Yes. I intend to go on about it for the rest of my life.'

'I better get used to it, then.'

He said, 'Yes, you had.' And took her hand under the covers.

This afternoon he had overheard her say something that had greatly amused him. A plumber had come to fix the pipe under the sink which was leaking.

'I thought it might have been blocked,' Mattie told him. 'I gave it a go with the plunger thing, but I think maybe the pipe needs to be replaced.'

'Maybe you should have left it to your old man.'

'I'm perfectly capable of unblocking a sink,' said Mattie.

'Doesn't your husband do these things?' said the plumber.

'Sometimes,' said Mattie. 'Though I fix the fuses and suchlike. There's nothing mysterious about any of that.'

'I always think those are men's jobs.'

'What are you saying? That my husband isn't a man? I can assure you he is. He's ten times the man you are. And he does very fine flower arrangements too.'

This had made John laugh, and feel tenderly towards Mattie. Though he had no idea what the plumber made of it. Still, what did he care? The pipe was now fixed.

'I'm worried about Marie,' said Mattie. 'What if Andy gets the children? She'll be heartbroken. Nobody should have to go through something like that. I mean, what if he takes them out of the country and she never sees them again? How could she go on with her life?'

'What if? What if? What if? You're letting your imagination

run away with you. What if, nothing. It won't happen. He won't get the kids. I think he won't. Lily thinks he won't. He won't.'

'But . . .' said Mattie.

'No buts,' said John. He took her in his arms. 'Everything will be fine.' He felt her relax against him. 'Let's try the Harley Davidson position.'

'That is so typical,' said Mattie. 'You get a woman in your clutches. You feel her relax, and you take advantage. I have no intention of trying the Harley Davidson position. I would feel ridiculous. I wouldn't enjoy it. I'm quite happy to go missionary.'

He kissed her. One of those long, deep kisses she and Rita Boothe had sighed over months and months ago on the beach at Mattie's picnic.

Everything That Makes You . . .

By the time Lily arrived home from Edinburgh, Rory had gone back to Isabel in Paris.

'Excellent sex,' Art said. 'A total bust-up, he gets thrown out, then allowed back. Fantastic making-up to be done. Great shagging.'

Lily kicked off her shoes, left them lying at odd angles to one another. Threw her coat on the sofa and said, 'My fucking family.'

Art had rarely heard her swear. Oh, the odd bloody now and then, perhaps ever a bugger when she was pushed. But this was an uncustomary full-blown adult four-letter word. It sounded strange; somehow she neutralised the word. It lost its sting when it fell from Lily's lips. It made him want to laugh.

'What about your fucking family?'

'Do you know what happened?'

'Yes, you rushed up there and Grandpa wasn't dead. In fact he was eating rice pudding. You phoned and told me.'

'Yes. And.' She lifted her hand and started to count on her fingers. 'One. Grandpa's alive. Two. Mattie hadn't bothered to tell me. Three. Marie wants to borrow fifteen thousand pounds. Four. It's because Andy's returned out of the blue and wants the kids. Five. Marie hadn't told Mattie, so I had to. Six. John is spending all day out in the shed making some kite thing and hardly talking to Mattie. Seven . . .' She stared at her hands. She'd made so many points she'd finished the fingers on her left hand and had moved on to the right. 'Well, isn't that enough? *And* there's Rory. So that's seven.'

She slumped on to a chair, legs splayed before her. 'My fucking family.'

Art said, 'Could we rewind to three in that list. Fifteen thousand pounds? We haven't got fifteen thousand pounds. I think your sister has romantic notions about our bank account.'

'We'll have to sell the car,' said Lily.

'I happen to like that car,' said Art.

'What can we do? She needs the money to pay for her court case, and she sure as hell hasn't got fifteen grand. I'll have to help out. She's my sister, Art.'

'Couldn't you just sort of mediate between Marie and Andy, make them sit down and talk things out? No lawyers.'

Lily stared. Art shrugged.

'All this is because one night four years ago my sister got caught by her husband shagging someone else.'

'You don't know that.'

'Oh,' said Lily, 'I know that. If Andy had been totally in the wrong he'd have just gone away and never come back. But he went away because he was hurt, then he decided to come back because he wants his kids. No, it was Marie, and it's going to cost me fifteen grand. My fucking family. They are all intertwined, weaving in and out. Sharing secrets with one person, and not another. Don't tell this and don't tell that. And bickering and making up and sharing jokes and stupid stories and planning things that never work out and wishing and dreaming and hoping and wondering why this one hasn't phoned and have they phoned that one instead and does that person know something I don't and have another helping of rice pudding, Lily. My fucking family. They are everything that makes me . . .' She couldn't think what her family made her. Mad? Frustrated? She couldn't quite get hold of the right word.

'They are everything that makes you,' said Art.

Lily reached out her hand; he took it.

'Oh my God,' she said. 'I have to go into work tomorrow and tell them my grandfather didn't die after all. It's going to be awful. Nobody will believe me. My fucking family.'

Art said, 'Well, don't go. Stay away for a week. Why face the embarrassment? They don't know your family. They don't know Grandpa was lying on the grass sleeping and Mattie thought he was dead and panicked. I'd rather just hide away for a week than go in and admit all that. Stay off and finish your piece about Rita Boothe.'

310

'I couldn't do that. And what happens when Grandpa really dies?'

'Tell them it's your other grandfather. They won't know.' He looked at her. 'Do you fancy going to bed? Why should Rory and Isabel have all the fun?'

'Why, indeed,' agreed Lily.

So Lily stayed off work and finished her piece about Rita Boothe. It had taken her over eight months. It was the cookbook, in the end, that brought the inspiration. Not the relaxed, happy-go-lucky recipe timings – cook for three songs on the radio, leave in a moderate oven for as long as it takes to make love, sigh, kiss and kiss again and have a gentle conversation about something you like to talk about, put in very hot oven for about as long as it takes to check what's on television tonight in the newspaper.

They amused Lily, though they didn't always work. But she learned something. Some things needed precisely measured ingredients, and some things could be put together casually, things added here or there as she fancied – slivers of lemon peel in a stew, dill or tarragon and honey to a roast chicken. Her kitchen shelves filled with spices. She didn't jump up and do the dishes as soon as she and Art stopped eating. She could cook some things without really thinking about it, leaving her free to contemplate other matters. She started to enjoy her kitchen. She laughed more.

It has been suggested that Rita Boothe blew her chances, Lily wrote. *No, she simply lived the way she wanted to, followed her instincts. When her instincts told her to get in touch with her inner self, she took LSD and went into therapy, and hated everything about both experiences. Self-Awareness Sucks, she wrote. She had found the inner woman, and didn't like her at all.*

Nearing forty at the end of the sixties, she could hardly be described as a flower child. But the dreams of that era enthused her. She got caught up in it, the music, the politics, the issues. Never one to plot a career path, she has always followed her instincts. Done what she wanted to do.

Still, she has given us a cookbook, long out of print, that tells us to enjoy what we do. It offers a recipe for the bleedin' obvious – cook what you like to eat and have fun while you are doing it. It invites us to relish what we cook, who we cook with, and who we cook for.

311

It would come as a surprise to her that she is considered a lost icon. An icon? She'd take issue with that, since she never sought to be one. Lost? She's never that, she has simply stayed where she was happiest, and watches the rest of us go, wishes us well, and hopes one day we come to our senses and join her.

Lily printed it out, and sent it off. She was rather proud of it. Waited a couple of weeks to hear what her editor thought of it, and when she heard nothing, decided to wait a little longer. People were busy.

It took two weeks to sell the car. She stuck a notice on the side passenger window and put an advert in the paper. She'd thought she would be glad to see the back of it. But no, she felt regret slice through her, and stood at the edge of the pavement watching it move away from her. It was indeed a lovely thing, and she had been too filled with self-loathing and remorse to enjoy it. That, and the price she got for it fell far short of the sum Marie needed.

'I should have driven it more,' she said to Art. 'I should have swished about town, roof down, opera roaring on the CD player. I'm a fool.'

'You don't even like opera,' said Art.

'I would have got to like it in that car,' said Lily. 'Too late now. It's gone, it's sold. And I'm left with the payments, what with Marie getting the money.'

Art said it was her call, she'd bought the car, she'd sold it. She didn't *have* to give the money to Marie.

'She's my sister,' said Lily.

'So you already told me,' said Art. 'Does that mean you have to sacrifice your car?'

'Yes,' said Lily. 'I look at it this way. I couldn't bear for Marie to lose her kids. I couldn't bear for her to be utterly devastated and miserable. I couldn't bear not to see Agnes and Tod grow up. I couldn't bear what Mattie would be like. And I couldn't bear to spend the next twenty or so Christmases sitting listening to Mattie going on about how nice it would be if Agnes and Tod were here. I mean, she goes on about lots of things, but that would make us all cry. So I'd rather she went on about the sledge. It isn't tragic, and you can amuse yourself by making a bet on how long it will take her to get round to it.'

Art watched her stump back into the building and into their flat. He thought she'd changed. Last night he'd found her in the living room wearing her yoga pants and a skimpy spaghetti-strap top. She'd been standing beside the sofa, fists clenched, swearing.

'I will not plump the cushions. I fucking won't.'

'What are you doing?' he asked.

'I'm willing myself to go to bed and leave this room the way it is. I won't tidy the books we've been reading. I won't take the cups to the kitchen. I won't plump the cushions. I will leave it all till tomorrow.'

'So leave it and come to bed.'

'I will. I will. But it's hard.'

'No it isn't.' He took her hand and led her from the room. Shut the door behind them. 'You just leave it.'

This morning Lily had got up, had a glass of orange juice and gone out running. She didn't tidy. She'd come home, showered, dressed for work, made herself coffee and toast, and left the house. And didn't tidy. Home just after five, and still she hadn't tidied. Art was a little unnerved now. What was coming next?

He didn't really want Lily to change. She was kind, good, still prone to getting up from the sofa to straighten the curtains or align her shoes neatly side by side, envious, occasionally impulsive and generous. He thought it a lovable enough mix.

He didn't think a cookbook could be life-changing. But Rita Boothe's lay on their kitchen unit, covered with drops of olive oil, butter and remnants of ingredients Lily had used. She used it every day. She hummed small songs as she cooked, sometimes she laughed, played CDs or stood beside some simmering pot, eyes shut, imagining the length of a lingering kiss. She had learned to lighten up.

After six weeks, she phoned her publisher. 'Could I speak to Donald Brindley-Shand, please?'

'I'm afraid he left the company two months ago. Would you like to speak to his replacement, Jessica Hughes?'

'Yes,' said Lily.

She got his replacement's PA, Louise. 'I'm afraid Jessica's in a meeting at the moment, can I help?'

'Yes, I'm Lily Raphael, I'm phoning about the piece I wrote about Rita Boothe for your *Lost Icons* book.'

'*Lost Icons*? Rita Boothe?' said Louise. 'I'm sorry, I've only been here for a few weeks. I'll have to look it up on the computer.' Silence. 'Oh yes, sorry about that, it went to the printer's about two months ago. It should be available in the shops sometimes early next year.'

'What?' said Lily. 'But I was to write one of the sections in it.'

'I don't know anything about that,' said Louise. 'Wait a minute.'

Lily heard papers being riffled through.

'I've got it here, your piece. Yes, Jessica is sending it back to you. You were a bit late with it. But Mr Brindley-Shand should have got in touch before he left. Sorry about that.'

Lily said nothing.

'I'll pop it back to you in the post this afternoon. Sorry about all this.'

'And I suppose I won't get paid,' said Lily. 'What about my expenses? A flight to Scotland. A hired car. A night in an hotel.'

'I don't know about any of that,' said Louise. 'You'd have to take it up with Jessica. Sorry.'

Lily rang off. She had a feeling she'd not get any of her money back. When Art came home, she told him about it.

'My God, Lily,' he said. 'You missed the boat. How incredibly Rita Boothe of you.'

'Yes,' said Lily. 'I was thinking that. She would be delighted if she knew.'

Rita Boothe was content. The nights were starting to draw in. The world outside her door smelled of damp earth, and the deepening autumn chill. Afternoons, she'd sit with a cup of Earl Grey and watch the starlings gather on the sycamore tree at the bottom of her garden. She'd listen to their thick throaty chorus and wait for the magic moment when they all took off as one. They'd silence in unison, as if someone had switched them off. Then up they'd go into the sky like leaves thrust into the air. Sometimes Rita thought it looked almost as if the tree was exploding.

Give a Little

Waiting for the court case, Marie watched *Kramer vs. Kramer* over and over. She could speak along with Dustin Hoffman and Meryl Streep.

'He won,' she said to Mattie.

'No he didn't. They found in favour of her, her being the mother and all, even though she had walked out. She chickened out in the end. But she won.'

'So they found in favour of the one who walked out,' said Marie.

'The mother,' said Mattie. 'The mother always wins in these things.'

'Yeah, but only when they're good,' said Marie.

'You're good,' said Mattie. 'You're very good.'

Marie looked down into her coffee cup. No I'm not, she thought. Mattie noticed this, recognised it from years ago when Marie was a teenager and had a guilty conscience about something, but wouldn't confess what.

'Where did you go last night, Marie?'

'Oh, just round to Connie's for coffee.' Marie sitting staring into her breakfast cup of coffee. They'd been in the pub, drinking vodka and orange and eyeing up the local rugby team.

'Have you been smoking, Marie?'

'No-o,' in a voice trilling through a couple of scales. And looking into the depths of her Nescafé. So Mattie suspected she had and told her to stop.

But what was it that Marie was feeling guilty about right now? Mattie had no idea.

'How's Sebastian?'

'Fine. I'm thinking of breaking up with him, though.'

'Why? He's lovely.'

'I'll tell him you said that. It's nothing to do with him. It's just I think I'd look like a better, more devoted mother if I didn't have a boyfriend.'

'Rubbish. You have to have a life. Besides, Andy has a girlfriend. It makes you seem like a proper rounded person. Do you think he's serious about you?'

'We haven't spoken about it.' Marie gazed into her cup. She and Sebastian had discussed the state of their affair the last time they were together.

'I wouldn't mind a kid of my own some day,' Sebastian had said.

'Oh,' Marie had replied. 'What sort?'

'Boy or a girl, one of those. Not sure which. Though a boy would balance things up. There being two girls in your family.'

'You were planning to have a baby with me, then?' Marie had said.

'I suppose I was. Now you mention it. I mean, if you put it like that. You're the only person in my life at the moment that I do anything with that's likely to start a baby.'

'That's gratifying,' Marie had said. 'But it could be problematic, what with you in Newcastle and me in Edinburgh.'

'I could move, or you could move,' Sebastian had suggested.

'So what if I move to Newcastle? That means moving the children – new schools and all that. Or what if you move here, and we have a baby, there's not enough room. So, we get a bigger place, and you go off me. I'm stuck. I couldn't afford the bigger place on my own, and it'd be years before I got to the top of the housing list.'

'I wouldn't go off you. But if I did, I'd move out and you could have the house. I'd have to pay alimony, so you'd be fine.'

They both looked ahead at the television. Both realising what he'd said. If he had to pay alimony, they'd be married. But neither of them wanted to go into this, really. So they left it at that.

Last week Claire Bradley, Marie's solicitor, had called and said that a Mrs Evans, a social worker, had been asked to write a report on Tod and Agnes's home situation, and would it be all right to give her Marie's number so they could make the arrangements between them. Marie agreed, and a little while later Mrs Evans called. She'd come to the house yesterday shortly before five o'clock.

'How did it go yesterday?' Mattie asked.

Marie sighed and shrugged. 'Hard to tell. She interviewed the children alone. I wasn't allowed in the room. She had a good look round at the house, though.'

'Well, she'd have found nothing to complain about there,' said Mattie.

Mattie had spent yesterday morning in Marie's house, cleaning. She had scrubbed the kitchen floor, bleached the unit counters, wiped everything in sight. She had vacuumed, dusted, polished with such thoroughness, Marie felt uncomfortable walking about her house when she came home. The children had looked about in mild awe. Marie knew they'd mention this strange, unsettling cleanness to the social worker when she came.

She had arrived at half past five, as Marie was cooking the evening meal. She was tall, cropped hair, carried a bulging handbag that clanked when she put it down. It was stuffed with papers, and a copy of the *Guardian* stuck out at the top. She spoke in a clipped, shorthand way, reporteese, Marie called it, missing out the definite and indefinite articles. 'If children are OK with it, I'll chat to them alone, here in living room.' She was assertive, but mildly so. Marie felt she was in the presence of a woman who had seen drastic things, and had to make drastic decisions, and in the company of her colleagues resorted to black humour to maintain her sanity.

'She looked at the carpet,' Marie said to Mattie.

'Well, she wouldn't have found a speck on it. Looking for burns, no doubt. I've read about that. They look to see where you've dropped your cigarette when you've keeled over, drunk in charge of your children.'

'Cheek,' said Marie. 'I don't think I'll ever forgive Andy for putting me through that. It was horrible.'

'What sort of things did she ask Agnes and Tod?' asked Mattie.

'Don't really know. Tod just said she asked a load of stupid questions and went off to watch *The Simpsons*.'

'What did Agnes say?' asked Mattie.

'Much the same,' said Marie.

She had quizzed Agnes after the interview and been told that Mrs Evans had asked if Sebastian ever touched her.

'I said of course he did.'

'What!' said Marie.

'Well he does, when he picks me up and puts me on his shoulders and when he buttons my coat.'

'I don't think that's what the lady meant,' said Marie. 'What else did she ask?'

'She wanted to know if I'd like to live in Daddy's flat.'

'And what did you say?'

'I said, "Where would I sleep?" And she said I'd have my own bedroom and so would Tod. I said that would be great. Especially if the cat was there.' Then, after a moment, Agnes said, 'It would be better if the cat came here.' Then she said, 'Where would *you* sleep if we go and live with Daddy?'

'I'd sleep here,' Marie had said. 'I'm not going.'

'Well, I'm not going if you're not going,' said Agnes.

'I wish you'd said that to Mrs Evans,' said Marie.

'She never said you weren't going. She just asked if I wanted to go. I thought she meant you and me and Tod and Lauren too.'

Now, Marie looked into her cup. 'I have no idea what Agnes said.'

Mattie watched and knew Marie had a good idea what Agnes had said to the social worker, and wasn't going to tell her. That was how awful it was. She'd be up tonight, sitting at the kitchen table, in the cold, drinking tea and worrying. Probably Marie would be too.

'They shouldn't put children through all that,' she said.

'Stuff the children,' said Marie. 'They're fine. It's me who's a wreck.'

Isabel was eight weeks pregnant. She was quite glad that Rory had come back to her, though she was increasingly sure she would manage perfectly well without him. She had, in the end, taken her mother's advice and, without telling him, stopped taking her pill. She judged she must have been two weeks gone when she threw him out, though she hadn't known it at the time.

She'd thought that if Rory were presented with a child, he'd love it. His change of heart was a relief to her. But something had happened between them. Though their time apart had only been a few days, while Rory stayed with Art and Lily, it seemed, to Isabel, that she had been without him for longer than that.

There had been his weeks of drifting and dreaming, staring into space, not communicating. When all that had been going on, Isabel, too, had withdrawn. She had been surprised and hurt at Rory's refusal to talk about what was troubling him. She knew exactly what she wanted from a relationship – companionship, laughter, shared opinions, shared chores, a lot of sex. When you had a disagreement you spoke about it, you put your point of view forward, discussed it and found a compromise. Silence, smoking dope, sulking were the stuff of teenage nonsense, an indulgence. Isabel had no time for it. She had seen a side of Rory she disapproved of. She wondered if he'd make the husband and father she was grooming him to be. So far he was scoring two (one for having succeeded in making her pregnant, and another one for telling her he now quite fancied having a child, not a baby, but a child) out of a possible ten. For the next few weeks she'd be watching Rory, assessing him, deciding if he was up to the task she had in mind for him – a further three children.

At the end of September Rita Boothe decided it was high time she invited John and Mattie to lunch. It had been months since she'd been on that delightful picnic and eaten quite the most delicious cheese sandwich she'd ever had in her life.

She and Mattie spoke regularly on the phone. By now they recognised one another's voices and could quickly flow into easy conversation. They'd talk about little things, what they'd been doing, their gardens, something they'd both seen on television the night before. But at first they'd mostly discussed Marie and Sebastian.

'She's good for him,' Rita had said. 'She's so grounded. Sebastian's always been a bit dreamy. Head in the clouds, you know.'

'Really,' Mattie'd said. 'He doesn't come across that way. Of course Marie hasn't always been grounded. She was the impetuous one. Did something, then thought about it later. But having to manage the kids on her own has been good for her. She's blossomed.'

'She's lovely,' Rita had said. 'It's so exciting them being together. Perhaps they might even . . .'

'Let's not think about that,' Mattie had said. 'Best not to. I find as soon as I think about something, it doesn't happen.'

'I know,' Rita'd said. 'Best not hope. But it would be lovely, wouldn't it. I'd be a grandmother, of a sort.'

'So you would. Oh my. Isn't it strange how things turn out?'

'Well, we'll have to wait and see,' Rita had said. 'And not interfere. That would put them off.'

Mattie had agreed: interfering was indeed off-putting.

After the subject had been addressed, Mattie and Rita often returned to it. They went through the finer points of each of their children's childhood. Both Marie and Sebastian's natures were scrutinised. And, at last, their hoped-for marriage examined. Would it work? They were, after all, very different people.

'That's what will make it – the difference,' Mattie had suggested.

'A voyage of discovery,' Rita had thought. 'Every day something new to talk about.'

'Exactly,' Mattie had agreed.

After that the finer details of child-minding came up.

'If,' Rita had said. 'Big if. But if they get married you could all come up here for the odd weekend. You and John and the kids. I'm sure I could find room. It'd give Sebastian and Marie time together. They'll need that. Newly-weds, you know.'

'Absolutely,' Mattie had said. 'And you'll have to come here for all the birthday parties and school concerts. That is, if it happens. We don't want to rush things. Or interfere or anything like that.'

No, they'd agreed. They couldn't interfere, so very, very off-putting.

Today Rita phoned to ask John and Mattie for lunch. 'I've been meaning to invite you for ages. Don't know why I haven't.'

'We'd love to come,' said Mattie. 'No. No. It's not too far. St Andrews is only an hour or so away. John loves driving. Twelve o'clock next Sunday. We'll be there, looking forward to it.'

She was in heaven when she told John about it. 'Rita's invited us to lunch,' she said. 'Who'd have thought it?'

John thought about telling her that it was about time.

The picnic had been months ago, he was beginning to think her rude. But in the end he thought better of it. Why spoil her moment?

They arrived ten minutes early. Mattie tried to insist they spend the time till twelve o'clock, or perhaps ten past, sitting in the car. It didn't do to turn up on people's doorsteps before the allotted time.

But John would have none of it. 'I'm not sitting in the car outside someone's house for twenty minutes. I've been sitting driving for almost two hours. I need a pee.' So he got out and walked up to Rita's front door. Rang the bell.

Mattie pulled down the car's sun visor, looked at herself in the mirror. Didn't really like what she saw, but freshened up her lipstick and ruffled her hair anyway. She climbed out of the car and looked round. It was a wonderful street, houses tacked on to houses. Beech hedges, lavender spilling on to the pavement, a scattering of sparrows bickering on a tiny front lawn.

'What a beautiful street,' she said to Rita when she opened the door.

'I like it,' said Rita. 'I do believe I am happy here. Though I'm not totally sure. Happiness is elusive, and when it comes to me I don't quite give in to it. It doesn't do to relax and think everything's going to be fine. That's when tragedy strikes, when you've let down your guard.' She opened the door wider, so they could come in.

John wanted to know where the bathroom was.

'Upstairs, door facing you,' said Rita. Then she took Mattie's jacket and showed her into the kitchen. 'This is where the action is. Have a seat while I get everything ready. Help yourself to wine.'

The table in the kitchen where Mattie sat was set for three. In front of her, beside a square glass vase containing thirty white roses, was a bottle of chilled Pinot Grigio and a bottle of San Lorenzo. She didn't know which to pour, but chose the white, thinking this most appropriate to start with. Rita looked at her and smiled. Mattie was pleased, she'd made the right choice. Though, in fact, Rita didn't care. She thought people should drink what they wanted to drink, eat what they wanted to eat, do what they wanted to do, as long as they didn't hurt people, especially people they loved, in the process.

'You have a lovely house,' said Mattie, looking round at the old wooden butter churn in the corner and the ancient scales on the kitchen unit and the row of old glass jars and bottles on the shelf. 'All those antiques.'

'You have antiques,' said Rita.

'Oh yes,' agreed Mattie. 'Things that have become antique. They were new when we bought them. That's how old we are.'

Rita served the first course, a garlicky mussel soup. It was to be followed by roast beef, crisp and mustardy on the outside, slightly pink within, with potatoes roasted with rosemary and green beans with almonds. Then a pear flan. She had judged John to be a pudding man. Now, of course, with no lover to kiss or frolic with, she timed her dishes in a different way. Leave roast beef till the smell deepens, thick, brown. Leave pears to poach for as long as it takes Maria Callas to sing 'Casta Diva'. Join in if you're feeling a little lonely.

'It's so nice to get away,' said Mattie. 'Things are a bit fraught at home, what with Marie's court case coming up.'

'I know,' said Rita. 'You must be worried.'

John said that the soup was lovely. And no, he wouldn't have any wine. But he would have a drop of the Italian stuff with his main course. You had to watch when you were driving.

Rita asked how his kite was going.

'Almost done,' said John. 'We're planning to have the big flight on Christmas Eve, though, when all the family's there.'

'You must come,' said Mattie. 'This soup is wonderful. Sebastian will be there, and Marie, and Tod and Agnes, we hope.'

'I'd love to come,' said Rita. 'And Tod and Agnes will be there. Marie will win the case. No doubt about that. Claire Bradley is a top-class lawyer. She never loses.'

'You know Claire Bradley?' said Mattie. Her spoon was poised halfway to her lips.

'Of course I do,' said Rita. 'It was . . .' She stopped, looked at Mattie, saw surprise, and was that a little hurt on her face? She had been going to say that it was her who had suggested to Marie which lawyer she go to. She had been going to tell Mattie and

John about the phone call all those months ago, when Marie was so desperate and needed someone to talk to. And in that moment realised that Mattie wouldn't want to know that her daughter had turned to someone who was a relative stranger. Any mother would want to think her child, in a moment of need, had turned to her for comfort and advice.

'It was so clever of Marie to find her. She must be shrewd, just like her mother,' she said. And leaned over and patted Mattie's hand.

John saw this, and allowed himself a couple of glugs of the white wine. He raised his glass to Rita. In that moment he'd seen what had happened. Sebastian had told Marie to phone Rita, and she had told his daughter who to turn to. She had no doubt offered words of comfort, and assured Marie that everything would turn out well. She had given out hope.

Rita thought, So that's how it's done. You tell little lies. You protect people's feelings. That's what the starlings do, they say, 'Don't mind John if he's grumpy. He only ever wanted the best for his family. And don't hurt Mattie, she's lovely. She just cares too much. Tell Marie everything's going to be fine, even if you're worried it won't be, she needs to know that.'

Give a little, Rita thought, be nice. Sometimes it doesn't do to be overly honest. My God, I'm over seventy. You think I'd have learned that by now.

Burning, Gleaming, Shining Hate

The court case was set for the beginning of November. Marie had become used to the night. The shifts and creaks of her house, the journey of the moon and stars across the sky. She could pull back the kitchen curtains at four in the morning, look up, note the positions of the constellations she now recognised, but couldn't name, and know what time it was. She knew that she had a neighbour who left at five when the first creeping light of dawn glimmered just beyond the rooftops over to the left. A cat crossed her garden every night, not long after the moon was directly above the rooftops. And the milkman's van rattled along the road when the moon was shifting to the right, not long before her neighbour's car started up.

She worried. But now she was past presenting herself with a series of dire what-ifs; now it was just a churning in her stomach, a tension in her jaw, an ache in her shoulder. She was almost used to it. Sometimes, at work, she would start to shake, and would have to walk out of her office to stand in the corridor, leaning against the wall, breathing, telling herself to get a grip. And by now, she was so convinced she was going to lose, she and Claire Bradley had started to discuss what terms Marie should demand when it came to visiting rights. 'More than once a week,' Marie had said. 'I want to see them for meals at least two or three times. They mustn't think I've forgotten them. And two weekends a month.'

By now Tod knew that his father wanted him to live with him, and resented it. He had started to refuse to go on their weekend outings. Agnes knew too, but had decided she wasn't going. She was so convinced of this, she was less upset than her brother.

Once Andy had tried to show Tod the room he would have when he came to stay and had asked how he would like it decorated. Tod had shrugged. 'Don't care.' Then he had phoned Marie and told her to come and get him. 'I don't like it here.'

At first Marie had refused. 'I can't come, Tod. Why don't you just relax and enjoy being there? You'll be home soon.'

But Tod had cried and taken a tantrum. He started to sob down the phone. 'Come and get me. I hate it here.'

So Marie had put Lauren in the car, driven to Andy's flat and picked him up. When Agnes saw Tod going home, she decided she wanted to go too. 'I want to play with my toys. I never get to see them these days,' she said.

'Look at what you're doing,' Marie said to Andy. 'Look at the state Tod's in. Do you really think he's going to settle down and live with you?'

'Kids are very adaptable,' said Andy. 'He'll come round.'

Three days after that, Andy got a letter from the Child Support Agency telling him he owed his wife four years' payments. He phoned his lawyer. 'Who did this to me? Who reported me?'

He was told it would have been his wife, probably on her lawyer's instructions.

The next time Andy picked up Tod and Agnes, he said, 'That was a shit thing to do, Marie.'

'Wasn't it?' said Marie. 'I'd do it again. I'll do anything, I don't care how far I go. I don't care how much I hurt you. I'm not letting you just take my kids.'

The force, the venom with which she spoke shook Andy. He noticed how pale Marie was, face thin, drained, and eyes wide, burning, gleaming hard, shining hate.

'I didn't think you were like this,' he said.

'Neither did I,' said Marie. 'But I am. I'm so angry, I think I could kill you. Only it wouldn't do any good. I'd really lose Agnes and Tod if I did. But know it as you walk about living your life: someone utterly loathes you for what you are trying to do.'

Last night she had told Sebastian to leave. 'Just go,' she said. 'I don't want to see you any more. You are spoiling my chances of keeping my children.'

He'd got up and gone to the door.

'Come back,' Marie said. 'Please. I want you here. What's the point of you going? Andy and his lawyer and that social worker know all about you, anyway.' All he had done was walk away, a few yards across the room, and she missed him.

He'd held open his arms and she came to him, let him hold her, and tell her that everything would be all right. She needed to hear someone say this to her several times a day, every day.

Andy took the letter from the Child Support Agency to his lawyer. 'What do you make of this?'

'I'd advise you to pay it. It won't look good for you in court if you don't. Haven't you been providing for your children?'

'I opened a trust fund.'

'That's good,' said his lawyer. 'Where do you have it? Is it under Tod's name? Have you opened a separate one for Agnes?'

'It's in my name. I needed to be able to transfer it over here. It's a high-interest account. Nobody can touch the money for ten years. By then Tod will be looking to go to university.'

'But it's in your name, so you can't prove the money is for your children.'

'But it is,' said Andy.

'Andy,' said his lawyer, 'I have to tell you, I don't think you're going to win this. In fact I'm sure you're not. You are fighting for children you haven't had meaningful contact with for four years to come live with you. You have not provided for these children financially on a day-to-day basis. I have had dealings with Mrs Evans before, so I spoke to her. She doesn't quite believe the things about your wife and her lover. She has a gut feeling it's something the little girl said in all innocence. She indicated that her report would say Agnes and Tod are happy and secure and benefiting from being in an extended family. They see their grandparents every day. They are cared for and loved. I should imagine she'll say she finds no good reason to remove them from their present home. Furthermore, Tod seems to be emphatic he wants to stay with his mother. He is considered old enough to know what he wants. If he stays, then it's likely the court will want Agnes to stay as well.'

Andy said, 'But she cheated. She was in bed with . . .'

He was told that had no bearing on the case. What the court would want to know was whether Marie was caring for the children. And she seemed to be. He would probably lose. He would have to pay costs, and maybe even Marie's costs. Then there was the Child Support Agency to deal with.

'I wouldn't be being fair,' his lawyer said, 'if I didn't advise you to drop the case.'

That night Andy told Lucy, his new partner, what his lawyer had said.

'Well thank God, sense at last,' said Lucy. 'Quite frankly, I don't think I want your children here. Not Tod anyway. I don't want some truculent, upset child sulking and crying around the place. You'll make him miserable. He might end up hating you. He might keep running home to his mother.'

Two days later Andy phoned his lawyer and told him he wasn't going to pursue his fight to have his children any further. 'It's over.' He put down the receiver. But the bitch wasn't going to get away with it. 'I'll get her back. Revenge.'

Marie was at work when Claire Bradley called and told her that the case had been dropped. She started to cry. Then, when she was off the phone, swamped with relief, she put her head on her desk and sobbed. Her boss, finding her shaking and unable to speak, told her she was of no use to anyone in that state. 'Go home.'

Once there, she stood beside the phone. She was overwhelmed with relief. She felt that for the last few months she had been battling through her life. It was as if she had been running uphill against a force ten gale, and suddenly it was over. Ever since the letter from Andy's solicitor had arrived she had been unable to really enjoy anything – a favourite television programme, playing with her children, making love to Sebastian – for thinking about it. Now it was over, she could start to live again. She needed to tell somebody, everybody. Who to call first? She dialled Sebastian's mobile.

Then she called Lily. Well, she had to tell Lily; after all, she'd come up with the money.

Then she called Rory. And, finally, Mattie.

'Oh, that's such good news,' said Mattie. 'What a relief. I'm going to cry.'

Marie could hear her mother's voice thicken, she heard a tissue being pulled from the box, being blown into.

'Where are you?' said Mattie.

'Home,' said Marie. 'My boss told me to get out of the office. I was in such a state I was no use to anybody there.'

'Well come over,' said Mattie. 'I want to hear all about it. And stay to supper. We'll celebrate.'

Marie phoned Lily again. 'I'm going over to see Mum. We're going to celebrate.'

'I wish I could be there,' said Lily.

'So do I,' said Marie.

'Roast chicken,' said Lily. 'And I bet she makes a trifle. Buy some wine, will you? Use some of that money I gave you.'

'Thanks,' said Marie. 'You don't need to persuade me.' She was starting to cry again. 'I'll be able to give you your money back.'

'Yep,' said Lily. 'You surely will.'

'I'll send you a cheque.' Marie was a bit sorry about this. Lily's money in her back account had made her solvent for the first time in years.

Lily thought that now she'd be able to pay off her car loan, but still quietly lamented the loss of the convertible. Ah well, she was back where she'd started. Well, not quite.

'So,' said Andy. 'You won. You would. It's hardly fair.'

'No,' said Marie. 'I agree it probably isn't. Though I have been looking after the children on my own for years. But nothing is fair, I'll give you that.'

'I'll send you the money the support agency demanded.'

'Don't bother. I've managed. I'll continue to manage.'

'I want to help support my children.'

'Of course you do. So help. But I don't want the back payments. Put them in the bank for the children.'

He said the money would probably go towards paying his lawyer.

'Let's call a truce,' said Marie. 'There's no reason you can't see more of Tod and Agnes, and get to know Lauren. She's lovely.

They could come to you after school sometimes. We don't have to stick to what the lawyers decide on visiting rights. You can see them whenever you want. Take them to the cinema, whatever.'

He said he knew, and he would take his children more often, and he would get to know Lauren.

Marie said, 'Truce, then?'

'Yes,' said Andy. 'But not till I get my revenge. I need that.'

Marie laughed. 'Well, get your revenge then. Should I watch my back?'

'No. No,' said Andy. 'No backstabbing. Just some inconvenience, I think.'

It took Andy a few weeks to decide on how to avenge his dropped court case. He wanted to make Marie's life hell without alienating his children. He was driving through Holyrood Park when he saw the solution. A woman was pushing a small child in a buggy, trying to keep two older children in check whilst being dragged along by an enormous dog. Poor soul, he thought.

Then the idea struck, one of those glistening brainwave moments. A dog. He knew Agnes wanted one, and Marie didn't. He would have to give it to Agnes on one of her visiting days, so she would be bonded with it when she went home. It would have to be a puppy and not house-trained, it would have to be hairy and grow enormous. It would have to eat huge volumes of food. And his children would have to dote on it, and think of him every time they saw it.

He bought a book on dogs, and selected a St Bernard. Extremely large, prone to shedding hair, gentle and loving. He noted with relish that it was recommended the dog be fed on tripe. How excellent. The smell of boiling tripe would permeate every room in Marie's home.

He phoned the Kennel Club and found a breeder with puppies for sale. It wasn't cheap. In fact it was ludicrously expensive, but worth every penny, Andy decided.

The next time he picked up Agnes and Tod he told them he had a very, very special surprise for them back at his flat. Tod was hoping for a remote-controlled car, Agnes, having long given up on getting a dog, wanted a bike.

The puppy, however, pleased them both. They spent the afternoon playing with it, and anxiously watching it sleep so they could play with it again. Andy told them it was very important their new puppy was allowed to get plenty of sleep, because it was, oh joy, growing. And it was going to be very, very big.

Marie was in the kitchen when Agnes and Tod arrived home. She heard them talking to William, and assumed they were chatting to Agnes's toy dog. She went to meet them, and saw the puppy sitting in the middle of the hall, looking round. Agnes beamed at her.

'It's our puppy. It's got a lead and a bowl and everything. Daddy bought her for us.'

Marie said, 'Daddy bought it?'

'Yes. She's called William,' said Tod.

'That's a boy's name,' said Marie.

'She doesn't know that. She's a dog.'

'What kind of dog?' said Marie. Though she didn't really have to ask. She had a horrible suspicion she already knew.

'A St Bernard,' said Agnes. 'They grow really big.'

Marie said to take the dog into the kitchen, she'd just slip outside and have a word with their daddy, she could see the car was still at the door.

Andy waited till he saw Marie come out of the front door, then he started the engine. He watched her run down the path. He could see the furious and horrified expression on her face. Wonderful. He drove off. In the rear mirror he could see her running down the street after the car. She was waving for him to stop. He had the window down and clearly heard her shout, 'Bastard.' Excellent result.

Sometimes, a Perfect Moment

It had been months since Grandpa contacted Nina, his internet friend. But early in December he emailed her, apologising for not being in touch. He had, he said, been hiking in the Andes, seeking inner calm.

Nina replied, telling him she'd wondered what happened to him. She thought it was very selfish to go off leaving John and Mattie. *They need you*, she told him.

He wrote back saying that they didn't. He told her that he was in fact very old. John was his grown-up son, Mattie his daughter-in-law. Lily and Rory were his grandchildren, as was Marie who had given him three great-grandchildren. Telling lies over the internet is getting me down, he said. Sylvia would think me a foolish old man.

Nina never replied. Grandpa missed her. Or rather, he missed her emails. He liked the optimistic moment when he read *You have one message*, and the lovely ding-dong clarion when it arrived. At first, he'd found it thrilling to flirt, he'd thought he was past such things. But the lies got him down. Lies led to more lies and even more lies. It was hard to keep track of them all. Thrills never last, he told himself.

Lily was pregnant, and it was all Mattie's fault.

'Good one,' said Art. 'I thought it had more to do with me.'

'It was Mattie phoned me to say Grandpa was dead. And then forgot to let me know he wasn't. I rushed out of the house and forgot to take my pills. Mostly because Rory was hanging about wondering if he should come too. So it is also his fault.'

Art was delighted. A girl, he thought.

'Then,' said Lily, 'I came back here and you wanted to go to bed. So it's your fault.'

'And nothing to do with you,' said Art.

'Nothing at all.'

'Only,' said Art, 'you could have taken your pill when you got home.'

'But I didn't,' said Lily. 'And I didn't take it the next day or the day after. I wanted to see what would happen.'

'And this happened.'

'Yes,' said Lily.

They both looked down at her stomach.

'Bloody hell,' said Art.

Lily said, 'Exactly.' She stroked where she thought the baby might be lying. 'Little baby.'

Art said, 'I know. Little baby.' He couldn't stop smiling.

'I'm pleased. I'm all misty-eyed and maternal. Who'd have thought it?'

They stared at one another. Then Art said he wanted a girl. Lily wanted a boy. Art wanted to call her Kirsten. Lily preferred Jake.

'My tits hurt. I feel queasy. Nothing will ever be the same. It'll be feeding and teething and where's the best school and riding lessons, or maybe the piano. Unless he wants to learn judo or something. Who's going to take him to school in the morning? Me. I want to do it. What if when he's a teenager he wants a tattoo? What am I going to tell him?'

Art thought she was rushing things a bit. But smiled. 'Christ, we've really done it now.'

Mattie looked at the calendar: the fifth of December. She should make a Christmas list, get things going. She sat at the kitchen table and started, jotting things down on the back of the electricity bill envelope. *Turkey*, she wrote. *Brussels sprouts. Bacon. Onions. Garlic. Champagne, wine. Check tree lights. Buy cards and post early to catch second-class mail. Cheeses. Buy pudding from Tesco. Present for William?* Then, *Two new grandchildren, goodness.*

John came in, and while she made him coffee took over the list. 'I don't think the dog needs a present. Shall I put down mince pies?'

'Oh yes,' said Mattie. 'You have to have them. Everyone likes mince pies at Christmas, even if they don't eat them. They're comforting, reassuring. It wouldn't be Christmas without mince pies.'

So he added them to the list. Then wrote, *Imagine*, because that was playing on the radio. And drew a line of little Christmas trees.

'I'm going to the post office to get a new tax disc for the car,' said Mattie. 'Do you want anything while I'm there?'

The front door opened and Marie shouted, 'It's us.'

Mattie heard the clatter of children and dog running down the hall. She laid out Rice Krispies, milk and sugar on the table. Muesli for Marie, put toast on for John. And filled the dog's water bowl, put it on the floor beside the sink.

'Lauren will be at nursery next year,' she said. 'Then it will be just us and Grandpa.'

'And William,' said John.

'Yes,' said Mattie. 'She's going to be awfully big. But at least you don't have to bend down to pat her. I think that's why some little dogs are yappy. It's lonely down there, and people find it too far to go to join them to say hello and stroke their heads.'

'Good theory,' said John.

Marie sat at the table and poured some muesli into a bowl. 'Not making your Christmas list already? It's ages yet.'

'No it isn't. Christmas just leaps out at you if you don't watch out,' said Mattie.

'Can Sebastian come to dinner?' said Marie.

'Of course,' said Mattie. 'Does that mean Rita will be alone?' No, she thought, not Rita Boothe. She'll have wonderful friends. She imagined Rita Boothe's Christmas, the witty, erudite people in velvet jackets, the glowing log fire, brandy in balloon glasses, the flowing conversation, the laughter.

'Sebastian says she usually just has a baked potato by the fire and watches television,' said Marie.

'I don't believe you. Not Rita Boothe,' said Mattie. 'He's teasing you.'

'No,' said Marie. She drank the last of her coffee. Gathered her handbag and coat, said she had to dash. She kissed each of the children, Mattie and John. Bent down and rubbed William behind the ears. 'Be good, you.' Then left.

'She's quite besotted with that dog,' said Mattie.

When she'd come back into the house, after chasing Andy's car shouting, 'Bastard,' Marie had looked at the dog, and her heart had melted.

'We better take you to the kitchen and feed you,' she said.

Not having any dog food, she'd scrambled it some eggs and finely chopped some chicken to mix through them and had topped it all up with brown bread. Then she'd taken it into the garden, hoping it would pee there rather than on the kitchen floor. It did.

'We might have the beginnings of a relationship,' she told it.

Now the dog followed her everywhere. And lay at her feet in the evenings when she fell asleep on the sofa. She found it a comfort, a soul to talk to who never criticised or disagreed. The dog adored her, even though it spent most of its time with Mattie and John.

After she'd returned from taking Agnes and Tod to school, Mattie put William on the lead and walked to the post office. There was a queue. She stood looking around her. It was a small branch, sold greetings cards, newspapers and magazines. There was a noticeboard where people advertised things for sale, and lost property.

Lost, small black and white cat, answers to Jasper. Phone . . .

Wanted, cleaner, three mornings a week. Good rates.

Found in post box in Findbury Avenue, one television remote control. Sony. Please enquire at desk.

Mattie bought the tax disc for the car, three sheets of stamps and asked about the remote control. 'We've lost ours,' she said. 'I can't tell you the trouble it caused. But it couldn't be ours. I mean, how would it have got into the post box?'

'That's what we asked,' said the woman behind the counter. 'The postman found it there when he was collecting the mail last year. He looked through all the letters to see if one had burst open, but no. Then he left it here thinking maybe someone's kids had done it. The notice has been up since last December. Nobody's claimed it.'

She fetched the remote control from the back room.

'That's it,' said Mattie. 'That's our remote control. How on earth did it get into the post box?'

'Kids?' said the post office woman.

'Well, I have grandchildren. That's all I can think of. This isn't like them, though. Oh, they get up to things. But posting the remote control isn't their style. But thank you for finding it, and keeping it all this time.'

'Hasn't taken up much space,' said the post office woman.

Mattie came home waving the remote control. 'It was in the post office. No wonder I couldn't find it. In a million years I'd never have thought of looking there. Someone posted it.'

Grandpa, in the kitchen, heard this and asked Lauren if she'd like to go for a stroll in the garden.

John took the remote control to the living room, switched on the television, and started zapping through the channels. 'Still works.'

'I've become used to not having it,' said Mattie. 'You do tend to be more selective about your viewing when you can't just flick between channels.'

John put it on the mantelpiece. 'There, that's where it is. I don't know how it got to the post office. It'll have to be one of the family mysteries.'

He said he was off upstairs to work on the plans for the Binghams.

He had taken Lily's advice and advertised in the local paper. *Plans drawn up. Extensions, conservatories, conversions. Experienced draughtsman. Advice given. Reasonable rates.*

Now he had two clients. Mattie wrote the estimates for John's plans, and for the work to be done. She sent bright chatty letters which John, at first, hated, but now had to admit seemed to put people at ease. People found her gentle informality pleasing. She had a way of saying things that sounded human. *I definitely wouldn't start this extension before Christmas*, she had written to the Binghams. *It's tricky enough without all the building mess when you are serving the turkey. In fact, I'd leave it till early spring. By then John will have helped you find a reliable builder. They do exist, you know.*

'You can't send that,' said John. 'You have to sound professional, businesslike.'

'You have to sound human,' said Mattie. 'That's the problem these days. Too many formal letters. People want you to sound human, as if you understand their pain. And getting the builders in is painful.'

So she'd sent her letter, and it worked. Not only did the Binghams ask John to draw up their plans and help them supervise the building of their extension, they recommended him to friends who wanted their loft converted into a bedroom and study.

'Now we have two clients and a remote control,' said Mattie. 'Things are looking up. I'm off to phone Rita and invite her for Christmas. We can't have her sitting alone with a baked potato. Though I don't believe that for a minute.'

Rita said she couldn't possible intrude. 'Not at Christmas.'

'But Sebastian will be here. And Lily and Art and Rory, though I don't know about Isabel. She usually goes to her parents. Only she and Rory are engaged now, it could make a difference. Anyway, you know us all now. You're one of us.'

It was the phrase that won Rita over. One of us, part of the gang, she'd never been that. And had secretly longed to be. 'I suppose I could,' she said. 'It might be fun.'

'Of course it will be fun,' said Mattie. 'We're always having fun. Did I tell you about the time John built a huge sledge that the whole family could sit on. He wanted us all to whoosh down the hill together. Sledges are usually little, they only take one or two people. So you have to wait your turn. He wanted us all to enjoy the thrill at the same moment.'

'Oneness,' said Rita. She knew she was going to hear this story again and again. Every time she saw Mattie.

'Only it didn't happen,' said Mattie. 'The damn thing stuck in the snow.'

'I think it did happen,' Rita told her. 'You have the memory. You all have the story to tell.'

'I never thought of that,' said Mattie. 'Perhaps you're right. Anyway, come along on Christmas Eve, we're having the maiden flight of John's kite. Everyone'll be there.'

At half past one on the twenty-fourth of December, the White family, along with Isabel, Art, Sebastian and Rita, arrived in Holyrood Park. John and Mattie started to lay the kite out on the ground. Everyone else milled around, chatting, and keeping clear of the bickering. Behind them Arthur's Seat loomed; the people far above them clambering up its slopes seemed almost tiny.

Sebastian thought it wonderful a city should have a huge hill, an almost wild place, right in the middle of it.

'Lots of cities have parks and green spaces,' said Marie.

'But not like this. This is unkempt.' They looked up and watched geese flying over. The wind bit their faces, chill nipped round them.

Mattie and John wrestled with the kite. 'It's taking up a huge amount of space,' she said.

'It's public property. We're allowed,' said John.

'A kite this big, it could be a danger to passing aircraft.'

'Don't be stupid. It won't go that high.'

'It'll blot out the sun,' said Mattie.

'It'll join the sky,' said John. 'Then we'll all grab hold of it together, and join the sky as one. The oneness of being a White.'

Mattie didn't argue with that, she thought it a grand notion. But secretly doubted it would happen.

Rory joined Marie, and Sebastian went over to chat to his mother.

'So, when's the wedding?' said Marie.

'After the baby's born. Isabel wants to wait till she's got her figure back. That's if there ever is a wedding. Isabel is watching me. Testing me. I think I'm getting marks out of ten.'

'What's your score so far?'

'Dunno, not very high. I'm trying. But I don't think it's going to work.'

'Don't say that,' said Marie.

'It all terrifies me,' he said.

'Everyone is scared when they are going to have a baby. First they're delighted, then they think about it, a whole new human being to look after, and they get jittery.'

'Not the baby. Isabel. I'm trying, but what do I do to please her?'

'Don't take drugs. Don't get drunk more than once a fortnight. Don't run after other women. Give her a cuddle when her pregnancy gets her down and she is feeling huge and retaining water. And don't keep your socks on in bed.'

'That it?'

'Yeah,' said Marie. 'More or less.'

'Works for you?' said Rory.

'Absolutely,' said Marie. 'Though I've been alone a while. Maybe my standards have slipped.'

'I didn't have a lot of luck with the magic words of comfort. There, there, never mind made Isabel furious. She said it was patronising.'

'Really?' said Marie. 'Like I said, what would I know? It did the trick for me.'

He smiled and watched Mattie and John. 'It'll be Isabel's baby. I'll be Isabel's husband. We'll live in Isabel's house. Isabel's life. I don't think I can do it.'

Marie linked her arm in his. 'Bummer.' Then smiled and said, 'There, there, never mind.'

Rory considered this. Looked at Marie and said, 'Isabel's right. It's patronising.'

It was windy. Arranging the kite was taking a while. Rita pulled her coat round her and asked Sebastian if he was going to marry Marie.

'Haven't asked her.'

'Why not? She's lovely. You couldn't do better.'

'I know that. But I'd have to move to Edinburgh. She won't leave. She likes being near her folks.'

'Quite right, you should apply for a job up here.'

'I have,' he told her. 'I've been offered a post. It's a big step. A wife, three kids and a dog.'

'So take the step. Stop thinking about it. Thinking gets you nowhere. I never thought about things, I just did what felt right. And look at me.'

Sebastian said, 'Exactly.'

Rita said, 'OK. So I made mistakes.'

Sebastian said, 'What happens happens. We'll see. I just want us all to be happy.'

'Happy?' said Rita. 'Don't be stupid. Nobody's happy, well, not all the time. I'll tell you what will happen. You'll marry Marie. You'll have kids, and mess and problems and debt, and your hair will go grey. And one day you'll look back and think: Have I been happy? And you'll think: Well, there have been moments. That's all there is – moments. Moments dire and dreadful, moments tedious and tiresome, moments vile and embarrassing, moments fat and golden. We move through them, from one to another. Treasure the good ones.'

The kite was flapping, lifting restlessly into the air. It was blue. John had originally planned to make it red and black and write a furious slogan about pension funds on it. But now it was blue, to join the sky.

Lily and Art joined Marie and Rory. Isabel, who had stayed in the car, because it was windy and cold, came over too.

'So,' said Lily. 'How long?'

'Fifteen minutes,' said Rory.

'Too soon,' said Marie.

'Sebastian will be there, she'll be anxious to tell him the story.'

'Twenty-three,' said Marie.

Rita and Sebastian joined them.

'Twenty-three?' said Sebastian. 'Twenty-three what?'

'Every Christmas we take a bet on how long it will be before Mum mentions the sledge,' Marie told him. 'I say twenty-three minutes after she's sat down to eat her main course.'

'Is that the starting point? Can I join in?'

'Of course,' said Lily. 'You're almost part of the family now.'

Sebastian thought. 'Twelve minutes.'

'Rubbish,' said Marie. 'She has to fuss. She has to make sure everyone has sprouts and stuffing and has their glass filled. She has to cut up Lauren's food. She has to say, "Has everybody got cranberry sauce?" And, "Are the roast potatoes crisp enough?" '

'I say seventeen,' said Lily. 'She'll be making an extra fuss because of Sebastian and Rita.'

'Sixteen minutes,' said Art. 'She'll be keen to tell Sebastian, thinking he doesn't know the story. Or Rita, come to that.'

'Oh,' said Rita, 'I've heard the story. I say, let's see – fuss, fill glasses, take a mouthful of turkey and stuffing together, enjoy. Feel mellow and content, happy that the family's all round her. Look at Sebastian, want to draw him into the group. Eighteen minutes.'

'Good try, Rita,' said Rory. 'Want to put a fiver on it?'

'I do indeed,' said Rita. 'What does Grandpa say?'

'He doesn't know,' said Lily.

'Well he should,' said Rita. 'You mustn't leave him out.'

'He can't keep a secret,' said Rory.

'I'm pretty sure he can,' said Rita. 'Nobody gets to his age without a secret or two.'

'This is terrible, to laugh at your mother like this,' said Isabel.

Rory said it was a family tradition. A joke. 'It's affectionate.'

'I find it strange,' said Isabel. 'I'd hate my children to do it to me.'

'Well, babe,' said Rory. 'They will. One way or another, they'll grow up and tell stories about you.'

Isabel sighed, and supposed it was true. 'Fifteen minutes. She hasn't told me the story either.' She smiled. 'I'll never understand your family.'

Recently she'd been judging Rory, almost by the moment. His bout of dope-smoking had depressed her. She liked people to be consistent. She had dipped back to the sort of superstitious beliefs she'd had as a child. If I can hold my breath till I get to the end of the street, everything will be all right. If I can bounce my ball forty times non-stop, everything will be all right.

She applied this to her relationship with Rory. If he offers to make coffee after dinner, everything will be all right. If he wants to go to the clinic with me, everything will be all right. If he remembers to water the plants, it will show that he has a nurturing nature, and everything will be all right.

The kite flapped into the air. And the wind caught it, gusting underneath it. It spread out, hovering a few feet off the ground.

John shouted for everyone to come, to hold it as it joined the sky.

If Rory goes and takes hold of the string, thought Isabel, it will show he is a family man, and everything will be all right.

Tod and Agnes ran to take hold of the kite. Lily and Marie looked sheepish, and walked slowly forward, as did Rory. Then the whole thing struck him as absurd. He stood, watching. This was another of his father's ludicrous notions. He couldn't do it. He turned and walked back to Isabel.

The kite moved upwards. It was soaring, its hugeness buffeted in gasping whirls of wind. John, holding the guiding strings, was being pulled along. Running below it. He was shouting for his family to come join him.

Lily and Marie walked reluctantly towards him. Both had their hands in their pockets, and both stared at the ground, trying to look as if they were not part of this fiasco.

'I thought you'd be running to help, Lily,' said Marie. 'As ever.'

'Nah,' said Lily. 'It's unbecoming for a pregnant woman to rescue middle-aged men from kites.'

Marie said, 'I never imagined you wanting children.'

'I didn't really,' she said. 'It was a mistake. But I'm pleased about it.'

'You? A mistake?' said Marie. 'When's it due?'

'On the twenty-sixth of May at twenty past two in the afternoon.'

Marie took this in. 'It doesn't work like that, Lily.'

'I seem to have had no control over the conception,' said Lily. 'I will have over the birth.'

Marie looked at her, jaw agape.

Lily sniggered. 'I know, nappies, teething, sleepless nights, feeding problems. All the stuff. My pristine life is over. Don't look so smug about it.'

Marie said she was trying. She looked at Lily, at Lily's stomach. A slight bulge. Damn, she thought, four months and she's hardly showing. I was huge. It's just not fair. Nothing's fair.

Lily said, 'It looks like you might lose your kids after all. That kite might just disappear over the horizon taking them and John and Mattie.'

Marie said, 'Christ.' And ran to help.

Rita went over to Grandpa, who was sitting on a bench watching.

'Absurd,' he said. 'Always absurd.'

'I think it's wonderful. Wanting everyone to join the sky together.'

'There's that. You don't want to ever stop having notions. It's the notions that count.'

'Do you want to join the bet?' said Rita. 'We're all putting money on how long it will take Mattie to mention the sledge at

Christmas dinner.' She didn't say the bet had been going on for some time now at family gatherings. It might hurt his feelings to discover he'd been left out.

'She always mentions it, doesn't she?' He thought about it. 'Twenty minutes.'

She sat beside him. 'You don't mind if I call you Martin, do you? Only I'm a bit uncomfortable with Grandpa. You're not my grandfather, after all. And I've had two of those. I don't need another. In fact, I'm too old to have a grandfather.'

'I'd like you to call me Martin,' said Martin. 'That's who I am. How much for the bet?'

'A fiver,' said Rita.

'Fine,' said Grandpa. 'Might as well join in. I probably won't be here next Christmas.'

'Where are you going?' asked Rita.

'With my luck, hell.'

'You're planning to die sometime next year?'

'Thought I might. It's going to happen sometime.'

'Well I might die too. So might John or Mattie or anybody really. I don't like to think about it,' said Rita.

'Neither do I,' said Grandpa. 'But the thought just creeps up on me, and there it is in my head.'

'Yes, I know,' said Rita. 'Me too. That's just the sort of thing I'd do. Die. Just when I'm starting to get along with my son.'

Cars were stopping. People were staring, pointing. The kite spread and momentarily took to the sky, then collapsed, folded in on itself and sank to the ground. Mattie said, 'Typical.'

But John said, 'It flew. There was a moment when it flew.'

'I think Mattie's got herself a new story to tell, Martin,' said Rita.

'Yes, I do believe you're right, Rita,' said Martin.

In bed that night Mattie said, 'Lily and me had a chat once about which it was better to be, totally accepted for what you were, or beautiful.'

Sleepily John said, 'Oh, really?' He wasn't interested.

'I said I wanted to be accepted. But I've changed my mind. I want to be beautiful. Like you.'

'I'm not beautiful, Mattie. Couldn't you say I was handsome?'

'Oh, but you're not handsome. Never have been. Not like Art. But you are beautiful. It's not just how you look, it's how you are that's beautiful. I thought that when I saw you in the park struggling with that kite. My God, he's beautiful, I thought.'

'I don't know what I think about that. I don't know if I want to be beautiful,' said John.

'Don't worry about it,' said Mattie. 'I'm the only that thinks it. I don't think anybody else has noticed.'

John spooned into her. 'Thank Christ for that.' Then, 'You fancy trying the Harley Davidson position, then?'

'No, I don't. The children are in the house. They'd hear us. Anyway, I'm too fat to try stuff like that.'

John told her she wasn't fat. She was acceptably plump. 'Perfect for the Harley Davidson position, whatever it is.'

Mattie told him it was a big day tomorrow. They should get some sleep.

Downstairs, Lily stood by the Christmas tree. She breathed in the scent of it, deep green pine. There was a tingle about it. She felt refreshed by its light, its softness. She was drinking a cup of tea. Art came and stood beside her.

'I know, we should go to bed. I was just standing here for a minute.'

He put his hand on her stomach. 'This time next year, there will be three of us.'

She put her hand over his. 'I know.'

Sometimes a perfect moment arrives unplanned. It is sudden, unexpected, like cresting a hill and there is a view fabulous enough to take your breath away. This moment was still, simple and so fragile, it could easily be broken. But she would keep it, treasure it. She didn't know what to say, she might spoil it. She put her hand on Art's cheek, smiled, and he said, 'Nice one, Lil.'

On Christmas Day, Mattie fussed. She filled glasses. She worried that the roast potatoes weren't crisp enough. She cut up Lauren's food. She asked Isabel if the turkey was tender, and what did they have in France? She told Rita to help herself to bread sauce.

'Isn't this lovely?' she said. 'All of us together. I love when this happens. Have some more wine, Rita. John, have you got sprouts?'

John said he had a few, and when it came to sprouts a few was enough.

'This is a new stuffing I tried. Got it from Delia. It's very nice,' she said.

Everyone agreed. And waited.

'Wasn't that fun with the kite?' said Mattie. 'I think it even beats the sledge.' Then she looked at Sebastian. 'Have I ever told you about the time John built this huge sledge for all the family?'

Sebastian smiled and said, 'No.'

'Well,' said Mattie. 'It was a snowy January and John had spent most of the year before building the sledge. It was green and red and . . .'

Twenty minutes. Grandpa won. Hardly surprising, he thought. He'd been watching these people for years.

Rita looked at her watch. Three o'clock. The starlings would be gathering on the tree at the foot of her garden. Jostling and croaking their throaty song. She'd see them again tomorrow, and was looking forward to that.

She still thought this family like starlings, flying together, whooshing apart, then joining one another again, milling and calling, coming back to where they'd started. She knew, of course, that she'd never truly be one of them; she just hoped that now and then they'd invite her to stand back and observe their flight.